Critical Security Studies

BORDERLINES

Critical Security Studies

Concepts and Cases

KEITH KRAUSE AND MICHAEL C. WILLIAMS, EDITORS

BORDERLINES, VOLUME 8

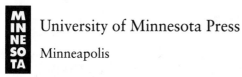

University of Minnesota Press

Minneapolis

Published by the University of Minnesota Press
111 Third Avenue South, Suite 290
Minneapolis, MN 55401-2520
Printed in the United States of America on acid-free paper

Library of Congress Cataloging-in-Publication Data

Critical security studies : concepts and cases / Keith Krause and
     Michael C. Williams, editors.
          p.   cm. — (Borderlines ; v. 8)
     Includes bibliographical references and index.
     ISBN 0-8166-2856-4 (hc : alk. paper). — ISBN 0-8166-2857-2
(pb : alk. paper)
     1. Security, International.   I. Krause, Keith.   II. Williams,
Michael C.   III. Series: Borderlines (Minneapolis, Minn.) ; v. 8.
JX1952.C735   1997
327.1'7—dc20   96-32885
                                                                      CIP

The University of Minnesota is an equal-opportunity educator and employer.

Contents

Preface: Toward Critical Security Studies

MICHAEL C. WILLIAMS AND KEITH KRAUSE

This book emerged out of a desire to contribute to the development of a self-consciously critical perspective within security studies. Intellectually, the rationale for this is straightforward: security studies (however broadly defined) has been among the last bastions of orthodoxy in International Relations to accept critical or theoretically sophisticated challenges to its problematic. Yet lurking in the interstices of the discipline, one can without much effort find a wide range of scholarship that is "about" security (and its core subject matter), but that its authors, or the discipline, refuse to label as such.[1] Simply bringing together some of these perspectives serves to make the challenges to orthodoxy more clear, and to signal that critical approaches to security studies are more than a passing fad or the idiosyncratic obsession of a few scholars.

Ultimately, this is healthy for security studies as a whole. For some time now, security studies has been treated as a theoretically impoverished cousin to the sturdy children of International Relations, which could include (depending on your preference) liberal and radical approaches to international political economy, neoliberal institutionalist analyses, regime theory, and so forth. Debate among competing approaches, and a greater conceptual clarity, can only strengthen the claims of security studies scholars for intellectual respect. Moreover, it is possible to argue that far from falling into desuetude with the end of the Cold War, many of the most interesting theoretical issues in International Relations—concerning, for example, identity politics, the role of multilateral institutions, the development of norms and practices, and so-called new issues in world politics—can be most usefully studied through a prism labeled "security studies."

Our main goal in this volume is not to invoke a new orthodoxy of critical security studies or to participate in polemical recriminations, but to engage directly with issues and questions that have been taken as the subject matter of security studies. We have tried to do this in two ways. First, we have solicited contributions from a variety of critical perspectives on security studies that address a diverse scope of theoretical concerns, ranging from the place of the Third World in security studies, to the conceptions of "the political" that underlie prevailing approaches. Second, we have encouraged some authors to examine substantive issues in security studies, such as the emerging issue of weapons proliferation (and how it is defined), the role of multilateral institutions in peace and security operations, or the changing meaning of security for actors in the erstwhile East-West conflict, in order to demonstrate that critical approaches can descend from the level of metatheory to tackle issues that are at the heart of the classical problematic of security studies: the causes of war and the conditions of peace. Obviously, this book does not pretend to present a comprehensive overview of alternative approaches to security studies. Our choices were in part guided by a desire to present a broad survey and to complement the worthy contributions that have already been made. Hence, for example, there is no chapter that directly addresses the environment and security, nor one that examines the complex dimensions of gender and international security.[2] Equally, we have not sought to define a precise meaning of the term *critical* in either a methodological or political sense.

This may risk seeming to some (at any point of the theoretical map) as if we have avoided important issues and left out important perspectives. Undoubtedly, we have. But part of the development of a broader conception of security studies (and critical security studies) requires that its growth not be straitjacketed by the imposition of criteria of inclusion and exclusion or by a renewed call for definitive answers. Indeed, it might be fair to say that these disciplining dynamics within so much of contemporary security studies are part of the problem, and that there is therefore a double need to resist them in the fostering of alternative positions. This collection, we hope, marks a small move in such a direction.

POLITICS, THE STATE, AND THE DISCIPLINE OF SECURITY STUDIES

There are still, of course, some guiding themes within this collection. One of these (which emerged from a series of discussions among many of the contributors) is that only by coming to terms with the shifting nature of "the political" in International Relations can we understand the various axes of the contemporary debate in security studies. In this light, the very name of the field—security studies—should give us pause. The implication is that scholars in the field are studying security. But what, precisely, does this mean? A moment's reflection reveals a basic problem: security is a derivative concept; it is in itself meaningless. To have any meaning, *security* necessarily presupposes something to be secured; as a realm of study it cannot be self-referential.

To some, this no doubt seems pedantic. But that the question seems nonsensical or uninformed illustrates an important point. To be a member of the security studies community has traditionally meant that one already *knows* what is to be studied. Both the object of security (what is to be secured) and the means for studying it are treated as largely given and self-evident. In this way, the discipline provides a shared framework, a common analytic culture for understanding. While there is room for considerable argument within this framework, the framework itself is not seen as subject to debate, and challenges to its way of understanding the world have been vigorously met. Thus, Stephen Walt seems to argue that one of the biggest threats to security is the seductive appeal of contrary methods for understanding it.[3] The security of the discipline, in this view, is made into an element—perhaps even a prerequisite—of security itself!

What is it that needs to be secured (both intellectually and practically) within the conventions of security studies? A simple and not wholly misleading answer is, "the state."[4] Recent trends in world politics and intellectual developments in International Relations have challenged this answer in many ways. New issues and perceived threats, the twin dynamics of the fragmentation and integration of existing states, and the challenges to sovereignty from a range of transnational and subnational forces have provided considerable grist for current discussions of the nature of security and the adequacy of a state-centric definition of the question. But simply to focus on the assumption that the state is the foundation for security studies, and then to claim that current transformations in world politics render this assumption inadequate is to underestimate seriously the issues involved. It is not simply a claim about the historical centrality of the state that is at the heart of traditional conceptions of security. What is at stake is also a particular understanding of how the state resolves the problem of political order itself. This is perhaps the central reason why the orthodoxy of security studies has been so resistant to taking account of current transformative trends (usually by denying their relevance) that seem to challenge its analytic assumptions.

The concept of security is not empty; it implicitly invokes and relies on a series of accepted prior visions of what is to be secured. As R. B. J. Walker has stressed (in this volume and elsewhere), what characterizes such approaches to the study of International Relations is not a claim about international relations per se, but a prior claim about the possibility of politics. Realists' accounts, for example, rest on a theory of domestic politics and defend a particular vision of the possibilities of political order—the political—that sees it as inextricable from the modern conceptions of sovereignty and the state. Its conception of security follows and is similarly derivative: its claims are a priori and deductive, not objective in any straightforward sense.

However paradoxical the outcomes of this understanding of security may become (think of nuclear deterrence theory or the rendering "insecure" of the entire citizenry), or however anachronistic its views may seem in light of many contemporary dynamics in world politics, this vision of politics and security maintains its purchase because the sovereign state is viewed as the only possible locus of political life. The conception of state or national security on which the traditional approach to security studies rests has certain limitations: its sense of the real and the possible is not derived wholly, or even primarily, from a practical assessment of contemporary dynamics in world politics. On the contrary, its appraisals are significantly predetermined by the construction of the political, which provides the foundation for its conception of security.[5]

Critical or critical?

Our appending of the term *critical* to *security studies* is meant to imply more an orientation toward the discipline than a precise theoretical label, and we adopt a small-*c* definition of *critical* for both practical and intellectual reasons. Practically, a broad definition allows many perspectives that have been considered outside of the mainstream of the discipline to be brought into the same forum, with attendant benefits for intellectual dialogue and debate. Hence this volume includes a contribution from Mohammed Ayoob that adopts a subaltern realism that is at odds with recent scholarship questioning the importance of the state, yet that does not fit comfortably within the core tenets of the mainstream understanding of security. Likewise, Thomas Risse-Kappen's contribution points to an important tension within competing accounts that could be labeled critical and takes its distance from much of poststructuralist International Relations. Similarly, contributions that lean on Ludwig Wittgenstein to analyze the transformed discourse of East-West relations in the 1980s, or that focus on the struggles to redefine security in framing policy responses to the war in the former Yugoslavia, or that attempt to apply work on metaphor to the construction of the "problem" of proliferation all come under our broad umbrella.

Because we have no wish in this context to engage in the ongoing debates within International Relations over the precise meaning of the term *critical*, a precise definition is unnecessary. Perhaps the most straightforward way to convey our sense of how *critical* should be understood in this volume is Robert Cox's distinction between problem-solving and critical theory: the former takes "prevailing social and power relationships and the institutions into which they are organized . . . as the given framework for action," while the latter "calls them into question by concerning itself with their origins and how and whether they might be in the process of changing."[6] Our approach to security studies (dealt with in our contribution to this volume) thus begins from an analysis of the claims that make the discipline possible—not just its claims about the world but also its underlying epistemology and ontology, which prescribe what it means to *make* sensible claims about the world.

Security studies, like any academic discipline, is underpinned by a culture of inquiry, and the orthodox approach to security to which all of our authors are responding rests on a claim about the necessary nature and limits of politics and political order. By making the definition of the *political* a question rather than an assumption, one can illuminate the dynamics of contemporary security debates, at both the policy-making and scholarly levels. In both realms it is the object of security, and consequently the corresponding concept of political order, that is at stake. In each case, the claims of the sovereign state are under strain. These tensions not only generate new problems that may require new explanatory frameworks (such as Barry Buzan's realms of political, military, economic, environmental, and societal security), but they also provide an opening for critical thinking as a result of the disarray and confusion into which prevailing approaches have been thrown. If the objective (or at least the outcome) of much scholarship in security studies has been to render the question and problem of security apolitical and largely static, critical theory takes the question of change as its foundation, in both an explanatory and an evaluative sense.

As regards the foundations of the field, our goal, to borrow a metaphor from Steven Shapin and Simon Shaffer, is to show that while the accepted practices of security studies appear like a ship in the bottle, we need "to see that the ship was once a pile of sticks and string, and that it was once outside the bottle."[7] One means of acquiring this critical distance lies in adopting a distinction between "member's accounts" and "stranger's accounts." Approaching the field of security studies as a culture of inquiry, we can begin to see how both engagement within it and critical distance from it are essential. As Shapin and Shaffer put it:

> Being a member of the culture one seeks to understand has enormous advantages. . . . Nevertheless, unreflective membership also carries with it serious disadvantages to the search for understanding, and the chief of these might be called "the self-evident method" . . . in [which] the presuppositions of our own culture's routine practices are not regarded as problematic and in need of explanation.

The stranger has "one great advantage . . . over the member in explaining the beliefs and practices of a specific culture: the stranger is in a position to *know* that there are alternatives to those beliefs and practices. The awareness of alternatives and the pertinence of the explanatory project go together." The perspective of the stranger is thus a useful analytic stance to adopt in attempting to come to terms with the discipline of security studies. On the other hand, however, playing the stranger poses intrinsic difficulties. Among the most substantial of these difficulties is that the member's account, and its associated self-evident method, have great instinctive appeal; the social forces that protect and sustain them are powerful. The member who poses awkward questions about "what everybody knows" in the shared culture runs a real risk of being dealt with as a troublemaker or an idiot. Indeed, there are few more reliable ways of being expelled from a culture than continuing seriously to query its taken-for-granted intellectual framework.[8]

In our view, a critical approach to security studies may adopt the position of a stranger, but not that of an outsider. As useful as the concept of playing the stranger may be as a critical strategy, it contains tensions, dilemmas, and pitfalls that emerge both from within the culture it is attempting to understand and from other critical perspectives outside of that culture. From within the culture of security studies, a stranger's account may face challenges that are disciplinary in the full sense of the term. Indeed, as our own contribution to this volume attempts to illustrate, this discipline has been exercised in contemporary debates on the reconstruction of security studies, a fact of some importance in developing critical approaches to security.

Yet although a critical distance may be invaluable in allowing us to step back from the claims of security studies, it is also incomplete. For where, precisely, does the stranger stand? This question moves to center stage as one shifts from a negative or deconstructive critique of existing positions to a positive or reconstructive stance. A failure to make this shift has precisely been the major charge leveled by practitioners working with prevailing conceptions of security studies against critical challenges. It is also a question that divides much of critical theory.

FROM CRITIQUE TO RECONSTRUCTION

The reconstructive agenda of critical security studies is more difficult to discern at this point. The claims of states-as-actors and the identification of security exclusively with citizenship that underpin the orthodox conception of security studies can be exposed as problematic, its epistemological claims can be shown to be suspect and inadequately grounded, and its view of the relationship between theory and practice can be demonstrated as insufficient. But what underlies the dismissal of alternative approaches is at heart a fear that unless one adopts its conceptions of the state and sovereignty (and the practices that follow from this), scholars will be incapable of saying anything useful or practical in (and about) the world.

However unconsciously security studies scholars have adopted the assumption of state sovereignty as their premise and object, the concept of the modern state and sovereignty embodies a coherent response to many of the central problems of political life. Viewed more fully and historically than it often is in strategic studies (and unfortunately in some critical theory), sovereignty must be seen not just as an assumption that can be challenged but as a sophisticated resolution to difficult questions. The fact that this resolution has always been incomplete, and that in the contemporary world it is coming under increasing strain, does not mean that the questions it originally attempted to settle no longer need to be addressed. The emergence and development of the modern state and its concept of sovereignty cannot be understood without reference to attempts to control and restrict the role of organized violence in political life.[9] And the question of the place of violence in political life does not vanish at the first challenge to the foundations of the state or sovereignty.

If a critical theory involves de-essentializing and deconstructing prevailing claims about security, then the question of how security is to be redefined seems necessarily to follow. Realism's construction of the possibilities for political order, of the realm of politics, and thus of security yields both an object to secure (the territorially defined political community) and an agent to pursue this end (the state). As the contributions to this volume by R. B. J. Walker and Simon Dalby point out, at the broadest level of theoretical reflection a consciousness of the dilemmas within security fragments its easy identification with the state. Processes of globalization highlight and exacerbate these tensions, and a recognition of these tensions and paradoxes is a continuing element in critical appraisals of security studies.

But this raises the question at the heart of much critical theory: is there a new grounding for political order that can provide both a referent and an actor in a globalizing and fragmenting world? And if so, what are its relations to other claimants and to the continuing claims and structures of state security? The question of where to root a critical position that can be the ground for theory and provide the subject and/or object of practical action has long bedeviled critical theories of society. The quintessential example, of course, is Marxism's myriad debates over the relationships between class and state, structure and agency, ideology and social power. Feminist approaches, too, have sought to show the prevalence of gender relations both nationally and transnationally, and the ways in which categories of gender can inform analysis of traditional security questions (for example, militarism) and broaden the understanding of security itself. But here as well, the question of whether such analyses can provide a cross-cultural or transnational conception of security from a feminist perspective, or can create a political force or actor capable of acting in its name, is a theoretically contested and practically unresolved matter.

Finally, there are the loosely defined postmodern orientations. Deeply suspicious of any universalizing claims, postmodernism is happy to participate in the deconstructive movement shared by these other theories. But it resists the desire to replace discredited certainties with new ones and celebrates the fragmentation, prizing difference over identity. Claims to absolute identity (whether epistemological or political) are seen as sources of exclusion and violence. But postmodernism cannot avoid entirely the question of political practice. An awareness of difference (as can be seen in Bosnia and Rwanda) can all too often lead not to celebration but destruction. In itself, this may not be a compelling criticism of postmodernism, as it overlooks the distinction between difference and Otherness, where violence arises most forcefully when the inescapability of difference is transformed into the oppositional category of Otherness. Yet in a context where oppositional violence against the Other exists—the condition par excellence of security studies—then the question of what to do, of choosing a side or taking a stand, is inescapable. Postmodern approaches have yet to confront this challenge convincingly.

These (and other) critical perspectives have much to say to each other in the construction of a critical theory of international relations and, in turn, to contemporary security studies. While elements of many approaches may be found in this volume, no one perspective dominates. If anything, several of the contributions to this volume stand more inside than outside the tradition of security studies, which reflects our twofold conviction about the place of critical perspectives in contemporary scholarship. First, to stand too far outside prevailing discourses is almost certain to result in continued disciplinary exclusion. Second, to move toward alternative conceptions of security and security studies, one must necessarily reopen the questions subsumed under the modern conception of sovereignty and the scope of the political. To do this, one must take seriously the prevailing claims about the nature of security.

Many of the chapters in this volume thus retain a concern with the centrality of the state as a locus not only of obligation but of effective political action. In the realm of organized violence, states also remain the preeminent actors. The task of a critical approach is not to deny the centrality of the state in this realm but, rather, to understand more fully its structures, dynamics, and possibilities for reorientation. From a critical perspective, state action is flexible and capable of reorientation, and analyzing state policy need not therefore be tantamount to embracing the statist assumptions of orthodox conceptions. To exclude a focus on state action from a critical perspective on the grounds that it plays inevitably within the rules of existing conceptions simply reverses the error of essentializing the state. Moreover, it loses the possibility of influencing what remains the most structurally capable actor in contemporary world politics.

CONTRIBUTIONS TO THE VOLUME

This volume attempts to address some of the issues we have raised through both conceptual and research-oriented contributions. Part one deals with a range of theoretical issues surrounding how we might approach critical security studies. The first chapter, by Simon Dalby, adopts an explicitly globalist (or "postsecurity") orientation, which treats security as an "essentially contested concept" that unavoidably presents scholars and practitioners with dilemmas. Dalby's analysis is oriented around poststructural and feminist questioning of the discourse of security, which he examines in light of three issues that pose dilemmas for security policy and analysis: economic competition, the drug trade, and environmental degradation. He concludes that it is not only difficult to broaden the concept of security beyond its Cold War military-oriented parameters, but that broadened understandings are vulnerable to being co-opted within orthodox formulations of policy and analysis. The chapter that follows, by the two of us, attempts to uncover some of the epistemological and conceptual foundations of the orthodox conception of security, as a way of highlighting the resilience of this conception to challenges, and the difficulties encountered in recent attempts to reorient the concept of security around individuals, citizens, and humanity as the subjects of security.

The remaining three contributions to part one invoke distinctive perspectives on the meaning of *critical*. The most explicitly postmodern perspective is that of R. B. J. Walker, who shares Dalby's analysis of the transformations of political life to which we are all witness but is skeptical about the broader notions of political community (and hence security) that are often invoked as a necessary consequence. On this account, the major confusion in current debates over the meaning of security arises from a dilemma: on one hand, it is not clear whether more broadly defined forms of political community can be realized; on the other hand, a trenchant denial of the very possibility seems historically myopic. A direct counterpoint to Walker (and to Ken Booth) is presented by Mohammed Ayoob, who argues that although the orthodox formulations of security do not adequately grasp the central concerns that motivate Third World state rulers, a too-broad definition of security is analytically useless and, politically, even potentially dangerously naive. He opts for a reformulated or subaltern realist perspective that is more sensitive to the dynamic of state formation and its impact on security in the developing world than formulations that downplay the role of the state. His contribution highlights both the narrow Western foundations of orthodox conceptions of security studies, and the practical and conceptual difficulties that confront some of the more radical reformulations of the concept of security. Perhaps the most unusual perspective is that of Ken Booth, whose autobiographical exploration of a "fallen realist" takes seriously the feminist admonition that the personal is the political. Booth emphasizes the everyday way in which the disciplinary structures of the profession operate within strategic or security studies and discusses the institutional or professional changes that he thinks are necessary for the future development of security studies under the framework of "utopian realism."

Part two brings various perspectives that can loosely be labeled "constructivist" to bear on a series of specific case studies.[10] The chapter by Beverly Crawford and Ronnie Lipschutz examines the Western response to the war in the former Yugoslavia, by analyzing the way in which this response depended on a particular construction of the causes of the conflict that framed the dominant policy of inaction. It also highlights the problems inherent in this construction, by focusing on the competing security claims of different ethnic and religious groups and the relatively recent creation of the animosities that fueled the conflict, and by drawing attention to an alternative formulation of the causes of the war that focuses on the role of tensions between state institutions and civil society. David Mutimer's research looks at the construction of the problem of proliferation in the post-Cold War period. It concentrates on the role of metaphoric constructions in framing our understanding of security challenges in such a way as to highlight certain aspects of the process of weapons production and diffusion and to occlude or obscure other aspects. The dominant metaphors of proliferation—balance and stability—are shown to privilege policy solutions that concentrate on strategies of technology denial, but that therefore downplay the importance of dual-use-technology imports for economic development and minimize the significance of the political and economic interests behind the supply of weapons technology. Finally, Karin Fierke examines the collapse and reconstruction of the East-West relationship. Her analysis brings to bear themes from Wittgenstein's linguistic analyses in order to demonstrate the way in which a shared discourse or language of security helped to constitute the identities and actions of NATO and the Warsaw Pact. She concentrates on the extended metaphoric use of notions of families and homes in the construction, renovation, and reconstruction of the European security architecture, and she concludes that the foundational metaphors have shifted away from those of a family toward those of a club, in which one makes investments or purchases insurance against a new range of unspecified risks in a fluid international environment.

The contributions to part three highlight the convergence of debates surrounding security and "world-order imperatives," which can be found in efforts to redefine the scope of United Nations actions to achieve international peace and security, or at the intersection of universalist and regionalist perspectives on security orders. The chapter by Thomas Risse-Kappen returns to the social constructivist themes evoked above and contrasts a rationalist account of multilateral cooperation in the security realm to a constructivist one, in which the preferences and interests of actors are explicitly part of the explanatory framework rather than exogenously given. This leads him to a focus on the changing normative and prescriptive content of Security Council resolutions and United Nations actions in the post-

Cold War period, and to conclude that a rationalist approach cannot explain the emergence of new norms of multilateralism, but that these norms have to date been only weakly implemented and enforced in recent UN operations. Amitav Acharya's contribution focuses on regional conflicts in the Third World and the ways in which understandings of security derived from the Western experience need to be adapted to the manifold security challenges of the developing world. He advocates an increased concentration on region-specific approaches to security, whether these are manifest in different institutional arrangements or in different understandings of how order is maintained and security created. Finally, the chapter by Ken Booth and Peter Vale on southern Africa discusses the way in which critical understandings of security could be brought to bear on the construction of a regional security order in postapartheid southern Africa. More explicitly activist than most of the other chapters, it advocates a rethinking of who must be secured, what the agenda of threats will be, and what the role of South Africa may be in the emerging regional order. It also discusses possible regional security orders in terms of some familiar concepts, such as Karl Deutsch's security communities, the notion of comprehensive security, and the possible role of regional security institutions.

CONCLUSION

In spite of the diversity of orientations and approaches represented in the chapters that follow, the contributors were united on two things. First, they shared a dissatisfaction with the "renaissance" account of strategic/security studies, in which new issues and challenges are being subsumed under old (and unexamined) approaches to the discipline. Second, they were perhaps equally dissatisfied with a simple "expansionist" agenda for security that celebrates the end of the Cold War as an opportunity to remove military and security issues from center stage and replace them with diverse challenges to individual and collective well-being or human survival.

Obviously, one edited volume cannot capture the entire range of contributions that can be made to a broader and more critical conception of security studies. Seen as part of an emerging and ongoing project, however, this volume contributes to a reinvigorated debate that compels scholars, students, and practitioners to think seriously about the conceptual limitations of orthodox conceptions of security, the difficulties inherent in attempts to redefine or broaden the concept, and the practical research questions and strategies that can be used to move beyond critique toward more intellectually satisfying reformulations of security studies. The task is important, both in scholarly and practical terms, if security studies is to help us meet the challenges of world politics in the twenty-first century.

NOTES

1. To illustrate, five examples from debates concerning nuclear weapons and deterrence would include Hugh Mehan, Charles Nathanson, and James Skelly, "Nuclear Discourse in the 1980s: Unravelling the Conventions of the Cold War," *Discourse and Society* 1:2 (1990), 133–65; G. M. Dillon, "Modernity, Discourse and Deterrence," *Current Research on Peace and Violence* 12:2 (1989), 90–104; Timothy Luke, "What's Wrong with Deterrence? A Semiotic Interpretation of National Security Policy," in James Der Derian and Michael Shapiro, eds., *International/Intertextual Relations* (Lexington, Mass.: Lexington Books, 1989), 207–29; Michael C. Williams, "Rethinking the 'Logic' of Deterrence," *Alternatives* 17 (1992), 67–93; Bradley Klein, *Strategic Studies and World Order* (Cambridge: Cambridge University Press, 1994), 106–22.

2. For major contributions to the former, see Thomas Homer Dixon, "On the Threshold: Environmental Changes as Causes of Acute Conflict," *International Security* 16:2 (Fall 1991), 76–116; Patricia Mische, "Ecological Security and the Need to Reconceptualize Sovereignty," *Alternatives* 14:4 (1989), 389–427; Jessica Tuchman Mathews, "Redefining Security," *Foreign Affairs* 68:2 (Spring 1989), 162–77; Daniel Deudney, "The Case against Linking Environmental Degradation and National Security," *Millennium* 19:3 (1990), 461–76. On the latter, see J. Ann Tickner, *Gender and International Relations: Feminist Perspectives on Achieving Global Security* (New York: Columbia University Press, 1992); Rebecca Grant, "The Quagmire of Gender and International Security," in V. Spike Peterson, ed., *Gendered States* (Boulder, Colo.: Lynne Rienner, 1992), 83–98; Cynthia Enloe, *Bananas, Beaches and Bases: Making Feminist Sense of International Politics* (London: Pandora, 1989).

3. Stephen Walt, "The Renaissance of Security Studies," *International Studies Quarterly* 35 (1991), 211–39. See also our contribution to this volume.

4. As Barry Buzan acknowledged in *People, States and Fear*, 2nd ed. (London: Harvester Wheatsheaf, 1991), 22–23.

5. A classic recent example of this is John Mearsheimer, "Back to the Future: Instability in Europe after the Cold War," *International Security* 15 (1990), 5–57. See also John Mearsheimer, "The False Promise of International Institutions," *International Security* 19:3 (Winter 1994/1995), 5–49.

6. Robert Cox, "Social Forces, States and World Orders: Beyond International Relations Theory," in Robert Keohane, ed., *Neorealism and Its Critics* (New York: Columbia University Press, 1986), 208. There are, of course, important weaknesses with this distinction that need not concern us here.

7. Quotations in this paragraph and the next are from Steven Shapin and Simon Shaffer, *Leviathan and the Air Pump: Hobbes, Boyle and the Experimental Life* (Princeton, N.J.: Princeton University Press, 1985), 4–7.

8. Shapin and Shaffer, *Leviathan and the Air Pump,* 6.

9. See Charles Tilly, "War Making and State Making as Organized Crime," in Peter Evans, Dietrich Rueschemeyer, and Theda Skocpol, eds., *Bringing the State Back In* (Cambridge: Cambridge University Press, 1985), 169–91; Karen Rasler and William Thompson, *War and State Making* (Boston: Unwin Hyman, 1989); Charles Tilly, *Coercion, Capital and European States* (Oxford: Blackwell, 1990).

10. For more explicit articulations of approaches to International Relations that could be labeled "social constructivist" (although not all the authors do so), see Alexander Wendt, "Anarchy Is What States Make of It," *International Organization* 46:2 (Spring 1992), 391–425; Roxanne Doty, "Foreign Policy as Social Construction: A Post-Positivist Analysis of U.S. Counterinsurgency Policy in the Philippines," *International Studies Quarterly* 37:3 (1993), 297–320; Audie Klotz, "Norms Reconstituting Interests: Global Racial Equality and U.S. Sanctions against South Africa," *International Organization* 49:3 (Summer 1995), 451–78; David Campbell, *Writing Security: United States Foreign Policy and the Politics of Identity* (Minneapolis: University of Minnesota Press, 1992).

Acknowledgments

This volume, and the conference that preceded it, could not have come about without intellectual and practical contributions from a wide range of people. The initial ideas were developed at the York Centre for International and Strategic Studies (YCISS) in Toronto, where for many years students and faculty have been working in an extremely congenial scholarly environment on a variety of alternative approaches to security and security studies. David Dewitt and Paul Evans suggested and encouraged the project throughout. Funding was obtained from the (now sadly defunct) Canadian Cooperative Security Competitions Programme. Organizational and administrative support for the conference was provided by the YCISS, in particular by Heather Chestnutt, Rose Edgecombe, Wendy Kubasik, and Steven Mataija. Support for preparation of the draft and final manuscripts was also provided by the Graduate Institute of International Studies (Geneva), in particular by Denise Ducroz.

We have also benefited from comments on various parts of the argument and manuscript from Lars-Erik Cederman, Pierre Lizée, Jennifer Milliken, David Mutimer, Heikki Patomäki, and all the participants in the original conference. Various people also provided many provocative and enlightening comments at presentations of our coauthored chapter at the British International Studies Association conference in York in December 1994, and at the International Studies Association conference in Chicago in February 1995. Finally, thanks to two anonymous readers for the University of Minnesota Press, whose detailed and insightful comments improved the volume considerably and helped us in the drafting of our preface.

I

Conceptual Debates and Approaches

eign and security policies by many states, and noticeably by the NATO alliance.

These policy debates have been paralleled by discussions, within the academy in general and within international relations in particular, about how security should be reformulated to adapt to new circumstances.[2] The global security *problematique,* it is often argued, now encompasses much more than the contest for political supremacy in the processes of superpower rivalry. Often under the rubrics of "common security" or "cooperative security," the themes of nonoffensive defense, economic security, environmental security, societal insecurities, drug threats, even human rights and the autonomy of civil society have been added in attempts to reformulate security policies to encompass many new items on the global political agenda.[3] Simultaneously, it has been suggested, by feminists in particular, that security needs to be rethought to downplay the use of military force, to recognize the violent consequences of its conventional formulations and the limited applicability that these political strategies have for dealing with structural inequality and environmental degradation.[4] Beyond this, one prominent scholar with a theoretical inclination has suggested the reformulation of security to encompass various aspects of human liberation.[5] Another recent analysis shifted the focus from state to societal security, although without apparently resolving many of the difficulties that a solely state-centric formulation traditionally posed.[6]

These extensions and simultaneous questionings of security raise the crucial issue of whether the discursive practices of Cold War security policy, premised on the necessity of ensuring military preparedness, maintaining secrecy, and working out strategies for using nuclear weapons in international conflict, really offer a useful policy approach or scholarly framework for dealing with political problems of economic dislocation, political violence, the growing numbers of refugees, environmental degradation, and the failure to think or act seriously concerning questions of sustainable livelihoods around the globe. During the Cold War critics of the Western use of the term *security* and of the practices of strategic studies pointed out that they were both used to maintain the dominance of American political priorities on the global scene. Little in the policy literature on the future of Western security and NATO suggests that this usage has disappeared.[7] Indeed, it might be argued that the dilemma of academic security discourse after the Cold War is precisely that its conceptual infrastructure has long outlived any usefulness it might have once had and has mutated into a number of discourses that operate to maintain the unjust political order of developed and underdeveloped and overconsumption in the developed world at the expense of degradation of the global environment.[8]

Extending the ambit of security without simultaneously investigating the formulation of what it is that is being rendered secure is a particularly tempting strategy for analysts and practitioners of national security, now that the certainties of the Cold War confrontation have evaporated, but it is one that begs precisely the questions that should be asked. The question then is whether, in the process of extending the ambit of threats requiring a military response, one is not further militarizing society rather than dealing more directly with political difficulties. As Lothar Brock puts it in discussing the possibilities of environmental security as a policy focus, "defining environmental issues in terms of security risks is in itself a risky operation. . . . we may end up contributing more to the militarization of environmental politics than to the demilitarization of security politics."[9] Taking this point further, contemporary global problems suggest the necessity for fairly dramatic political change in numerous contexts.[10] Can security studies make this theme clear? The political order itself may generate insecurity, in which case security studies may well need to be a subversive enterprise. But national and international security, premised on the desirability of order, are usually understood as precisely that which is not subversive.

It might be possible, and it is perhaps much easier, to challenge conceptualizations of security by drawing on literature in peace research, peace studies, or a number of other literatures to somehow formulate a better understanding of what security should be. But *security* is a crucial term, both in the political lexicon of state policy makers and among academics in the field of international relations. Precisely because of the salience of security, the current debates about reformulating it provide, when read as political discourse in need of analysis rather than as a series of solutions to problems, a very interesting way to come to grips with what is at stake in current debates about world politics and the constitution of the post-Cold War political order. Instead of reformulating the security *problematique* from outside, this chapter reads the contemporary formulations of security discourse in its own terms, working with the difficulties and dilemmas of security to explore the discursive terrain of this important and "essentially contested concept."[11]

Thus the rest of this chapter attempts to work with the dilemmas of security as a concept and simultaneously to engage with the political implications of its contemporary reformulations. The thrust of the argument suggests that the contemporary additions, enlargements and reformulations of the concept of security, premised on the assumed virtue of security in the modern world, turn out to be very difficult to add to security as it was conventionally understood for most of the Cold War. They are, however, vulnerable to being co-opted into the Cold War geopolitical formulations of militarized foreign policies. *Security* is a contested term, one with multiple meanings, some of which are not at all necessarily logically linked to conventional understandings. Most interestingly, as far as the analysis presented in this chapter goes, the additions to, and expansions and reformulations of, *security* can be read as destabilizations and contestations of the term itself. The implications of these readings of security suggest that the concept and its related practices can be understood as a number of political problems, ones that have, among other consequences, profoundly unsettling implications for the field of security studies, as well as more widely for International Relations.

WHOSE SECURITY? THROUGH GENDERED LENSES DARKLY

During the Cold War, security was often presented as protection and safety, but the threat of nuclear destruction in particular undermined in many ways the assertions of safety, calling into question the possibility of the technological provision of security. During that time the dangers of nuclear warfare also rendered all women vulnerable to violence as a consequence of the political arrangements that supported nuclear-weapon-based security policy. Precisely these political arrangements marginalized the role of women. It is not surprising that in a world of mutually assured destruction those with no direct stake in the military institutions often understood technological violence, the use of resources for military purposes, and the persistence of geopolitical divisions as the political problem rather than as a solution to problems of insecurity.

Technology, surveillance, and the political division of space substantially shaped the discourses of security during the Cold War.[12]

The conventional understandings involved the threat, and sometimes the imposition, of military force, the operation of surveillance technologies that produced huge volumes of information, and the careful demarcation of spheres of interest and defined carceral spaces that were technologically patrolled and controlled. The possibility of politics was constrained by structural anarchy and the radical disjunction of geopolitical spaces. Seeing through gendered lenses, being sensitive to the different social experiences of different genders, and looking at how pervasive conceptual and terminological dichotomies often have gendered attributes, it is not hard to argue that built into these masculinist definitions of power are all the modernist assumptions of control, domination and surveillance that premise security in one way or another on violence and spatial control.[13] This point is important in unraveling the dilemmas of security in the current context. In reconsidering security through feminist lenses in particular, the assumptions of power, control, knowledge, and the resort to violence look increasingly suspect as appropriate modes of response to contemporary political problems.[14]

The feminist investigations of global power relations, perhaps clearest in Cynthia Enloe's contemporary writings, suggest a very different understanding of power in global politics, one that challenges the conventional focus of states as autonomous actors and raises the difficult question of what is being secured in the provision of security as conventionally defined.[15] By looking at the lives of women in numerous places and social positions, from diplomatic wives to migrant domestic workers, Enloe argues that conventional international-relations practices render women insecure and subject to violence in numerous ways but also make them an indispensable part of these contemporary political practices. Just as their rights to land ownership are limited in many parts of the world, so too their status as passport holders has often been limited and their rights to travel restricted.[16] Thus, masculine spaces define women's places in numerous politically important ways beyond the most obvious social segregations and the construction of the spheres of the masculine public and the feminine private that have been the focus of much feminist attention. The feminist arguments that security (in terms of masculinist modes of domination) secures patriarchal relations of power and renders women insecure precisely because they are women undercuts the state-centric logic of the security discourse.

Such arguments challenge the essential rationale of state security in supposedly providing citizens with physical safety within the political community that is defined in terms of the territorial container of the state.

In rethinking international relations in these terms, feminist analyses raise perhaps most directly the crucial point that is so often silenced in the conventional neorealist premises in contemporary security studies. They ask the simple question of who and what precisely is being rendered secure by the provision of national and international security.[17] Looking at the fate of women in the societies that are supposedly made safe by the policies of security provision offers a powerful line of critique by pointing out that in many ways national security operates to render women insecure. Masculine definitions of appropriate behaviors in military organizations leave women vulnerable to abuse and rape and often limit the socially accepted roles they can perform. Women in these societies are not secure in many meaningful ways. Put directly, this is the dilemma of using violence as the mode of preventing violence. Can security be provided by the social implements of violence that are the ostensible cause of insecurity because of their possession by Others? Ultimately, this logic leads to the question of whether, in a world of nuclear-armed states, security in any general sense can be provided by nuclear weapons.[18] It also raises the question of whether it can be provided by the security practices that Carol Cohn has termed "technostrategic" discourse.[19]

Similar logic works in the case of broader definitions of security. Resources spent on military preparation are not available for the provision of social services, and hence, security understood in the broad sense of welfare and the provision of basic needs can also be undermined.[20] Women's livelihoods and environmental sustainability in underdeveloped states facing the financial constraints of "structural adjustments" are not easily understood in the terms of either Cold War security discourses or contemporary notions of global security as being provided by international organizations.[21] But these factors directly affect physical survival, the most basic premise of security. As is the case with development, conventional notions of security cannot provide food, health care, and shelter to poor women across the South.[22] Nor can global climate change be controlled or dealt with by these ways of thinking and acting. Indeed, given the military's roles as a polluter and user of petroleum fuels, in most cases they are seriously aggravated by conventional security practices. All of these questions raised by feminist writers, but until recently absent in academic discussions of international security, force attention on the politics of security provision and, crucially, on the social arrangements that are being secured.

Based on these considerations, the feminist critiques (like the post-structuralist writers discussed below) point to the political order of modernity as a series of social and political constructions.[23] This analysis challenges the ontotheological status of the taken-for-granted formulations of anarchy that inform so much of security thinking. Hence, states and alliances are not the assumed starting point for analysis of state behavior and the application of strategic planning, but the political problem to be analyzed. Taken further, this shift in focus to analyze the power structures implicit in the provision of security suggests that rather than operating in game theoretic modes, premised on masculinist-defined rational actors, security analysts should investigate the operation of power and violence in a sociologically sensitive manner. Unraveling the contingency of the supposedly universal anarchy of states and refuting the gender-specific notions of states of nature disentangles the practices of security discourse, calling into question both its foundational assumptions in supposedly Hobbesian or Rousseauian metaphors, and how its practices act to perpetuate the militarization of international politics.[24]

SECURITY DISCOURSE AS POLITICAL PRACTICE

This leads the discussion to the crucial geopolitical formulations of security and the policing functions of the political spaces of security states. Security as conventionally formulated is about the protection of a political community of some sort, with community understood as a population with attributes in common. These attributes are usually articulated in terms of territorial community having commonalities that external Others imperil in ways that require violence or the threat thereof to dissuade.[25] Difference is posited as threatening when identity is premised on a supposedly vulnerable sameness. The question then arises, can security be rethought in terms that do not necessarily equate difference with threat and that recognize the possibility of conducting foreign policy in terms of an "ethics of heteronomous responsibility"?[26] Among other things, this requires a recognition of the flows and the interconnections of transboundary interactions with the formulation of political identity and responsibility. Such an approach to foreign policy making would, in Michael Shapiro's terms, require a very different series of practices of "making foreign," and a recognition that sovereignty understood simply as autarkic control over territory is not tenable.[27]

The poststructuralist dissidents in international relations also question the whole operation of security as a discourse for making sense of contemporary politics.[28] They argue that discourse implicates practitioners in the practices that they claim to be only observing from some detached, neutral vantage point.[29] More so than most, security has been a state policy practice as much as an academic activity. Among other themes, the critics point to the politics of security discourse and the importance of media representations in legitimating political orders in numerous locations.[30] The intimate relationship between foreign policy making and academic research and teaching is also obvious in the sociology of the disciplines involved and the dynamics of academic conferences where practitioners and scholars so frequently rub shoulders and blur the boundary lines.

Academic tools of analysis are often closely related to the social institutions that manage social phenomena, formulate state policy, and oversee its administration. This was particularly so in matters of strategy and security during the Cold War, where expertise involved a series of security discourses that structured analysis and policy prescription.[31] David Campbell has shown that security is a policy discourse that has frequently worked to constitute political order rather than to initiate social change.[32] National security has very often been a conservative formulation equating the political status quo with desirable order. Likewise, the assumption that Western political identities are unproblematic, not to mention universally desirable, and that all political matters are to be judged by their criteria leads all too quickly to the attribution of difference as a threat. Formulating social problems other than direct violence in terms of security too easily results in militarization or violence as a solution to what is defined as a problem. Thus, social theory is a political practice in that it situates actors, articulates identities, and legitimizes organizations and institutions.

Three episodes from the Cold War support the contention that security discourses are constitutive of the *problematique* that, according to the positivist contention, their practitioners supposedly merely observe. First is the importance of the U.S. National Security Council document NSC-68, the key policy formulation that articulated the American national security interest in terms of a military threat from the Soviet Union in 1950. The point that both Charles Nathanson and Robert Latham make clearly, albeit in different ways, is that there were other possible political scripts, ones that would not necessarily have led to the militarization of the Cold War confrontation, a militarization that George Kennan, the supposed architect of the policy of containment, was later to repudiate.[33] The NSC-68 was a deliberate choice to conduct politics in a certain discursive framework. Second, a quarter of a century later, in the 1970s during the policies of detente, the Cold War geopolitical precepts were no longer the unchallenged premises of policy formulation in Washington. The Committee on the Present Danger's campaign to render them once again hegemonic in Washington provided, with the accession of Ronald Reagan's administration to power, a specification of the geopolitical situation that facilitated the remilitarization of U.S. foreign policy.[34]

Third, and more recently, it can be convincingly argued that an important part of the unraveling of the Cold War system came about as a result of Soviet reconceptions of security in the 1980s.[35] Michael Mccgwire's widely ignored analysis suggests clearly that the Soviet leadership rethought their security policy quite drastically in the mid-1980s, in the aftermath of the war scare of 1983 and the accession of a new leadership to power in the Kremlin.[36] Key to understanding the processes of perestroika and Mikhail Gorbachev's innovative foreign policy was a clear decision that the Leninist strategic code, concerning the likelihood of war triggered by imperialist ambitions and crises, no longer held. The assumption that the superpower relationship could be managed politically rather than militarily is crucial to what subsequently transpired. These innovations occurred before the economic collapse and political implosion of Soviet power. Indeed, one can argue that the shifting of Soviet security priorities was crucial to initiating the drastic changes in Eastern Europe in 1989.[37]

It is interesting to note that, like many other contributions, Edward Kolodziej's meditations on the end of the Cold War occlude this whole theme of shifting Soviet priorities by simply arguing that the Soviet Union was a political and security failure.[38] The significance of

tance of specifically strategic minerals are sometimes vulnerable to the simple charge of circular reasoning. Military aircraft use substantial quantities of relatively rare metals whose known sources are in remote and politically unstable regions. To ensure access to these materials, it is then argued, requires the production of military equipment capable of guaranteeing continued access to the raw materials needed to produce the military equipment. In the face of increasing globalizations, these geoeconomic arguments to reassert access to resources in the South also challenge the arguments for international trade that suggest that global interdependence is necessary to ensure prosperity. The dilemmas here are also fairly clear, albeit not exactly new. One set of security priorities points to autarky, the other clearly to international interdependence.

Dilemma 2: The War on Drugs

Extending the theme of security to matters such as the so-called drug war in the United States suggest the dangers to a broadly conceived notion of security. In the case of the war on drugs through the 1980s, the security discourses and the practices that go with them were very obviously in play in U.S. policy debates.[46] Where drugs are portrayed as an external threat to the social fabric of the state, their importation is viewed in analogous terms as an invasion, a violation of sovereignty. Frontiers are being violated, we are told; interdiction and military action are obviously the solution to the problem. What follows is the strengthening of police forces and the escalation of violence against the suppliers of the narcotics and the users of these controlled substances. The crucial assumption built into the (security) discourses of drug wars is that the source of the problem is external supply of substances, not an internal matter of health or social policy.[47] Dealing only with the supply side perpetuates the problem by doing nothing to reduce the demand for drugs.

Those opposed to drug wars point to the hazards of militarization, the increased use of violence by both drug dealers and police, and the perpetuation of the criminalization of addicts who might be much better dealt with through the very different discursive practices of therapy and medical treatment.[48] Taken one step further, the drug war militarizes social relationships in the areas of the South that receive military assistance to tackle drug production, processing, and distribution as a military problem, without necessarily solving the key problems of poverty and underdevelopment that force so many into drug production and distribution as a way of economic survival. The argument for decriminalization of drugs and the regulation of their distribution suggests a very different reading of what constitutes the problem. Focusing on the social conditions that support the drug economy and subculture suggests that there are many flaws in the polity that offers little hope of social success to many people.

To argue that security is the most important lens through which to view this issue implicitly constructs the political identity that is being rendered secure as unproblematic and as the desired political order.[49] Shoring it up by imputing external threats to and internal subversion of that political order is an important political strategy, one that usually works against social reform and defines as beyond consideration policies designed to deal with social problems through strategies that accept the need for domestic political reform. Understanding the problem as one analogous to traditional national-security preoccupations produces a dilemma in that what is being secured is the power of the state to intervene in a variety of social arenas, but the personal health and security of the individuals actually using the substances is not improved. The ostensible reason for conducting a war on drugs in the first place is displaced in a way that perpetuates rather than solves the problem. The dilemma is quite clear: in this case security (broadly defined to refer to the national population) cannot be secured by the application of traditional national-security practices.

Dilemma 3: Environmental Security

Early advocates of linking problems of environmental degradation to traditional security discourses were hopeful that the rhetorical ploy would result in increased priority being given to matters of environment in the policy-making circles in the U.S. and other Western states. Some writers explicitly argued that environmental degradation would trigger conflict.[50] But despite some early suggestions by Gro Harlem Brundtland and others, the term *environmental security* was apparently eclipsed by the discussions of other matters at the Earth Summit.[51] Vice President Al Gore's writings before the 1992 election included suggestions for a strategic environment initiative, but little was heard on these themes as a focus of policy action from the Clinton administration until early 1994. Then Robert Kaplan's alarmist article about the future of global politics in the *Atlantic*

Monthly magazine, which predicted a "coming anarchy" because of conflict caused by environmental degradation, generated considerable attention.[52]

Environmental security is a *problematique* that clearly reveals the difficulties of thinking about security if the complex contexts of environmental politics and security policy are critically examined. The conflation of the themes exposes a number of dilemmas that call into question either one or the other term's political efficacy.[53]

Three dilemmas are fairly clear. First, the haste with which at least some parts of the U.S. military were willing to adopt environmental themes in the immediate aftermath of the Cold War gives pause for thought. The military record on environmental protection in many societies is much less than reassuring. The environmental legacy of Cold War nuclear test ranges, weapons-making facilities, and abandoned toxic waste at military facilities in many states is one aspect of the issue.[54] But beyond this is the parallel concern that institutions concerned with secrecy and centralized control, not to mention frequently being exempt from environmental regulation under some variation of doctrines of sovereign immunity, are simply not appropriate social organizations for dealing with environmental issues.[55]

Second, conventional formulations of security that support maintaining the North's political status quo implies maintaining consumer lifestyles, which in turn require protection of Northern access to resources around the world. On this large scale the environmental-security discourse raises once again the simple but fundamental question of what exactly is being rendered secure. Whatever political arguments may have been made at the time, the United States was in a war in the Persian Gulf in 1991 at least in part to ensure the maintenance of oil supplies to the industrialized world. The economic patterns of industrial production in developed parts of the world depend to a large extent on oil. It is precisely this dependence that is the major contribution to the changing composition of the global atmosphere, with all the possible consequences that flow from this in terms of climate change and environmental disruption. If environmental security is, at least in part, about protecting societies from disruptions caused by anthropogenic climate change, then maintaining the American (and the rest of the developed world's) way of life based on the huge use of fossil fuels is obviously not contributing to environmental security in the sense of protecting environments.

Third, the dilemmas of linking environment and security also refer to enlarging the operation of the formal commercial sector in the South. Security based on modernization and the promotion of economic growth often leads to environmental destruction. Forests are stripped and clear-cut in the search for profits for development, while water supplies are contaminated and indigenous peoples deprived of subsistence. Modernization is secured at the cost of disrupted ecologies and the denial of subsistence, as seen in the recent political turmoil in Southern Mexico. The Chiapas revolt early in 1994 was at least in part about control over land. The link between the turmoil and the North American Free Trade Agreement was made by a number of human-rights watchers. Commercial interests hoping to expand external markets are, so their reports say, enclosing and clearing land that traditionally was used by indigenous and peasant peoples for their subsistence. This is a frequently heard theme in conflicts over resources and land in the underdeveloped world.[56] The desperation of the dispossessed has, it seems, led to political unrest and widespread insecurity. But the reimposition of political order by the military reinforces the disruption of these people's lives, perpetuating violence and encouraging migration to the cities of Latin and North America. The politics of modernization often involve these conflicts; the political order protected by national-security policies in many underdeveloped states is related to the destruction of ecosystems, most obviously of tropical rain forests. Once again, securing modernity seems to be antithetical to environmental protection.[57]

On this point it is also worth remembering that the premise of the notion of sustainable development is precisely that conventional notions of development are not sustainable. In terms of the debates in academic literature on these matters as they relate to security, the dilemma can be perhaps most clearly seen in Barry Buzan's discussions of the possibility of a mature anarchy's providing for international security on a global scale.[58] His theory in part suggests that security is premised on much of the world's becoming advanced industrialized democracies. If this is impossible because of ecological limitations (rather than resource shortages, as earlier arguments suggested), then the prognosis for a global future of peace and security, if security is understood as requiring conventional industrial development, is not good. Ecological limitations suggest that the industrial-democratic assumptions present a dubious (ethnocentric?) premise on which to construct the edifice of a security order.

These dilemmas lead to the argument that either security or environment has to be rethought to allow for an easy conflation of the terms. Security understood as the perpetuation of the modern order seems antithetical to the preservation of the environment. Preserving the environment in turn seems antithetical to the preservation of the modern political economy that is, according to conventional thinking, the referent that should be secured. The dilemma of environmental security is this simple, but none of the suggested reformulations is easy.

THE POLITICS OF SECURITY DISCOURSE

The difficulties of expanding security to encompass themes such as environmental degradation or drug wars, and the problems of reconceptualizing security if feminist and poststructuralist critiques of its conventional formulations are taken seriously, together raise the question of the political functions of security discourse and the role of the academic study of international security issues after the Cold War. A number of writers have recently argued that conventional thinking in international relations is deeply flawed both by its failure to predict or understand the dramatic political changes of 1989 to the present, and its apparent inability to adjust its conceptual tools to deal with global political changes.[59] Viewed from the perspective of global environmental changes, and the apparent complete failure of state governments to come to terms with the nature and scale of worsening poverty and environmental degradation around the world at the Rio conference of 1992, this question of what the purpose of security discourses are after the Cold War seems particularly pertinent.[60] More specifically, this question is also germane given the apparent failure of substantial institutional reform in the U.S. military in the past few years, where large military budgets continue despite changed political circumstances.[61]

But there are now many arguments, not least those that point to the erosion of democratic oversights and the distortions of economic life by military production, to add to the antinuclear arguments of the 1980s against militarized versions of security.[62] These suggest that the triumphalism of Francis Fukuyama's arguments, or for that matter of the NATO officials who suggest that containment and liberal democ-

racy won the Cold War (and are therefore sacrosanct institutions precisely because of their supposed victory), is an idea that very seriously
misreads the global political situation. But defining the world in
terms of the triumph of liberal democracy, as opposed to the recently
vanquished and hence obviously inadequate alternatives, blinds the
discourse to all the pressing issues of global degradation.

More specifically, given the primacy of order in the thinking of
international relations theorists of the realist persuasion, and the security intellectuals who continue to see the world in terms of military
threats, one can easily argue that these modes of reasoning are powerful tools in the arsenals of those who are uninterested in dealing
with questions of injustice, degradation, and human rights. As Mick
Dillon has long argued, politics is about the definition of danger.[63]
Dangers of military threats and drug importation are a lot easier to
mobilize concerned publics and policy communities to tackle than
the more amorphous threat of environmental degradation. Indeed, it
is precisely because the new threats are not (yet?) enemies that they
are less easy to formulate in the conventional terms of security or
other traditional forms of political discourse.[64] But it is not hard to
imagine a reimposition of geopolitical discourses in international
politics under the guise of Western-led global environmental man-
agerialism, where environmental refugees and economic migrants
are constructed as external threats requiring extensive surveillance
and military responses.[65]

There also remains a nagging ethnocentric doubt about the whole
discursive enterprise of international security studies, one that paral-
lels the doubts about the use of more explicitly geopolitical rhetoric
after the Cold War. As a number of writers have noted, the Cold War
was only partly about the superpower confrontation.[66] It was also a
mode of hegemony whereby the United States dominated the planet's
political life and constructed a geopolitical order in terms of "us"
and "them," friend and foe. It has also been repeatedly noted that
International Relations is very much an American (and much less so
a British) social science.[67] Bradley Klein has gone further than this,
arguing that security studies can be understood as a series of discursive practices that provided the policy coordination that went with
incorporation into the U.S. political sphere.[68] Seen in these critical
terms, the whole political preoccupation with security is less a matter of a pregiven political reality and more a matter of the social con-

struction of political orders, which is premised on this particular mode of understanding international politics that has so often supported hegemonic policies.

This is not necessarily to make a simplistic claim that international relations as a discipline is some kind of vast ideological disinformation campaign. It is, however, to note that its recent critics have been persistently pointing to the huge difficulties that the conventional categories of analysis offer to attempts to reconceptualize global politics and place new items on the global agenda.[69] The definitions of politics in neorealist scholarship are narrow and constraining, in few places more so than in how they make it difficult to think about politics in such terms as the *local* and the *global,* terms that often seem to have more resonance with political experience than do the geopolitical rituals of statecraft. They are even more constraining in the way that they operate in terms of security as "the normalization and extirpation of differences" promoting the political efficacy of tropes of violence as appropriate political practice while contingent complexity is simultaneously elided.[70]

Reviewing power and security through feminist lenses suggests focusing on structural inequities and the social relationships of both domination and cooperation as a better approach to understanding the social dynamics of conflict. Getting away from competition and the dynamics of polarization and concentrating instead on diplomacy, cooperation, and the construction of communities across spatial boundaries offers a very different view of security.[71] To put matters crudely, it extends the assumptions of the logic of common security focusing on the common vulnerabilities of people in a variety of different locations and arguing that the political structures of modernity, patriarchy, and capitalism are the sources of insecurity. But such a reformulation of *security* is so different as to call into question whether the term itself can be stretched to accommodate such reinterpretations. Inescapably, it puts into question the utility of the term in political discourse after the Cold War.

THE END OF SECURITY?

But if one removes the term *security* from the political lexicon, what then? As Michael Williams has asked, "if you take away security, what do you put in the hole that's left behind?"[72] Maybe the answer is that there simply is not a hole. After all, the hole is in many ways a relatively recent creation. Despite the frequent invocation of the name of Thomas Hobbes as the architect of contemporary notions of security, it was only in the middle of this century that security became the architectonic impulse of the American polity and, subsequently, of its allies. The emergence of security states elsewhere is often more recent. In the United States, the National Security Council, the National Security Agency, the Central Intelligence Agency, and related institutions were early Cold War creations. Their rationale came from a period of perceived danger to American interests which for the first time were truly global in scope as a result of the U.S. victory over the Axis powers. Coupling fears of Soviet ambitions, of a repeat of Pearl Harbor, and of nuclear war, these institutions formed the heart of a semipermanent military mobilization to support the policies of containment militarism.[73]

If this context is no longer applicable, the case that the national security state is not an appropriate mode for social organization in the future is in many ways compelling. If security is premised on violence, as security-dilemma and national-security literatures suggest (albeit often reluctantly), perhaps the necessity of rethinking global politics requires abandoning the term and the conceptual strictures that go with it. Likewise, perhaps the discourse of international security studies, if not all international relations, and for that matter, more specifically geopolitical modes of reasoning, are also not practically functional as the discursive frameworks for any political arrangement that can hope to deal with some of the more pressing global difficulties. As noted above, the difficulty of extending security to deal with pressing political items is by now obvious. Perhaps the time for a new language to encompass the political agendas of the post-Cold War era has finally arrived.

The questions that this line of argument suggests include the following: Can security be reformulated to incorporate James Der Derian's admonition to celebrate rather than fear difference?[74] Might such sensitivities at least facilitate more cooperative approaches to international political difficulties and tighten the leashes on the dogs of war? Can security also be articulated to demilitarize the provision of security and reformulate it in terms of compassion and caring, as some feminist arguments suggest? Can it also be rearticulated to emphasize diversity, adaptability, and built-in redundancy, as the conflation of ecology and security seems to require in the more far-reaching understanding of environmental security as a political desideratum? Can security be reformulated to recognize the plethora of insecurities that confront most societies and to adapt to the premise that certainty is a political impossibility? Finally, can a new security politics operate in ways that displace the rituals of power that reproduce the spatializations of authority facilitating the construction of conventional security dilemmas? The scope of these questions is obviously huge. But they are the questions that confront scholars thinking critically about security, sovereignty, and geopolitics after the Cold War.

SECURITY STUDIES AFTER SECURITY

A number of tentative suggestions for critical themes and questions that might structure security studies follow from these arguments. First, the argument presented above suggests that the difficulties with reformulated conceptualizations of security in part may lie in the conflation of numerous political and military factors. The links between threat and militarized response are less than helpful when dealing with either drugs or environment. Clearly, a case can be made convincingly for de-linking these themes from security discourses and returning them to the ambits of traditional diplomacy and (domestic) social-reform-policy discourses. But doing so challenges the political order of the national security state that Cold War militarization supported for four decades. Rethinking security as a concept and as an intellectual and pedagogic practice clearly means taking this point seriously. Security is profoundly political; neorealist assumptions usually elide this basic point; what it is that should be rendered secure is an essential component of any discussion of security.

Second, military threats may well be best dealt with as such, as a matter of defense in the absence of diplomatic accomplishment. This is the logic of Patrick Morgan's recent suggestion that "it is important to confine the concept of 'security' to physical safety from deliberate physical harm inflicted internationally, i.e. across national boundaries."[75] For this topic, strategic studies as a specialist discourse is clearly appropriate. Ironically, such a pedagogic stance would also find favor among more conservative military minds, particularly those advocates of a Clausewitzian approach to military strategy.[76] There is much to recommend the reformulation of defense in terms of narrowly defined military strategy and to disconnect the military dimension from international politics as much as possible. As critics of Cold War politics have long argued, maintaining conditions of partial military mobilization in times of ostensible peace erodes what little democratic control might be possible over foreign policy making and consumes resources that might well be spent otherwise.

Third, in the aftermath of the collapse of the Soviet Union there is no longer an external ideological threat to Western institutions. Security is no longer credible in Western states, if it ever was, as part and parcel of a policy of internal repression, monitoring, and harassment of the political left. The ideological dimension of security confuses political orientation with subversion. National propaganda is no longer a conceivable part of what security might possibly involve in the current political period. But these functions of the "security apparatus" are likely to remain part of the political scene in Southern states that are potentially unstable for reasons relating to poverty, injustice, or ethnic composition.[77] Here, security forces may remain the greatest threat to the population that neorealist theory assumes they are protecting. A critical security studies cannot ignore the politics of security provision in differing political circumstances.

Fourth, the focus on economic espionage and the logic protecting the knowledge base within a state for national competitiveness suggests the persistence of a geopolitical understanding of security as a matter of inviolate borders. This language suggests that the "territorial trap" remains alive and well in international relations thinking and foreign policy making.[78] In a world where international trade is so often intrafirm trade, this whole formulation is dubious indeed. Economic security in a globalized economy is surely an anachronistic formulation for an outmoded notion of national sovereignty. All this may suggest the necessity of promoting international cooperation and regimes, if not an international society. But more than this, the question of economic production and the incorporation of most societies into the international capitalist market calls into question the capabilities of states in the era of globalizations.[79] This is not to argue that they are likely to disappear; rather, it is to raise the question of the capabilities of states to guarantee prosperity in a rapidly changing world economy. It is also to note the questionable assumptions in formulations of security like Buzan's that suggest that security is likely to emerge contemporaneously with rich, liberal democratic polities. If either theories of uneven development or environmental limits to growth are even partly correct, the possibilities for all states to be-come rich are precluded. Thus, security for all cannot be limited to assumptions about conventional development strategies. This in turn politicizes the concept of security by again focusing on who is to be secured.

Fifth, all of these suggestions challenge the assumptions of Inter-national Relations theory concerning the status of the state. The au-tarkic territorial state is still often taken for granted in international relations theory.[80] Its ontological status has structured much of the debate about security dilemmas and political behavior. The argu-ment in this chapter suggests that the state is the political entity that needs investigation in terms of its supposed provision of security, rather than having its provision of security taken for granted as the starting point for analysis. Clearly, this argument is in line with Michael Williams and Keith Krause's call for a more historically nuanced and interpretative international studies project.[81] It further suggests the necessities of thinking of security as only one possible mode of governmentality.[82] Understanding politics as about more than territorial community is not easy in the terms of modern politi-cal theory, but the limitations of so doing are particularly clear in international relations.

Finally, possibly the most important reason for unbundling the the-oretical dimensions of security is related to the epistemological and political matters implicit in the positivist assumptions of neorealism. The assumption that most, if not all, things are both knowable and hence predictable through the application of social scientific methods and reasoning is intimately related to the formulation of security as the management and control of risks and threats. But just about any social or natural phenomenon can potentially be hazardous; protect-ing against every eventuality is clearly impossible. But the assump-tions of control and predictability suggest that political and military interventions offer the possibility of managing international politics. As so much of the past decade's political history suggests, however, this may be a dangerous illusion. The will to power that is implicit in the positivist epistemology of neorealism suggests that other less am-bitious approaches deserve to be taken more seriously.[83]

None of these conclusions necessarily charts a precise course for the future of security studies. All they do is suggest themes for the critical examination of contemporary security discourses. The social contexts of security discourse have changed in the aftermath of the Cold War. The dilemmas of reformulating security suggest that it is time to reconsider seriously the whole concept, its rise to political prominence with the origins of the Cold War, and the possibility of thinking about global politics in ways that are not reduced to the territorial and ethnocentric discourses of (national) security.[84] Perhaps more important are the political questions of the possibilities of organizing global action around pressing issues of poverty, development, and environmental degradation without formulating them in terms of a security framework where technocratic and managerial modes of governmentality are invoked in the absence of a more flexible political imagination.[85] The possibilities for such a postsecurity security discourse may not be very bright as yet, but the task of rethinking this important theme in contemporary politics in the face of burgeoning global crises is surely worth the effort.

NOTES

1. Gregory D. Foster, "Interrogating the Future: The Question of Long Term Threats," *Alternatives* 19:1 (1994), 53–97.

2. Stephen Walt, "The Renaissance of Security Studies," *International Studies Quarterly* 35 (1991), 211–39; Edward A. Kolodziej, "Renaissance in Security Studies? *Caveat Lector!" International Studies Quarterly* 36 (1992), 421–38.

3. Independent Commission on Disarmament and Security Issues, *Common Security: A Programme for Disarmament* (London: Pan, 1982); Ken Booth, ed., *New Thinking about Strategy and International Security* (London: HarperCollins, 1991); G. Evans, *Cooperating for Peace: The Global Agenda for the 1990s and Beyond* (St. Leonards, N.S.W.: Allen and Unwin, 1993); J. E. Nolan, ed., *Global Engagement: Cooperation and Security in the 21st Century* (Washington, D.C.: Brookings Institute, 1994); M. T. Klare and D. C. Thomas, eds., *World Security: Challenges for a New Century* (New York: St. Martin's, 1994).

4. V. S. Peterson, "Security and Sovereign States: What Is at Stake in Taking Feminism Seriously," in V. S. Peterson, ed., *Gendered States: Feminist (Re)visions of International Relations Theory* (Boulder, Colo.: Lynne Rienner, 1992), 31–64.

5. Ken Booth, "Security and Emancipation," *Review of International Studies* 17:4 (1991), 313–26.

6. Ole Waever, Barry Buzan, Morten Kelstrup, and Pierre Lemaitre,

Identity, Migration and the New Security Agenda in Europe (London: Pinter, 1993).

7. Bradley S. Klein, *Strategic Studies and World Order* (Cambridge: Cambridge University Press, 1994).

8. Wolfgang Sachs, "Global Ecology and the Shadow of Development," in Wolfgang Sachs, ed., *Global Ecology: A New Arena of Political Conflict* (London: Zed, 1993), 3–21.

9. Lothar Brock, "Security through Defending the Environment: An Illusion?" in Elise Boulding, ed., *New Agendas for Peace Research: Conflict and Security Reexamined* (Boulder, Colo.: Lynne Rienner, 1992), 98.

10. Richard Falk, *Explorations at the Edge of Time: The Prospects for World Order* (Philadelphia: Temple University Press, 1992).

11. On "essentially contested concepts" see W. B. Gallie's "Essentially Contested Concepts," in Max Black, ed., *The Importance of Language* (Englewood Cliffs, N.J.: Prentice Hall, 1962), 121–46; William Connolly, *The Terms of Political Discourse* (Princeton, N.J.: Princeton University Press, 1983).

12. James Der Derian, *Antidiplomacy: Spies, Terror, Speed and War* (Oxford: Basil Blackwell, 1992).

13. See Simon Dalby, "Gender and Critical Geopolitics: Reading Security Discourse in the New World Disorder," *Environment and Planning D: Society and Space* 12:5 (1994), 595–612.

14. V. Spike Peterson and Anne Sisson Runyan, eds., *Global Gender Issues* (Boulder, Colo.: Westview, 1993).

15. Cynthia Enloe, *Bananas, Beaches and Bases: Making Feminist Sense of International Politics* (London: Pandora, 1989); and Cynthia Enloe, *The Morning After: Sexual Politics at the End of the Cold War* (Berkeley and Los Angeles: University of California Press, 1993).

16. Rudo Gaidzanwa, "Citizenship, Nationality, Gender and Class in Southern Africa," *Alternatives* 18:1 (1993), 39–59.

17. R. B. J. Walker, "Security, Sovereignty, and the Challenge of World Politics," *Alternatives* 15:1 (1990), 3–27.

18. This, of course, is the old question of the relationship of means and ends in strategic planning. Lawrence Freedman used this reasoning to suggest that the term *nuclear strategy* might well be oxymoronic, in his book *The Evolution of Nuclear Strategy* (New York: St. Martin's, 1983).

19. Carol Cohn, "Sex and Death in the Rational World of Defense Intellectuals," *Signs: Journal of Women in Culture and Society* 12 (1987), 687–718.

20. J. Ann Tickner, *Gender and International Relations: Feminist Perspectives on Achieving Global Security* (New York: Columbia University Press, 1992).

21. Fiona Mackenzie, "Exploring the Connections: Structural Adjustment, Gender and the Environment," *Geoforum* 24 (1993), 71–87.

22. Vandana Shiva, *Staying Alive: Women, Ecology and Development* (London: Zed, 1988).

23. Christine Sylvester, *Feminist Theory and International Relations* (Cambridge: Cambridge University Press, 1994).

24. M. Cooke and A. Woollacott, eds., *Gendering War Talk* (Princeton, N.J.: Princeton University Press, 1993).

25. R. B. J. Walker, *Inside/Outside: International Relations as Political Theory* (Cambridge: Cambridge University Press, 1993).

26. David Campbell, *Politics without Principle: Sovereignty, Ethics, and the Narratives of the Gulf War* (Boulder, Colo.: Lynne Rienner, 1993).

27. Michael Shapiro, *The Politics of Representation* (Madison: University of Wisconsin Press, 1988), 100. On the important theme of why sovereignty is not just sovereignty, see Cynthia Weber, *Simulating Sovereignty* (Cambridge: Cambridge University Press, 1995).

28. James Der Derian and Michael Shapiro, eds., *International/Intertextual Relations: Postmodern Readings of World Politics* (Toronto: Lexington, 1989).

29. See Bradley S. Klein, "After Strategy: The Search for a Postmodern Politics of Peace" *Alternatives* 13:3 (1988), 293–318; Hugh Gusterson, "Realism and the International Order after the Cold War," *Social Research* 60:2 (1993), 279–300.

30. For a critical overview, see Sankaran Krishna, "The Importance of Being Ironic: A Postcolonial View on Critical International Relations Theory," *Alternatives* 18:3 (1993), 385–417; and a reply by James Der Derian, "The Pen, the Sword and the Smart Bomb: Criticism in the Age of Video," *Alternatives* 19:1 (1994), 133–40.

31. Simon Dalby, *Creating the Second Cold War: The Discourse of Politics* (New York and London: Guilford and Pinter, 1990).

32. David Campbell, *Writing Security: United States Foreign Policy and the Politics of Identity* (Minneapolis: University of Minnesota Press, 1992).

33. Charles Nathanson, "The Social Construction of the Soviet Threat: A Study in the Politics of Representation," *Alternatives* 13:4 (1988), 443–83; Robert Latham, "Liberalism's Order/Liberalism's Other: A Genealogy of Threat," *Alternatives* 20:1 (1995), 111–46.

34. Dalby, *Creating the Second Cold War*.

35. Jim George, *Discourses of Global Politics: A Critical (Re)Introduction to International Relations* (Boulder, Colo.: Lynne Rienner, 1994).

36. Michael MccGwire, *Perestroika and Soviet National Security* (Washington, D.C.: Brookings Institute, 1991).

37. I have done so in "Post Cold War Security in the New Europe," in

John O'Loughlin and Herman van der Wusten, eds., *The New Political Geography of Eastern Europe* (London: Pinter, 1993), 71–85.

38. Edward A. Kolodziej, "What Is Security and Security Studies? Lessons from the Cold War," *Arms Control* 13:1 (1992), 1–31.

39. Ronald Steel, "After Internationalism," *World Policy Journal* 12:2 (1995), 49–51.

40. Although Barry Buzan distinguishes between defense dilemmas and power-security dilemmas, his discussion of these matters is particularly useful; see his *People, States and Fear: An Agenda for International Security Studies in the Post-Cold War Era* (Boulder, Colo.: Lynne Rienner, 1991).

41. Joseph J. Romm, *Defining National Security: The Non-Military Aspects* (New York: Council on Foreign Relations, 1993).

42. Two classic statements of these themes at the end of the Cold War are Jessica Tuchman Mathews, "Redefining Security," *Foreign Affairs* 68:2 (1989), 162–77; and T. C. Sorensen, "Rethinking National Security," *Foreign Affairs* 69:3 (1990), 1–18.

43. Gearóid Ó'Tuathail, "Japan as Threat: Geo-Economic Discourses on the USA-Japan Relationship in US Civil Society, 1987–91," in Colin Williams, ed., *The Political Geography of the New World Order* (London: Belhaven, 1993), 181–209.

44. T. H. Moran, "The Globalization of America's Defense Industries: Managing the Threat of Foreign Dependence," *International Security* 15:1 (1990), 57–99; Beverly Crawford, "The New Security Dilemma under International Economic Interdependence," *Millennium* 23:1 (1994), 25–55.

45. V. M. Hudson, R. E. Ford, D. Pack, with E. R. Giordano, "Why the Third World Matters, Why Europe Probably Won't: The Geoeconomics of Circumscribed Engagement," *Journal of Strategic Studies* 14:3 (1991), 255–98. For a critical review of this theme in the Cold War literature, see Ronnie D. Lipschutz, *When Nations Clash: Raw Materials, Ideology and Foreign Policy* (Cambridge, Mass.: Ballinger, 1989).

46. Waltraud Queiser Morales, "The War on Drugs: A New US National Security Doctrine," *Third World Quarterly* 11:3 (1989), 147–69.

47. William O. Walker III, "The Foreign Narcotics Policy of the United States since 1980: An End to the War on Drugs?" *International Journal* 49:1 (1993–94), 37–65.

48. R. Elias, "Drug Wars as Victimisation and Social Control," *New Political Science* 20 (1991), 41–61.

49. Campbell, *Writing Security.*

50. For a review of the earlier literature, see Simon Dalby, "The Politics of Environmental Security," in Jyrki Kakonen, ed., *Green Security or Militarized Environment?* (Aldershot: Dartmouth, 1994), 25–53. The conventional case for considering environmental factors as a security threat is made

in Norman Myers, *Ultimate Security: The Environmental Basis of Political Stability* (New York: Norton, 1993); see also Peter Stoett, "The Environmental Enlightenment: Security Analysis Meets Ecology," *Coexistence* 31:2 (1994), 127–47.

51. See Gro Harlem Brundtland, "The Environment, Security and Development," in *SIPRI Yearbook 1993: World Armaments and Disarmament* (Oxford: Oxford University Press, 1993), 15–26.

52. Al Gore, *The Earth in Balance: Ecology and the Human Spirit* (New York: Plume, 1992); Robert Kaplan, "The Coming Anarchy," *Atlantic Monthly* 273:2 (1994), 44–76.

53. For an earlier articulation of these points, see Simon Dalby, "Security, Modernity, Ecology: The Dilemmas of Post-Cold War Security Discourse," *Alternatives* 17:1 (1992), 95–134.

54. See Seth Shulman, *The Threat at Home: Confronting the Toxic Legacy of the U.S. Military* (Boston: Beacon Press, 1992); Murray Feshbach and Alfred Friendly, *Ecocide in the USSR: Health and Nature under Siege* (New York: Basic, 1992); Mike Davis, "Dead West: Ecocide in Marlboro Country," *New Left Review* 200 (1993), 49–73.

55. Daniel Deudney, "The Mirage of Ecowar: The Weak Relationship among Global Environmental Change, National Security and Interstate Violence," in I. H. Rowlands and M. Greene, eds., *Global Environmental Change and International Relations* (London: Macmillan, 1992), 169–91; Matthias Finger, "Global Environmental Degradation and the Military," in Kakonen, ed., *Green Security or Militarized Environment?*, 169–91.

56. *The Ecologist*, ed., *Whose Common Future? Reclaiming the Commons* (London: Earthscan, 1993).

57. D. Faber, *Environment under Fire: Imperialism and the Ecological Crisis in Central America* (New York: Monthly Review Press, 1993).

58. Buzan, *People, States and Fear*. Other suggestions for extending contemporary Western economic patterns are also vulnerable to this critique.

59. Jim George, "Of Incarceration and Closure: Neo-Realism and the New/Old World Order," *Millennium* 22:2 (1993), 197–234. This is a failing shared, for many of the same reasons, by scholars in Soviet studies. See Michael Cox, "The End of the USSR and the Collapse of Soviet Studies," *Coexistence* 31:2 (1994), 89–104.

60. Neil Middleton, Phil O'Keefe, and Sam Moyo, *Tears of the Crocodile: From Rio to Reality in the Developing World* (London: Pluto, 1993).

61. P. Morrison, K. Tsipis, and J. Wisner, "The Future of American Defence," *Scientific American* 270:2 (1994), 38–47; see also Robert Borosage, "Inventing the Threat: Clinton's Defense Budget," *World Policy Journal* 10:4 (1993–94), 7–15.

62. Kevin J. Cassidy and Gregory A. Bischak, eds., *Real Security: Con-*

verting the Defense Economy and Building Peace (Albany: State University of New York Press, 1993).

63. Mick Dillon, "The Alliance of Security and Subjectivity," *Current Research in Peace and Violence* 13:3 (1991), 101–24.

64. See Gwyn Prins, ed., *Threats without Enemies: Facing Environmental Insecurity* (London: Earthscan, 1993).

65. Simon Dalby, "The Threat from the South: Environmental Security and Global Justice," in Daniel Deudney and Richard Matthews, eds., *Contested Grounds: Security and Conflict in the New Environmental Politics* (Albany: State University of New York Press, 1996).

66. Mary Kaldor, *The Imaginary War: Understanding the East-West Conflict* (Oxford: Basil Blackwell, 1990).

67. The standard arguments on these lines include Stanley Hoffmann, "An American Social Science: International Relations," *Daedalus* 51 (1977), 41–59; and E. Krippendorf, "The Dominance of American Approaches in International Relations," *Millennium* 16:2 (1987), 207–14.

68. Klein, *Strategic Studies and World Order.*

69. In particular, see R. B. J. Walker, *Inside/Outside.*

70. James Der Derian, "The Value of Security: Hobbes, Marx, Nietzsche, and Baudrillard," in David Campbell and Michael Dillon, *The Political Subject of Violence* (Manchester: Manchester University Press), 97.

71. Betty A. Reardon, *Women and Peace: Feminist Visions of Global Security* (Albany: State University of New York Press, 1993).

72. Michael C. Williams, personal communication, December 1993.

73. The classic account of the formation of the "national security state" is Daniel Yergin, *Shattered Peace: The Origins of the Cold War and the National Security State* (Boston: Houghton Mifflin, 1977).

74. Der Derian, "The Value of Security." David Campbell comes to a similar conclusion in *Politics without Principle.*

75. Patrick M. Morgan, "Safeguarding Security Studies," *Arms Control* 13:3 (1992), 470.

76. H. G. Summers, *On Strategy II: A Critical Analysis of the Gulf War* (New York: Dell, 1992).

77. Mohammed Ayoob, *The Third World Security Predicament: State Making, Regional Conflict and the International System* (Boulder, Colo.: Lynne Rienner, 1995); Brian Job, ed., *The (In)Security Dilemma: National Security of Third World States* (Boulder, Colo.: Lynne Rienner, 1992).

78. John Agnew, "The Territorial Trap: The Geographical Assumptions of International Relations Theory," *Review of International Political Economy* 1:1 (1994), 53–80.

79. Joseph Camilleri and Jim Falk, *The End of Sovereignty?* (London: Edward Elgar, 1992).

80. John G. Ruggie, "Territoriality and Beyond: Problematizing Modernity in International Relations," *International Organization* 47:1 (1993), 139–74.

81. See the chapter by Michael C. Williams and Keith Krause in this volume.

82. G. Burchell, C. Gordon, and P. Miller, eds., *The Foucault Effect: Studies in Governmentality* (Chicago: University of Chicago Press, 1991).

83. Richard Ashley's critique remains apposite here. Richard Ashley, "The Poverty of Neorealism," *International Organization* 38:3 (1984), 225–86.

84. On alternative formulations of security that challenge the conventional state-centric formulations of political community and much else, see R. B. J. Walker, *One World/Many Worlds: Struggles for a Just World Peace* (Boulder, Colo.: Lynne Rienner, 1988).

85. Ronnie Lipschutz and Ken Conca, eds., *The State and Social Power in Global Environmental Politics* (New York: Columbia University Press, 1993).

2

From Strategy to Security:
Foundations of Critical Security Studies

KEITH KRAUSE AND MICHAEL C. WILLIAMS

INTRODUCTION

The nature of security has become one of the most widely discussed elements in the intellectual ferment that has been triggered by the end of the Cold War. Optimists have declared that the end of the century is ushering in a new era of peace and cooperation, based variously on liberal democracy, transnational capitalism, international organizations, or a combination of the above.[1] The more pessimistic offer warnings of an anarchic future filled with intercivilizational or ethnic conflict and weapons proliferation.[2] Still others, less absorbed with questions of military statecraft, have focused on new threats or new understandings that require a basic rethinking of security itself. Economic and environmental security have often taken center stage here, although numerous other voices, from human rights to gender to indigenous cultures, can be heard.[3]

Behind this chorus of voices lies a more disciplinary debate over how the object of study should be defined. This can be framed in terms of the tension between strategic studies and security studies. One position in this debate argues that the proper umbrella or title should be security studies, but that it should retain a relatively narrow (or only slightly enlarged) understanding of its scope and purpose.[4] Another position argues that the shift from strategic to security studies ought to expand the categories and areas of analysis considerably beyond their traditional purview, with strategic studies retaining its more narrow purpose and scope while being embedded within the broader ambit of security studies.[5] A basic challenge that expanded conceptions of security must confront is the charge that they are not *about* security at all.

This chapter does not address in any detail the many alternative conceptions of security that have emerged in recent years. Our goal is to make the debate between different approaches and orientations theoretically self-conscious, as a prelude to greater understanding of their respective strengths and weaknesses. It is driven by the conviction that many of the current debates broach but fail to address critical theoretical issues, and that the uncovering of their underlying premises and commitments will allow the discussion to move beyond the premature theoretical closure sought by advocates of a narrower definition of security.

Contemporary debates over the nature of security often float on a sea of unvoiced assumptions and deeper theoretical issues concerning to what and to whom the term *security* refers.[6] It is even difficult to gain a perspective on how the central claims and assumptions of the various strands of debate are related to controversies over the theory and practice of security.[7] As Barry Buzan has noted, although few today defend a narrow definition of *national security*, "that advance does not, however, mean that a consensus exists on what a more broadly constructed conception should look like."[8] Or, as Helga Haftendorn notes, there is no "common understanding of what security is, how it can be conceptualized, and what its most relevant research questions are."[9]

What most contributions to the debate thus share are two inter-related concerns: what security is and how we study it. Underneath these lurk significant theoretical divergences, which can in part be addressed by asking not just how we study security, but what it is that is being secured. In the dominant (neorealist) conception, the primary referent for security has been the state. While many current arguments challenge the adequacy of this statecentric conception, they have rarely examined systematically the implications of so doing. Two elements are necessary in such a reconsideration. First, one must come to terms with the reasons why the statecentric conception still holds such sway and exercises such disciplinary authority. To challenge it necessarily involves understanding its claims at a

deeper level, especially because defenders of the neorealist conception have mounted a spirited defense of the prevailing intellectual
order. Second, the construction of different conceptions of security
also requires a retheorization. While many analyses provide useful
insights into areas traditionally ignored, or into new challenges that
need to be taken account of, they have rarely reflected fully on their
own foundations.

A result of this disciplinary turmoil is that reconceptualizing security has often come to resemble a grab bag of different issue areas,
lacking a cohesive framework for analyzing the complementary and
contradictory themes at work. Simply articulating a broad range of
newly emerging or newly recognized threats to human survival or
well-being will not in itself move security studies away from its traditional concerns. This is particularly well illustrated in Robert Dorff's
reaction to Charles Kegley's attempt to broaden the agenda of security studies in Kegley's contribution to a recent text, *Security Studies
for the 1990s*.[10] While he agrees that economic, ecological and social
questions represent issues of real concern, Dorff denies that they represent security issues:

> There is no conceptual thread in the Kegley list that holds them all to-
> gether except that they are "problems." This is not to downplay the
> serious nature of some of these problems, but "problems" is not a
> concept. It does not help us organize the content of what we teach let
> alone how we teach. "Problems" provides us with no ordering of re-
> ality that we can use to create a common understanding of what it is
> that we are talking about and the range of possible policy approaches
> to addressing those problems.[11]

It is important to be clear about what is at stake here. The issue of
the distinction between threats and problems is a conceptual one. It
determines their status not according to their significance for human
welfare and survival, but by their relationship to prevailing conceptual structures and analytic categories of security studies. To argue,
as Dorff does, that certain issues are problems not threats, the study
of which will "lead us down an unproductive intellectual path," is a
self-referential claim. The prevailing conception of what it is to study
security (and thus what threats are) defines the terms within which
competing conceptions of threats are found wanting. At bottom, it
amounts to saying that threats are what current schools of security

liefs was not confined to strategic studies (narrowly defined) but "has become, during almost two centuries, so deeply embedded in Western consciousness that many adherents refuse to accept it as a 'mode' of thinking at all."[16] Moreover, as Shy goes on to note, this mode of thinking has played a long-standing role in defending strategic studies from criticism, as "contemporary strategists echo [Henri de] Jomini (in his defense against [Carl von] Clausewitz) by insisting that [their] critics fail to meet the urgent demand of strategy for clarity, rigor and utility."[17] Defenders of the prevailing intellectual order of security studies stand clearly within this tradition.

By presenting an evolutionary vision of knowledge that draws on a particular conception of science, and by identifying neorealist theory as the expression of this process within security studies, Walt attempts to anchor the legitimacy of neorealist security studies to a claim to authority within the field. This unarticulated foundation then provides the conceptual context within which the debate takes place. It is precisely this move that allows Dorff so easily to make the claims about what is legitimate analysis, about what is conceptually acceptable and what is not.[18] Threats are what prevailing conceptions say they are, and security follows suit. This claim to authority, in turn, is justified by a commitment to a form of knowledge that is presented as self-evident and authoritative, but never fully articulated.

But it is not just a claim about evolutionary and scientific knowledge that underlies neorealist security studies. Supported by this metahistorical and epistemological foundation is a series of foundational claims that are now presented as unproblematic facts. The most important of these concerns the centrality of the state as the subject of security and provides the basis for the exclusion of issues other than those of traditional military diplomacy from the field. Walt, for example, defines the scope of the discipline as "*the study of the threat, use, and control of military force. . . . it* explores the conditions that make the use of force more likely, the ways that the use of force affects individuals, states and societies, and the specific policies that states adopt in order to prepare for, prevent, or engage in war."[19]

No one would deny the significance of these issues. Yet given the challenges that have been raised to thinking about security in these narrowly traditional terms (not to mention the broader claims that so state-centric a conception of International Relations is no longer tenable), how is it that Walt and the vision of security studies he represents are so easily able to present these as the preeminent facts and concepts generated by the historical evolution of knowledge about security? Answering this question requires that we again go behind the overt claims of neorealist security studies to examine the unspoken premises that make them possible, to uncover the foundations that allow it to claim that states and anarchy are the essential facts of world politics, and that the preeminent foundation and concern of security are the threats that follow from these facts.

States Are the Subjects; Anarchy Is the Condition; Contractarianism Is the Solution

Despite its consistent invocations of the concept of structure, the neorealist theory of International Relations is fundamentally grounded in a particular conception of states and state action.[20] The sovereign nation-state is declared to be the subject within (or objective reality of) international relations, although this claim itself is never justified. It is simply taken as apparent or sufficiently demonstrated elsewhere. While it would be foolhardy to deny the relevance of states, it is also evident that the claim that states comprise the most important elements in the contemporary world is one of the most hotly debated issues in contemporary analysis. These debates usually take the form of a dispute over what the relevant facts are: transnational corporations and capital networks, international organizations, and interstate cooperation, for example, are heralded as facts that better represent the objective reality of the current world than statecentric conceptions of international anarchy. These disputes, for example, have been at the heart of the divergent analyses concerning the future of European security.[21]

Given the multiplicity of facts with which one is confronted, then, how is it that neorealism claims that states and anarchy are the essential components in understanding international relations? Neorealism's key theoretical moves here involve a conception of the individual subject that provides both a positivist epistemological foundation and a conception of the sovereign realm of domestic politics. Both elements are grounded in an understanding of human subjectivity as self-contained instrumentally rational actors confronting an external reality to which they relate objectively.[22] Although this does not explicitly commit the field to a positivist conception of science (in the Weberian appraisal of Hans Morgenthau, or in the more overtly socioscientific idiom of microeconomics and rational-choice theories favored by many contemporary analysts), the conception of state action as the instrumentally rational pursuit of self-interest is the foundation of theoretical analysis for the neorealist approach to security studies.[23] Here the "logic of cooperation" and its antithesis, the logic of conflict, engage their long-standing confrontation. Although cooperation is not excluded, it can only arise under circumstances in which each actor rationally calculates interest-maximizing strategies.[24] The analytic assumptions of instrumentally rational actors (and the commitment to rationalism), however, remain the same.

In a conception most commonly (if somewhat erroneously) identified with Thomas Hobbes, the individual subject as autonomous rational actor is confronted by an environment filled with other similar actors. These others are a source of insecurity, hence the classic security dilemma. Whether this insecurity results from the nature of the actors or from the situation in which they find themselves is here less important than recognizing the common foundation from which both possibilities spring: the wholly self-contained, instrumentally rational subject. From this starting point, there can be no security in the absence of authority, the state.

The state accordingly becomes the primary locus of security, and with it, authority and obligation. Obligations between citizens represent the limit—underwritten by the authority of the state—of effective coordination of collective action, or community (depending on the metaphor chosen). Either way, the security of citizens is identified with that state, and, by definition, those who stand outside it are threats, whether potential or actual. Relations between states are, on this basis, thereby rendered purely *strategic,* in the instrumental sense of the word. It is from this theoretical conception that neorealist security studies begins in its claim to construct an objective theory of security.

How, from the so-called facts of self-regarding, autonomously constituted, and sovereign states, do we get international anarchy? A particular state, as the individual rationalist, looks to its own interests first and foremost. Despite the fact that in the long term this interest might be better served through cooperation, each state cannot rationally assume that all states would act in a cooperative fashion;

therefore, it acts solely in its own interest, and all others do the same. The classic analogy here, of course, is Jean-Jacques Rousseau's parable of the stag hunt, used so effectively by Kenneth Waltz and others.[25] As Richard Ashley has noted, this account rests on "an understanding of international society . . . in which . . . there exists no form of sociality, no intersubjective consensual basis, prior to or constitutive of individual actors or their private ends."[26]

The declaration that the state is the subject of security, and anarchy the eternal condition of international relations, is premised not on objective facts but is grounded in a deeper set of claims about the autonomous nature of subjectivity and its relationship to sovereignty. This underlying methodological individualist premise is shared by neorealist and neoliberal approaches. The clearest illustration of this is offered by the framing of the debate between the two: as Alexander Wendt notes, both neorealist and neoliberal accounts share a "rationalist" conception in which "questions about identity- and interest-formation are therefore not important."[27] This can only make sense within a commitment to some version of what C. B. Macpherson called "possessive individualism," which treats "human beings as individually autonomous, 'related to each other as proprietors of their own capacities and of what they have acquired by their exercise.'"[28] It is but a short step from this conception to the neorealist view of state action.

Anarchy becomes an objective fact because international relations are defined by the absence of that which is necessary for political order at all: the state. Anarchy, then, is derivative: it is a conclusion based on an a priori claim about the nature of the individual human subject and the kind of political order that this subjectivity necessarily requires. The essence of the neorealist conception of international relations is thus not simply the postulate of anarchy, positing a world of self-regarding states operating under the security dilemma and autonomously defining their own interests, but the assumption of a particular form of individual rationality in state action as both the source and outcome of that anarchy. Both state and anarchy, as the foundations of the neorealist conception of security, are premised on these more fundamental claims.

These contractarian foundations then provide the basis within which neorealism's second theoretical move can take place: the claim to the authority of science. Neorealism and neoliberalism do not claim simply to represent bodies of opinion regarding international relations. On the contrary, they claim to ground and justify their analyses in strict opposition to the vicissitudes of opinion and subjective interpretation, holding, rather, that they are founded on the more secure tenets of science, of the objective representation of reality. Hence, neorealism or neoliberalism entail not simply a claim about the nature of international relations but a claim to *know*: specifically, a scientific claim to know objectively the reality of international relations. This belief in the appropriateness of the physical sciences as the model for knowledge, and the desire to separate objective truth from subjective opinion, continues—despite considerable diversity in its embodiments—to unite the mainstream approaches to the study of international politics.[29] Robert Gilpin (whom Walt cites with approval) provides an explicit restatement of its centrality for realist thought: "An offspring of modern science and the Enlightenment. . . . Realism is based on the practice of states, and it seeks to understand how states have always behaved and presumably always will behave."[30]

If the discipline of International Relations is to proceed toward the necessary knowledge, it must conform to the tenets of objective knowledge as they have developed in other sciences. In neorealist theory, the key to understanding the rational nature of reality is rationality itself.[31] In epistemological terms this means that the discipline must treat the phenomena under consideration as *objects*.[32] The nature of human action and subjectivity has provided a consistent difficulty for such an epistemological stance. In the tradition of thought from which the neorealist theory of International Relations emerges, this problem is overcome through an appeal to the universality of rational self-interest.[33] The positing of a unitary state-as-actor as the bearer of this rationality provides the solution to this fundamental problem. The concept of rational self-interest provides the theoretical bridge in neorealism's conversion of subjectively grounded state actions into the externally observable objective phenomena required by a positivist epistemology.

The neorealist reduction of individuals to instrumentally rational actors, embedded in a contractual theory of sovereignty and tied up within a specific claim about scientific knowledge and its progress, is a powerful theoretical move. The terms of the debate have been set in such a way that they privilege existing conceptions. The ability of what used to be called strategic studies to adopt the mantle, and define the agenda, of security studies within narrow traditional terms rests on a claim to authority and knowledge grounded in a series of assumptions deeply embedded in the culture from which it emerges. This is both a source of its power and a reason that it has reacted so strongly against attempts to broaden the agenda of security studies. Not only the field, but its entire worldview is threatened (both intellectually and practically) by the new challenges to security. Again, Walt is clear on this point: expanding the field of security studies to include issues such as poverty, environmental hazards, pollution, or economic recessions "would destroy its intellectual coherence and make it more difficult to devise solutions to any of these important problems."[34] The world may have many "problems," but security studies, at least, has been made secure by this move.

CHALLENGES TO THE TRADITIONAL CONCEPTION
Individuals as Persons, Citizens, and Humanity

The neorealist vision of security effectively makes it synonymous with citizenship. Security comes from being a citizen, and insecurity from citizens of other states. Threats are directed toward individuals qua citizens (that is, toward their states), and the study of security accordingly strives to mitigate these threats through concerted action by the representatives of the citizenry—the state leaders. This underlying rationale allows neorealism to call for the continued restriction of the agenda of security studies. Yet, while to be a people without a state often remains one of the most insecure conditions of modern life (witness the Kurds or the Palestinians), this move obscures the ways in which citizenship is also at the heart of many structures of insecurity and how security in the contemporary world may be threatened by dynamics far beyond these parameters. One way to grasp these challenges is to link them to analogous debates over the nature of subjectivity, the state, and security that have become among the most vibrant and diverse areas of debate in contemporary International Relations.

One set of challenges has been united by a common desire to treat the object of security not as the sovereign state but as the individual: security is a condition that individuals enjoy, and they are given primacy both in the definition of threats and of who (or what) is to be secured. Rather than presuming an identity (by means of sovereignty) of the individual with the security of the state (as in neorealism), concentrating on individual security exposes the ways in which this may conflict with claims of state security. But from this basic reorientation, three overlapping arguments have emerged that treat individuals as rights-bearing persons, as citizens or members of society, or as members of a transcendent global community (humanity).[35]

The first possibility, making individuals qua persons the object of security, opens up the state for critical scrutiny. Protection of individuals within a community is not equated with support for states, and this leads to a focus on individual human rights and the promotion of the rule of law, which protects persons from each other and from predatory state institutions.[36] The focus often becomes the security of the person, a theme that find its most prominent expression in a stress on the rights of individuals against their own states in areas such as freedom from torture or wrongful imprisonment, or protection from everyday violence and privation. Internationally, this plays itself out in the renewed debate over humanitarian intervention, as illustrated by former United Nations Secretary-General Javier Perez de Cuellar's assertion that "we are clearly witnessing what is probably an irresistible shift in public attitudes towards the belief that the defense of the oppressed in the name of morality should prevail over frontiers and legal documents."[37] While its implications in policy terms remain unclear and contested, this focus represents a clear challenge to the claim that state sovereignty provides the sole locus of authority and security for its citizens.[38]

The second possibility (focusing on individuals qua citizens) illuminates a central dynamic in contemporary life that is consistently obscured by neorealism: the way in which the most direct threats to individuals can come not from the anarchic world of international relations and the citizens of other states, but from the institutions of organized violence of their own state. This has been highlighted in the work of scholars such as Mohammed Ayoob, who argues that the state-centric and contractarian tenets of the classic neorealist conception obscure the fact that in many places the state is not the guarantor of security but is rather the greatest threat to its citizens.[39] It is also echoed in the notion of "societal security" developed by Ole Waever.[40] The doctrines of sovereignty and national security become a justification for the use of state institutions against political opposition: citizenship paradoxically becomes a source of insecurity, and the claims of citizenship become the justification of violence. The claims of the state to authority over citizens *as* citizens provide a source of its ability to exert violence against them. The national security state is the extreme, if unhappily familiar and oppressive, outcome as the situation in many Central American or Middle Eastern states, for example, has historically illustrated. Conversely, the identification of "us" becomes a precondition for actions against "them" (as illustrated by ethnic cleansing in the former Yugoslavia). This dynamic of state formation and the reciprocal relationship of threat and insecurity between regimes and citizens is difficult to accommodate within the statist assumptions of neorealism. Focusing on the security of individuals qua citizens, however, makes these dynamics capable of theoretical and practical engagement, although, again, precisely how represents one of the central dilemmas of contemporary theory and policy: witness Bosnia and Rwanda.

The third aspect, individuals as the objects of security, treats them as members of a transcendent human community with common global concerns. Shifting the focus of security to the individual paradoxically allows an engagement with the broadest global threats. This allows issues such as environmental security to emerge from the neorealist shadows as threats to the security of humankind, and often as threats that cross political boundaries. Environmental degradation poses (common) threats to individuals that transcend particular states and exclusive conceptions of national security.[41] Proponents of broadening the definition of security in this fashion almost always suggest that external threats of organized violence are far less urgent than, for example, the consequences of continued environmental degradation or economic growth and transformation. Moreover, this focus also illuminates dynamics that do fit within prevailing categories (albeit problematically), such as the potential rise of intra- and interstate conflicts over environmental degradation or resource depletion.[42]

Each of these three threads of argument challenges the vision of sovereignty underlying the neorealist conception of security. In the first case, the claims of sovereignty must be limited by the more basic rights claims of individual persons. In the second, the state as a source of threat to citizens themselves, and the disjuncture between state and society, is highlighted. In the third, narrow conceptions of national interest and state sovereignty are seen to limit our ability to deal with security issues whose source and solution stand beyond statist structures and assumptions. Making the individual the object of security provides the conceptual shift that allows these perspectives to take their place as central elements of any comprehensive understanding of security.

But making the individual (in various guises) the focus of security is also a double-edged sword, one that risks simply replicating the difficulties it seeks to overcome. One danger lies in treating individuals as purely abstract, that is, as ungrounded in any social or historical context. This problem leads to the often-stated criticisms of human-rights standards as culturally specific, or as being an attempt to impose Western standards on others.[43] Even more fundamentally, if we also regard individuals (qua persons) as abstract actors, then a return to a contract theory of the state is almost inevitable.[44] If we treat individuals solely as persons, then the following question arises: why and in what ways are they responsible for each other's security, and how are these responsibilities institutionally expressed? This is the problematic of contract theory, and its resolution results in precisely the limitations on the understanding of security previously discussed. It makes the move back from individuals to states seemingly unavoidable, and one is caught again in the traditional dualisms of universal and particular orders.

This also sets the parameters for the circular debates between neoliberalism and neorealism that have underlain many of the most notable clashes over security in the post-Cold War world. Neoliberals, for example, argue for the emergence of a peaceful Europe on the basis of a broadening commonality of individual interests that transcend and to some extent redefine more narrowly defined state interests. Neorealists simply adopt the same foundation for analysis and question the capacity for the peaceful coordination of individual actions in the absence of the state (domestically) or a hegemon (internationally). While not without advantages, then, treating the individual as the object of security risks simply replicating the Lockean and Hobbesian alternatives of contract theory that it seeks to replace. Moreover, treating abstract individuals as the foundational objects for thinking about security leads to an inability to grasp the dynamics of ethnic conflict and the (often violent) fragmentation of existing sovereignties. In these cases, the neorealist assumption of the state is inadequate, but so, too, is the appeal to abstract individuality as that which is to be secured. Rather, these conflicts must be seen in part as conflicts over the constitution of collective identity that provides much of their impetus. Similarly, the dilemmas over how to think about them are part of the reason for the international discord and ineffectiveness in dealing with them, as evidenced in Bosnia and Somalia. Likewise, the cosmopolitan conception of humans as members of a global community that emerges from the third perspective elides more than it explains and contains no concrete vision of how such a community could (or should) be realized.

Security, Community, and Identity

A second set of challenges is raised by the argument that the appropriate referent for thinking about security is identity and its connections to community and culture.[45] Individual security cannot be severed from the claims of group and collective structures within which individuals find their identity and through which they undertake collective projects. Although this is one of the insights of classical realism, it was subsequently reified into an unreflective assumption by neorealism, and it also appears to have dropped out of the analysis in other approaches.[46] The competing claims to identity, and the argument that legitimate sovereignty lies in the ability of the group to govern itself, are at the heart of many current nationalist conflicts.

As with the focus on individuals, this way of looking at things also challenges the assumption of the state as given, but it does so in significantly different ways. Most prominently, it is the existence of competing claims to sovereignty, rather than the competition of existing sovereignties, that provides the source of conflict and the appropriate understanding of what is to be secured. In opposition to the empiricist predilections of neorealism, the source of conflict in these cases (and what is attempting to be secured) is an idea. This is not to say that material elements are unimportant, but such conflicts simply cannot be reduced to the competing interests of pregiven political objects. They are about the creation of these objects, and the way in which different identities are constitutive of them.[47]

The implications of this recognition highlight some of the shortcomings of the neorealist position, something illustrated clearly by the neorealist response to the fragmentation of existing states, a dramatic feature of world politics since the end of the Cold War. Such a development is beyond the conceptual grasp of neorealism, which can only comprehend the new forms of violent ethnic and nationalist conflict by placing these phenomena within neorealism's objectivist epistemology and generating another uncritically grounded claim about the foundations of sovereignty. Groups simply replace states as the objects of analysis and security. Barry Posen's attempt to analyze ethnic conflict through the lens of the neorealist "security dilemma" illustrates this: it assumes the unproblematic prior existence of ethnic groups, treats them as protostates, and focuses on the acuteness of the security dilemma when defensive and offensive capabilities are indistinguishable, and offensive action enjoys superiority over the defense.[48] Precisely the most important features of ethnic and nationalist conflicts (the struggle over identity) are excluded from such an account, which requires theorization of the state, not just an assumption of its existence.

Posen concludes by advocating, among other things, that "groups drifting into conflict should be encouraged to discuss their individual histories of mutual relations. Competing versions of history should be reconciled if possible."[49] Aside from the apparent naïveté of this observation, it cannot be made within a realist understanding of independently constituted, self-interested actors. Indeed, the conflicts connected with political fragmentation and identity formation arise in part out of precisely the categories that neorealism takes as given: legitimacy, authority, and obligation. Rather than residing in a contract or an existing structure of authority, sovereignty lies in the self-governance of the group or nation.

While this may move toward addressing issues in a more plausible way than the neorealist stance, it hardly provides us with a clear capacity for thinking about security, for at least two reasons. On the one hand, the foundations of group identity must be adequately theorized if they are not to remain ultimately arbitrary. Further, if group identity is to become the locus of security, it raises the dilemma of thinking about the forms of security relations possible between these groups. The risk is that a shift from abstract conceptions of sovereignty to a prima facie focus on structures of exclusionary group identity will merely replicate the inside-outside structure of anarchy in a different form. In this case, the assumption of anarchy can be transformed into a "clash of civilizations" in which neorealist convictions take on a new mantle.[50]

None of the issues raised in this chapter thus far has easy answers. But while approaches that seem to broaden the agenda may contain many unanswered questions, their failure to conform to the tenets of existing conceptions of what security is (and how one ought to study it) cannot be considered a compelling argument for a narrow definition of the question.

EPISTEMOLOGICAL IMPLICATIONS AND SHIFTS

The challenges to the conventional understanding of security and the object to be secured also necessitate an epistemological shift in the way security is to be understood and studied. What is involved is a shift in focus from abstract individualism and contractual sovereignty to a stress on culture, civilization, and identity; the role of ideas, norms, and values in the constitution of that which is to be secured; and the historical context within which this process takes place. Epistemologically, this involves moving away from the objectivist, rationalist approach of both neorealism and neoliberalism, and toward more interpretive modes of analysis. While these issues have gained some prominence in debates over the nature of regime theory and the study of international organizations, they have made little impact on security studies.[51] This is clearly illustrated by Helga Haftendorn's attempts to broaden the ambit of security studies. On method, she concludes that the goal of security studies is "to construct an empirically testable paradigm," which involves defining the "set of observational hypotheses," the "hard core of irrefutable assumptions," and the "'set of scope conditions' that . . . are required for a 'progressive' research program." Although she admits that "we might do well to follow [Robert] Keohane's counsel to apply somewhat 'softer,' more interpretive standards," there is little room in this approach for studying norm change and the role of ideational elements in *constituting* the historical context within which actors take specific decisions.[52] Despite Haftendorn's goal of incorporating new issues that are normatively driven, the subordination of normative and reflexive conceptions of agency to objectivist visions of method remains largely undisturbed, and she remains committed to the fact-value distinction.

To understand security from a broader perspective means to look at the ways in which the objects to be secured, the perceptions of threats to them, and the available means of securing them (both intellectual and material) have shifted over time.[53] New threats emerge;

new enemies are created; erstwhile fellow citizens become objects of hatred and violence; former enemies can be transformed into members of the same community. The status of Others is uncertain, needing to be deciphered and determined.[54] To comprehend these processes requires an understanding of the problematics of security as constituted by self-reflexive historical practices. The knightly code of honor, for example, was both a central structuring practice of late-medieval conflict and a central object that was to be secured. Honor was an integral part of conflict in its genesis as well as its practice. To view the military conflict of the late-medieval world as a competition between instrumentally rational actors in the modern sense is to misunderstand it in both form and content.[55]

The shift to interpretive models of understanding (broadly conceived) also yields a different vision of the transformation of practices. As historically grounded, the practices of security become capable of conscious transformation through the process of critical reflection. No longer objective in the sense of a fixed reality that the analyst can only mirror, reality as the realm of subjective practices and structures becomes self-reflexive. This is most emphatically not to say that security studies needs to move away from studying the role of ideas, institutions, and instruments of organized violence in political life. In this respect, the continuing defenders of traditional strategic/security studies are correct (although this formulation will probably leave them uncomfortable). But if we are to understand these realities, we must take them more seriously than the abstractions of neorealism allow. We must grasp the genesis and structure of particular security problems as grounded in concrete historical conditions and practices, rather than in abstract assertions of transcendental rational actors and scientific methods. We must understand the genesis of conflicts and the creation of the dilemmas of security as grounded in reflexive practices rather than as the outcome of timeless structures.[56]

An approach to security that begins from the foundation of practice provides new ways of understanding the nature and genesis of particular conflicts and security challenges. It also, however, provides new ways of thinking about solutions to those conflicts, and about the conditions of stability, peace, and security. Rather than remaining within the theory of hegemonic stability or the balance of power, structures of cooperation and security can be seen as underpinned by deeper commonalities. They need not depend on the existence of external threats, nor on the presence of a hegemon in the neorealist sense.

In this view, cooperation, as some recent work in international organization has shown, is based on shared norms and values that provide the foundation for collective action. Security arrangements are capable of being understood in the same way. Indeed, as Bradley Klein has argued, the stress on shared culture and norms is essential in grasping an institution such as NATO, and, as he has also noted, this is not a radically new insight.[57] Indeed, it was one part of the classical realist understanding of Hans Morgenthau, which has been largely obscured by neorealism. This is not to say that perceptions of threat and interest are irrelevant, but the questions become how these threats and interests are constructed, how the actors involved are constituted, and how these processes may change.

CONCLUSION

All of the alternative ways of studying security that have been advanced in this chapter possess their difficulties, and they also all present considerable epistemological challenges.[58] Questions of relativity, values, and evidence remain central to social science and security studies. While the categories of neorealist empiricism in International Relations are frequently (and implausibly) invoked as standards against which interpretive approaches must be judged, the issues involved here remain complex and difficult to resolve.

Equally importantly from the perspective of security studies, the relationship between these approaches and the traditional concerns of the discipline has not often been considered in any depth. Most significantly, the question of military power and the instruments of violence is crucially undertheorized in interpretive (or alternative) approaches. Interpretive approaches may be able to provide a much fuller understanding of conflict, and perhaps of the conditions under which stability and even security can be achieved, but they have been conspicuously vague or even silent about how those conditions are to be achieved. The importance of the ideas, institutions, and instruments of organized physical violence has been greatly understated.[59] It is perhaps unfair to look at the situations in Bosnia, Somalia, and Rwanda, and (parodying Mao) to argue that "interpretation comes out of the end of a gun," but the question of violence in its direct and brutal form cannot be avoided in security studies. It is scarcely adequate to argue the textuality of all existence if the destruction of one's text is at issue in the conflict.

The question here is practical in a dual sense. A shift from objectivist rational-actor theory to a focus on historically and reflexively constituted practices provides a more insightful way of understanding the various forms of conflict and security in the contemporary world. In this context the almost ritualized neorealist's criticisms of alternative approaches as failing to generate a research program that conforms to prevailing conceptions of theory and method are misplaced. Neorealism's emphasis on how practical and useful knowledge is to be generated does not provide an unproblematic standpoint from which other conceptions can be judged.[60] But its underlying claim that *some* orientation toward practice must be at the heart of security studies represents a basic challenge for alternative approaches. Included in this is the question of who or what is being secured, and how change is effected. If an expanded agenda for security studies moves (at least partly) away from answering these questions in state-centered terms, then it becomes necessary to think of audiences and forms of political relevance beyond (but not necessarily excluding) those of state leaders. The experience of Western policy makers in dealing with so-called ethnic conflicts highlights one aspect of this issue.

The question of the relationship of theory to practice is particularly difficult in the late-twentieth century, when little kindness is shown to grandiose visions of the end of history or the heroic travels of its chosen agents. Neither nation, nor class, nor civilization appears up to the task. More recent intimations in support of liberal individualism (democracy), or woman, or even the earth itself as the latest bearer of the historical task are not yet particularly convincing either. Equally, strategic/security studies has hardly provided understanding or guidance for achieving security in the post-Cold War world. Thinking about security in light of these alternative conceptions moves the inquiry far afield from the supposed certainties of neorealist strategic studies, but it is a path that must be followed further (and with much more sophistication) if we are to develop understandings of security more adequate to human survival and well-being.

NOTES

1. See, for example, Steven van Evera, "Primed for Peace: Europe after the Cold War," *International Security* 15:3 (Winter 1990–91), 7–57; Carl Kaysen, "Is War Obsolete?", *International Security* 14:4 (Spring 1990), 42–64; Bruce Russett, *Grasping the Democratic Peace* (Princeton, N.J.: Princeton University Press, 1994).

2. See John Mearsheimer, "Back to the Future: Instability in Europe after the Cold War," *International Security* 15:1 (1990), 5–57; Samuel Huntington, "The Clash of Civilizations," *Foreign Affairs* 72:3 (Summer 1993), 22–49.

3. Among others, see Theodore Moran, "International Economics and National Security," *Foreign Affairs* 69:5 (Winter 1990–91), 74–90; Jessica Tuchman Mathews, "Redefining Security," *Foreign Affairs* 68:2 (Spring 1989), 162–77; Brad Roberts, "Human Rights and International Security," *Washington Quarterly* (Spring 1990), 65–75; J. Ann Tickner, *Gender and International Relations: Feminist Perspectives on Achieving Global Security* (New York: Columbia University Press, 1992); Rebecca Grant, "The Quagmire of Gender and International Security," in V. Spike Peterson, *Gendered States* (Boulder, Colo.: Lynne Rienner, 1992), 83–98; Robert A. Rubenstein, "Cultural Analysis and International Security," *Alternatives* 13 (1988), 529–42.

4. This is the position staked out by Stephen Walt, "The Renaissance of Security Studies," *International Studies Quarterly* 35 (1991), 211–39; Joseph Nye and Sean Lynn-Jones, "International Security Studies: A Report of a Conference on the State of the Field," *International Security* 12 (1988), 5–27; Richard Schultz, Roy Godson, and Ted Greenwood, eds., *Security Studies for the 1990s* (New York: Brassey's, 1993). Nye and Lynn-Jones draw the lines clearly: on one hand, "a subject that is only remotely related to central political problems of threat perception and management among sovereign states would be regarded as peripheral," while on the other, "the name strategic studies . . . might exclude some of the more basic theoretical questions about the causes of war or the relationship between international economics and international security." Nye and Lynn-Jones, 7.

5. Barry Buzan, *People, States and Fear*, 2nd ed. (London: Harvester Wheatsheaf, 1991), 23–25, is the most clear exponent of this view.

6. For an excellent illustration of this, see the list of definitions collected by Barry Buzan, and his commentary on them. Buzan, *People, States and Fear*, 16–18.

7. Central contributions to the debate have been Buzan, *People, States and Fear*; Helga Haftendorn, "The Security Puzzle: Theory-Building and Discipline-Building in International Security," *International Studies Quarterly* 35 (1991), 3–17; Walt, "Renaissance"; Edward Kolodziej, "What Is

Security and Security Studies? Lessons from the Cold War," *Arms Control* 13:1 (April 1992), 1–31; Edward Kolodziej, "Renaissance in Security Studies? Caveat Lector!", *International Studies Quarterly* 36 (1992), 421–38; Ken Booth, "Security in Anarchy: Utopian Realism in Theory and Practice," *International Affairs* 67:3 (1991), 527–45; Mohammed Ayoob, "The Third World in the System of States: Acute Schizophrenia or Growing Pains?", *International Studies Quarterly* 33 (1989) 67–79; R. B. J. Walker, "The Concept of Security and International Relations Theory," unpublished paper. Other important sources will be cited below.

8. Buzan, *People, States and Fear,* 14.

9. Haftendorn, "The Security Puzzle," 15.

10. Charles Kegley Jr., "Discussion," in Schultz et al., eds., *Security Studies for the 1990s.*

11. Robert H. Dorff, "A Commentary on *Security Studies for the 1990s* as a Model Core Curriculum," *International Studies Notes* 19:3 (Fall 1994), 27.

12. Walt, "Renaissance"; Nye and Lynn-Jones, "International Security Studies," 5–27.

13. Walt, "Renaissance," 222. See also his treatment in Stephen M. Walt, "The Search for a Science of Strategy," *International Security* 12:1 (Summer 1987), 140–65.

14. This issue is beyond the scope of the present chapter. For some reflections on the question, see R. Keat and J. Urry, *Social Theory as Science*, 2nd ed. (London: Routledge and Kegan Paul, 1982); Peter T. Manicas, *A History and Philosophy of the Social Sciences* (Oxford: Basil Blackwell, 1987); John G. Gunnell, *Between Philosophy and Politics* (Albany: State University of New York Press, 1986). The paradigmatic treatment in this vein remains Kenneth Waltz, *Theory of International Politics* (Reading, Mass.: Addison-Wesley, 1979). Two recent treatments of the entire question of neorealism, epistemology, and social theory are David Campbell, "Recent Changes in Social Theory: Implications for International Relations," and Jim George, "The Study of International Relations and the Positivist/Empiricist Theory of Knowledge: Implications for the Australian Discipline," both in Richard Higgott, ed., *New Directions in International Relations? Australian Perspectives* (Canberra: Department of International Relations, 1988).

15. Azar Gat, *The Origins of Military Thought* (Oxford: Oxford University Press, 1989), 29. See also Azar Gat, "Positivism, Romanticism and Military Theory, 1815–1870," in his *The Development of Military Thought: The Nineteenth Century* (Oxford: Clarendon Press, 1992), 1–45.

16. John Shy, "Jomini," in Peter Paret, ed., *Makers of Modern Strategy* (Oxford: Clarendon Press, 1986), 184–85.

17. Ibid., 184.

18. And it is thus hardly surprising to find that Dorff's first citation is to Walt's history of the field.

19. Walt, "Renaissance," 212, emphasis his. Nonmilitary phenomena are excluded on the twin grounds that including them "would destroy [the] intellectual coherence [of the field] and make it more difficult to devise solutions to any of these important problems," and that "it would be irresponsible . . . to ignore the central questions [of war and peace] that form the heart of the security studies field." Walt, "Renaissance," 213. On the realist premises underpinning this, see Robert Keohane, "Realism, Neorealism and the Study of World Politics," in Robert Keohane, ed., *Neorealism and Its Critics* (New York: Columbia University Press, 1986), 1–26.

20. Richard K. Ashley's "The Poverty of Neorealism," in Keohane, ed., *Neorealism and Its Critics*, 255–300, remains an especially clear treatment of this theme. See also Jennifer Milliken, "State Action in International Relations: A Critique," unpublished paper, 1995.

21. Mearsheimer, "Back to the Future"; "Back to the Future, Part II: International Relations Theory and Post-Cold War Europe," *International Security* 15:2 (Fall 1990), 191–99.

22. For a sophisticated theoretical treatment, see R. B. J. Walker, *Inside/Outside: International Relations as Political Theory* (Cambridge: Cambridge University Press, 1993).

23. An analysis of Morgenthau as a Weberian is well traced in R. Turner and S. Factor, *Max Weber and the Dispute over Reason and Value* (London: Routledge and Kegan Paul, 1984). For a critical analysis, see Philip Lawrence, "Strategy, the State and the Weberian Legacy," *Review of International Studies* 13:4 (April 1987), 295–310.

24. The classic account is Robert Axelrod, *The Evolution of Cooperation* (New York: Basic Books, 1984). For an overview of recent contributions, see David Baldwin, ed., *Neorealism and Neoliberalism: The Contemporary Debate* (New York: Columbia University Press, 1993). For a trenchant critique of rational choice accounts, see Donald Green and Ian Shapiro, *Pathologies of Rational Choice* (Princeton, N.J.: Princeton University Press, 1994).

25. See Kenneth Waltz, *Man, the State and War* (New York: Columbia University Press, 1959), 159–86. Although the idiom differs in his *Theory of International Politics* (Reading, Mass.: Addison-Wesley, 1979), the essential position remains unaltered. See Michael Williams, "Rousseau, Realism and Realpolitik," *Millennium* 18:2 (Summer 1989), 163–87.

26. Ashley, "The Poverty of Neorealism," 276. See also Friedrich Kratochwil, *Rules, Norms and Decisions* (Cambridge: Cambridge University Press, 1989).

27. Alexander Wendt, "Anarchy Is What States Make of It: The Social Construction of Power Politics," *International Organization* 46:2 (Spring

3

The Subject of Security

R. B. J. WALKER

SECURITY AND CHANGE

What are the conditions under which it is now possible to think, speak, and make authoritative claims about what is referred to in the language of modern politics as "security"? This is the crucial question that must be addressed, given the widely shared sense that we hardly know what we are talking about when this term rolls so easily off the tongue to circulate among the practices of modern violence.

The most obvious answers to this question depend on the degree to which modern accounts of security have been articulated in relation to the structures and practices of the modern state, the determinations of the systemic relations in which states engage with other states, and the historical transformations through which those structures, practices, and determinations have changed from, say, the era of gunpowder and pirates to that of the strategists and merchants of nuclear threat. These conditions are well known and require very little rehearsal, although the narrative details and the lessons drawn from them may be deeply contested. Many have been lulled into thinking that to understand them alone is sufficient to respond to the widespread sense of uncertainty informing demands for more sensible policies or more sophisticated accounts of the relation between security and shifting historical circumstances. There are, however, distinct limits to a political imagination that focuses too intently on the supposed necessities of state and the state system. These limits converge in and are sustained by a powerful consensus that the state does indeed provide a satisfactory—sometimes merely adequate, sometimes laudable, sometimes simply natural and uncontestable— answer to the most fundamental questions about the character and location of political life.

This consensus retains a certain plausibility, as much because of the absence of any sustained agreement about alternative answers as because of any clear evidence that it remains adequate to contemporary circumstances. To accept the plausibility of this answer, however, is to be faced with a well-known discourse of repetitions, with a ritualized and institutionalized play of affirmations and negations that leave our understanding of security more or less where it is supposed to be. Indeed, despite their rhetorical linkage with hardheaded claims about the way the world is, modern claims about security are at root primarily normative both in their commitments and their effects, as even a rapid glance through professional journals like *International Security* will readily show. The forms of political realism that play such a crucial role in the legitimation of contemporary security policies affirm the way things should be far more clearly than they tell us how things are. Moreover, these claims are always in danger of breaking the one cardinal rule of political wisdom: things change.

Consequently, the primary conditions under which it may be possible to think creatively about security now, I will argue, involve, first, a certain skepticism about the claim that the modern state and states system offer the only plausible way of responding to questions about the political; second, a clear awareness of the essentially normative, indeed radically idealist character of claims about national security; and third, a sense that if things are indeed changing, they are unlikely to be doing so in ways that are foretold in the normative visions of the modern state, which are, after all, visions preoccupied with containing change within territorial boundaries and legal codes.

Change does seem to me to be upon us, and with a vengeance. And the incoherence of modern accounts of security is closely related to our incoherent sense of how things are probably changing. In this context, one would expect to witness a rather desperate clinging to answers, and their consequences, that have at least had the advantage of being worked out over some centuries and refined through the legitimation practices of the most powerful institutions of modern societies. One would also expect to see a certain rage against the violence perpetrated in the name of answers that carry less and less conviction and generate more and more hypocrisy.

I share much of this rage, while also recognizing that a desperate clinging to familiar answers is to a considerable extent unavoidable given the political and intellectual uncertainties in which we are all caught. But I also believe that complaints about the complicity of modern accounts of security with practices of intolerable violence in the modern world must be harnessed to an attempt to work through more persuasive answers to those questions about the character and location of political life to which the state and states system have seemed such a natural response for so many for so long. Questions about security cannot be separated from the most basic questions of political theory, but they also cannot be left in the care of those who have allowed questions of political theory to curdle into caricature. These questions are not susceptible to easy answers. The conditions under which we are able to ask questions that might prove productive, however, do seem to me to be susceptible to some useful clarification.

EVERYTHING AND NOTHING

Whether analytically or rhetorically, claims about security increasingly have an air of slovenly imprecision. A word once uttered in hard cadences to convey brutal certainties has become embarrassingly limp and overextended. It is perhaps the case that claims about security have long thrived on a denotative imprecision that has been carefully calibrated. Notions of national security, most notoriously, have invoked realities and necessities that everyone is supposed to acknowledge, but also vague generalities about everything and nothing. Much of the rhetorical force and political legitimation expressed through modern discourses of security rests ultimately on this simultaneous appeal to the hard and the vacuous, the precise and the imprecise, the exaction of blood and sacrifice in the name of the grand generalization.[1]

Those who once thundered loudly that the supposed realities of international order and necessities of state must be taken seriously have now retreated to their scattered hideaways, although some remain well fortified and funded in specialized institutions devoted to their preservation. Not even their practiced talent for rhetorical bombast can disguise a crippled geopolitical vision. But it has become increasingly evident that crippled vision is not the burden only of the discredited security intellectuals of old. Although students of contemporary politics, international relations, strategic studies, peace research, and so on, are regularly encouraged to develop "alternative" concepts of security better suited to changing structural and historical conditions, or at least less likely to intensify the dangers that policies promising security are supposedly intended to avoid, the obviousness or urgency of the task does little to mitigate the sheer difficulty of thinking about what security could or should now involve.[2] It was never hard to recognize the intellectual banality and political priorities of the discourses that traded in claims about security during the Cold War era, whatever the improbability that institutions and practices thriving on intellectual banality might be budged. But it has long been clear that the difficulty of speaking about security in any other way is not a consequence of entrenched political and institutional interests alone. The sociology of knowledge has only a limited purchase on the way we have all become caught up in habits of speaking that now seem not only dangerously out of touch with the times, but even trite and more than faintly ridiculous. Laughter has once again shown its episodic virtue as a principle of epistemological rectitude.

To ask about the conditions under which we might now speak usefully and coherently about security is, in the first instance, to ask about immediate historical and structural contexts. Here, the end of the Cold War now provides the most popular point of departure. The reigning Cold War orthodoxies had become widely offensive long before 1989, but the possibility of capturing complex historical and structural transformations in a single year of exhilaration also offered a glorious chance to rehabilitate the longing for a tabula rasa, the blank slate of the "new world order." Discussion could then proceed to a remarkably expansive itemization of new dangers and new contexts. New geopolitical configurations, regional variations, and apocalyptic visions of cultural, ethnic, ecological, and economic collisions, as well as a desperate scanning of horizons for new enemies, have come to delineate a landscape in which claims about security once again threaten to encompass both everything and nothing. This time, vague generalities are increasingly articulated under the sign of the global rather than of the reason of state. Where claims about security could once be expanded to cover the most totalizing necessities of statecraft, the sovereign power in its state of emergency, changing historical conditions are now increasingly said to require broader visions and perspectives. These stretch out in two quite different directions, although both are in direct conflict with the claims of states and those always potential states of emergency on which modern claims about security ultimately rest.

First, demands are made for a broader understanding of just what security itself involves, of what it means to be secure as well as what one is to be secured from.[3] Mere physical survival, it is said, is not enough, and power comes not just or even primarily from the barrel of the gun. It is then possible to define the meaning of security in relation to social, cultural, economic, and ecological processes, as well as to geopolitical threats from foreign powers. Hence, for example, the insistence on the need to break down artificial distinctions between security and development. Hence, also, the elaboration of concepts like structural violence as a way of avoiding simplistic distinctions between peace and war. Now even the most respectable voices of sovereign authority are likely to tell us about their fears and insecurities in the language of trade, sustainability, or the technologies of human reproduction rather than of the barracks and the war college.[4]

Second, and more crucially, demands are issued for a broader understanding of whose security is at stake, and usually for a more persuasive account of the security of people in general and not just for the citizens of particular states.[5] Hence, the resort to concepts like collective, common, as well as world security, despite a widespread sense that such terms merely underline the political incoherence of claims about the collective, the common, and the world.[6] These demands are usually reinforced by accounts of the transformative character of the modern age, especially of the increasingly interdependent character of something that may be appropriately called a world politics rather than just interstate or international relations.

In this way, discussion of the conditions under which we might now make some sense of claims about security begins to shift away from competing accounts of contemporary events and trajectories, away from those admittedly often-pressing scenarios of dangers here and there, of coming catastrophes on a global scale or the minor tragedies of forgotten, thirsty peoples whose poverty, sickness, and exclusion clearly demands—from some points of view—to be counted as a state of emergency. It moves away, also, from the analysis of discourses associated with particular elites and around particular technological regimes like the illogical language of logic ascribed to the deployment of nuclear weapons. It may be that the conditions under which we are now able or unable to speak about security are in considerable part understandable in relation to the experiences of the Cold War, the institutionalized foibles of national security elites, the fetishization of nuclear deterrence, and so on. But they are also related to the limits of our ability to speak about and be many things other than secure, and not least of our ability to be citizens, democrats, and even humans. It is no doubt difficult enough to keep up with those situations and technologies that can readily be categorized as matters of security as conventionally understood. Demands for broader accounts of security risk inducing epistemological overload. Nevertheless, claims about security are a serious matter. They cannot be dissociated from even more basic claims about who we think we are and how we might act together.

SUBJECTS OF SECURITY

In some ways, the limits of prevailing accounts of security are straightforward and uncontentious. Both the general historical narratives of the twentieth century and the deployments of destructive force that are such a visible part of the contemporary structures of everyday life are enough to give pause to the most serene of myopias. Despite the temptation to exaggerate the dangers confronting one's own epoch, a temptation that is perhaps never far from the contrary temptation to exaggerate that epoch's achievements and superiorities, the argument that we live in especially dangerous times carries considerable plausibility. Yet many of the dangers of concern to most prevailing accounts of what is dangerous are not entirely novel. The key issue here is not some corollary of some permanent defect in the human condition, some inherent flaw or original sin of human nature. Nor is it the supposed security dilemma that is said to always arise from conditions of competition among more or less equal actors, the basic ontology of modern liberalism in the disguise of a "state of nature" or an obscure parable about stag hunters. It concerns, rather, the contradictions that are expressed by the historically specific claims of the modern state. Claims about a security dilemma tend to trade on images of ahistorical determination, of structural necessities to which states can only respond as they must. As expressions of the claims of the modern state, however, modern security discourses rest on historical and political judgments. Appeals to necessity that now flow so easily from claims about security simply obscure the historical practices through which political judgments are made, and made to stick.

Even in the classic source of modern wisdom about security, Thomas Hobbes's paradigmatic legitimation of the sovereign authority of the modern state in his *Leviathan*,[7] there is an explicit recognition that the state is likely to be a major source of insecurity as well as the only source of order that could make a secure life for more or less equal individuals possible at all. Whatever inspiration might be drawn from chapters 11 and 13 of that text for a reading of the states system as a form of anarchy, the subsequent chapters on the constitution of the sovereign power in law, on the transition from natural to political necessity (the precondition for "liberty"), are of crucial relevance to the manner in which modern accounts of security have become plausible. In Hobbes's judgment, whatever the sovereign does cannot be as bad as the condition of unrestrained competition that Hobbes himself had rather cheekily portrayed as a natural condition of human existence. Many others, following John Locke's paradigmatic example, have been deeply skeptical of this judgment, and a large proportion of contemporary debate about security continues to oscillate around it. For some, strong states are still necessary to ensure, say, basic human rights, and indeed are precisely the primary material condition under which the notion of human rights has become even thinkable, let alone an ambition that might be achievable. Others are more persuaded that strong states have a nasty tendency to erode basic human rights, whatever they are taken to be. To the extent that contemporary debates about security avoid this well-worn path, they tend to express diverging judgments about how historical transformations have or have not changed the conditions under which it might be rational to gamble that Hobbes was right.

States have always been dangerous, say some; for others, whatever capacities they once had, states no longer serve as a plausible place of safety and may well be making our existence more precarious than ever. In one form or another, these twin arguments offer a fairly persuasive account of the need to think about security in a radically different manner. They have done so for quite some time. But the persuasiveness of these arguments does little to suggest how it might be possible to come to terms with the conditions under which we have learned to make a connection between the demand for security and the presence and legitimacy of modern states. This is in large measure because states, or the absence of states, have come to be framed not only as the source of security, or of insecurity, but also as that form of political life that makes it possible for us to imagine what security, or insecurity, could possibly mean. In this respect, Hobbes remains a crucial figure, athough certainly not because of his supposed insights into the permanent condition of human insecurity. Like most of those who have been canonized among the theorists of International Relations, Hobbes is concerned almost entirely with the constitution of particular societies. To the extent that such figures remain relevant for contemporary thinking about security, it is necessary to focus on what they have achieved, or what they have been taken to express and legitimize, in relation to the claims of particular states.

It has become increasingly apparent that the primary condition under which we are or are not able to rethink the concept of security involves the derivation of our dominant understanding of security, and, perhaps more crucially, our dominant understanding of what it would mean to articulate an alternative to this dominant understanding of security, from a prior understanding of what we mean by the political. The difficulties of analyzing the meaning of security, and of finding ways in which this meaning might be reinterpreted or reconstructed, derive less from its notorious imprecisions or susceptibility to propagandistic abuse than from its derivation from a prior account of who or what is to be secured. The crucial subject of security, in short, is the subject of security.[8] And the crucial understanding of the subject of security focuses precisely on the claims of the modern sovereign state to be able to define what and where the political must be. In one way or another, the twin arguments that dominate contemporary debates about security—about the state as both source of and solution to the pervasive insecurities of modern life and the continuing relevance or increasing irrelevance of the state as solution if not as source—tend to work well within a statist account of what it means to have a subjectivity that might be made secure.

Security cannot be understood, or reconceptualized, or reconstructed without paying attention to the constitutive account of the political that has made the prevailing accounts of security seem so plausible. It may be true that the intellectual certification sought by modern security discourses through appeals to the tradition and necessities of political realism can hardly withstand even an amateur dose of critical scrutiny, but such discourses did successfully insist on and illustrate some of the crucial limits of modern political imagination in this respect.

Consequently, to try to rethink the meaning of security must be to engage with a variety of attempts to rethink the character and location of the political (and not simply what is usually framed as "international relations"). This in turn, I believe, demands a considerable degree of skepticism toward the modern principles of autonomy and sovereign subjectivity. (This is why at least some elements of the so-called critical turn in contemporary social and political theory are of some relevance to the process of rethinking.) It also demands that the process of rethinking security must respond especially to questions about whose security is being assumed and under what conditions. (This is why the complex debates about political identity that have come to be so influential in literatures on, for example, feminism and postcolonialism, cannot be avoided in this context.)[9] Consequently, also, interrogations of security must contend with practices that are apparently abstract, practices whose concrete powers derive precisely from their apparent abstraction. (This is why recent critical accounts of discourse and the politics of representation are so important in a field that still insists on crudely dualistic theories of language, culture, and ideology.)[10]

In all these contexts, the claims and practices of political identity and legitimate authority expressed by the spatiotemporal demarcations of state sovereignty must be taken especially seriously. The claims of state sovereignty do not express a simple fact of life, as so many of those who work with prevailing conceptions of security so often insist. Nor can they be wished away in the name of some common humanity, as many who issue demands for an alternative account of security often seem to believe. They are a specific historical articulation of relations of universality/particularity and self/Other, an articulation that depends in the final instance on a capacity to distinguish a territorial or spatial boundary between a historical politics inside and a merely contingent nonpolitics outside the modern state.[11]

There are no doubt many analysts who would insist on the irrelevance and even irresponsibility of questions that are posed in such a resolutely theoretical form. This insistence may be voiced as a gruff appeal to apparently brute realities, like the intrinsic place of violence among the defining characteristics of the human condition or the dismal historical record of warfare among human collectivities. Or it may be voiced as a more elevated appeal to the achievements of scholarly traditions that congratulate themselves on identifying the recurring patterns of violence and warfare, and the precise methodological procedures that will allow us to analyze these patterns even more precisely in the future. In either case, the prevalence of such appeals in the specific disciplinary institutions of modern security studies is one of the conditions that demand critical analysis. There are, nevertheless, three general reasons why it is important not to dismiss prevailing notions of security too hastily, reasons that also suggest a certain degree of caution about some accounts of what it means to develop alternative accounts of security.

First, there has been significant progress in working through some of the more fruitful implications of moving from assumptions about the inevitability of conflict to the possibility of cooperation given the logic of the so-called security dilemma.[12] The general move here is perhaps usefully framed in relation to a prior shift in early-modern European politics "from the passions to the interests," to use Albert Hirschman's telling phrase.[13] To oversimplify even more crudely from Hirschman's already oversimplified tale, one can identify a gradual shift from early-modern claims that capitalism and individualism are both morally and existentially dangerous (thus the sin of usury and Hobbes's "state of nature") to the later celebration of the public benefits of self-interest (the wealth of nations and the magic of the market). In the present context, the move is usually framed as one from national security to common security. The details are worked out in terms of a commitment to arms control, the privileging of nonprovocative defense postures, and the cultivation of confidence-building measures among elites and detente from below among broader communities. The shift from self-interest to common interest is marked by commitments to interdependence and some understanding of a more broadly defined form of political community. The difficulty here, of course, is that it is not at all clear what it means to invoke a more broadly defined form of political community in this way.

Second, the claims about political realism that still echo in discussions about security serve as a crucial reminder that accounts of imminent historical transformation are invariably overdone and that claims about alternatives are very likely to express a continuing, even if veiled, commitment to those practices that are supposedly obsolete. Especially when framed in relation to the complex of claims that have emerged around the concept of peace, attempts to elaborate alternative accounts of security have been susceptible to a familiar repertoire of co-optations and appropriations.

Third, they may be read as expressions of a hegemonic normative commitment to the way the world must be. Like the theory of International Relations, claims about national security can be read as expressions of the legitimation practices of modern states more readily than as empirical explanations of the practices of such states. Like the doctrinal claims of political realism, the discourses of national security are explicitly normative (or idealist) in that they idealize the sovereign state as the norm against which international anarchy is projected by negation. Modern discourses of security essentially work as sites of transgression, as places where violence and knowledge can legitimately converge; and transgressing the norm at the limit then works to affirm the continuing legitimacy of the norm within the limit.

All of these three lines of analysis ultimately return us to the central claims expressed through the principle of state sovereignty. Beginning with an affirmation of the absolute priority of the claims of citizenship over all other claims to political identity and allegiance, discussion of security can contemplate increasing cooperation between groups of citizens—states—but not the possibility of any other subject. Claims about common security, collective security, or world security do little more than fudge the contradiction that is written right into the heart of modern politics: we can only become humans, or anything else, after we have given up our humanity, or any other attachments, to the greater good of citizenship. Modern accounts of security are precisely about subjectivity, subjection, and the conditions under which we have been constructed as subjects subject to subjection. They tell us who we must be. And then they offer to tell us how we might stay this way. Many will continue to believe this to be the best way of resolving all contradictions in a less than perfect universe. They can try to read the codes of modern subjectivity in a more constructive manner than Hobbes did. Others may protest that we are in fact not what the modern discourses of security tell us we must be, and that in any case the conditions under which the modern state could guarantee the subjectivity/subjection of its subjects are visibly dissolving.

OVER AND OVER

According to the formal claims of state sovereignty, International Relations cannot turn into an analysis of world politics,[14] and there can be no alternative to national security except anarchy or empire. National security can only be framed in relation to a continuum that expresses the paradoxes of self-interested behavior in a competitive system of equal units, although the continuum can be distorted by the degree to which the equality condition is actualized in practice, and thus the degree to which the states system is structured by hegemonies or approximates the logic of empires. Hobbes remains noteworthy here as someone who explicitly denied the logic of anarchy to which his name is so frequently attached precisely because he denied the equality condition that is crucial to his account of the "state of nature" as a factor in the "state of war."[15] Consequently, even if it is admitted that we are all now participants in common global structures, that we are all rendered increasingly vulnerable to processes that are planetary in scale, and that our most parochial activities are shaped by forces that encompass the world and not just particular states, it is far from clear what such an admission implies for the way we organize ourselves politically. The state is a political category in a way that the world, or the globe, or the planet, or humanity is not. The security of states is something that we can comprehend in political terms in a way that, at the moment, world security cannot.

This is an elementary point, and it is often made in a regrettably crude and ahistorical way. People, it is said, have competing interests and allegiances. They are always likely to put the interests of their own society and state above any claims about a common humanity. In any case, the ongoing record of large-scale violence shows just how naive it is to hope for any political arrangements that give priority to some general human interest over the particular interests of states. Consequently, typical forms of this argument go, if you want peace, prepare for war.

The security of states dominates our understanding of what security can be, and who it can be for, not because conflict between states is inevitable, but because other forms of political community have been rendered almost unthinkable. The claims of states to a monopoly of legitimate authority in a particular territory have succeeded in marginalizing and even erasing other expressions of political identity, other answers to questions about who we are. This success did not come about lightly. Much of the history of the last half-millennium can be written as an account of the energy and violence required to ensure that the monopolistic claims of states be respected. Whether through appeals to the nation, the flag, or the national interest, states continue to deploy immense resources on an everyday basis to ensure that this monopoly is maintained.

The dominant understandings of what politics is all about, and thus of what security must mean, arise precisely because the very form of statist claims to a monopoly on legitimate authority challenges the possibility of referring to humanity in general—and by extension, to world politics or world security—in any meaningful way. Thus, to speak of security is to engage in a discourse of repetitions, to affirm over and over again the dangers that legitimize the sovereign authority that is constituted precisely as a solution to dangers. But it is important to remember that this discourse of dangerous affirmations becomes, in another guise, a discourse of excluded subjectivities. Just as the discourses of security keep returning to the same old affirmations of a self-constituting danger, they simultaneously exclude the possibility of admitting the presence of other subjectivities, most obviously those of class, race, gender, and humanity. Critiques of the gendered or ethnocentric character of modern security discourses are important not because it is possible to point to some essence of masculinity, femininity, national character, civilizational encounter, or any other identity (and not least for reasons spelled out in Hobbes's critique of Aristotle as well as the limitations of Hobbes's own nominalist critique), but because the forms of modern politics expressed in contemporary security discourses admit only one— although largely abstract—identity, in relation to which struggles among all other identities are expected to take their proper place.

State sovereignty defines what peace can be and where peace can be secured: the unitary community within autonomous states. Consequently, it also defines a place where neither peace nor security is possible for very long: the noncommunity of contingencies, Others, and mere relations outside the boundaries of the state. In addition to this, state sovereignty raises hopes that at some point in the future, the kind of political life attained within (at least some) states might be projectable from inside to outside, from the national community to the world community. But at the same time as these hopes are raised, state sovereignty denies that they can ever be fulfilled. It does so through a claim that only through the state is it possible to resolve all contradictions—between universality and particularity, space and time, them and us—in a politically plausible manner. Claims about world politics, world order, world security, and so on, it suggests, can offer no credible way of responding to counterclaims about the need for autonomy, freedom, national identity, or diversity in general. Instead, it is said, such claims must either disguise a dangerous yearning for hierarchical authority and empire or an equally dangerous refusal to understand that universalist claims about humanity or the planet as such have no effective political expression.

Once locked into this logic, this discourse that is at once ritualized into disciplines and clichés and enshrined in the most powerful structures of violence the world has ever known, only two options seem to remain open before us. One is to push this logic to its extreme. If the world is in fact organized as a series of sharp divisions between inclusion and exclusion, community and anarchy, civilization and barbarism, then the maxim that preparations for war are the only guarantee of peace does make some sense. And it is precisely because disciplines like strategic studies and the cultural codes of the Cold War era have pushed this logic to extremes that the crudest fanaticism has been able to masquerade as realistic and responsible policy. The corollary of this option, of course, is that once the world outside is no longer treated as completely different, it is treated as essentially the same. The new world order is ready to be written, and then smudged, on the blank slate of the new beginning.

The other option is to relax this logic in order to permit accommodation, cooperation, arms control, and the rest. The legitimacy of the modern state is left essentially unchallenged, but our understanding of what this means is no longer informed by pseudo-Hobbesian accounts of anarchy and the security dilemma. This is the option that informs many of the more optimistic scenarios of contemporary security discourse. But it is an optimism that is always haunted by its pessimistic condition of possibility, the appeal to a logic of anarchy in the final instance: a logic that is itself made possible through a constitutive form of political community that lures the more relaxed codes of accommodation and cooperation toward an idealized image of collectivity that can never be reached.

Once we know who we are, because we know our place in the universe as citizens of modern states, claims about security oscillate back and forth between the extremes that have come to be coded as political realism and political idealism. Realism in this sense is the code that affirms the limits of modern politics. Idealism is the prior code that idealizes the moral community within the state that produces realism as the limit, although now projected outward and forward into a world that is apparently without limit. This oscillation generates a discourse of tremendous power. It induces illusions of permanent hopes and permanent tragedies. It legitimizes an account of political necessity that can excuse the most intolerable barbarism. Indeed, intolerable barbarism, in this account, cannot be separated from the highest aspirations of modern politics. Modern politics, the political realists insist, is inherently hypocritical. And in this insistence, political realism works as a mode of political critique as well as a mode of normative legitimation. The moment of critique may have been largely effaced by the hyperidealism that has recently masqueraded under the guise of a neo- or structural realism, but it would be a mistake to lose sight of the degree to which, for all its association with the crudest of reifications, the most dogmatic of disciplinary practices, and the most tedious repetitions of the apparently obvious, discourses about security have necessarily expressed a critical edge because modern politics has always teetered critically on the edge.

CHANGING SUBJECTS

Viewed in this way, attempts to rethink the notion of security through a process of broadening pose significant problems. Some fear that once the concept begins to open out to encompass new accounts of what security means, or to whom it refers, it will cease to have any specific referent at all. At least, one might argue, established accounts do permit us to refer to identifiable threats, to concrete dangers, to institutions and people who do things. Security, it can be said, is the proper preserve of the Department of National Defense; or perhaps of the Ministry of the Interior and the police force; or the Ministry of Finance; or the Minister of Health, or Environment, or even Culture; or at least to some such Ministry of Uncertain Things. The uncertainty of certain things is, of course, precisely the problem. For in the end it has never been possible to pin security down to concrete practices or institutions with any great precision, no matter how insistent the voices of military and defense establishments might be. The whole point of concepts of security that are tied to the claims of state sovereignty is that they must expand to encompass everything within the state, at least in its ever-potential state of emergency. So, in this context, broadening the concept as such is not really the problem; difficulties arise only with the kind of broadening that is envisaged.

Similarly, some fear that to try to broaden the notion of security will lead to the extension of behaviors deemed appropriate to the demands of national defense to the rest of social life. The fear here is primarily democratic in inspiration. Democratic politics depends on the exclusion of the state of emergency from the interstices of civil society quite as much as the democratization of states and civil societies depend, in the last instance, on a willingness to declare a state of undemocratic and very uncivil emergency. Concerns about extending the practices of security policy into other spheres of political life may be well founded in this respect, but the extent to which practices of security are already part of the broader social, political, economic, and cultural arenas is not something that can be simply wished away. Again, the problem involves the kind of broadening that is envisaged.

Furthermore, there is a crucial sense in which it is necessary to refuse many of the sentiments associated with the more familiar attempts to broaden our understanding of what security involves in a rather different direction than the expansive potentials inherent in claims about security within states. These are the sentiments that affirm the need to make a move from the particular to the general, from the territory to the planet, from the citizens of states to citizens of the world. For the need to broaden out in *this* way is exactly the wrong conclusion to draw from the more convincing claim that the state is in some trouble as the place in which to gamble that Hobbes was right. It is a conclusion based on the false premise that modern insecurities arise from a system of political fragmentation. Because there are many states, and because these many states tend to be in conflictual relations with each other much of the time, the familiar narrative goes, it is necessary to move from a state of fragmentation to a state of greater integration: to broaden out toward cooperative, or common, or world security.

Yet the state and the states system do not express a principle of fragmentation, at least not in the first instance. Some, indeed, would argue quite the reverse: that the fragmentation of the states system depends on the prior existence of some underlying unity, whether of a European or modern culture that requires, for example, all states to organize themselves on the modern principle of sovereignty, or of a specifically capitalist global economy that ultimately drives the geopolitical behavior of all states. In my view, however, this opposing stance also misreads the historical achievement of modern states, and of the principle/practice/institution of state sovereignty, in forging a very specific relationship between the claims of universality and those of diversity. It is this specific relation between these opposing claims that is in trouble, and it is not obvious that we might cope with the consequences of its dissolution by hoping to erase one set of claims in favor of the other. It is because of its insistence on the absurdity of this move, in fact, that the old junker of political realism can remain on the road and even keep some of its critical potentials alive in some places.

The modern state expresses the modern aspiration to be able to resolve all contradictions between universality and particularity through the body of the modern subject: through the autonomous individual and the sovereign territorial state. The upside of this resolution is expressed inside, as the possibility of reconciling our autonomous subjectivity as individuals with some universalizing account of humanity as such; Immanuel Kant's categorical imperative can be read as the crucial regulative principle in this context. The downside is expressed outside: all our grand hopes for unity in diversity, for humanity through citizenship, depend on the potentially violent inscription of the boundary between inside and outside that makes the resolution possible in the first place. Thus, any attempt to simply broaden our understanding of security by taking the inside outside, by extending the upside of statist community to the world of conflict outside, is fundamentally misguided. Any such attempt will necessarily lead back to an insistence on the adequacy of the modern resolution of all relations of unity and diversity on the terrain of the modern state. All that is then left to argue about is the extent to which the modern principle of autonomy is compatible with some kind of social and political order, whether inside or outside the modern state. Hobbes will still serve to remind us that a basic liberal account of equal individuals leads to anarchy, and Kant will continue to name the utopian hope of reconciling all particularities in the perpetual peace of universal reason.[16] Thinking about security under these conditions has gone on for long enough. Whether under the auspices of Hobbes or Kant, it harbors nostalgia for a normative vision that never did say much about the way the world is, only as it must be.

If the subject of security is the *subject* of security, it is necessary to ask, first and foremost, how the modern subject is being reconstituted and then to ask what security could possibly mean in relation to it. It is in this context that it is possible to envisage a critical discourse about security, a discourse that engages with contemporary transformations of political life, with emerging accounts of who we might become, and the conditions under which we might become other than we are now without destroying others, ourselves, or the planet on which we all live. Where so much recent debate about security has been predicated on the impossible dream of absolute invulnerability (the counterpart of the impossible dream of absolute freedom), a critical engagement with security would envisage it precisely as a condition of being vulnerable to the possibility of being otherwise than one has already become. A latter-day Machiavelli might even consider this a species of *virtù*.

NOTES

1. See Bradley S. Klein, *Strategic Studies and World Order: The Global Politics of Deterrence* (Cambridge: Cambridge University Press, 1994); David Campbell and Michael Dillon, eds., *The Political Subject of Violence* (Manchester: Manchester University Press, 1993).

2. The fate of the ambitions of peace research are especially interesting in this context; for an analysis that has implications considerably beyond its

explicit focus, see Peter Lawler, *A Question of Values: Johan Galtung's Peace Research* (Boulder, Colo.: Lynne Rienner, 1995).

3. The relevant literature here is enormous. Typical examples, each referring to extensive literatures and debates, include Barry Buzan, "New Patterns of Global Security in the Twenty-First Century," *International Affairs* 67:3 (1991), 431–51; Jessica Tuchman Mathews, "Redefining Security," *Foreign Affairs* 68 (1989), 162–77; Thomas F. Homer-Dixon, "Global Environmental Change and International Security," in David Dewitt, David Haglund, and John Kirton, eds., *Building a New Global Order: Emerging Trends in International Security* (Toronto: Oxford University Press, 1993), 185–228; Simon Dalby, "Security, Modernity, Ecology: The Dilemma of Post-Cold War Security Discourse," *Alternatives* 17:1 (Winter 1992), 95–134; Daniel Deudney, "The Case against Linking Environmental Degradation and National Security," *Millennium* 19 (1990), 473–74; David V. J. Bell, "Global Communications, Culture and Values: Implications for Global Security," in Dewitt, Haglund, and Kirton, eds., *Building a New Global Order*, 159–84; Robert Cox, "Production and Security," in Dewitt, Haglund, and Kirton, eds., *Building a New Global Order*, 141–58; James Rochlin, "Redefining Mexican 'National Security' during an Era of Post-Sovereignty," *Alternatives* 21:3 (July–September 1995), 369–402; Costas M. Constantinou, "NATO's Caps: European Security and the Future of the North Atlantic Alliance," *Alternatives* 20:2 (April–June 1995), 147–64; Caroline Thomas, *In Search of Security: The Third World in International Relations* (Boulder, Colo.: Lynne Rienner, 1987); J. Ann Tickner, "Re-Visioning Security," in Ken Booth and Steve Smith, eds., *International Relations Theory Today* (Cambridge: Polity, 1995), 175–97; Gregory D. Foster, "Interrogating the Future of Long Term Threats," *Alternatives* 19:1 (Winter 1994), 53–97; Phil Williams, "Transnational Criminal Organizations and International Security," *Survival* 36:1 (Spring 1994), 96–113; Gabriel Sheffer, "Ethno-National Diasporas and Security," *Survival* 36:1 (Spring 1994), 60–79; and the special issue on "Searching for Security in a Global Economy," *Daedalus* 120:4 (Fall 1991).

4. Thus, to give one example among many that can be culled from contemporary public debate, in the wake of the UN Cairo conference on population and development, U.S. Secretary of State Warren Christopher was quoted as saying that "I see proof every day that population [that is, the population explosion] harms regional and global and ultimately jeopardises America's security interests. It strains resources, stunts economic growth, it generates disease, it spawns huge refugee flows, and ultimately it threatens our stability." "Third World Population Threatens US: Christopher," *The Times of India*, 22 December 1994, 15.

5. Again, among many others, see Ken Booth, "Security and Emancipation," *Review of International Studies* 17:4 (October 1991), 313–26; and

Richard Falk, *On Humane Governance: Towards a New Global Politics* (Cambridge: Polity, 1995).

6. Andrew Mack, "Concepts of Security in the Post-Cold War World," *Working Paper 1993/8*, Australian National University Department of International Relations, Canberra (December 1993); Michael Klare and Daniel Thomas, eds., *World Security: Trends and Challenges at Century's End* (New York: St. Martin's, 1991).

7. Thomas Hobbes, *Leviathan*, ed. C. B. Macpherson (London: Penguin Books, 1968).

8. The tendency for many attempts to rethink the concept of security to reify the modern subject is most tellingly exemplified by what is generally regarded as the most sustained recent attempt to rethink the concept of security, Barry Buzan, *People, States and Fear,* 2nd ed., (London: Harvester Wheatsheaf, 1991). Critiques of reification in this context are developed in R. B. J. Walker, *Inside/Outside: International Relations as Political Theory* (Cambridge: Cambridge University Press, 1993); Campbell and Dillon, eds., *The Political Subject of Violence*; David Campbell, *Writing Security: United States Foreign Policy and the Politics of Identity* (Manchester: Manchester University Press, 1992); and, in the context of recent attempts to develop alternative accounts of security in the Third World by affirming modern statist subjectivities, Mustapha Kamal Pasha, "Security as Hegemony," *Alternatives* 22:3 (July–September 1996).

9. Among a rapidly expanding feminist literature, see, for example, Patricia Molloy, "Subversive Strategies or Subverting Strategy? Toward a Feminist Pedagogy for Peace," *Alternatives* 20:2 (1995), 225–42; J. Ann Tickner, "Inadequate Providers? A Gendered Analysis of States and Security," in Joseph A. Camilleri, Anthony P. Jarvis, and Albert J. Paolini, eds., *The State in Transition: Reimagining Political Space* (Boulder, Colo.: Lynne Rienner, 1995), 125–37; J. Ann Tickner, *Gender and International Relations: Feminist Perspectives on Achieving Global Security* (New York: Columbia University Press, 1992); V. Spike Peterson, ed., *Gendered States: Feminist (Re)Visions of International Relations Theory* (Boulder, Colo.: Lynne Rienner, 1992); Christine Sylvester, *Feminist Theory and International Relations in a Postmodern Era* (Cambridge: Cambridge University Press, 1994); and M. Cooke and A. Woolacott, eds., *Gendering War Talk* (Princeton, N.J.: Princeton University Press, 1993).

For literature on postcolonialism, see for example, Sankaran Krishna, "Cartographic Anxiety: Mapping the Body Politic in India," *Alternatives* 19:4 (Fall 1994), 507–21; and Ashis Nandy, ed., *Science, Hegemony and Violence* (Delhi: Oxford University Press, 1988).

10. For exemplary analyses in this mode, see Michael J. Shapiro, "Images of Planetary Danger: Luciano Benetton's Ecumenical Fantasy," *Alternatives*

19:4 (Fall 1994), 433–54; Timothy W. Luke, "Discourses of Disintegration, Texts of Transformation: Re-Reading Realism in the New World Order," *Alternatives* 18:2 (Spring 1993), 229–58; William Chaloupka, *Knowing Nukes: The Politics and Culture of the Atom* (Minneapolis: University of Minnesota Press, 1992); and James Der Derian, *Antidiplomacy: Spies, Terror, Speed and War in International Politics* (Oxford: Basil Blackwell, 1992).

11. R. B. J Walker, *Inside/Outside*; Jens Bartelson, *A Genealogy of Sovereignty* (Cambridge: Cambridge University Press, 1995); Cynthia Weber, *Simulating Sovereignty: Intervention, the State and Symbolic Exchange* (Cambridge: Cambridge University Press, 1995).

12. Ken Booth, "Steps towards Stable Peace in Europe: A Theory and Practice of Coexistence," *International Affairs* 66:1 (January 1990), 17–45.

13. Albert O. Hirschman, *The Passions and the Interests* (Princeton, N.J.: Princeton University Press, 1977).

14. R. B. J. Walker, "From International Relations to World Politics," in Camilleri, Jarvis, and Paolini, eds., *The State in Transition*, 21–38.

15. This is seen most explicitly toward the end of chap. 13 of *Leviathan*, although the entire argument can be read as a denial of a simple isomorphism between individuals and states.

16. Kant's name, of course, has become associated with many things that are difficult to reconcile with the texts he wrote. For helpful recent readings in this context, see Michael C. Williams, "Reason and Realpolitik: Kant's Critique of International Politics," *Canadian Journal of Political Science* 25 (1992), 99–119; Jens Bartelson, "The Trial of Judgement: A Note on Kant and the Paradoxes of Internationalism," *International Studies Quarterly* 39:2 (1995), 255–79; and Mark Franke, "Immanuel Kant and the (Im)Possibility of International Relations Theory," *Alternatives* 21:3 (July–September 1995), 279–322.

4

Security and Self:
Reflections of a Fallen Realist

KEN BOOTH

What is being discussed in this book and this chapter is no trivial matter. It begins in a debate in which there is agreement that security is crucial, but disagreement about what security is and how it should be studied. This debate within security studies over the past few years is now largely polarizing between the post-Cold War updaters of established strategic studies and the proponents of what is now labeled—as a result of the York conference that gave birth to this book—critical security studies. It is not simply an academic dispute over professional turf—about the boundaries of a subfield and how it should be studied. Fundamentally, it is part of a debate about the focus, direction, and meaning of the study of International Relations at the end of one era and the beginning of another. To the extent that this branch of academic life has political influence, it is therefore part of a struggle over the next set of worldviews of Western opinion.[1]

Personal experience has always been an explicit feature of feminist theorizing. Making sense of one's own life has been seen as a way of making sense of the lives of others. The personal, the political, and the international are a seamless web. In this chapter I want to make some reflections, in a similar spirit, about self, profession, and world politics. Instead of purporting to describe or explain the world "out there," as is one's professional training, I want to reflect on the world "in here,"[2] in my professional head. This is academically and temperamentally a somewhat difficult thing to do. It is especially out of line with the traditions of several decades of security studies, which involved "telling it as it is"—"it" being a realist account of the purported state(s) of the world. As a profession, security studies has not been particularly self-reflective. At the start of the 1960s we were invited by Herman Kahn to think the unthinkable, yet "we" remain out of bounds. At what is thought to be a period of intellectual crisis in security studies, "we" should not be, as we are both part of the problem and part of the solution. Hence, the risky personal nature of the approach adopted below.

This chapter, the bulk of which is an experiment in autosociology, has several specific aims: to show from personal experience how the discipline (security/strategic studies) has actually worked in trying to discipline its students and teachers; to encourage students new to the subject area to think about the sociology of knowledge rather than simply assuming that the bundles of knowledge that arrive in neat packages into libraries, like tubs of butter into supermarkets, are in some way untouched by human hand; to illustrate from my own career as a university teacher the development of how we (an increasingly incoherent we) think about security; and to provide a framework for commenting on some current controversies about where the subject (whatever it is) has been, is, and should be. There are some obvious dangers in such an approach, including those of overgeneralizing from personal experience and mistaking memories about one's own past. The risks are trivial, however, if the exercise helps us think constructively about the crucial debate identified in the opening paragraph.

OUT THERE

The established image of positivist International Relations is that academics take issues—European integration, the Cuban Missile Crisis, foreign-policy behavior, security, or whatever—and place them under their social-science microscopes. They then try, objectively, to describe and explain the phenomena in view. Occasionally, there will be enough changes in a particular pattern of thought or behavior to lead to a reconsideration of an issue, or of how it should be studied. The assumption of this approach is that our conception of security derives entirely from changes "out there"—in what is thought to be the real world of international affairs—rather than changes "in here," in the mind of the analyst. Cold wars rise and fall, new technologies develop, and with such shifts come changes in academic theories, agendas, and relevant expertise. But it is not as simple as the natural-science analogy suggests. The relationship between the observer and observed is not as direct, as commonsensical, as in the idealized laboratory model. The events and facts of world politics sometimes thrust themselves under the microscope (World War II, for example), but sometimes they have always been there, usually unnoticed (poverty, for example). It is too simple to believe that changes in theory and agenda result from the demands of the observed, "out there," as opposed to the reinventions "in here." The facts of world politics do not exist independently. They look back through the microscope and examine the mind of the observer, as well as the other way around.

It is already a cliché that the end of the Cold War produced a major change in the way International Relations scholars conceive security. Like all clichés, it has at least a grain of truth, but it is an exaggeration. Realization of this is helped by grasping Cynthia Enloe's insight about the *endings* of the Cold War rather the simpler image that it had one neat conclusion.[3] This insight underlines that what happened means and meant different things to different groups of people. Except for the congenital "keepers of the threat" (the Cold War warriors and worriers on both sides), attitudes about security had already shifted significantly before 1989. There had already been plenty of signs of discontent about Cold War conceptions of "national" and "international" security by the early 1980s, if not earlier, among proponents of alternative defense, peace research, and the many supporters of global civil society committed to nonviolence, human rights, environmental sustainability, and so on.[4]

From the late 1970s and early 1980s, "new thinking" about strategy and international security gradually expanded, particularly in Europe (both East and West). In place of the traditional statist and militarized perspective on international security, which had dominated academic strategic studies from the mid-1950s on, alternative thinkers emphasized nonoffensive defense, common security, democracy, human rights, disarmament, confidence building, and civil society—in short, a broader conception of security, with a wider agenda and changed practice. A significant body of opinion labeling itself "alternative defense" had developed, and in the East as well as the West.[5] This movement played some part in creating a radically different group of experts in Moscow from those that Soviet leaders had usually drawn on. As a result, when Mikhail Gorbachev came to power in 1985, he gave superpower backing to those who were challenging Cold War ways of practicing the military dimension of security. Critics of the established way of thinking about the theory and practice of security (which equated safety with the accumulation of military power) could not but recognize that the Cold War was deadly, but they also believed that it was being directed by policies that ran on rote rather than reason. There was an understanding, even if not always perfectly articulated, that the iron curtain and what it symbolized imprisoned us all, East and West, into old thinking about the games nations played. What kept the Cold War going was the Cold War. What kept Cold War strategic studies going—which the mainstream saw as synonymous with security studies—was the dominance of Cold War intellectuals.

One of the features of the post-Cold War debate about security has been the issue of broadening the concept from its Cold War norms. One harbinger of this, from within neorealist International Relations, was Barry Buzan's *People, States and Fear,* written in the early 1980s.[6] The issue of broadening had potentially been on the agenda for decades, but it had not been taken up by security experts of the day because the issue areas opened up by broadening were seen as belonging to peace rather than to security studies. Between students of peace and security in the Cold War, there was a conceptual, professional, and ideological chasm. Consequently, the teachers of strategic/security studies during the Cold War rejected as irrelevant (or worse) the work of those "radicals" in peace research or world-order studies whose conception of peace and security was far broader than the high politics of mainstream security studies. Prominent among the radicals (although their epistemology was not radical) were Johan Galtung's writings about structural violence (as opposed exclusively to direct violence); Kenneth Boulding's concept of stable (as opposed to unstable) peace; John Burton's individualist rather than statist worldview; and Richard Falk's world order as opposed to realist values.[7] Such approaches, which promoted a broad conception of peace and security, gained some supporters but very few in mainstream Western International Relations; I would argue, however, that their insights constitute a more original set of contributions to the present security debate than any of the articles that

have been filling space in the workaday security journals at the clos-
ings of the Cold War.

The historical point being emphasized here is that those I regard as
the true redefiners of contemporary security studies predated the end
of the Cold War. In addition to the radical and neorealist approaches
just mentioned, several advocates of distinctive Third World security
perspectives also challenged dominant Anglo-American Cold War
conceptions of security before 1989.[8] Significantly, none of these
people I am identifying as the true redefiners of security was prominent on the reading lists of mainstream Western strategic/security
specialists even at the time the Berlin Wall was being demolished.

After this brief introduction, it should be evident that the much-
touted intellectual crisis in security studies on the cusp of the Cold
War's endings exists more or less exclusively in the camp of those
previously dominant security specialists who want to rescue the assumptions of Cold War strategic studies as the basis for approaching
security in the post-Cold War world. Some in this group are in crisis
because everything seems to have changed except their assumptions.
Critical security theorists, long before 1989, realized that change is
the essence of world politics, and that change was taking place "out
there" and "in here," and that it needed to.

SELF

Against this background I want to emphasize the complex inter-
relationship between theorizing and the theorizer. In so doing I want
to illustrate from experience the falsity of the positivist assumptions
that social truth exists out there independently of the observer, and
that the norm is that changes in theory flow directly from new issues
placing themselves under the security analyst's microscope, with the
result that the analyst is led to reconsider approaches, agendas, referents, and so on. The latter may happen. In 1945 the atomic bomb
without doubt dropped itself under the microscope. I want to illustrate, however, that what goes under the microscope in the name of
security may be the result of changes within the theorist—"in
here"—rather than as a result of any significant changes in the world
"out there." By discussing, as frankly as possible in a short space, the
construction of the self as a security analyst, and the interrelation-
ship between the changing theorizer and theorizing about security, I
hope to encourage new students of security to be more self-conscious

about why they think what they think. The following quotations are a good starting point. The first is from Anaïs Nin: "We see things not as they are, but as we are." The second is by Mahatma Gandhi: "We must be the change we wish to see in the world." The words of Nin are a succinct summary of the differences between the spirit of positivism and the agenda of postpositivism, while those of Gandhi make us think about academic inquiry and political change. Both quotations raise crucial question for students of security. What, for example, does Nin's apparently simple phrase "we are" mean? Who and what are we? Do we (women, men, humans) have unchanging natures, or are we socially constructed beings ("women," "men," "humans")? As well as inviting such questions, Nin's words also suggest a seamless web between the realm of the political and the identity of the personal. This links directly to Gandhi's words, which for present purposes invite us to consider whether, before we reinvent the study of security, we first have to reinvent ourselves. If we decide on the latter, how do we do it (whoever "we" are)? Furthermore—and this is a troubling question for academics—are universities the best means by which to create and re-create the people who might offer some promise of meeting the challenges to global security in the next century? In order to help us think about all this, it is necessary to make several points about identity (we are all now, to a degree, identity theorists).

In the sociological tradition of thinking about identity, especially that of the symbolic interactionists, we do not come into the world as formed individuals but are constructed out of the interaction between our individual genetic makeup and the various social structures in which we develop. People have to maintain those structures, and so communication and language are crucial in the development of identity.[9] These general remarks are basic to the sociology of security. The issue of identity—who *I* really think I am, who *one* actually believes one is, who *they* think they are, what makes *us* believe we are the same and *them* different—is inseparable from security.

Role theory or role playing is central to the sociological tradition of thinking about identity. A role is defined by Peter Berger as "a typified response to a typified expectation."[10] In this formulation, society provides the script, individuals slip into assigned roles, and the social play proceeds as planned as long as everybody plays his or her appropriate part. Role playing consists of individuals who adapt their behavior and goals to the expectations others have of them. Then the role "forms, shapes, patterns both action and actor."[11] Berger summarizes the significance of role theory by saying that "identity is socially bestowed, socially sustained and socially transformed."[12] Each role has a certain identity; some are trivial and temporary, others are not. It is doubtful, incidentally, whether anybody would disagree with the proposition that during the Cold War the roles and identity of those Western academics who were strategic studies and national security experts were fundamental to their sense of self. For strategic studies specialists during the Cold War, their professional identity derived from the belief that they were playing an important role in probably the most important political job of the era—containing the power of the Soviet Union. And with this important role came important bonuses such as position, promotion, research support, media presence, and a certain glamour. Hence, the strategist's versions of Descartes's cognito: "I am a strategist, therefore I am important"; "I am protecting the free world against barbarism, therefore I am a hero"; "I am defending the innocent, therefore I am a man"; and "I get research grants, therefore I am a success." Changing identity is not easy, especially when it risks losing all the identity-bearing bonuses that go with it. The conservatism that is encouraged by the pressures to maintain loyalty to a highly valued label no doubt played its part in the self-disciplining of the discipline of Cold War strategic/security studies.

The roles and identities just mentioned referred to adults. George Herbert Mead, in a key text, emphasized the importance of such ideas in relation to children.[13] The discovery of the self—the process of creating and being created—is simultaneous with the discovery of society. Children learn to play roles, both with respect to significant others (mothers and so on) and the generalized other (society and so on). Identity is not something given but "is bestowed in acts of social recognition."[14] Berger goes on to argue that every act of social affiliation entails a choice of identity, and that, conversely, identity requires specific social affiliations for its survival:

> The individual locates himself in society within systems of social control, and every one of these contains an identity-generating apparatus. *Insofar as he is able* the individual will try to manipulate his affiliations . . . in such a way as to fortify the identities that have given him

satisfaction in the past. . . . In many cases, of course, *such manipulation is not possible*. One must then do the best one can with *the identities one is thrown*.[15]

In addition to the identification of the individual with masculine pronouns, this passage is noteworthy for what Berger suggests about the scope for choice and, more particularly (as the emphasized words show), the lack of choice. For many people in many situations identities are simply thrown at one—"woman," "Serb," "black." Before some of the implications of these remarks for security specialists are discussed, it is useful to clarify Mead's distinction between *I* and *me*.

According to Mead, the human self is a reflexive being, made up of an "I" and a "me."[16] The latter is socially constructed whereas the former is more the product of subjective choice (although this subjective choice is also in part the product of social circumstances). The me is known through social interaction, but the I might be unknowable. To relate this to the previous discussion, it is me who is allotted the role (by micro/macro society), but it is I who chooses how to play it. In Mead's words, "the 'I' is the response of the organism to the attitudes of the others; the 'me' is the organised set of attitudes of others which one himself assumes. The attitudes of the others constitute the organised 'me,' and then one reacts toward that as an 'I.'"[17] In terms of the development of individuals as academic specialists, the me is the identity ascribed by the profession to an individual (and therefore the identity taken on through seeing oneself in relation to those of the same profession); the I is the inner self, which, to a lesser or greater degree, may subjectively want to play the role differently. One's identity as a security specialist evolves through the interplay of I and me, psychology and culture, the individual and social structures.

This sociological interpretation of the making of the self has been echoed by some postmodern accounts of social change.[18] The importance of feeling, instinct, personality, and "other conditions of the self" are emphasized in the way that texts are read and deconstructed. Jan Aart Scholte discusses this in relation to Michel Foucault and his account of the history of ideas. Writers expressing other postpositivist approaches have written along similar lines. Jürgen Habermas's theory of "life worlds" and communicative action involves the interplay between self-identity and the construction of meaning. In addition to Scholte, Alexander Wendt is one of the few International Relations scholars who has addressed this additional dimension to the inside/outside phenomenon.[19]

This brief survey of some standard sociological literature yields several concepts that are useful for thinking about the critical turn in security studies: self, roles, socialization, I/me. One might also add Erik Erikson's notion of "identity crisis" (dating from World War II), by which he meant a "lost sense of personal sameness and historical continuity."[20] Such crises are said to characterize some life stages—particularly for youths—where there is confusion about identity until a new social ideology is found that provides "a convincing world image." It is significant for our present discussion that Erikson believed that such problems were more acute at times of great historical change.[21]

There are, of course, many so far unmentioned variables that in practice affect evolving interrelationships between I and me, including gender, race, national group, upbringing, and so on. These are questions that students of International Relations and security studies have generally ignored but cannot continue to do so without seriously impoverishing the quality of their analysis.[22] Humans are a meanings-making species, and the creation and re-creation of identity are fundamental to the meanings we make of international politics. And how we conceive international politics is at the root of the meanings we make of security.

The point of these introductory remarks is that if Nin and Gandhi are correct, and we see things as *we* are, and *we* need to be the change, then it is necessary for security specialists to worry more about the implications of the reality of subjectivity than the aspirations of objectivity. Who do we think we are? What is the relationship between our identity and our interests? What do we think we are doing? Who do we represent? What values are we promoting? And why? Why do we give priority to certain issues and ignore others? What are our grounds for claiming special competence? To what extent is the profession prone to "group think?" What are the assumptions at the base of the profession's "conventional convictions?" Do we need to reinvent ourselves before reinventing the profession? If we do, can we? And how can we? What is or should be the relationship between study in a university and the political world? Who becomes a security specialist, and why? And if the scope and method of security is defined by *me*, should not *I* become more assertive?

The academic subject of security studies is ultimately what we make it; it is the (temporary) historical outcome of the interplay between a socially constructed profession and the (part social, part biochemical) individuals who are employed to profess it. In the working out of the relationship between the many me's and I's, security studies will be replicated or revised, as specialists in security studies talk and act what they think they play.

ME

As security specialists—graduates or junior faculty—we begin with the me in the ascendant. We know relatively little, and we are, to a degree, what our teachers make us. Put at its crudest, if we had not passed their examinations, our careers as security specialists would not have begun. We must therefore consider the making of me-the-security-analyst. Here begins the personal experience, which some may find indulgent, but which I think is one direct way of making sense of the contested subject of security.

Almost all those who were students of International Relations (in Britain) in the 1960s lived on a diet of realism. For the most part it was not high-cuisine realism (the actual works) of the founders of this school, but a form of fast-food realism. By the 1960s realism showed rather little of the complexity, sophistication, and moral anguish of Reinhold Niebuhr and the other founding fathers (as Nicholas Wheeler keeps reminding me). By the 1950s realism was a body of ideas neatly packaged for teaching purposes in order to make them easily palatable to students. It was made into a persuasive story. The fast-food version was also very congenial to politicians and officials. If realists are now easily caricatured, they have only themselves to blame. They had become caricatures by their own self-description.

Realism, and particularly its offshoot, strategic studies, helped make and was made by the Cold War. It is difficult for young academics today to imagine the mood and experience of students of the subject more than thirty years ago. For International Relations students in the early 1960s World War II was only yesterday. For those of us whose first schoolyard jokes were about Hitler, Mussolini, and Churchill (learning that the world was run by strong leaders), who played after school around the neighborhood air-raid shelter, whose first experience of "important" films (marked by a free ticket from school funds and a half-day holiday) was to watch major war movies about Dunkirk or D-Day (in which our teachers and relatives had participated), and whose first awareness of newspapers and television was of global crises such as those over Berlin in the late 1950s— for that generation of International Relations students, who learned power politics through our skins, the realist account of the world that we were later taught seemed exactly to fit the images we already had had imprinted.

Having been brought up on the statecentric and militarized news media and popular culture of the Cold War, my generation of students was primed to believe that a theory of what, in Raymond Aron's phrase, "diplomats and soldiers" did, explained world affairs. Just as children are primed to expect the mince-pies eaten and the brandy drunk on Christmas morning, so students of International Relations in the 1960s were primed to expect an account of ministers rushing between conference halls and missiles at the ready. So, just as the Father Christmas story constitutes and then "explains" the crumbs on the plate by the chimney to the satisfaction of wide-eyed and believing children, so realism helped constitute the behavior in world politics, which it then, in a self-fulfilling way, explained to wide-eyed and primed students. Instead of positivism's seeing is believing, the social world is in important ways constructed by the phenomenon of believing is seeing. There is another parallel. The Father Christmas story and academic realism are also both deeply masculinized. Within departments of International Relations in the 1960s the concept of gender was neither seen nor believed.

Those who were good students of realism, and who passed their teachers' examinations, were offered places in the academy and became teachers themselves. To be accepted it was necessary to take on what Charles Manning—who dominated the department at the London School of Economics for several decades—used to call the "conventional convictions" of the profession. Thus, the junior-faculty me was one largely created by the teaching and expectations of a generation of realists-positivists. Like many students of that time I was attracted to the growing subfield of strategic studies. This seemed to be where the action was, literally and academically.

In order to be a teacher at the heart of power politics it was necessary to become adept at, and share in the assumptions of, what the strategic studies community identified as the basic ideas of peace and security. These ideas—nuclear deterrence, arms control, limited war, and crisis management—were elaborated from the mid-1950s to the mid-1960s in what John Garnett called the "golden age" of strategic theory.[23] The ideas of those who questioned the morality or rationality of so-called nuclear strategy, or those who challenged Cold War assumptions about Soviet behavioral patterns, were ignored completely or dismissed as irrelevant or idiosyncratic or lacking in realism or soft on communism. This attitude now seems astonishingly anti-intellectual as well as politically naïve. It also reveals an important warning for those students of the social world who believe that they are capturing timeless truth. When we look back at centuries of political theory, it is evident that particular theorists were more or less "men of their time" (and place). This does not mean, however, that some have nothing to say to others in different times and cultures, but it does underline that truth in the social world is pragmatic and intersubjective. As far as strategic studies is concerned, it did not take long for critics, and changing international circumstances, to show that all that glitters is not gold. But for many of us, for a time, it dazzled, and like junior faculty everywhere, what one had been taught only a short time before, one tended to teach to one's own students. Last-minute lecture preparation makes corner-cutters of us all. Other professional pressures also exercised an influence. To be one of the boys—with all that entailed—it was necessary to share the same assumptions. Significantly—and what I now think of with some shame—my student criticism of the war in Vietnam in 1965–67 evolved in 1968–69 into the explanatory language of realpolitik. Pursuing the goal of "stability" now seemed more important than criticizing the "arrogance of power." It was not the war in Vietnam that had changed, or my knowledge of it; what had changed was that I had become a defense intellectual. It was not a difficult script to follow, for it involved powerful stories and heroic images, and the duty to be responsible.

While the professionally constructed me continued to enjoy the challenges thrown up by the attempt to understand some of the great issues of peace and war, I began to have serious disquiets about some aspects of the subject. In particular, when I began to teach strategic studies in 1967, it came as a stunning surprise that almost all those strategists around me whose professional lives had been and were in-volved with "the Soviet threat" and devising cosmic counters knew little or nothing about the Soviet Union itself. Moreover, they did not seem to think it mattered. They were confident in their belief that we, the West, were faced by a (super) powerful adversary, whose en-mity was such as to justify any counter, however "unthinkable."[24] This was my first academic shock. I had entered the powerhouse of the study of power politics only to discover that those who were paid to profess it in universities were curiously incurious about other countries and other cultures—even enemies. And repeated experi-ences convinced me that many of them did not care. Looking back, this discovery of the profound realist incuriosity about the world was a critical turning point. I have been criticized in recent years for vulgarizing realism on occasion: I can say in defense that, if I have, I have never managed to do it as blatantly as some of its proponents.

This professional shock—felt more strongly as a result of an ear-lier visit to the Soviet Union in 1964—convinced me that strategic theory should never be separated from area studies. Consequently, when I started teaching such topics as nuclear strategy and U.S.-Soviet relations I tried to develop an understanding of the evolution of Soviet military and foreign policies. An enormous piece of luck in this regard was finding Michael MccGwire in my class as a student. He had recently taken early retirement from the Royal Navy, where he had been a senior and original intelligence analyst working on the Soviet Union.[25] As well as being a student, he was also directly involved in major policy debates about Soviet strategy. He taught me more than I taught him. Shortly afterward, as a professor he organized a series of seminars at Dalhousie University in the early 1970s on Soviet naval developments that brought together some of the best Soviet specialists available and encouraged a range of sig-nificant research, from how to think about shipbuilding programs to discussions of the semantic differences between the Russian and Anglo-American words for *deterrence* and *defense.*[26] These meetings generally confirmed the conclusion that I had reached in the late 1960s that the West should be relaxed about the Soviet threat. The Soviet Union's power was exaggerated by Soviet and Western pro-paganda and it was often more threatened than threatening.[27] Try-ing to understand the Soviet Union, and the variety of Western thinking about it, revealed the ethnocentric character of Anglo-

American strategic studies in particular and International Relations in general. What gradually dawned was that what purported to be rational and objective strategic theory was often a rationalization of national prejudice, and that strategic practice was best understood as applied ethics—a continuation of (moral) philosophy with an admixture of firepower.[28] Strategic theory helped to constitute the strategic world, and then strategic studies helped to explain it—self-reverentially and tautologically.

The realization that we live within structures that are theories, that the material circumstances of strategy are the manifestations of theories, that theories about security deliver our strategic facts, and that there is more than one strategic logic led to a growing disquiet with realism and its familiar positivist methods. But what did it mean to believe that reality is in the eye of the beholder? That there is more than one version of the (strategic) logic of anarchy? That social truth is a product of history rather than timeless common sense? And that human nature is not natural? I had no clear idea, but in 1974 I started collecting material and ideas about the ethnocentric character of strategic theorizing and practice. This effort was encouraged by James King, the director of research at the U.S. Naval War College in the mid-1970s, and he made it possible for me to spend some time there writing up the material in 1977. Jim King was a great and unselfish supporter of younger colleagues, and one of the very few true scholars in postwar strategic studies—and so his career was not destined to survive long at the War College.[29] Neither was mine, given that the late 1970s coincided with a slowly developing professional identity crisis. The changing (collapsing) relationship between the academic strategist (me) and the uncertain self (I) was summed up in the dedication of *Strategy and Ethnocentrism* (1979), the book that eventually emerged out of the growing discontents about strategic man.

It was fortunate that the opportunity to study at the U.S. Naval War College had been firmly fixed by Jim King, for in the previous year there had been a sharp termination of my personal naïveté about the relationship between academics and policy makers, in this case in the shape of important players in the U.S. Navy. For a number of years, following an opportunity to spend a term alongside officers of my own age at the Royal Naval College in Greenwich, I had been writing and lecturing regularly about navies and foreign policy, and this work had converged with that of some key groups in the U.S. Navy. During this period I lectured on several occasions at the War College and got the chance to meet some impressive people and see amazing technology.[30] But I was abruptly dropped by the U.S. Navy, after what very senior officers saw as a hostile attack on their raison d'être. To an audience of senior naval commanders on NATO's southern flank, including commanding officers of the U.S. Sixth Fleet, I gave a paper entitled "If the Sixth Fleet Did Not Exist Would You Invent It?" My answer was "no," and I think I won the first round on points, hence the determination of the counterattack. A knockout blow came in round two, as I was never again asked to talk to the U.S. Navy, except for one fixed commitment, and so I felt directly what previously I had only read, namely, that practitioners see academics as only more or less useful bureaucratic resources.[31] (Jim King was also a victim of the less scholarly, more technocratic and policy-relevant research regime that took over the U.S. Naval War College.) One of the lessons I learned from this, very forcefully, is that practitioners only allow in those critics who share, or seem to share, every assumption with them. Academics are allowed to become insiders in order to help practitioners win; they are not there to supply wisdom or speak truth to power. Partly as a result of these events, my own work, quite erroneously in my opinion, became seen as anti-American. It should, more accurately, have been seen as critical commentary on some of the policies of the U.S. government. Later, with the Reagan administrations, there was of course much more to criticize.

Together, the public policy concern over the issue of the Soviet threat, the theoretical concern over the ethnocentric character of the discipline, and the realization that academics and policy makers make uncomfortable bedmates, had converged to create a sort of professional identity crisis about the subject, the subject matter, and my own role as a university teacher. The professionalized "me" was slipping away, but what would take its place? I knew what "I" was reacting against—the assumptions, presumptions, assertions, and prescriptions of mainstream strategic studies—but did not know where this reaction would ultimately take me. I still do not. Academic life changed from being the confident teaching of established wisdom to an uncertain, agonizing, and always unfinished search for ways of revisioning and relating to world politics. There have been some occasional flashes of what I hope is insight along the road, but the paradigm gained, like the paradigm lost, was not a singular event but rather a steady accumulation over years of trying to fit the bits together in a different pattern.

I

I only attempted to become self-conscious about this process of ontological reinvention recently, when a student tagged me as a "fallen realist." It is worth briefly relating how this came about because there is a tendency to assume that changed conceptions of the world are, for academics, either the result of being persuaded by a decisive book or being shocked by major events in world politics. People seem determined to make us either simply disciples or positivists. There are other possibilities.

What follows is largely a story of the influence of three individuals outside mainstream International Relations; it is not the stuff of Cold War strategic/security studies, but it is perhaps a story of increasing relevance for global security studies for the twenty-first century. It is not a story in which new facts are discovered, but one in which old ones are seen in a new way. Together, and almost at the same time, these three individuals led me to rethink what, how, and why I thought about security in International Relations. It is interesting to discuss this process of rethinking in relation to the Waltzian level of analysis problem because for me, like many other students of the subject, Kenneth Waltz's work has been an important stimulus and provocation; and the three levels of analysis or "images" that he discusses in his major work *Man, the State and War* were a formative influence.[32] If, in the 1970s, I was conscious of moving away from the realist fatalism of Waltz's logic of anarchy, it took ideas and stimuli outside the literature of the subject to clarify alternative logics of anarchy and give my discontents direction. I will account for the three new "images" in a chronological rather than Waltzian order.

The State

An Australian friend, Dale Trood, tried seriously in the mid-1970s to interest me in the work and spirit of Amnesty International. She failed. Interfering in the business of other states ran against the realist norms of academic International Relations and the society of states, while the implication that any nongovernmental organization could be a serious player in world affairs ran counter to the litany that states are the most powerful actors. By chance, a couple of years later, in a different place, Dale got another try. I dipped in my toe, and it made me rethink all that I had been taught. The more I thought about the individual cases that are the staple of Amnesty's work, the more I thought about the significance of thinking about international relations from the perspective of individuals rather than states. For me, the experience of writing those first letters to governments about perfect strangers—victims of those governments—was a real turning point. Here were some names and sometimes faces of the hitherto unseen casualties of the structures of international relations. It is not only war that produces casualties. This turning point was almost as vivid—although obviously neither as personally life threatening or other life saving—as it was for Oskar Schindler, in Steven Spielberg's film, when he focused, through all the carnage, on the solitary little girl in a red coat. At least this is how I read the moment in the film: the reality of gross human wrongs suddenly becomes clear in the image of a single stranger. One consequence of this visualization for me was the wish to read literature previously ghettoized by realist ideology. As a result, individual victims came to be seen not simply as a feature of domestic politics, but as a part of an international system that, through a mixture of rationality and historical happenstance, had developed into the business of power politics rather than into the exploration of common humanity. The individual/bottom-up/victim perspective began to change what I thought about the state, state types, social power, security problems other than the military inventories of the superpowers, the state as the exclusive security referent (which legitimized nuclear deterrence), and states as a source of threat rather than as a source of security. The sovereign state came to be seen as an important part of the problem of insecurity in world politics, not the solution.

War

A Canadian peace campaigner, Peggy Hope-Simpson, refused to accept that somebody she took to be sane and knowledgeable could actually believe what I was teaching students about nuclear deterrence and arms control. She insisted that I talk to her and her group (Project Ploughshares) about such realist truisms as the "inescapable" war system, the "impossibility" of disarmament, the "rational" relationship between military power and national security, the "perpetual" nuclear peace, the "just" nuclear deterrent, and this as "the best of all possible worlds." In the course of one particular lecture it became apparent that "me" was mouthing a strategist's script—written by myself—that "I" no longer really believed. Strategists are not supposed to be doubting Thomases, but doubts kept accumulating and led to the conclusion that anarchy in a multicultural world might not only deliver different logics of strategy (the subject of the book on ethnocentrism) but also that interstate anarchy invites different logics of foreign policy and, indeed, of international relations. Alexander Wendt recently expressed such a shift very neatly in the title of his much-cited article "Anarchy Is What States Make of It" (although I would want to add that anarchy is much more than what those contested units called states make of it!).[33]

The conceptual jump involved here was from thinking of war as a structural phenomenon to thinking of it as a cultural phenomenon, albeit a deeply entrenched one. War should be regarded as a cultural phenomenon (and hence a cultural problem) because human political groups have not always fought. The existence of societies without war undermines reductionist and determinist arguments about human nature and the interstate structure; certainly, human political groups have often fought, but the meaning of that violence that we label "war" has changed radically. If war is a cultural phenomenon, then it can be transcended. The theory of power politics and self-help got us into this security predicament; better theories—the theories and practices of global moral and political obligation—can get us out. The latter is obviously easier said than done, and it is always worth remembering Karl Marx's cautioning words that "men make their own history, but they do not make it just as they please; they do not make it under circumstances chosen by themselves." This changing view of the war system led to the need to rethink structures and agents and to reconsider the whole subject of International Relations. I did not see it this way at the time but later realized that I was struggling against what Roberto Unger came to call "false necessities."[34]

Men

Eurwen Booth—my daily reminder for more than thirty years that there are other than English, strategic, and masculine ways of thinking—got a job with Welsh Women's Aid, which deals with battered women. Her feminist consciousness rocketed and dragged me along in its slipstream. This did not come naturally to a professional strategist and lad from Yorkshire in the north of England. Nevertheless, the gendered character of the social and political world was then blindingly obvious once it was pointed out (although dealing with it appropriately was another matter). What with hindsight is now remarkable is how invisible this dominating fact of life had previously been. It is a perfect illustration of believing is seeing. When I was growing up, I could not see my mother's life as anything other than natural. Once I believed it was not, it looked very different. I had not seen the marriage Eurwen and I had lived as other than natural until I and we believed that we had been social sleepwalkers. Some still argue that gender has nothing to do with international relations in general and security in particular, but in time I have come to believe that it has everything to do with them. To talk about security without thinking about gender is simply to account for the surface reflections without examining what is happening deep down below the surface.

US

"We are as we are because we got that way" is one of the many insightful Kenneth Boulding-isms for which we should be grateful. The world is as it is through the interplay of the marketplaces and battlefields of competing theories through history. The corollary of this is that we (human society in whole or in part) might become what we hope to be: such a viewpoint places a totally different perspective on the timeless present of realism and the necessitous nature of International Relations as taught during the Cold War. This open-ended view of human potential is also important in thinking about the construction of the self in relation to being a security specialist. The important message here—especially for young colleagues, but also for others—is that the self is an unfinished journey: above all, one should not assume that the end of the history of one's own self will or should come in postgraduate and junior-faculty years. Too often, however, individuals are trapped and trap themselves in the subject areas and intellectual convictions of their early twenties (the Ph.D. millstone). Our work as academics, like ourselves, should never be regarded as finished. Our books and articles should be seen as explorations not destinations, and so should our own individual lives. In a way never understood by those who saw and see the study of International Relations and other social sciences as comparable with natural science, we are what we do and we do what we are. Our lives are our work as well as our books. This was Gandhi's point.

But we do not work alone. There are a variety of circumstantial factors, as indicated above, that affect one's explorations. The "me" is constrained by place, time, and community, but so is the exploring "I." Luck, as well as curiosity, is a factor. To complete the brief autobiography, I want to suggest a number of influences that helped give direction in the 1980s to the fallen realist of the 1970s.

First, the matter of place can be important. As the disquiets grew about what I had been taught, and the complacent attitudes of the then-leading lights of strategic studies in Britain, it was helpful that I then moved to Canada for two years. The critical distance this created, with relative freedom from immediate loyalty tests and the absence of familiar peer pressure, undoubtedly made it easier to reassess my position and change my mind. This experience seems to provide support for at least some academic mobility and is certainly a confirmation of the old adage about the purpose of travel not being to discover new places, but to return and see one's country for the first time (and in this case, also one's profession). There are two other points to make about place. I grew up in Featherstone, a mining village in West Yorkshire, which is in England but in important ways was not then of "England"; and then, after I was eighteen, I have lived most of the time in Aberystwyth, a small town on the west coast of Wales, which not only is the home of the oldest department of international politics in the world, but also probably has a higher number of books per capita than anywhere else in the world (the quirks of history gave this town of twelve thousand people not only a university but also a national library, one of the major depository libraries of English-language books in the world). In terms of identity, Featherstone was an experience of class and industry, and Aberystwyth one of nationalism, biculturalism, and education. Living on such margins, I am pleased to say, inculcated a distaste for that view of the world represented by the Britishness embodied in the likes of Margaret Thatcher, with its jingoism, false nostalgia, simplistic history, metropolitan-mindedness, ethnocentrism, nationalistic and individualistic complacency, and comic-book world politics.

We are all, in different ways, creatures rather than creators of our times, and in the story just related, another important contextual consideration was that the working out of some of these changes coincided with the renewed debate about nuclear weapons that began in the late 1970s. This proved to be a convenient focus for thinking about issues such as the role and morality of nuclear deterrence. It was a helpful coincidence rather than a provocation, although Erikson's point about identity crises and periods of historical change is worth bearing in mind. Without doubt, the process of trying to think through previously held positions on peace and security was given a particular focus and clarity by the posturing of Ronald Reagan, Margaret Thatcher, and Leonid Brezhnev. The points made at the beginning of this chapter should not be read as implying that changes out there are always irrelevant to the way we think about security—only that they are not necessarily the most important or even crucial. It often takes new circumstances to crystallize what may be going on in here.

Finally, most academics need to belong to a community. Some in this community may be theorists, others activists; the contact may be direct or through writing; some will be like-minded strangers, while others close friends. But what matters will be the support of the treasured few. In the 1980s, as the world became increasingly wired, it became apparent that in many countries there existed a community of strangers who disagreed profoundly with the conventional strategic/security convictions of the elites in their different countries. But this community of strangers generally lacked the financial backing that enabled the proponents of Cold War structures, attitudes, and policies to meet frequently and air their views in fancy hotels in fancy locations. Nevertheless, a congenial and transnational alternative defense community grew. For the most part, academic work seems a solitary activity, but it is often a team effort. In my own case, what helped put the critique of the 1970s together into a sense of direction in the 1980s were the long-term perspectives and ferocious criticism offered by Michael MccGwire; the stimulus to think in wider theoretical terms given by Nicholas Wheeler; and the alternative defense networking made possible in Eastern and Western Europe and North America by Just Defense in Britain and the Institute for Defense and Disarmament Studies in Boston.

CRITICAL SECURITY STUDIES

With hindsight, it is possible to see the story above as a struggle away from realist strategic studies toward what some of us now call critical security studies. In this struggle it was the inadequacies of realism rather than the attraction of any other particular alternative that did all the early work, and indeed, it took a considerable time before all the other strands came together in the notion of "utopian realism."[35] The latter is an idea whose theory and practice I am still working out but whose assumptions—the utopian element being a belief that world politics do not have to be this way and the realist element being a recognition that we have to begin where we are—fit firmly within the notion of critical security studies.

The birth of critical security studies was both to be expected and is to be celebrated at a time when world events are even more complex and confusing than ever, when old political and philosophical certainties are challenged, and when the study of International Relations is rent by divisions over ontology, epistemology, agenda, and method. When thinking about international political theory is at a crossroads, so must be the way we think about security. Although it is rarely made explicit—especially by those wedded to traditional (military) security theory—the debate about security studies is only one aspect of a more fundamental debate about politics, including the increasingly important context of world politics. The contemporary debate about the meaning of security—and how it should be studied—is only part (but a very important one because of the political salience of security issues) of the uncertainty about what it means to be living, thinking, and teaching at the end of the twentieth century. And thus, at least implicitly, it plays a part in what it will mean to be a human political and social agent in the twenty-first century.

At the heart of the personal account earlier was the move away from the narrow realist definition of what constitutes *the political,* and the ethnocentric subject of Cold War international relations, toward a critical perspective that gradually embraced a less top-down, Anglo-American definition of *international politics* and a broader meaning of *politics.* It goes without saying that not all my colleagues have gone down this same path. While some of us became increasingly dissatisfied with aspects of the training we had received in Cold War International Relations, others continued to see strategic/security studies as simply part of an innovative and heroic age for academics. The latter version would be amusing if it had not been so powerful. This is evident in the views of those who lionize the strategic studies archive and even claim a "renaissance." The classic exemplar of this is Stephen Walt's much-cited 1991 article, "The Renaissance of Security Studies" in *International Studies Quarterly*.[36] What Walt describes is not a renaissance, at least not a rebirth of anything worth reviving. The article attempts to legitimize what in fact needs to be challenged: it is relentlessly U.S.-centric; it discovers what others have known for a long time; and it criticizes those who would broaden the concept of security in favor of the traditionalist military conception (although apparently without appreciating the statist political theory that goes with it). The "norms and ethos" of the "strategic studies community" are strongly endorsed at the end of Walt's article without subjecting their statism, ethnocentrism, masculinism, parochialism (of time as well as space), and positivism to scrutiny.

Stephen Walt and those who think like him have got it wrong. What he was describing was not a renaissance but "late strategic studies."[37] There is still an important job to be done in analyzing the military dimension of international politics (see below), but only as a branch of a more broadly defined understanding of security studies. The true renaissance in security studies these days is being brought about not by those seeking to prioritize and modernize the theories of peace and security that dominated the Cold War, but by those struggling to develop, at the end of a century of violence and change, a postrealist, postpositivist conception of security that offers some promise of maximizing the security and improving the lives of the whole of humankind—the security studies of inclusion rather than exclusion, of possibility rather than necessity, and of becoming rather than being.

It is not easy to change academic minds or shift direction, and the struggle is not an even one. The overwhelming number of today's security specialists were obviously trained during the Cold War, within the norms and ethos of that professional community. As a result, there are now hundreds of experts able to talk about nuclear deterrence, arms control, limited war, and crisis management—invariably from the perspective of East-West relations. There is nothing like the same body of expertise to deal with internal conflicts, identity, ethnic disputes, political theory, conflict resolution, methodology, confidence building, conventional war, regional security in the Third World, and so on. The opening up of the security problematic has created an enormous research agenda, and the insecurity community of Cold War strategic specialists is not well equipped to deal with it. It will take time for a critical security community to grow.

Critical security studies begin in a rejection of traditional security theory.[38] The approach rejects, in particular, the definition of politics that places the state and its sovereignty at the center of the subject; the moral authority of states; the belief that the state is and should be the key guardian of peoples' security; the priority of strategic studies' descriptions of the reality of world affairs; the assumptions and presumptions implicit in the simple binaries of mainstream International Relations; the regressive view of human nature evident in the classical preachings of realism; the utter dominance of structure over agent evident in neorealism; the unreflecting positivism implicit in much of the method of traditional International Relations; and the "false necessities" that restrict the vision, and weigh down the spirit, of so many students of International Relations.

Security is what we make it. It is an epiphenomenon intersubjectively created. Different worldviews and discourses about politics deliver different views and discourses about security. New thinking about security is not simply a matter of broadening the subject matter (widening the agenda of issues beyond the merely military). It is possible—as Barry Buzan has shown above all—to expand "international security studies" and still remain within an asserted neorealist framework and approach.[39] Although the subject of critical security studies also broadens the agenda it is fundamentally different because the agenda derives from a radically different political theory and methodology; the former is based on deeper understandings of the meaning of the political, and the latter on discontents with the presumptions of positivism.

A school of critical security studies that develops from what might be called "global moral science,"[40] rather than the traditional security theory deriving from the "dismal science" of Cold War International Relations, sees as crucial the relationship between theory and its historical/social/political context; it is more concerned with the search for meaning than the endless accumulation of knowledge; it believes that social and political science cannot be separated from life but are inseparable from social and political criticism, replication, and practice; it believes that theory is constitutive rather than explanatory; that the invention of an emancipatory future is more urgent than the discovery of ultimate philosophical foundations; that the role of academics is not (and cannot be) that of a dispassionate observer but is rather that of Antonio Gramsci's "organic intellectual" or of Mary Midgley's socially engaged philosopher; and is based on the belief that, because human potential is barely tapped, politics on a global scale must be regarded as open-ended rather than determined, and based on ethical choices rather than on supposedly natural instincts. One of the attractions of the critical turn in security studies is that it should never settle into the complacency of that it seeks to overthrow; the essence of a critical approach is that it expects change. By turning its own technique in on itself, it invites regular renewal, as times and material circumstances change.

Critical security studies as just described do not—should not— ignore or play down the state and the military dimensions of world politics. What is being challenged is not the material manifestations of the world of traditional realism, but its moral and practical status, including its naturalization of historically created theories, its ideology of necessity and limited possibility, and its propagandist common sense about this being the best of all worlds. There is an important place in critical security studies for the study of the threat and use of military force, but the study of (military) strategy should no longer be synonymous with security studies, as was the case in Cold War International Relations, and as some still want to maintain it (the line of argument associated with Stephen Walt discussed earlier). In the hyperinflated militarization of the Cold War, it was not surprising that strategic studies got too big for its roots. But the subject area can now be seen in proper perspective, as the military dimension of international relations (focusing on relations between states), which itself is a subsystem of world politics—who gets what, when, and how on a global scale (to extrapolate Harold Lasswell's famous definition of politics).[41] Military strategy is a subject area within critical security studies, but it is only one aspect—although sometimes a crucial one—of a wide agenda and one with security referents other than the state (which hitherto has given strategic studies their meaning). This can be illustrated by the example of the "security dilemma," which in many respects has been seen as the quintessential dilemma of international relations because pervasive

"Hobbesian fear" is seen as resulting in insecurity, even when no malevolence is intended. Rather than seeing the security dilemma as the quintessential dilemma, however, a critical perspective might regard it as a sometimes important phenomenon in relations between states, but fundamentally as an epiphenomenon of fatalistic and hegemonic reasoning and practices through time.[42] The latter need to be understood in order that self-constituting human societies and society can learn new practices to help mitigate and then perhaps one day transcend the traps of security dilemmas. In order to transcend the traditions, it is necessary to work at two levels: first, at the level of mitigating the symptoms of the epiphenomenon itself (by confidence-building measures, nonprovocative defense postures, and so on); and second, at the deeper level of the structures that give rise to the epiphenomenon, which, depending on one's political outlook and strategic preferences, may involve the building of the grand schemes of structural idealists, such as world government or world communism, or the "process utopian" schemes of contemporary agents of global reform, such as the world-order values promoted by transnational civil society.[43]

The foregoing is a sketch of what I take the critical-security-studies approach to be at this stage. Because the idea (or more precisely the label) is only of recent coinage (May 1994), and because it has been the focus of only a couple of academic papers, critics should not expect too much too soon. The subject is being worked out; it is presently at the takeoff stage, waiting to happen, in some ways comparable to strategic studies in the mid-1950s, when the subject was a handful of books in search of an academic label. For the immediate future, those attracted to the idea of critical security studies have two agendas, one largely intellectual and the other, what might be called professional. The latter includes building up a network of like-minded individuals, starting courses, and providing materials—in short, institutionalizing the idea within an academic context. The intellectual agenda crystallizes around four tasks: to provide critiques of traditional theory, to explore the meanings and implications of critical theories, to investigate security issues from critical perspectives, and to revision security in specific places. Already the approach and agenda developing under the critical security studies label have come under attack from traditional strategic/security theorists, and I want to close this section by addressing some of the more familiar. This can be done under the headings "critical," "community," "emancipation," and "security."

Critical

What does "critical" mean in the label critical security studies? As it happens, this is likely to be a real focus of disagreement among the body of people who agree that there is a serious crisis in Western thought in general and in particular in that area that discusses security. The division is between the Critical Theorists who trace their intellectual ancestry to the Frankfurt School and postmodern/ poststructuralist critical writers. The former approach is cosmopolitan, self-consciously progressive, emancipatory, postpositivist, post-Marxist, open-ended about human possibilities, Enlightenment-inspired, and epistemologically self-conscious.[44] The latter approaches have shown themselves to be more concerned to expose what is seen as the crisis of representation in Western (Enlightenment) thinking—specifically, issues of foundationalism, closure, difference, hierarchies of knowledge and opinion, metanarratives, and so on— rather than to engage in political projects of their own.[45] My own way of dealing with this critical debate is to say I welcome any approach that enables us to challenge the dismal norms and ethos of Cold War strategic studies and then rethink security, as long as there is a commitment to emancipation (as opposed to leaving power where it is) and to a notion of common humanity (as opposed to forms of cultural or communitarian essentialism).

Community

One of the aims of critical security studies must be to reconsider the distinctions between "us" and "them" in a political sense—in short, to reconsider global political organization in a way that will best deliver security. This is obviously something that cannot be worked out in theory and, still less, in practice overnight. Extending notions of community, and having overlapping communities (thereby accommodating contemporary ideas of multiple and overlapping identities), is a promising way ahead, but there is far to go, and it is here where critical regional security specialists can be very helpful. The sovereign state system has been around for about 350 years, and, globally speaking, it has been a normative failure; at the level of theory we still ask whether states are "global gangsters" or "guardian angels."[46] Against this standard, students of newly created critical security studies can be relaxed against the charge that they have not sorted out the details of their preferred political organization for the twenty-first century.

Emancipation

Whereas traditional International Relations theories privileged power and order as the bases for security, critical security studies—at least in my conception of it—privileges emancipation. For some reason, the notion of emancipation causes traditional security theorists a quite exaggerated degree of irritation. There may be two explanations: first, it opens up the possibility of political programs that they see as being against their interests (as academics/Westerners/men); and second, they are uncomfortable with what is an inherently dynamic concept, whereas so much of traditional theory is based on static concepts (nuclear deterrence, above all). From my perspective, it is simply not possible to say what emancipation *looks like*, apart from its meaning to particular people at particular times. Emancipation *means* freeing people, as individuals and groups, from the social, physical, economic, political, and other constraints that stop them from carrying out what they would freely choose to do.[47] As circumstances change, so will the goals of emancipation. Emancipation has been an issue throughout the twentieth century—for colonies, blacks, women, workers, and so on—and there is no reason to suppose the twenty-first will be different. Indeed, emancipation is a worldwide though not universal cultural norm; it is not universal because it is resisted by traditionalist power structures. "What is emancipation?" and "who will be emancipated?" are the urgent questions for students of critical security studies and the victims of world politics.

Security

A frequent criticism addressed toward those who would broaden the concept of security from its Cold War state/military/status quo focus is that the broadening of the notion of security so extends it that it becomes meaningless; security will encompass everything. (There once was a time, some of us remember, when *strategy* was similarly criticized for being synonymous with *policy*.) I acknowledge that the concept of security does become less coherent the more it is broadened, and that the security agenda risks becoming overloaded. But I welcome both these developments without reservation. This point needs to be set alongside the crucial political fact that the word *security* has enormous political significance, and that to get an issue onto a state's security agenda is to give it priority. With that in mind, it is easy to justify a broadened conception of security. To maintain the traditionalist ("intellectually coherent") concept of security simply perpetuates statist, militarized, and masculinized definitions of what should have priority in security terms, and to do that leaves the agenda in the hands of the traditional strategic/security specialists. Why should certain issues—human rights, economic justice, and so on—be kept off the security agenda? They are, after all, crucial security questions for somebody (if not those benefiting from statist power structures). At base, the question is, who will be secure? This is the fundamental issue, not intellectual incoherence. But even in regard to the latter, if one accepts different security referents other than the state, then there is intellectual coherence in the broadened concept of security—the problem becomes a political one of balancing different military and nonmilitary security demands, not an intellectual one concerned with understanding.

The broadening of the concept of security, to my mind, is the inevitable consequence of the (primary) aim of critical security studies to deepen our understandings of security. By *deepening* I mean investigating the implications and possibilities that result from seeing security as a concept that derives from different understandings of what politics is and can be all about, and specifically, politics on a global scale. Traditional security studies derived from statist norms and was characterized by positivist methods; one result was the legitimation of a strategy such as nuclear deterrence, whereby small sections of the world's population had no hesitation in justifying policies that included the threat of destroying civilized life in, at least, most of the Northern Hemisphere. In contrast to the statist horizons and cosmic dangers of traditional strategic/security studies, an attempt to deepen our understandings of security will lead to different conceptions of the political; these investigations will explore possibility rather than impossibility, openness rather than closure, inclusion rather than exclusion, common humanity rather than tribal sovereignty, nonnecessitarianism rather than false necessities, and emancipation rather than power. In short, critical security studies invites students to unthink the all-too-thinkable norms and ethos of established security studies and, instead, engage in the exciting journey of exploring the hitherto conventionally unthinkable.[48]

CONCLUSION

What, then, does it mean to study security, and the means to achieve it, in the late twentieth century? To begin, I want to assert two things that it does not mean. First, it should not involve the replication of the narrow statist, militarized, Anglo-American, masculinized version of security that was synonymous with strategic studies from the mid-1950s to the late 1980s. This period of strategic studies, defined by the Cold War and the nuclear revolution, can now be seen in its entirety, as based on an ethnocentric and time-bound set of theories of "peace" and "security." Second, this is not meant to imply that strategy and war are not important dimensions of the security problem. Far from it. War and therefore strategy are not going to disappear in the near future, and so they require due attention. The agenda, assumptions, and approaches of Cold War strategic studies, however, cannot be left to define security if we want to improve the prospects for human life at the level of individuals, societies, states, regions, and globally in the next half-century and beyond. Strategic studies is simply the label we should give to the military dimension of the study of international security.

The thrust of this chapter has been that there is a critical relationship between the me/I as a theorist of security and what it means to study security. The argument has been that the meaning of studying security is not simply or necessarily created by the changes out there in the world, but by the changes—or lack of them—in here (who we think we are, and what we think we are doing). I was taught to think of security in statist, military, Anglo-American, masculinized terms, and to see my activity as that of a realist-positivist. I later came to think of security in cosmopolitan, comprehensive, emancipatory terms and my role as that of a utopian realist. And in bringing about this change, most of the work was done not as a result of reading books or experiencing the impact of world events but was instead the influence of friends at particular crossroads of time and place. The university would seem to have shaped the me, but life shaped the I. This being so, it is important that university teaching eschews Sunday School—the learning by rote of supposed timeless wisdom—

and instead commits itself to opening up possibilities. For students of security, the shift from realism to critical security studies will represent pedagogical progress.

Change is the condition of modern life, it was argued earlier, yet understanding it is hampered by a cultural norm that seems to hold that the longer one has had an idea, the truer it is. The corollary of this is that it is somehow a weakness to change one's mind. The implication of this norm is that it supposedly strengthens an argument to begin "I have always thought that . . . "; the implication of this is that the ideas imposed on one or arrived at while a student/an adolescent/a child somehow have more value than those developed when one learned to think for oneself. It is a zany norm. Critical security studies gives space for change, of all sorts.

Nobody can be blamed for their upbringing, their teachers, their time, or their place. Those who purport to be academics *can* be criticized for not being open to different ideas and for the dogmatic (and usually ignorant) anti-intellectual dismissal of thoughts that come from outside the university (for example, from activists), from those critical of the hegemonic discourse (for example, those called radicals), from those with different time scales (utopians), from those said not to understand the real world (feminists), and so on. Those who always think what they have always thought (or were taught to think) are left with a security studies defined by the interests and agenda of policy makers and taught solely by those content to work within this framework. This would not only not be honorable (the phrase "academic Eichmanns" comes to mind), it would also be boring.

If, as argued earlier, security (and hence the subject of security studies) is what we make it, it follows that it will be made according to who we are and aspire to be (remembering the aphorisms of Nin and Gandhi). Consequently, I want to end by offering four sets of ideas about the we who might seek to push the critical-security-studies project in the years to come. By looking at area studies, political and social theory, political practice, and the role of the academic, it is possible to sketch the profile of a student of critical security studies at this juncture.

Area Studies

As is emphasized in the chapter in this collection by Peter Vale and myself on southern Africa, critical security studies should not remain confined to critique at the level of theory. Practice is the aim of theory, and so it is essential for students and teachers to have an area specialization (or specializations), as well as theoretical interests. And this area specialization should not be restricted to the country in which one happened to be born. The study of real people in real places outside one's immediate citizenship is crucial in breaking down ethnocentric outlooks and opening up fresh perspectives on the human predicament. Theory and method, without area studies, encourage thinking in a vacuum and are likely to legitimize dangerous policies (as was evident in the abstract theorizing about nuclear deterrence).[49] Unlike most of their counterparts in Cold War national security studies, students of critical security studies should become area specialists.

Political and Social Theory

Cold War security studies were not only notoriously ethnocentric, they were also notoriously inbred. Like the political realism from which they derived, they cut themselves off from the mainstream of political and social theory. In this way they were slow to see some of the reality they purported to describe and deprived themselves of many philosophical and other tools for accounting for the human security condition.

Theory and Practice

Security is concerned with how people live. An interest in practice (policy relevance) is surely part of what is involved in being a security specialist. The study of security can benefit from a range of perspectives, but not from those who would refuse to engage with the problems of those, at this minute, who are being starved, oppressed, or shot. It is therefore legitimate to ask what any theory that purports to belong within world politics has to say about Bosnia or nuclear deterrence. Thinking about thinking is important, but, more urgently, so is thinking about doing. For those who believe that we live in a humanly constituted world, the distinction between theory and practice dissolves: theory is a form of practice, and practice is a form of theory. Abstract ideas about emancipation will not suffice: it is important for critical security studies to engage with the real by suggesting policies, agents, and sites of change, to help humankind, in whole and in part, to move away from its structural wrongs.

The Role of Academics

During the Cold War, Western security specialists were particularly deferential to the worldview and agendas of governments. Politicians, diplomats, and military establishments have their own identities and interests that are not always shared by those for whom they supposedly speak. This is particularly the case where state and society do not coincide. This is why the growth of civil society is so important for security, cooperation, and development, whether regionally or globally. Within civil society, academics in many countries have a special and privileged role: they have knowledge and they are removed from the daily pressures of political life. With this in mind the role of academics in the "intellectual enterprise of security studies" might be defined as follows: to provide new knowledge and more helpful accounts of world affairs and human lives; to look at old facts in new ways; to unsilence the silenced; to help give longer-term perspectives than decision makers concerned with the next election; to expose the hypocrisies, inconsistencies, and power plays in language, relationships, and policies; to provide a more sophisticated language with which to analyze events and problems; to engage in dialogues with policy makers in order to try to open the latter's imaginations and minds about the ways in which concepts might be translated into better (more friendly to people and nature) policies; to expose false ideas and reveal the unstated assumptions of policies; to open up space for thought and action; to help students think for themselves; to develop new and more rational theories about global security; to cast a critical eye on all theories and all exercises of power, including one's own; and to speak for cosmopolitan values and to speak up for those who do not have a voice. To attempt to do less is to commit ourselves as university teachers and researchers to being clerks of the powerful, the priests of necessity (rather than architects of possibility), and fatalists about the geography of meaning.

NOTES

1. Several people criticized an earlier draft of this chapter and have helped to shape it. In particular, I want to thank Nalini Persram, Steve Smith, Nicholas Wheeler, Marysia Zalewski, and the editors of this book.

Richard Wyn Jones deserves a special mention because his own work on critical theory has shown me important signposts.

2. Peter L. Berger, *Invitation to Sociology: A Humanistic Perspective* (Harmondsworth: Pelican Books, 1966), 140.

3. This is a point she has made more explicitly in presentations than in her *The Morning After: Sexual Politics at the End of the Cold War* (Berkeley and Los Angeles: University of California Press, 1993).

4. For a list of the actors promoting such ideas, see Paul Ekins, *A New World Order* (London: Routledge, 1992); for a discussion of the influence of one group, the peace movement, see David Cortright, *Peace Works: The Citizen's Role in Ending the Cold War* (Boulder, Colo.: Westview, 1993).

5. Ken Booth and John Baylis, *Britain, NATO and Nuclear Weapons: Alternative Defence versus Alliance Reform* (London: Macmillan, 1989), especially chaps. 1 and 3.

6. Barry Buzan, *People, States and Fear: An Agenda for International Security in the Post-Cold War Era* (New York: Harvester Wheatsheaf, 1991. 1st ed., 1983).

7. See, among others, Johan Galtung, "A Structural Theory of Imperialism," *Journal of Peace Research* 8 (1971), 81–117; Kenneth Boulding, *Stable Peace* (Austin: University of Texas Press, 1979); John Burton, *World Society* (Cambridge: Cambridge University Press, 1972); Richard Falk, *A Study of Future Worlds* (New York: Free Press, 1975).

8. See, for example, Caroline Thomas, *In Search of Security: The Third World in International Relations* (Brighton: Wheatsheaf, 1987).

9. Berger, *Invitation to Sociology*, 81–141; John Schotter, *Social Accountability and Selfhood* (Oxford: Blackwell, 1984), 53–72, 195–217.

10. Berger, *Invitation to Sociology*, 123.

11. Ibid., 112–14.

12. Ibid., 116.

13. George H. Mead, *Mind, Self and Society* (Chicago: University of Chicago Press, 1934), 135–226.

14. Berger, *Invitation to Sociology*, 117.

15. Ibid., 119–20, emphasis added.

16. Mead, *Mind, Self and Society*, 173–78.

17. Ibid., 175.

18. Jan Aart Scholte, *International Relations of Social Change* (Buckingham: Open University Press, 1993), 113; see also 107.

19. Alexander Wendt, "Anarchy Is What States Make of It: The Social Construction of Power Politics," *International Organization* 46:2 (Spring 1992), especially 394ff. See R. B. J. Walker's *Inside/Outside: International Relations as Political Theory* (Cambridge: Cambridge University Press, 1993).

20. Erik H. Erikson, *Identity, Youth and Crisis* (London: Faber and Faber, 1968), 15–19.

21. Ibid., 30–31.

22. Marysia Zalewski and Cynthia Enloe, "Questions about Identity in International Relations," in Ken Booth and Steve Smith, eds., *International Relations Theory Today* (Cambridge: Polity Press, 1995), 279–305.

23. John C. Garnett, ed., *Theories of Peace and Security* (London: Macmillan, 1970).

24. See where the cult of national prejudice in the guise of rationality got us, in Herman Kahn's *Thinking the Unthinkable* (New York: Horizon, 1962).

25. The major works that eventually emerged were Michael MccGwire, *Military Objectives in Soviet Foreign Policy* (Washington, D.C.: Brookings Institute, 1987) and *Perestroika and Soviet National Security* (Washington, D.C.: Brookings Institute, 1991).

26. See, for example, Michael MccGwire, ed., *Soviet Naval Developments* (New York: Praeger, 1973); with John McDonnell and Ken Booth, *Soviet Naval Policy* (New York: Praeger, 1975); and with John McDonnell, eds., *Soviet Naval Influence* (New York: Praeger, 1977).

27. Ken Booth, *The Military Instrument in Soviet Foreign Policy, 1917–1972* (London: Royal United Service Institute for Defence Studies, 1974).

28. Ken Booth, *Strategy and Ethnocentrism* (London: Croom Helm, 1979), preface.

29. Jim King was such a perfectionist that some of his work, notably his *The New Strategy*, never reached the publisher at the right time or at the right length and so did not get published.

30. Some of the lectures were written up for publication in the college's journal: see "Foreign Policies at Risk: Some Problems of Managing Naval Power," *Naval War College Review* 29:1 (Summer 1976), 3–15; and "U.S. Naval Strategy: Problems of Survivability, Usability and Credibility," *Naval War College Review* 31:1 (Summer 1978), 11–28.

31. See, for example, Morton Halperin and Arnold Kanter, eds., *Readings in American Foreign Policy: A Bureaucratic Perspective* (Boston: Little Brown, 1973).

32. Kenneth Waltz, *Man, the State and War* (New York: Columbia University Press, 1959) and his *Theory of International Politics* (Reading, Mass.: Addison–Wesley, 1979).

33. See note 19 above.

34. Roberto Unger, *False Necessities: Anti-Necessitarian Social Theory in the Service of Radical Democracy* (Cambridge: Cambridge University Press, 1987).

35. Ken Booth, "Security in Anarchy: Utopian Realism in Theory and Practice," *International Affairs* 63:3 (July 1991), 527–45.

36. Stephen M. Walt, "The Renaissance of Security Studies," *International Studies Quarterly* 35:2 (June 1991), 211–39.

37. The history of academic strategic studies can be divided into four phases: prenuclear strategy, early strategic studies (1945–55), high strategic theory (1956–85); and late strategic studies (1985–91). See Ken Booth, "Strategy," in A. J. R. Groom and Margot Light, eds., *Contemporary International Relations: A Guide to Theory* (London: Pinter, 1994), 109–27. Post-Cold War strategic studies, as the military dimension of security studies, has yet to develop a distinctive character.

38. The analogy is to Max Horkheimer's classical critique "Traditional and Critical Theory," in Max Horkheimer, *Critical Theory: Selected Essays* (New York: Continuum, 1992), 188–252.

39. Buzan, *People, States and Fear.*

40. See Ken Booth, "Human Wrongs and International Relations," *International Affairs* 71:1 (January 1995), 103–26.

41. Harold D. Lasswell, *Politics: Who Gets What, When, How* (New York: Peter Smith, 1950).

42. Ken Booth and Nicholas J. Wheeler, *The Security Dilemma: Anarchy, Society and Community in World Politics* (London: Macmillan, forthcoming).

43. I tried to suggest how such a long-term approach might be thought about, in the context of what were then the Gorbachev years, in "Steps towards Stable Peace in Europe: A Theory and Practice of Coexistence," *International Affairs* 66:1 (January 1990), 17–45.

44. See, among others, Robert Cox, "Social Forces, States, and World Order," *Millennium* 10:2 (Summer 1981), 126–55; Jürgen Habermas, *The Philosophical Discourses of Modernity* (Cambridge: Polity Press, 1987); Mark Hoffman, "Critical Theory and the Inter-paradigm Debate," *Millennium* 16:2 (Summer 1987), 231–49; and Andrew Linklater, *Beyond Realism and Marxism: Critical Theory and International Relations* (Basingstoke: Macmillan, 1990).

45. See, among others, Richard K. Ashley and R. B. J. Walker, eds., "Speaking the Language of Exile: Dissidence in International Studies," *International Studies Quarterly* 34:3 (September 1990), special issue; David Campbell, *Writing Security: United States Foreign Policy and the Politics of Identity* (Manchester: Manchester University Press, 1992); James Der Derian and Michael J. Shapiro, eds., *International/Intertextual Relations: Postmodern Readings in World Politics* (Lexington, Mass.: Lexington Books, 1989); Bradley Klein, *Strategic Studies and World Order* (Cambridge: Cambridge University Press, 1994); R. B. J. Walker, "Security, Sovereignty and the Challenge of World Politics," *Alternatives* 15:1 (1990), 3–28.

46. Nicholas J. Wheeler, "Guardian Angel or Global Gangster: The Ethical Claims of International Society Revisited," *Political Studies* 44:1 (March 1996), 123–36.

47. Ken Booth, "Security and Emancipation," *Review of International Studies* 17:4 (October 1991), 313–26.

48. Herman Kahn (see note 24) got it wrong. From the very beginning of the nuclear age, the problem has been to unthink the thinkable, rather than vice versa.

49. See Michael K. MccGwire, "Deterrence: The Problem—Not the Solution," *International Affairs* 62:1 (Winter 1985–86), 55–70.

5

Defining Security:
A Subaltern Realist Perspective

MOHAMMED AYOOB

I

Recent attempts at broadening the definition of the concept of security beyond its traditional realist usage have created a major dilemma for students of International Relations. On the one hand, it is clear that the traditional definition of security that has dominated the Western literature on the subject is inadequate to explain the multifaceted and multidimensional nature of the problem of security as faced by the majority of members in the international system. On the other, the often indiscriminate broadening of the definition of security threatens to make the concept so elastic as to render it useless as an analytical tool.[1]

It is in this context that I attempt in this chapter to provide an alternative definition of security that, while preserving the valuable insights of the realist paradigm, goes beyond its ethnocentric obsession with external threats to state security. It does so by incorporating into the definition the principal security concerns of the majority of the members of the international system (the subalterns—those that are weak and of inferior rank). These states' major security preoccupations are primarily internal in character and are a function of the early stages of state making at which they find themselves.

Interestingly, these concerns mirror the major security concerns evinced by most West European state makers during the sixteenth to the nineteenth centuries, when these states were at a stage of state building corresponding to that at which most Third World states find themselves today.[2] Unfortunately, these historical concerns of West European states—the earliest to have attained the status of sovereign national (and, therefore, modern) states—have been lost sight of by the neorealists because of their obsession with the anarchic structure of the international system. This has led to a consequently glaring neglect on their part of domestic variables that have major (often determining) impact on the way state elites perceive and define the security problems of the large majority of states that inhabit the international system today. I shall return to a discussion of my concept of "subaltern realism" and its application to the field of security studies at the end of the chapter after having made the necessary arguments demonstrating its superiority as an analytical tool, both over neorealist as well as fashionably expansionist definitions of the concept of security.

II

The importance of going beyond the traditional realist paradigm of treating states as unitary actors primarily concerned with assuring their safety from external threats has been driven home by the fact that most conflicts since the end of World War II have been either primarily intrastate in character or have had an important intrastate dimension built into them. Furthermore, the overwhelming majority of conflicts since 1945 have been located within the Third World where the process of state making is far from complete.[3] As a result, most conflicts since the end of World War II have been, and are, intimately related to the process of state making (and its obverse, state breaking) and cannot be explained in terms of the traditional realist paradigm.[4] The *SIPRI Yearbook 1993* has dramatically made this point by presenting data that demonstrate that of the major armed conflicts that were waged in thirty locations around the world in 1992 all but one were intrastate in character.[5] There is abundant evidence, therefore, to support the conclusion that the overwhelming majority of conflicts in the international system since 1945 have been "a ubiquitous corollary of the birth, formation, and fracturing of Third World states."[6]

The end of the Cold War has not diminished the security predicament of Third World states and regions. In fact, changing international norms in the post-Cold War period, especially those pertaining to the recognition of secessionist states and the relegitimation of ethnonationalism, are expected to make this predicament more acute. The removal of the global overlay of superpower rivalry on Third World conflicts, both intrastate and interstate, is also likely to have mixed results as far as conflicts in the Third World are concerned, and its negative impacts are expected to neutralize the more positive ones.[7] This, I believe, will hold true both in the short and long terms (as long as one defines the latter in terms of decades and not centuries), given the historical juncture at which most Third World states find themselves in terms of their state-building odyssey. The current phase of Third World state making can be reasonably expected to last well into the next century despite the pressures on these states to complete this task within the shortest possible time.

These pressures emanate primarily from the international system in terms of the demonstration effect of the existence of effective, responsive, and representative (and, therefore, legitimate) states in the industrialized world, as well as the demand on Third World states to transform their juridical statehood into effective statehood, not merely within the shortest possible time frame but in a humane manner as well. This attempt to fit an evolutionary process such as state making into a time-bound straitjacket of ridiculously short duration and then expect it to be undertaken with due regard for the human rights of groups and individuals flies in the face of historical evidence.[8] It also raises expectations regarding the achievement of the final goal (and regarding the process through which it is supposed to be achieved) that increase the load on Third World political systems to such a degree that they are threatened with serious disequilibrium. The above pressures therefore provide a substantial part of the explanation for the high degree of domestic violence and insecurity plaguing most Third World states.[9]

In this context, it is surprising that many leading advocates of the view that the realist (or *neorealist,* to use the currently fashionable term) paradigm has the greatest power, of all paradigms, to explain the international realities of the post-Cold War era virtually ignore the security situation in the Third World, where most members of the international system are located and where most of the conflicts are concentrated. For example, Stephen Walt defines security studies, and by extension the concept of security, as *"the study of the threat, use, and control of military force,"* especially of "the specific policies that states adopt in order to prepare for, prevent, or engage in war." While Walt is clear that "military power is the central focus of the field," he is willing to concede that

> military power is not the only source of national security, and military threats are not the only dangers that states face (though they are usually the most serious). As a result security studies also includes what is sometimes termed 'statecraft'—arms control, diplomacy, crisis management, for example. These issues are clearly relevant to the main focus of the field, because they bear directly on the likelihood and character of war.[10]

It is clear that Walt's definition of security studies takes its philosophical cue from the fundamental realist assumption best summed up by Walter Lippmann half a century ago: "A nation is secure to the extent to which it is not in danger of having to sacrifice core values, if it wishes to avoid war, and is able, if challenged, to maintain them by victory in such a war."[11] Lippmann's definition, as Arnold Wolfers pointed out, "implies that security rises and falls with the ability of a nation to deter an attack, or to defeat it."[12]

In the traditional, predominantly realist, literature in International Relations the concept of security is therefore defined primarily in external or outward directed terms, that is, outside the commonly accepted unit of analysis: the state. It should be further pointed out that the tradition in International Relations that portrays states as unitary actors responding to external threats or posing such threats to other states has been stronger in the field of security studies than in the rest of the discipline, which has lately become more open to competing explanations of state behavior in the international arena. As has been stated earlier in this chapter, however, the reality of security problems faced by the vast majority of states in the international system belies this simplistic understanding of the security problematic. Furthermore, as Amitav Acharya points out in this volume,[13] the fact that the periphery, the Third World, may well have become the core, as far as conflict and security in the post–Cold War international system are concerned, has made the inapplicability of the realist definition of security to the vast majority of conflicts in the international system all the more glaring.

III

At the same time, it is important to guard against the temptation to make the concept of security so broad that it comes to mean all things to all people because this is certain to render the concept analytically useless. This latter tendency, however, has become very visible in the new critical discourse about security during the past decade. Such a discourse has tended to include everything from the violation of human rights to environmental degradation as a part of the security problematic. Thus, adjectives like human and environmental, in addition to economic, have been attached to the term *security* in an attempt to bring these diverse phenomena under the rubric of security.

However, there are major intellectual and practical hazards in adopting unduly elastic definitions of security. For example, Jessica Tuchman Mathews's attempt at portraying environmental decline and climatic change as major sources of insecurity in the last decade of the twentieth century, while valuable in pinpointing important challenges facing the human race as we move into the twenty-first century, confuses the issue by wrapping these problems in the security blanket.[14] It does so by attempting to make global management problems part of the national and international security agendas. This is the danger that an author as sympathetic to environmental concerns as Daniel Deudney warned against when he argued that

> national-security-from-violence and environmental habitability have little in common. . . . The rising fashion of linking them risks creating a conceptual muddle rather than a paradigm or world view shift—a *de-definition* rather than a *re-definition* of security. If we begin to speak about all the forces and events that threaten life, property and well-being (on a large-scale) as threats to our national security, we shall soon drain them of any meaning. All large-scale evils will become threats to national security.[15]

It is therefore imperative that analysts show greater discrimination in applying security-related vocabulary to matters pertaining to ecological or other global management issues. It would be wrong to assume that such issues automatically form part of the calculus of national or international security. In order to do so, they must demonstrate the capacity immediately to affect political outcomes. Short of that it would be wise to keep the two discourses analytically distinct in order to enhance our understanding of both phenomena and of the interconnections between them. Collapsing concepts can cause tremendous intellectual confusion.

Mathews herself demonstrates an understanding of the occasional, episodic, and diffuse nature of the impact of environmental degradation on security issues and, therefore, the usually indirect and difficult-to-decipher relationship between the two, when she states that "environmental decline occasionally leads directly to conflict, especially when scarce water resources must be shared. Generally, however, its impact on nations' security is felt in the downward pull on economic performance and, therefore, on political stability."[16] Greater awareness of the indirect and sporadic nature of this link and greater discrimination in the use of security rhetoric when dealing with environmental concerns are, therefore, imperative if one is to maintain the analytical usefulness of both the concepts of security and environmental degradation.

It has also become fashionable these days to equate security with other values that some analysts consider intrinsically more important than, and morally superior to, the political-military phenomena and objectives traditionally encompassed by the concept of security. For example, Ken Booth has argued that security should be equated with "emancipation." According to him, "emancipation is the freeing of people (as individuals and groups) from the physical and human constraints which stop them carrying out what they would freely choose to do. . . . Security and emancipation are two sides of the same coin. Emancipation, not power or order, produces true security. Emancipation, theoretically, is security."[17]

The problem with such semantic jugglery is that by a sleight of hand it totally obfuscates the meanings of both the concepts of security and emancipation. Booth's definition refuses to acknowledge that a society or group can be emancipated without being secure and vice versa. The emancipation of Kurds in northern Iraq from the Iraqi regime or of the Chechen from Russian rule did not necessarily enhance the security of either population, even though it may have brought them closer to their cherished goal of independence or emancipation for which they may have been willing to sacrifice the security provided to them, in however imperfect a measure, by the Iraqi or the Russian state. Similarly, the citizens of Damascus under the repressive rule of the Assad regime may have felt more secure in the period from 1975 to 1990 than their emancipated brethren in Beirut next door, who suffered immensely during the Lebanese civil war because of the weakness of the Lebanese state and its inability to provide them with even a minimum degree of order and, consequently, of security.

As the cases cited above demonstrate, such semantic acrobatics tend to impose a model of contemporary Western polities—of national states that have by and large solved their legitimacy problem and possess representative and responsive governments, which preside over socially mobile populations that are relatively homogeneous and usually affluent and free from want—that are far removed from Third World realities. It may therefore be possible to equate emancipation with security in Western Europe (although one has grave reservations even on that score), but it would be extremely far-fetched and, indeed, intellectually disingenuous to do the same in the case of the Third World, where basic problems of state legitimacy, political order, and capital accumulation are not only far from being solved but may even be getting more acute.

This is why to posit emancipation as synonymous with security and the panacea for all the ills plaguing Third World states can be the height of naïveté. Emancipation, interpreted as the right of every ethnic group to self-determination, can turn out to be a recipe for grave disorder and anarchy as far as most Third World states are concerned. This would result from a combination of two factors. First, ethnicity is a fluid and flexible concept and is subject to change depending on the context in which it operates at any point in time. Examples ranging from the secession of Bangladesh from the state of Pakistan to the failure of the state in Somalia bear adequate testimony to "the dynamic and changing character of contemporary ethnicity . . . [which] is in major respects contextual, situational, and circumstantial."[18] In the former case, Bangladesh seceded from Pakistan when the majority of its population decided to define their identity in ethnolinguistic terms as Bengalis rather than in ethnoreligious terms as Indian Muslims, a definition that had led to the creation of Pakistan in 1947. In the latter case, Somalia, not so long ago considered to be the only nation-state in Africa, has fallen prey to interclan warfare that has led to the virtual disintegration of the state itself, thus exposing the mutable nature of Somalian ethnonational identity.

Therefore, to link such a potent ideology as that of self-determination, which can be considered a major manifestation of emancipation, to a malleable idea like that of ethnicity and then legitimize this combination by reference to the principle of human rights of groups is bound to increase disorder in the Third World because of the multiethnic character of almost all Third World countries. Furthermore, the breakup of existing Third World states on the basis of the emancipation of ethnic groups is bound to increase rather than reduce ethnic strife and political intolerance because there are no pure ethnic homelands existing in the world today. As the example of the former Yugoslavia has demonstrated, minorities in ministates, which are dominated by one particular ethnic group that arrogates to itself the right to define the national identity of such a state, can be expected to receive much more brutal treatment—ranging from perpetual oppression to ethnic cleansing—than is the case with ethnic minorities in most Third World states that exist within their colonially determined boundaries.

In the context of the Third World (which means the large majority of states), where the legitimacy of states and regimes is constantly challenged and where demands for economic redistribution and political participation perennially outrun state capacities and create major overloads on political systems, the concept of security should not be confused with that of emancipation, as Booth tends to argue. In such a context an explicitly state-centric definition of security is likely to provide an analytical tool of tremendous value that should not be sacrificed at the altar of utopian thinking, even if Booth would prefer to call it "utopian realism."[19]

IV

Bearing the above-mentioned problems of too restrictive and too inclusive definitions in mind, and remaining sensitive to the nexus between domestic and external threats faced by Third World states, I would like to put forward a definition of security that I believe depicts the multifaceted nature of the concept, integrates these various facets into a conceptual whole, and does so while retaining its analytical utility by avoiding the pitfalls of undue elasticity.

To begin with, this definition of security, as I have stated earlier, purports to be state-centric in character, thus emphasizing both the primarily political connotation of the term and the major enterprise in which the large majority of countries in the international system are currently engaged, namely, state building. My definition of the political realm is based above all on the acceptance of David Easton's logic that "however diffuse political science may appear to be, there can be no doubt that 'political' refers to a separable dimension of human activity." Further, he explains that "political life concerns all those varieties of activity that influence significantly the kind of authoritative policy adopted for a society and the way it is put into practice." In other words, "the political" refers to that arena of human activity that is concerned with "the authoritative allocation of values for a society."[20]

Because it is the state that is (or, where it is not, is supposed to be) engaged in the authoritative allocation of social values within territorially defined political and administrative entities, it becomes the primary referent of security in my definition.[21] Expanded definitions of *the political,* like elastic definitions of *security,* do not help in clarifying the security problematic; they tend to obfuscate issues, confuse the discussion about security, and end up by de-defining rather than redefining the concept.

This emphasis on the primacy of the political realm in the definition of security, however, does not mean that the political realm can be, or should be, totally insulated from other realms of human and societal activity when it comes to dealing with or analyzing security issues. It means that while retaining its primacy in the definition of security the political realm must be informed by these other arenas of human activity. Yet, the influence of the other realms on matters that pertain to, or have a bearing on, security must be filtered and mediated through the political arena and must be directly relevant to that realm. In other words, when developments in other realms, ranging from the economic to the ecological, threaten to have immediate political consequences, or are perceived as having the potential to threaten state boundaries, political institutions, or governing regimes, then these other variables have to be taken into account as a part of a state's security calculus. Short of that, the political and security realm must maintain its distinctiveness from other realms. Phenomena like economic deprivation and environmental degradation should be analyzed as events, occurrences, and variables that may be linked to, but are essentially distinct from, the arena of security as defined here.

The definition of security advocated here is therefore explicitly political in character. So defined, the concept of security must be used in the relatively restricted sense of applying to the security of the state—both in terms of its territory and its institutions—and of those who profess to represent the state territorially and institutionally. In other words, security or insecurity is defined in relation to vulnerabilities, both internal and external, that threaten to, or have the potential to, bring down or significantly weaken state structures, both territorial and institutional, and regimes. According to this definition, the more a state and/or regime—and often it is very difficult to disentangle issues of state security from those of regime security in the Third World where most states in the system are located—fall(s) toward the invulnerable end of the vulnerable-invulnerable continuum the more secure it/they will be. Other types of vulnerability, whether economic or ecological, become integral components of our definition of security only if they become acute enough to take on overtly political dimensions and threaten state boundaries, state institutions, or regime survival. In other words, debt burdens, rainforest decimation, or even famine do not become part of the security calculus for our purposes unless they threaten to have political outcomes—as they may in certain instances—that either affect the survivability of state boundaries, state institutions, or governing elites or dramatically weaken the capacity of states and regimes to act effectively in the realm of politics, both domestic and international.

The measurement of a state's or regime's location on the vulnerable-invulnerable continuum must not be limited to its capacity merely to repress challengers and opponents by force. Its position on this continuum is likely to be determined as much, and probably more, by its possession of what Edward Azar and Chung-in Moon have termed "security software"—legitimacy, integration or societal cohesion, and policy capacity—as by security hardware, the means of coercion that states attempt to monopolize in their hands.[22] This is why a state like Denmark is, according to my definition, more secure than a state like India, despite the possession by the latter of much greater coercive capacity when compared to the former. Furthermore, the introduction of variables such as legitimacy and policy capacity in the measurement of security also denotes the fact that predatory authoritarian regimes, for example, the Mobutu regime in Zaire, that are unconcerned about the rights and conditions of their

citizens, whether as individuals or groups, are usually far more insecure than those, such as the elected government in India, that try to
accommodate societal demands regarding individual and group
rights, even if they are less than completely successful in this regard.

In this sense, Azar and Moon's attempt to introduce software into
the security calculus of Third World states, in addition to the traditional variables of threats and capabilities, is a commendable one.
Furthermore, their operationalization of the concept of security software primarily in terms of political variables both adds to the rich-
ness of the definition of security as well as clearly delimits the scope
of the term, thus making it intellectually manageable and analytically useful.

There has been a spate of writings recently that warn that environmental degradation, resource scarcity, and the skewed distribution of
available resources are likely to lead to conflict in the Third World.[23]
It needs to be pointed out, however, that the more incisive among the
authors writing on this subject recognize that these variables will
have to be mediated by, and filtered through, the political realm before they can be translated into threats to the security of states and
regimes. For example, Thomas Homer-Dixon, a leading analyst in
this field, has clearly emphasized "the perceived legitimacy of the
regime," "the role of *politics* in shaping a society's response to social
stress," and "the nature and rate of change of power relations among
states" as crucial intervening variables that mediate the relationship
between environmental degradation and conflict within and among
states.[24] All of these variables are eminently political in character.

V

The overriding importance of the state—both as a territorial unit
and as an institutional complex—to the political, and therefore security, realm in the case of the large majority of countries is justified in
the context of the historical juncture at which most members of the
international system (that is, the large majority that is located in the
Third World) currently find themselves. At this juncture their primary goal is the construction of credible and legitimate political apparatuses with the capacity to provide order—in many respects, the
foremost social value—within the territories under their juridical
control.[25]

This is the quintessential definition of the term *state building*. The fundamental importance of this enterprise is borne out by the fact that without the provision of political order by the state every other form of security is likely to remain elusive or, at best, ephemeral. Examples ranging from Afghanistan to Somalia and including such disparate cases as Liberia, Rwanda, Tajikistan, and Bosnia attest to the veracity of this conclusion. It was this realization, especially in the context of the civil war in Lebanon, that led a perceptive scholar of the Middle East to assert: "'Seek ye the political kingdom first'—not because it matters more, but because, in the lack of political order, no normal social development is possible. The state cannot replace society, but it must protect society. In the lack of political order, social and individual values are meaningless; they cannot be realized, nor can they be protected from assault, violence and chaos."[26]

Given the primary importance of state making in the political lives of a majority of states and the fact that much of the activity concerned with state making is carried out under the guise of a search for security, the concept of security becomes fundamental to our understanding of the political behavior of most states, especially those inhabiting the Third World. It also means that the security calculus of most states must take into account domestic as well as external threats because intrastate conflict is a major, in fact dominant, component of the state-building enterprise. In the case of a large majority of states, the domestic dimension of security is far more important than the external one.[27]

The importance of the domestic dimension is the result primarily of the fact that the three major categories of activities subsumed under the concept of state building are directed primarily inward and affect state-society relations much more than they affect interstate relations, although the latter are far from negligible in their impact on the process of state formation when it is concurrently undertaken by contiguous and proximate states. The primary ingredients of state making are the following:

1. The expansion and consolidation of the territorial and demographic domain under a political authority, including the imposition of order on contested territorial and demographic space (war, including internal or civil war). In most Third World states fighting internal insurgencies and imposing order on peripheral populations have become the predominant warlike activities of the juridically recognized state.

2. The maintenance of order in the territory where, and over the population on whom, such order has been already imposed (policing).

3. The extraction of resources from the territory and the population under the control of the state essential to support not only the war-making and policing activities undertaken by the state but also to maintain the apparatuses of state necessary to carry on routine administration, deepen the state's penetration of society, and serve symbolic purposes (taxation).[28]

The three broad categories of activities outlined above, however, depend on the state's success in monopolizing and concentrating the means of coercion in its own hands in the territory and among the population it controls. That is why the accumulation of power becomes so crucial to the state-making enterprise; the more primitive the stage of state building, the more primitive and therefore coercive the strategies employed to accumulate and concentrate power in the hands of the agents of the state. As Youssef Cohen, Brian Brown, and A. F. K. Organski demonstrated in a seminal article published in 1981, "the extent to which an expansion of state power will generate collective violence depends on the *level* of state power prior to that expansion . . . the lower the initial level of state power, the stronger the relationship between the *rate* of state expansion and collective violence."[29]

The early stages of state making therefore involve the almost inevitable use of violent means by the state as it attempts to extend and consolidate its control over contested demographic and territorial space, and counterviolence on the part of those segments of the population resisting the extension and consolidation of such control. This is the stuff of which civil wars and secessionist movements are made, and they pose much greater, and more immediate, threats to the security of the large majority of states than do external adversaries. The latter are, however, likely in many cases to take advantage of internal strife in, or become unwillingly drawn into the internal conflicts of, neighboring states, thereby turning domestic conflicts into interstate ones.[30] The high incidence of conflict between contiguous states, for example, India and Pakistan, Vietnam and Cambodia, Ethiopia and Somalia, Serbia and Croatia, Armenia and Azerbaijan, can be explained to a large degree by the fact that these states are simultaneously engaged in the state-making enterprise, which includes the attempt to extend their control over territories and populations at the expense of their neighbors. Such concurrent state-building activity is usually responsible for bringing such states into conflict with each other and feeding their perception that their neighbors form the principal source of threat to their security. It is this phenomenon that underlies the creation of "security complexes," to use Barry Buzan's terminology,[31] which dominate the security landscapes of discrete regions in the international system.

To conclude this part of the discussion, let me reiterate that a definition of the concept of security with adequate explanatory power must meet two criteria. First, it must go beyond the traditional realist definition of security and overcome its external orientation and military bias. Second, it must remain firmly rooted in the political realm while being sensitive to variables in other realms of societal activity that may have an impact on the political arena and that may filter through into the security calculus of states because of their potential capacity to influence political outcomes.

VI

Analyses that focus primarily on state making and state and regime security also are likely to furnish more realistic assessments of democracy's chances in postcolonial societies as well as help solve the dilemma regarding the relevance of the democratic peace theory to current international realities.[32] It should be pointed out that the democratic peace argument is very different from the assertion that democracies are less prone to interstate conflict than nondemocratic states. In fact, Steve Chan has assembled data from 1816 to 1980 that demonstrate that democracies have been associated with more, not less, interstate conflict.[33] In a study that attempts to correlate regime types with international conflict between 1816 and 1976, Zeev Maoz and Nasrin Abdolali conclude that even though democratic states have never gone to war with one another, they are neither more nor less prone to conflict than nondemocratic states.[34] Moreover, as Edward Mansfield and Jack Snyder have pointed out,

> Countries do not become mature democracies overnight. They usually go through a rocky transition, where mass politics mixes with authoritarian elite politics in a volatile way. Statistical evidence covering the past two centuries shows that in this transitional phase of democratization, countries become more aggressive and war-prone, not less, and they do fight wars with democratic states. In fact, formerly au-

thoritarian states where democratic participation is on the rise are more likely to fight wars than are stable democracies or autocracies.[35]

In light of this data, one wonders whether the latest wave of democratization in the Third World will make democratizing states more pacific or war-prone. Specifically, it raises the question of whether rival countries such as India and Pakistan, as democracies, will desist from warring with each other. Again, even if India and Pakistan do not go to war with each other, can this be attributed to the democratic nature of their regimes or to other factors, like their all-but-acknowledged possession of nuclear weapons? These questions and the corresponding doubts about the role of democracy raise the fundamental issue of whether democracy is the independent variable when it comes to determining the warlike character of states. Alternatively, one can argue that democracy, especially mature democracy, is a dependent variable itself, and its presence or absence is determined by factors that may also have more to do with determining whether a state is conflict-prone and to what degree.

Looking at the political realities in the Third World, especially at the early stage of state building at which most Third World countries find themselves, and comparing this situation with the relatively advanced stage of state making in the industrialized world, one can conclude that states can afford the luxury of stable, liberal democratic governance only if they are territorially and politically satiated, that is, finished with the process of state building: having concentrated coercive capacity in the hands of the agents of the state and achieved unconditional legitimacy for state boundaries, state institutions, and governing regimes; being socially and politically cohesive; and having reached a high level of industrialization, and, therefore, of affluence that is distributed relatively evenly. They can do so because only marginal differences remain in the population on the fundamental issues of political and economic organization of the society, and on the basic identity of the state. Furthermore, societal demands no longer threaten the integrity or the viability of the state. The absence of major differences on fundamental issues explains why "political struggles in a democracy do not need to degenerate into an all-or-nothing fight for the control of the state; prosperity and the enjoyment of economic and political rights do not depend on a life-and-death conflict over which group controls the government."[36]

The historical evolution of the industrialized democracies also explains the absence of conflict among them. These states have completed their process of state making over three hundred to four hundred years and are territorially satiated in relation to one another. They do not have residual state-making claims outstanding against each other.[37] Also, they have too much at stake in the global capitalist economy to go to war with each other, thereby upsetting the global economic apple cart. The nuclear factor, which has ruled out war in the global strategic heartland where most industrial democracies are located, provides further explanation for their pacific behavior toward each other and toward the members of the erstwhile Warsaw Pact.

The comparison with the industrialized democracies raises the question of whether these variables can come together in the same mix for most Third World countries so that they can also become stable democracies and maintain pacific relations with each other. Even if some or many Third World states have formally instituted or are likely to institute democratic forms of government, this is unlikely to signal that their state-making processes are complete, nor will it necessarily reduce their vulnerabilities to the extent that they can be considered internally stable and externally pacific. They may be democracies in the formal sense of the term, but they will be neither satiated nor stable democracies and will therefore be far from reaching the goal of democratic maturity.

Territorial satiation, societal cohesion, and political stability—all part of successful state making—have determined the generally pacific nature of the industrial democracies' relations with each other. In Western Europe and North America liberal democracy is a function of these factors, when they are present in the right combination, not their cause. As long as Third World states are not able to achieve these three goals, their formally established democratic institutions will continue to be vulnerable to internal challenges, and the gains of democratization could be reversed. This is why it is wise to heed Robert Rothstein's warning: "It is a mistake to jump too easily from the observation that democracies do not fight each other to the notion that a world of mostly democracies (many of them weak and potentially unstable) will necessarily be more peaceful, either internally or internationally."[38]

The adoption of a state-centric definition of security that is intimately tied to the understanding of the process of state making is therefore likely to provide us with valuable clues to sorting out the puzzle about the pacific nature of democratic societies in relation to each other, and the real reasons behind what has come to be known as democratic peace. It would also set the debate regarding the relevance of the democratic peace theory in proper historical perspective by bringing in the data for Third World states that happen to be at a stage of state making at which most industrial democracies were in the sixteenth to the nineteenth centuries. It would enrich the traditional realist model by going within the black box called the state and examining evolutionary and historical processes that determine state behavior in major ways. This, I believe, will be a major contribution to the field of international security studies.

VII

One of the main reasons why the study of security has become tied to the traditional realist billiard-ball model is that during the past four or five decades it has been widely viewed as an appendage of strategic studies, which by definition has been concerned almost exclusively with analyzing the balance of forces (not even the *balance of power*, in the broad sense of the term) between and among the major powers. Furthermore, as a result of the strategic culture that evolved during the Cold War era, strategic studies has become primarily a policy-prescribing enterprise, and it continues to suffer from that hangover even after the end of superpower rivalry. For strategic thinkers, therefore, the analysis of security cannot be de-linked from the interests of their great power patrons and their own interest in catering to the needs and demands of policy makers in the major capitals of the world.

This relationship between security and strategic studies has been summed up very well by Barry Buzan, who has argued convincingly that a major reason

> for the conceptual underdevelopment of security can be found in the nature of Strategic Studies . . . [which] is for the most part an offspring of Anglo-American, and more broadly Western, defense policy needs. . . . Its attachment to security is heavily conditioned by the status quo orientations of hegemonic countries safely removed from the pressure of large attached neighbours. Strategic Studies is policy ori-

ented, and therefore both empirically bound and constrained not to wander much beyond the imperatives of the national policy level.[39]

This policy orientation led during the Cold War years to the neglect of the study of the fundamental causes and the autonomous dynamics of conflict and security in the Third World, where the majority of states are located. Third World states figured in the arena of strategic studies primarily as pawns to be used in the global great game of superpower competition. Their analysis was undertaken largely from the perspective of global rivalry and, consequently, the roots of conflict, and therefore of security, in the Third World, were traced to the global machinations of the rival superpower rather than to the causes of conflict that inhere in the Third World, but which both the superpowers were equally willing to manipulate for their own ends.

This situation has, however, done a great disservice to the study of security as an academic enterprise, which, like the study of the overarching discipline of International Relations, as Hedley Bull has pointed out, "is an intellectual activity and not a practical one." Therefore, as Bull continues, "the search for conclusions that can be presented as 'solutions' or 'practical advice' is a corrupting element in the contemporary study of world politics. . . . Such conclusions are advanced less because there is any solid basis for them than because there is a demand for them which it is profitable to satisfy."[40] Bull's admonition applies with particular force to the study of security, which needs to be rescued from its unholy matrimony with strategic studies. It should once again be situated squarely within the mainstream of the discipline of International Relations and de-linked from the policy science that is strategic studies.

The study of security as an analytical enterprise must also be clearly distinguished from the ideology of the national security state and the pejorative connotations that accompany it. This can be done, once again, if one is able to restore the study of security to the realm of analysis and rescue it from its perceived connection with policy prescription and policy advice that had dogged it during the Cold War era because of its link with strategic studies. The national security state will then become a legitimate object of analysis by scholars interested in the study of security without their necessarily being perceived as apologists for such a political formation.

At the same time, it should be recognized, by those critics of the concept who consider it to be too narrow and who would like it to be broadened to encompass a very diverse set of human activities, that the concept of security is not designed to explain the entire human reality. It is but a conceptual tool that has the potential, if utilized with adequate discrimination and scholarly restraint, to explain an important part of that reality pertaining to the political domain. In other words, the concept of security must not be broadened to such a degree that it loses all analytical usefulness. While it is essential to move beyond an exclusively ethnocentric Western definition of security to include domestic and nonmilitary dimensions, especially issues of intrastate conflict and political legitimacy, in the construction of security paradigms, one should not, as I have stated earlier, run away with the concept to make it all things to all people. Scholars are not supposed to be in the business of expanding the constituency for security, although they must recognize that there are important constituencies that may be interested in just such an expansion; our only obligation is to sharpen the concept as an analytical tool so that it may help provide some of the answers, or at least help ask some of the right questions, in our study of the political realm. Intellectual modesty can in this case turn out to be the beginning of wisdom.

VIII

Finally, I would like to point out that my emphasis on the state as the linchpin of the political realm and my consequent preoccupation with the process of state making as the primary variable and the defining element within the security problematic of states comes from my two-decades-long study of the politics and international relations of the Third World. Like the Third World that I analyze, I do not find myself in a position to advocate the supersession of the state by suprastate or substate structures or entities for either moral or practical reasons. As long as the international system continues to be primarily a system of states, and state interests continue to be the primary motivation for international interactions, Third World polities cannot afford to relinquish their search for effective statehood.

Effective statehood is essential not only to provide domestic order but also to allow Third World societies to resist, even if imperfectly and to a limited degree, domination by the powerful, industrialized, established members of the international system and to prevent them from permanently remaining secondary actors in that system. Effective statehood—defined as a balanced combination of coercive capacity, infrastructural power,[41] and unconditional legitimacy[42]—is the only path to attaining full membership in the international system in more than just a legal sense. As the earlier European experience has clearly demonstrated, however, the road to effective statehood is strewn with violence and unavoidable internal conflict.[43]

In the case of the Third World the situation has been immensely complicated by the workings and the norms of an international system over which Third World states have little or no control. In fact, certain trends—ranging from political and economic conditionalities attached to foreign aid, to humanitarian intervention—that have become increasingly visible during the past few years lead one to believe that the process of state formation in the Third World has become, and will continue to be, subjected to greater external intrusion, following the removal of restraints imposed by the Cold War on major powers and international institutions.[44] This has made, and will continue to make, the transition from juridical to effective statehood far more difficult than was the case when the states of Western Europe were at a corresponding stage in their state-making processes.[45]

To expect Third World states, which form the large majority of the membership of the international system, to sacrifice their search for adequate stateness at the altar of emancipation (whether of ethnic groups or individuals) or global governance (whatever that may mean) is neither practical nor unambiguously moral, especially as globalist conceptions of world order, fashioned largely in the West, do not seem to come anywhere close to corresponding to international political or economic realities even after the end of the Cold War.[46]

One can, in fact, go to the extent of arguing that globalist and emancipatory conceptions of world order share the same neocolonial bias from which much of the realist literature has traditionally suffered. The neocolonial domination of International Relations discourse, and therefore the discourse on security, is demonstrated by the popularity both of conventional wisdom (realism, neorealism) and of its critical alternatives in the literature on the subject. Neither of these adequately describes the political reality in the Third World. This applies with particular force to their contribution (or lack of it) toward the understanding of the security problematic of the large majority of states inhabiting the international system. Only the adoption of a perspective that is both securely grounded in the political realm as defined above and is informed by the political realities that dominate the lives of the large majority of states, even if they are weak and peripheral in Western perceptions, can correct this glaring deficiency in International Relations literature, especially in the field of security studies.

IX

As I have stated at the beginning of the chapter, I have termed such a perspective *subaltern realism,* a combination that denotes its primarily political and statecentric character, on the one hand, and its sensitivity for the concerns of the large majority of states—the less powerful and, therefore, of "inferior rank," to quote the dictionary definition of *subaltern*—on the other. The term *subaltern,* Gramscian in its inspiration, is borrowed from the subaltern school of history, composed primarily of historians of India, which is engaged in studying the role of the less powerful elements—peasants, artisans, and so on—within societies, elements that form a majority within their societies but whose histories are ignored by elitist historiography of the traditional kind that tends to focus on the activities of the powerful.[47]

Third World states form the quintessentially subaltern element within the society of states, given their relative powerlessness and the fact that they constitute a large majority in international society. The traditional realist literature in International Relations, echoing elitist historiography, tends to ignore the concerns of these states and the problems that they face. Because of the ubiquitous nature of the problems of security in the international system and the neglect of the fundamental issues that have an impact on the security of the large majority of states in the study of International Relations, a good way to begin applying the subaltern realist perspective to the discipline of International Relations is to begin with the field of security studies. Such an approach, while broadening and deepening the realist understanding of international politics, can at the same time act as a bulwark against the fashionable excesses of undue elasticity, which in their mistaken zeal for redefining the concept of security and the meaning of the political threaten to de-define two of the most important concepts in International Relations, indeed, in all of political science. This chapter is but a preliminary attempt to introduce the community of scholars to such a perspective and to its applicability to the study of security in the hope that it will stimulate further thinking and writing on the subject.

NOTES

1. I have wrestled with this problem earlier in my article "The Security Problematic of the Third World," *World Politics* 43:2 (January 1991), 257–83.

2. For the European experience of state making and the domestic conflict and violence that this process entailed, see Charles Tilly, ed., *The Formation of National States in Western Europe* (Princeton, N.J.: Princeton University Press, 1975).

3. For one tabulation that brings home this point very clearly, see Evan Luard, *War in International Society: A Study in International Sociology* (New Haven, Conn.: Yale University Press, 1986), appendix 5, 442–47. Also see Kalevi J. Holsti, *Peace and War: Armed Conflicts and International Order 1648–1989* (Cambridge: Cambridge University Press, 1991), table 11.1, 274–78.

4. For details of this argument, see Mohammed Ayoob, "State Making, State Breaking, and State Failure: Explaining the Roots of Third World Insecurity," in Kumar Rupesinghe, P. Sciarone, and Luc van de Goor, eds., *Between Development and Destruction: An Enquiry into the Causes of Conflict in Post-colonial States* (London: Macmillan, 1996).

5. Ramses Amer, et al., "Major Armed Conflicts," *SIPRI Yearbook 1993: World Armaments and Disarmament* (Oxford: Oxford University Press, 1993), 81.

6. K. J. Holsti, "International Theory and War in the Third World," in Brian L. Job, ed., *The (In)Security Dilemma: National Security of Third World States* (Boulder, Colo.: Lynne Rienner, 1992), 38.

7. For details of the argument about the impact of changing international norms and the end of superpower rivalry on conflict and order in the Third World, see Mohammed Ayoob, "The New-Old Disorder in the Third World," *Global Governance* 1:1 (Winter 1995).

8. For the historical evidence regarding the lengthy, violent, and extremely repressive process of state making in Western Europe, see Tilly, *The Formation of National States in Western Europe*. Also see Keith Jaggers, "War and the Three Faces of Power: War Making and State Making in

Europe and the Americas," *Comparative Political Studies* 25:1 (April 1992), 26–62.

9. For details of this argument, see Mohammed Ayoob, *The Third World Security Predicament: State Making, Regional Conflict, and the International System* (Boulder, Colo.: Lynne Rienner, 1995), especially chap. 2.

10. Stephen M. Walt, "The Renaissance of Security Studies," *International Studies Quarterly* 35:2 (June 1991), 212–13. Emphasis in the original.

11. Walter Lippmann, *U.S. Foreign Policy: Shield of the Republic* (Boston: Little, Brown, 1943), 51.

12. Arnold Wolfers, *Discord and Collaboration: Essays on International Politics* (Baltimore: Johns Hopkins University Press, 1962), 150.

13. See the contribution by Amitav Acharya to this volume.

14. Jessica Tuchman Mathews, "The Environment and International Security," in Michael T. Klare and Daniel C. Thomas, eds., *World Security: Trends and Challenges at Century's End* (New York: St. Martin's Press, 1991), 362–80.

15. Daniel Deudney, "The Case against Linking Environmental Degradation and National Security," *Millennium* 19:3 (Winter 1990), 465. Emphasis in the original.

16. Mathews, "The Environment and International Security," 366.

17. Ken Booth, "Security and Emancipation," *Review of International Studies* 17:4 (October 1991), 319.

18. Crawford Young, "The Temple of Ethnicity," *World Politics* 35:4 (July 1983), 659.

19. Booth, "Security and Emancipation," 317.

20. David Easton, *The Political System: An Enquiry into the State of Political Science* (New York: Knopf, 1963), 99, 128, 129.

21. For a discussion of the inseparable connection among territoriality, authority, and sovereignty—the three pillars of the Westphalian order—see Janice E. Thomson, "State Sovereignty in International Relations: Bridging the Gap between Theory and Empirical Research," *International Studies Quarterly* 39:2 (June 1995), 213–33.

22. Edward E. Azar and Chung-in Moon, "Legitimacy, Integration and Policy Capacity: The 'Software' Side of Third World National Security," in Edward E. Azar and Chung-in Moon, eds., *National Security in the Third World: The Management of Internal and External Threats* (College Park: Center for International Development and Conflict Management, University of Maryland, 1988), 77–101.

23. For some of the best examples of this genre of writing, see Andrew Hurrell and Benedict Kingsbury, eds., *The International Politics of the Environment* (Oxford: Clarendon Press, 1992); and Nazli Choucri, ed., *Global*

Accord: Environmental Challenges and International Responses (Cambridge, Mass: MIT Press, 1993).

24. Thomas F. Homer-Dixon, "On the Threshold: Environmental Changes as Causes of Acute Conflict," *International Security* 16:2 (Fall 1991), 114–15. Emphasis in the original.

25. For details of this argument, see Mohammed Ayoob, "The Security Predicament of the Third World State: Reflections on State Making in a Comparative Perspective," in Job, *The (In)Security Dilemma*, 63–80.

26. Gabriel Ben-Dor, *State and Conflict in the Middle East: Emergence of the Post-colonial State* (New York: Praeger, 1983), 244.

27. For details of this argument, see Mohammed Ayoob, "Security in the Third World: Searching for the Core Variable," in Norman Graham, ed., *Seeking Security and Development: The Impact of Military Spending and Arms Transfers* (Boulder, Colo.: Lynne Rienner, 1994), 15–28.

28. For a detailed discussion of state making in the Third World and its impact on state and regional security, see Ayoob, *The Third World Security Predicament,* especially chap. 2. For highly perceptive discussions of the general process of state making, see Charles Tilly, "War Making and State Making as Organized Crime," in Peter B. Evans, Dietrich Rueschemeyer, and Theda Skocpol, eds., *Bringing the State Back In* (New York: Cambridge University Press, 1985), 169–91; and Jaggers, "War and the Three Faces of Power."

29. Youssef Cohen, Brian R. Brown, and A. F. K. Organski, "The Paradoxical Nature of State Making: The Violent Creation of Order," *American Political Science Review* 75:4 (1981), 905. Emphasis in the original.

30. For details of this argument, see Ayoob, *The Third World Security Predicament,* especially chap. 3.

31. Barry Buzan, "A Framework for Regional Security Analysis," in Barry Buzan, et al., *South Asian Insecurity and the Great Powers* (London: Macmillan, 1986), 3–32.

32. For recent contributions to the debate about the utility of the democratic peace theory as an explanatory paradigm for state behavior, see Christopher Layne, "Kant or Cant: The Myth of the Democratic Peace"; David E. Spiro, "The Insignificance of the Liberal Peace"; and John M. Owen, "How Liberalism Produces Democratic Peace," which are all in *International Security* 19:2 (Fall 1994), 5–125.

33. Steve Chan, "Mirror, Mirror on the Wall . . . : Are the Freer Countries More Pacific?" *Journal of Conflict Resolution* 28:4 (December 1984), 617–48.

34. Zeev Maoz and Nasrin Abdolali, "Regime Types and International Conflict, 1816-1976," *Journal of Conflict Resolution* 33:1 (March 1989), 3–35.

35. Edward D. Mansfield and Jack Snyder, "Democratization and War," *Foreign Affairs* 74:3 (May–June 1995), 79–80.

36. Robert L. Rothstein, "Weak Democracy and the Prospect for Peace and Prosperity in the Third World," in Sheryl J. Brown and Kimber M. Schraub, eds., *Resolving Third World Conflict: Challenges for a New Era* (Washington, D.C.: United States Institute of Peace Press, 1992), 32.

37. It should be pointed out that in those instances where industrialized states were not territorially satiated (for example, Germany between the wars) and when their democratic institutions were weak, they pursued policies that led to conflict with other industrialized states. It is instructive to note that Germany became a national state only around 1870. The weakness of democratic institutions in Germany can therefore be attributed to its relative newness as a national state, lacking societal consensus on fundamental issues of political and economic organization and struggling to establish its legitimacy and complete its state-building process.

38. Rothstein, "Weak Democracy and the Prospect for Peace and Prosperity in the Third World," 24.

39. Barry Buzan, *People, States and Fear: An Agenda for International Security Studies in the Post-Cold War Era*, 2nd ed. (Boulder, Colo.: Lynne Rienner, 1991), 10.

40. Hedley Bull, *The Anarchical Society: A Study of Order in World Politics* (New York: Columbia University Press, 1977), 319–20.

41. Infrastructural power has been defined by Michael Mann as "the capacity of the state actually to penetrate civil society, and to implement logistically political decisions throughout the realm." Michael Mann, "The Autonomous Power of the State: Its Origins, Mechanisms and Results," in John A. Hall, ed., *States in History* (Oxford: Basil Blackwell, 1986), 113.

42. For a discussion of unconditional legitimacy of state structures and regimes, see Mohammed Ayoob, "Security in the Third World: The Worm about to Turn?," *International Affairs* 60:1 (Winter 1983–84), 44.

43. For a perceptive analysis demonstrating the close relationship between state making and violence, see Cohen, Brown, and Organski, "The Paradoxical Nature of State Making," 901–10.

44. For a sophisticated statement of this argument, see Martin Doornbos, "State Formation Processes Under External Supervision: Reflections on 'Good Governance,'" in Olav Stokke, ed., *Aid and Political Conditionality* (London: Frank Cass, 1995), 377–91.

45. I have made this argument in greater detail in Ayoob, *The Third World Security Predicament*, especially chap. 4.

46. This is very clear from the more perceptive scholarship both in international politics and international political economy emerging after the end of the Cold War. For example, see Christopher Layne, "The Unipolar Illu-

sion: Why New Great Powers Will Rise," *International Security* 17:4 (Spring 1993), 5–51; Kenneth N. Waltz, "The Emerging Structure of International Politics," *International Security* 18:2 (Fall 1993), 44–79; Wayne Sandholtz, et al., *The Highest Stakes: The Economic Foundations of the Next Security System* (New York: Oxford University Press, 1992); Lester C. Thurow, *Head to Head: The Coming Battle among Japan, Europe and America* (New York: William Morrow, 1992).

47. For a collection of seminal writings in the field of subaltern history, see Ranajit Guha and Gayatri Chakravorty Spivak, eds., *Selected Subaltern Studies* (New York: Oxford University Press, 1988).

II

The Discourses of Security

6

Discourses of War:
Security and the Case of Yugoslavia

BEVERLY CRAWFORD AND RONNIE D. LIPSCHUTZ

INTRODUCTION

The agonizing war in the former Yugoslavia, the interminable parlays about what to do, the innumerable threats made and peace
plans offered, retracted, and made again have all served to highlight
the process by which Western decision-making elites have tried to redefine their own, and their countries', security in the post-Cold War
world. To the question, "What is to be done in Bosnia?" they have
answered, "Almost nothing." To the question, "Why?" they have
answered, "Because it does not threaten us." And, so, almost nothing has happened. In this chapter, we argue that this policy response
is directly related to conceptions of security and threats that have
structured the debate on the causes of the war as well as its potential
consequences. In turn, widespread acceptance of the dominant view
of those causes has justified a policy of relative inaction, in the
process virtually precluding future actions designed to prevent such
carnage from becoming an accepted feature of global politics.

The literature on the war in the former Yugoslavia grows daily, in
both quantity and quality. Much of it attempts to solve the puzzle of
violence and bloodletting, unleashed with the complicity of Europe,
the United States, the European Community, and Russia in what
most people agree was once a vibrant multiethnic society. Few analyses, however, have explored the connection between widely accepted

149

causal claims regarding the war and the policies pursued by the dominant powers. Nor have they examined how dominant explanations for the war serve to vindicate prevailing conceptions of specific security requirements. Such analysis is required to improve the level of debate, the effectiveness of policy, and our understanding of security in the post-Cold War world.

In this chapter we explore those connections at two levels. In the first part of the chapter, we examine the ways in which elite decision and opinion makers constructed an intersubjective understanding of the causes of war in the former Yugoslavia when the fighting broke out, relying on competing discourses of war. That story is essentially a chronological one. It shows how political forces in the West, rather than "objective" events on and beyond the battlefield, worked to undermine the initial interpretation of the conflict and replace it with an alternative one that required little or no active intervention. We make no claim here that the prevailing explanation is wrong in any positive sense. But we do argue that it is based on a state-centric conception of Western security, not on a conception of state security in the region or on a preference for the security of individuals in what was once Yugoslavia. Given the assumptions on which the interpretation is built, the prevailing explanation posits a narrow range of causal factors that might link Balkan violence to the security of Western European states and other states in the region. The conventional security assumption underlying all these causal claims is that peace is *divisible* in the post-Cold War world, and the causes of war in the former Yugoslavia will not lead to a widening of the conflict in ways that would impinge on the security of Western states. Therefore, not much *needs* to be done. Bolstered by a belief that Serbian aggression, compounded by centuries of hatred, was responsible for the initiation and continuation of the war, the policy response has become: "Nothing *can* be done."

In the second part of the chapter, we challenge two of the prevailing assumptions that undergird the dominant explanation for the causes of this war: that of centuries-old hatreds and the assumption about divisible peace. Historical evidence shows that ethnic animosities in the region are relatively new. We interrogate the concept of divisible peace by shifting the analytic focus from Western states to individuals in the region. This shift in focus opens the way for an alternative explanation of the causes of war. We present one possible alternative—that the institutions of the federal Yugoslav state played a double-edged role in the evolution of the conflict: they nourished regional and ethnic identities and even resentments, but they initially created working relationships among the ethnically defined regions and removed the potential sources of collective violence. The weakening of those federal institutions increased the insecurity of individuals whom they protected. Policy implications that flow from this critique of the prevailing claims focus on more, not less, intervention to restructure state institutions in areas threatened with similar conflicts in ways that might lead to peace and more security for individuals.

THREATS, SECURITY, AND WAR

What does the term *security* mean? The answer quite clearly depends on the object to which the condition refers. In the case of a state, to be secure is conventionally thought to refer to threats that originate from outside of the border of the state and, if fulfilled, could undermine the stability and integrity of the state. Yet it is clear on reflection that such threats can also originate from within the borders of the state, in the form of deliberate subversion or even the destabilizing of social arrangements as a result of the dissemination of new ideas, practices, and technologies. How the leaders of a state define security consequently relies a great deal on how those leaders conceptualize the state and its place in the world, and how they explain processes inside and outside the state that might conceivably undermine the state.[1]

How, then, might a war in a faraway place impact the integrity and stability of states outside of that place? There are several possibilities, and each provides a somewhat different vision of the state, its political and social constitution, and its internal coherence. One possible impact is enshrined in the venerable domino theory, which posits the spillover of war across borders as an almost automatic process. The Former Yugoslav Republic of Macedonia (FYROM) has at times been suggested as the potential flash point of a Third Balkan War that could expand to engulf not only the former Yugoslav republics but also Rumania, Bulgaria, Greece, Albania, and Hungary, eventually perhaps drawing in Western Europe, Russia, and the United States. The model for this causal process is, of course, World War I. The response is clear: stop the war before it gets out of hand, even if that means active intervention.

second possible impact is internal. The chaos and disruption
e Balkans has displaced millions and will, in all likelihood, dis-
: millions more, and these millions upon millions will all head
toward more peaceful places. The burden of so many refugees, especially on societies that are already under serious economic strain,
will inevitably disrupt internal stability, heighten social conflict, and
perhaps even lead to violence. Hence, the threat is one that can be
stanched either by closing borders and turning away from the war,
or intervening in the region. Closing borders is politically much
easier than intervention, and this is the most recent response of the
European Union to the chaos in the Balkans.

Third, there is the possibility that the war is strictly local—a civil
conflict, in effect—and has no spillover or other effects that merit a
military response. To be sure, there is a refugee problem, but this is
one that can be handled through appropriate administrative procedures. The war is unlikely to spread—no one has very much interest
in the Balkans anymore—and involvement, if necessary, should proceed through strictly diplomatic means. For the most part, however,
peace is divisible.

A final perspective—one that might be immanent but has yet to
be operationalized in a serious way—assumes the existence of an
"international society of states," which enjoins state leaderships to
impose a normatively based world order on regions engulfed in conflict.[2] Certainly, there has been much discussion about public pressure on governments to intervene in various places in order to stop
killing and restore order, but as the UN-American experience in Somalia, and more recent events in Bosnia, seem to have demonstrated,
such state-led intervention is rife with contradictions. Not the least
of these is that peacekeeping appears inevitably to lead peacekeepers
to favor one side over another, if only for tactical reasons.[3]

We will argue later that, in fact, none of these four discourses provided an explanation of the conflict, but that a discourse of "social
warfare," prosecuted at the level of individual, family, and civil society, would be much more accurate. As we shall see, however, this
type of war could not, and cannot, be handled through the existing
practices and institutions of the state system.

Each of these interpretations rests on a certain set of notions
about war and its consequences; each is, under certain specific conditions, a plausible outcome, and each demands a different response.

But plausibility—or probability—is not what is at issue here; politics is. The particular explanation that is advanced by political elites has to do with their estimation of what is politically possible inside and outside of their individual countries, and how to make the possible come true, not what is most likely to happen. Should they be proved wrong in their estimates, of course, the political cost could be quite high, and careers could be put on the line (as President Clinton's frequent changes of course on the issue suggest). But this is hardly news. What is news—and of some interest—is how these estimates change from one to another through the course of a war, with all-too-real effects on those caught in the middle of the carnage.

PREVAILING IMAGES OF WAR

By 1994 the prevailing explanation for the bloodshed in Yugoslavia could be characterized as Serbian aggression compounded by ancient hatreds on all sides in the conflict. Conveniently, this explanation minimized the need for outsiders to become involved, as there is no way to change such ancient hatreds through diplomatic or other means. Such an explanation, however, was not the one initially promulgated during the first six months of the war. More strikingly perhaps, this explanation evolved not in response to events on the battlefield but to parlays in conference rooms in Brussels and Washington, where envoys' definitions of the conflict became entwined with their own domestic political agendas. Indeed, the conventionally accepted interpretation of the war's causes was negotiated through a series of meetings in the European Community, largely driven by Germany's unwavering pressure to recognize Croatia as an independent state in the face of signs that this might lead to catastrophe. Recognition of Croatia demanded a justification, and the justification for it became Serbian aggression. Curiously, however, this interpretation was not the original one: when hostilities began in June 1991, there was a consensus among Western officials and scholars alike that a civil war was pending, whose cessation could be negotiated through diplomatic means.

Below, we trace the ways in which the competing discourses of war emerged in an authoritative fashion at the diplomatic level as a function of the political context within Europe, and came to blame Serbian aggression as the central causal factor, with its corollaries of primordial hatreds and divisible peace. We then analyze what that particular constellation of interpretations implied in the European context for Western definitions of security and formulation of policy.

THE OUTBREAK OF VIOLENCE IN THE FORMER YUGOSLAVIA

In the aftermath of the collapse of the communist regimes in Eastern Europe in 1989, it appeared to the West that Yugoslavia was also on the brink of liberalizing its economic and political system. It quickly became clear, however, that the central issue was not liberalization at all, but the future of the Yugoslav federation itself.[4] In the course of 1990 and 1991 presidents of the six Yugoslav republics met repeatedly to discuss that future. In those meetings, Slovenia proved uncompromising on the issue of independence.[5] Throughout the course of these negotiations—for that is really what they were—Serbian President Slobodan Milosevic declared that he would not accept the transformation of Yugoslavia into a loose association of sovereign states,[6] inasmuch as this would undermine the right of all Serbs, inside and outside of the Serbian Republic, to live in a single state. Tensions mounted as the ultranationalist Croatian Democratic Union (HDZ) party won the 1990 elections in Croatia, and they were further exacerbated as the new president, Franjo Tudjman, explicitly identified the Croatian state with the ethnic Croatian "nation," in spite of the large number of Serbs living within the state.

Meanwhile, during this period of escalating tension in Yugoslavia, U.S. and European leaders basked in the belief that the Cold War's end and the demise of Communism had ushered in a new era of peace in Europe; more specifically, they were preoccupied with the West's first post-Cold War military confrontation in the Persian Gulf. As a result, they paid scant attention to developments in the Balkans. By January 1991, however, political elites in the European Community (EC) could no longer ignore the fragmentation of established states on their borders. Soviet troops were putting down demonstrations for independence in Latvia and Lithuania; by March, referenda in Lithuania, Estonia, and Latvia showed overwhelming support for independence. With much less international attention, these moves were mirrored in Yugoslavia: the Slovenian parliament voted to invalidate Yugoslav federal law in Slovenia, and the Croatian parliament asserted its own veto power over federal laws. Slovenia, moreover, made no secret of the fact that it was seeking complete and unconditional independence from Yugoslavia.

Despite early indications that President Tudjman might be willing to compromise on Croatia's position with respect to a new Yugoslav federation, Slovenia's uncompromising stand on independence had the effect of pushing Croatia in the same direction, and this pressure ignited open hostilities between Croats and Serbs. On 6 June 1991, a gun battle in Borovo Selo, a town in northwestern Croatia, left twelve Croatian policemen and three ethnic Serbs dead. In response, the Serb-dominated Yugoslav National Army (JNA) went on alert and began to call up reserves. Nineteen days later, on 25 June, Croatia and Slovenia declared their independence. The JNA was mobilized to prevent the secession of the two states. Both resisted, and fighting broke out.

WHICH INTERPRETATION?

At this point, the question of how to explain the war arrived at center stage: was it a *civil* conflict, in which one or more of the involved parties was trying to alter the post-World War II borders legally reified in the Helsinki accords? Was it an *international* conflict, in which one state was trying to conquer territory that legitimately belonged to another, legally independent state? Was it a matter of *world order*, which required intervention by a coalition of like-minded states? Or was it an *ethnic* conflict, rooted in ancient hatreds that no one could control but that were unlikely to spread outside of the region? Each explanation drew on different cultural and political tendencies within Europe, each implied different policy options to preserve the peace, and each suggested different conceptions of Western security in a post-Cold War world.

Defining the conflict as a civil war suggested that political mediation and negotiation could halt the hostilities and keep the Yugoslav state together. The policy response on the part of the EC and the United States would be to exert diplomatic pressure on the constituent republics in order to preserve Yugoslavia's territorial integrity in the wake of Communism's collapse. This view coincided with the more general Western conceptualization of security immediately following the East European revolutions of 1989: postcommunist states were actively participating in Europe-wide political and security institutions, and the disintegration of those states threatened to weaken and discredit those institutions. Particularly, because most postcommunist states were moving toward democracy, self-determination through fragmentation would mean the loss of control over their territories by new democratizing governments, raising once again the specter of nationalism and nationalist rivalries in Europe.

The second explanation of the conflict, and one that would take the European Community down a different path, was to frame it as an act of Yugoslav-Serbian aggression against a new nation-state exercising its justifiable claim to independence. With this interpretation, the policy response would involve recognition of Croatia's and Slovenia's right to self-determination, grant them diplomatic recognition, and impose sanctions against Serbian aggression. Such a common Western policy on recognition would effectively internationalize the dispute, passing it to the United Nations. With this option, the focus of mediation and conflict resolution would move from the European Community to the UN and bring in the United States and NATO. Pursuit of this alternative would thus indicate a preference for international as opposed to independent regional practices of mediation and conflict resolution in a new and uncertain security environment for Western states; as such, this alternative would indicate continuity in the pursuit of transatlantic political and security cooperation and recognize the constraints of international law on external intervention.

The third interpretation, based on an international society concept, would justify intervention not only for humanitarian reasons but also in order to establish a political framework that would bring the post-Yugoslav republics into line with the global trend toward liberal democratic forms of governments. The rationale behind this view is that democracies do not go to war with each other, and that the spread of democratic governments contributes to the establishment of an international union of Kantian "republics."[7] Ideally, such intervention would take place under the combined auspices of the European Community (financing), the Organization for Security and Cooperation in Europe (negotiating), and the United Nations (peacekeeping), along the lines of the UN's reconstruction efforts in Cambodia.

The fourth interpretation, attributing war to primordialism and ancient hatreds, represented an effort to "read the Balkans out of history" and turn it into a place with no relevance to Europe's future. This explanation harkened back to the beginning of the twentieth century, the first two Balkan Wars, and the triggering of World War I in Sarajevo—events that were generally agreed to be outside of the realm of possibility (except for those favoring the ethnic domino theory, who were, in any event, mostly Americans). More to the point, because it was widely held that most of Europe had long since passed the stage of ethnic hatred, the Balkans could be regarded as a place sufficiently removed to be of little or no importance to Europe proper and therefore meriting little, if any, outside involvement. Obviously, such a view provides a curious reading of European geography, but there is ample historical precedent for regarding the Balkans as a backward and largely irrelevant place.

Within Western Europe, there was initially widespread consensual agreement on the first explanation. François Mitterrand and John Major argued that "the territorial integrity of a single Yugoslavia must take precedence . . . over the aims of Croatian and Slovenian nationalists." In February 1991, Helmut Kohl wrote to the prime minister of the Yugoslav Federation, Ante Markovic, that the "unity of the country and the ability of its peoples to live together could only be assured through a peaceful dialogue based on the principles of democracy, respect for human rights, and the rights of minorities."[8] The European Community initially agreed on the first interpretation of the conflict, regarding it as a civil war. The EC took the position that the Yugoslav state should be held together, but that a looser federation, retaining the same name, should be negotiated among the six republics. To this end, the EC would take the lead in mediating the conflict.

The substantive argument made on behalf of the second explanation of the war was that the right of self-determination had historically implied the creation of local and responsive government as a counter to totalitarian domination and control. Indeed, this right of self-determination of the East German people was precisely the argument used by Kohl in both internal debates over German unification and in the two-plus-four negotiations that brought external recognition of a unified Germany.[9] This particular argument was not initially popular in either Washington or Brussels; eventually, however, it would come to take on an aura of truth as a result of German political pressure.

The third argument held, and continues to hold, widespread appeal, especially among some sectors of Western publics. Scenes of violence and bloodshed from various zones of chaos around the world, broadcast over the Cable News Network, generated pressures on Western leaders to do something. President George Bush's decision in December 1992 to send troops into Somalia for humanitarian purposes and to restore the state was a model for such a "republican" commitment to order. Revelations of concentration-camp conditions in Bosnian Serb prisoner-of-war camps, and seemingly indiscriminate killings in Sarajevo, had similar effects. Yet as soon as it became clear that the combatants would not lay down their arms and welcome the arriving troops in a peaceful fashion, the costs of imposing peace proved politically unsustainable. The difficulties associated with the intervention in Somalia pretty much put paid to similar efforts in the future.

The fourth argument had no currency when war first broke out in Yugoslavia. It was only after the failure of various initiatives, such as the Vance-Owen partition plan, that some observers began to regard the situation as hopeless. This was the basis for Warren Christopher's gloomy view and for President Clinton's reluctance to commit U.S. troops to peacekeeping efforts in Bosnia. It was also, in essence, the basis for the solution offered by realists such as John Mearsheimer, who argued that Serbs, Croats, Bosnian Muslims, and the other ethnic groups would never get along, and that it was better that they be separated, armed, and allowed to keep the peace through a Balkan-wide balance of power.[10]

Why was the civil-war interpretation and policy response initially chosen? Two explanations can be offered. First, it could be argued that the EC foreign ministers wished to use the conflict as an opportunity to build a common European foreign and security policy, given that Yugoslavia was viewed as part of Europe, and in view of the impending Single Market, the European Community was attempting to strengthen its regional security institutions. Second, within the EC itself, a number of separatist movements had called on the principle of self-determination to justify their own claims for varying degrees of autonomy. Consequently, granting recognition—particularly of Croatia as a constituent republic of a multiethnic federal state—on the basis of self-determination was a sensitive issue for the constituent states of the EC. In advertisements in the *New York Times* as well as other venues, Catalonia was asserting its independence "as a country in Europe." Indeed, in early meetings of the European Council of Ministers, opposition to the right of self-determination was voiced most vociferously by the foreign minister of Spain. France and Belgium were facing similar problems with regions that had pressed for more independence. Further, it was widely believed that recognizing the right of self-determination without securing the protection of minority rights was imprudent and unjustifiable. Finally, the granting of collective rights and autonomy to any minority group ran counter to the dominant liberal principle protecting individual rights enshrined in EC law.[11]

During the following six months, Western states pursued policies in line with the civil-war interpretation of the conflict. Publicly, EC officials insisted that the principles of the Conference on Security and Cooperation in Europe (CSCE) with regard to borders, minority rights, and political pluralism would guide its approach toward resolution of the conflict, and the issue of aggression was not raised. The European Community insisted that Croatia and Slovenia suspend for three months any further steps toward independence in order to allow a negotiated revision of the 1974 Yugoslav constitution, and it threatened to withdraw $1 billion in aid to the federation unless a peaceful resolution of the crisis were negotiated.

In Germany, however, forces were at work to alter the EC's course by changing the dominant explanation for the war. The German press and, in particular, the influential *Frankfurter Allgemeine Zeitung* (FAZ), considered to be the German newspaper of record, began to propagate new images of the parties to the Yugoslav conflict. Croatia was portrayed as committed to European values, while Serbs were caricatured as being hardly European at all. The FAZ editorialized that the people of Croatia and Slovenia had voted democratically to secede and were being prevented from doing so by the violent response of Serbia's Communist government. After the revolutions of 1989 for self-determination and freedom from communist rule, one editorial questioned how democratic peoples could possibly continue to support centralized communist regimes.[12] The campaign proved influential: one by one, the leaders of the German political parties voiced their agreement with this view, with growing pressure on Kohl and Foreign Minister Hans-Dietrich Genscher to adopt this view and change EC policy.

Toward the end of August and the beginning of September 1991, events in the Soviet Union also began to undercut one of the principal reasons for the EC's interpretation of the conflict as a civil war and its insistence on continued recognition of federal Yugoslavia. In the wake of the August coup attempt, the republics of the Soviet Union began to declare their independence, a course to which virtually no one in the West voiced any objection. The EC, following the principle of self-determination, began to recognize the independence of these republics, and with this, its rationale for not recognizing the independence of Croatia and Slovenia began to weaken. The significance of this process was not lost on the leaders of the Yugoslav republics, especially Croatia's President Tudjman.

On 2 September 1991, the *New York Times* reported that Croatian officials thought that their drive for European support was boosted by the collapse of the Soviet coup, the willingness of the republics to defect from the Soviet Union, and West European recognition of the right to independence of the Baltic republics. The report further suggested that Tudjman was trying to convince Croatian radicals that they could portray themselves as the victims of Serbian aggression and thus gain the support of both Europe and the United States. Serbian victory in the field, he argued, might be translated into defeat at the negotiating table.[13]

Throughout the next three months, cease-fires between Croatia and the JNA (now representing Serb interests) were repeatedly negotiated and just as quickly broken. The Yugoslav army attacked Dubrovnik, on the Dalmatian coast, demanding the city's surrender and forcing EC peace monitors to leave the city. The JNA attacked and held Vukovar, leading Croatian officials to plead with the International Red Cross for help for the city's besieged citizens. The JNA's planes bombed militia positions on the outskirts of Zagreb.

The Croatians did not appear innocent amidst all of this: Amnesty International accused both Serbians and Croatians of committing atrocities against civilians,[14] and the Tudjman government's refusal to disavow the Croatian fascists who had ruled a puppet state in league with the Nazis in the 1940s proved disturbing to some European officials. German Foreign Minister Genscher went so far as to admit that Tudjman was "no ideal democrat."[15] And while the aims of the peace conference were attacked by the warring parties themselves, Germany's insistence on EC recognition of Croatia weakened the process from the inside, too. As long as the Western powers disagreed among themselves, there was little chance that they could bring pressure to bear on either Serbian President Milosevic or Croatian President Tudjman to end the conflict.

By December 1991, the German effort was rewarded with success, as the EC's position on the conflict began to shift publicly. Increasingly, Serbia came to be seen as the aggressor by both European political elites and the German public at large. German officials began to announce that the country would grant diplomatic recognition to Croatia, and Genscher put increasing pressure on the European Community to change its position. On 2 December 1991, the EC made this shift official by lifting trade sanctions against all of the former Yugoslav republics except Serbia and Montenegro. At the same time, Germany severed all of its transport links with Serbia and the Yugoslav government.[16]

Important voices continued to be raised, however, against this transformation in interpretation and policy. Lord Carrington, the EC's chief negotiator at the peace conference, complained to Hans van der Broek, the Dutch foreign minister who held the EC's rotating presidency, that German recognition would destroy the Hague peace conference. It would prompt Serbia to leave the negotiations and cause Croatia and Slovenia to lose interest in the proceedings. As if to confirm Carrington's concern, Milosevic threatened that recognition of Croatia would lead the JNA, which already occupied one-third of Croatian territory, to undertake further military action.[17]

France, Britain, and the United States made it clear that they would support recognition only as part of a larger peace settlement,[18] and so, throughout December 1991, the Western powers and the UN tried to convince Germany not to grant diplomatic recognition to Slovenia and Croatia. United Nations Secretary-General Javier Perez de Cuellar officially requested that Germany refrain from recognizing the two republics "in a selective and uncoordinated manner." He cited pleas from Bosnia and Herzegovina that unconditional recognition might lead to the spread of the conflict into other parts of Yugoslavia. Indeed, the president of Bosnia visited Genscher in November to plead against recognition, arguing that it could only lead to a move for Bosnian independence and thus invite Serbian and Croatian aggression against Bosnia.

Officials in the Dutch government were clearly convinced that the recognition threat would goad Serbia to seize as much territory as it could and tempt Croatia to provoke skirmishes in the hope of drawing foreign intervention on its behalf. While Croatian officials had stated publicly that recognition would intensify attacks, and although to this point all peace negotiations had been futile, it was by no means clear that German recognition would intensify the fighting in the long run.

SHIFTING INTERPRETATIONS: FROM CIVIL WAR TO SERB AGGRESSION

Nonetheless, Germany did not back down. And with the threat of unilateral German recognition of the two breakaway republics—a threat that would destroy efforts to construct a common European foreign policy—the EC declared a change of its collective interpretation of the causes of the conflict. This reinterpretation took place at an EC Council of Ministers meeting on 16 December 1991, during which the EC declared conditional diplomatic recognition of Croatia and Slovenia, placing the blame for the conflict on Serbia. Emerging from that meeting, Douglas Hurd, the British foreign minister, diplomatically called the outcome "an exceptional compromise"; EC President Hans van der Broek said that he hoped that the prospect of recognition would put pressure on Serbia to end hostilities against Croatia.[19] Serbia, of course, assailed the EC decision, warning that it would recognize the Serb-inhabited regions of Croatia and Bosnia as new, separate republics,[20] and the Serbian media described the new policy as part of an elaborate German plot to dominate Europe and establish the "Fourth Reich."[21]

On 29 February 1992, voters in Bosnia overwhelmingly supported independence in a republic-wide referendum. One month later, Bosnia found itself ravaged by war. On 7 April the EC and the United States granted Bosnia diplomatic recognition. Unable to stop the process of disintegration, national self-determination was now the guiding principle of European Community policy, at least where the Balkans were concerned. With recognition and a prominent place for the principle of self-determination, it became the conventional wisdom that Bosnian Serbs were the aggressors in the new war in Bosnia, that Serbia had been the aggressor in the war in Croatia, and that it followed that Serbia was also providing support to Serb forces now fighting in Bosnia.

In the recent, normal course of international relations, if aggression is clearly and consensually defined, there have been attempts to meet it through collective security measures. Certainly, this was the case with the Gulf War in 1991. In the Yugoslav case, however, the only collective security measure taken was a joint and porous embargo against Serbia and Montenegro. Between the period following the diplomatic recognition of Croatia and mid-1994, both European and U.S. leaders demonstrated extreme reluctance to intervene in the crisis with meaningful collective security measures.

There are two explanations for this reluctance: first, there was gradually emerging yet another explanation for the violence, based on "ethnic conflict." This not only replaced the civil-war account, but it also served to complicate the Serb-aggression account. Second, there was a growing consensual belief that peace in Europe was, indeed, "divisible," and that the Balkans did not matter much, except as the source of endless flows of refugees. Below, we analyze each construction in more detail and offer an alternative construction that points to a different explanation for the war.

ETHNIC CONFLICT AND DIVISIBLE PEACE

Laying the blame on Serbia for the war in Yugoslavia was complicated by the popular discussion of ethnic conflict involving century-old hatreds. Such a characterization has two components: first it assumes that such hatreds as were evident in the repeated episodes of ethnic cleansing in Croatia and Bosnia are "natural" and "ancient," as modern societies have managed to surmount them. Second, the reason that these ancient hatreds have emerged now, after 1989, is that they were simply repressed by centralized communist states. With the fall of Communism, goes the metaphor, the lid was blown off the pot, and the potent mix of ancient and natural hatreds quickly came to a boil. Oddly enough, such a characterization was not offered in the early discussions of the war within the EC. It only emerged gradually, becoming dominant after the recognition of Croatia. In the United States, the same argument was first promulgated during the Bush administration. Bill Clinton dismissed it as incorrect during the presidential campaign, but subsequently, both he and Secretary of State Christopher began to invoke "centuries" of "accumulated hatreds," with primordial origins, as the administration's rationale for doing nothing (especially in light of the debacle in Somalia).

This view found support among some Western scholars, who argued that the ethnic hatreds flowing from identity politics are both ancient and natural, going so far as to cite sociobiological explanations that "the urge to define and reject 'the other' goes back to our remotest human ancestors, and indeed beyond them to our animal predecessors." Balkan elites perpetuated this version of events as well. During World War II, for example, nationalist scholars in Croatia claimed that the first documented reference to Croatians could be found in 2,500-year-old Persian sources, which "proved" links to "Aryans" (who are themselves Persians).[22] According to these same Croatian intellectuals, moreover, enmity with Serbs dated back for centuries. Not only had this been used to justify Croatia's wartime alliance with Nazi Germany, but it was also the basis for the Ustasha's killing of hundreds of thousands of non-Croats. These works were revived during the 1990 election campaign in Croatia, in the process also providing support for Serbia's claim that the new Croatia was the same as the fascist one. But Serbia produced its own form of self-serving nationalist scholarship in the latter part of the 1980s, too, proclaiming a Serbian right to "greater Serbia," including parts of Croatia, Bosnia, and the Serbian "heartland" in Kosovo, which today is ethnically 90 percent Albanian.

In point of fact, however, Serb-Croat hostility is not ancient at all. Rather, it dates only from the Austro-Hungarian period, a result of political divisions that emerged as the Hapsburg Empire began to decay from within. Indeed, Yugoslavia was the creation of late-nineteenth-century nationalism that spread throughout Central Europe. Political elites in both Serbia and Croatia attempted to build a common state based on a shared "southern Slav" identity and a common ideology of humiliation and suffering at the hands of both the Ottoman and Hapsburg empires.[23] As a result, the 1921 constitution of the newly created state of Yugoslavia was a liberal one, enshrining civil and political rights for all of its citizens, regardless of ethnic or religious origin.[24]

Not all Yugoslavs, however, were happy with this new arrangement; many Croatian nationalists felt that they had freed themselves from Hapsburg domination only to be newly saddled with Serbian hegemony. They mistrusted the new constitution, arguing that it masked Serbian control over Croatia and that a national Yugoslav identity could not be created based on a Serbian king, his army, policy, and administration, and on the dominance of the Orthodox church. Indeed, argued such Croats, this "nation" really represented the submission of a Roman Catholic people on the periphery of civilized Europe to an inferior, Oriental culture.[25] Threats of Croatian secession, and the fact that large sections of the Croatian population did not accept the constitutional basis of the Yugoslav state, led to growing centralization of power in Serbia. This and mounting Croatian resistance came to dominate the country's political agenda and prevented the formation of interethnic political coalitions. Even so, the conflict was a relatively mild one, and the bloody battles that created such enmity between Serbs and Croats date only from World War II, when Nazi Germany encouraged and provoked violent conflict.[26]

Nonetheless, in spite of clear historical evidence that the origins of the conflict between Serbia and Croatia are of recent vintage, the primordial-hatreds account persists. It is bolstered, as noted earlier, by the argument that links the emergence of violence now to the fall of communist states. But this last point goes beyond the simple boiling-pot metaphor to suggest that more fundamental issues of identity are at stake. Thus, when the grip of central control is relaxed, "people reflexively grasp at ethnic or national identifications or what passes for them."[27] This argument is, however, tautological: because conflict has now appeared, it must have been repressed in the past by strong states and powerful empire. The policy implications of this argument are clear: if ethnic conflict does appear, it appears as a natural process. Hence, even though the explanation is deterministic, all sides, whether aggressor or not, bear at least some of the responsibility for any violence that does occur. The issue of proportionality does not enter into the discussion because this would suggest choosing sides. Consequently, intervention on behalf of a victim is neither warranted nor feasible.

The logic of this argument, in concert with the focus on Western states as the objects of security, inevitably led to a new and consensual perception about the requirements for peace in Europe. At the end of the Cold War, West European elites often invoked Mikhail Gorbachev's notion of a common European home as a political goal, and this vision was reflected in a flurry of activity to enlarge and strengthen institutions, such as the CSCE, to incorporate newly independent states into a European framework where divisions between East and West did not exist. But as pressures mounted for the diplomatic recognition of Croatia, EC officials began to change their views, speaking instead about a divisible peace in Europe. They argued that, in contrast to the pre-World War I period or 1939, conditions now were such that crises in the East would not inevitably draw in the West. Western interests in the East were minimal, and the ethnic conflicts in the Balkans were being fought over limited aims, none of which involved the EC nations directly. Certainly, war refugees presented a domestic political and social problem, but not a security threat.[28] Throughout the EC, this changing perception weakened any residual enthusiasm for either independent military action or collective security measures in Yugoslavia. Thus, in spite of periodic public demands for action, the crisis was transmuted into a foreign-policy issue, external to the EC and the United States, and not something that impinged on the security of Western states.

The entire process described here reflects the optimism and disappointments of the years since 1989. During the Cold War, because of superpower interests and commitments, there was always the possibility that a small conflict might grow into a large one, resulting in nuclear confrontation or world war. Peace was, in other words, indivisible. This was the discourse that dominated the U.S. confrontation with Iraq in 1990 and 1991. If, indeed, Saddam Hussein was, as President Bush claimed, a Hitler, could World War III be far behind? (One might have claimed, as some did, that Iraq's invasion of Kuwait was strictly an Arab affair, not requiring outside involvement. Indeed, that was the logic behind the localization of the Balkan wars.)

There was, however, another discourse available: that of civil war. Technically, the legitimate party in a civil war is usually considered to be the regime in power; practically, of course, such a distinction is difficult, and sometimes undesirable, to make. Nonetheless, one solution in such a situation—beyond defeat or exhaustion, both of which are now favored—is a compromise between the warring sides that somehow satisfies both. Civil wars, while potentially explosive, can be contained, but active intervention by outsiders is required for this to happen. Intervention involves, moreover, real economic and political expenditures, domestic as well as international.

Finally, there was a third discourse available that simply wrote off the regions of conflict as lost to history and the victims of primordial blood lusts, thereby dismissing them as irrelevant to the flow of modern politics. Ancient and primordial forces were at work, and there was nothing that diplomacy, money, or military power could do to stop them: if they ran out of bullets, they would use rifles as clubs, and when the rifles were broken, they would pick up sticks and stones. Hence, the best strategy would be to walk away and deny the importance of the war to Europe as a whole. But this third account of the war in Yugoslavia is not quite so easy to walk away from. If, indeed, the bloodshed is primordial, or even genetic, anyone might fall victim to it, even Western Europe. Consequently, if the tragedy of Yugoslavia were regarded, and treated, as a part of preindustrial history, no one would be conceptually safe. Today, Serbia, Croatia, Bosnia; tomorrow, Wallonia and Flanders; Catalonia and Spain; Lombardy and Italy. Reading Yugoslavia "out of history" is, so to speak, a strategy of denial: it cannot happen here. It represents, in other words, a woefully shortsighted conception of security.[29]

AN ALTERNATIVE DISCOURSE: ENTREPRENEURS AND INSTITUTIONS

It would be irresponsible of us to stop here, without offering our assessment of the security implications of the Third Balkan War.[30] This assessment rests in part on a different framing of the referent object of security and, indeed, of the significance of the ethnic fragmentation under way in the former Yugoslavia and elsewhere. Our argument is not a "discourse" in the sense used above—it is not authoritative in having been adopted by political elites and offered as a prescription for action or inaction—but it does, on the one hand, generalize the implications of the Yugoslav case while, on the other hand, offer greater precision, we believe, in linking these implications to European and Western security.

If the origins of the Yugoslav and other ethnic conflicts are seen not as primordial or natural but, rather, as a consequence of the intersection of global forces with the domestic politics and histories of individual countries, it becomes evident that no community is necessarily immune. Denial is not only potentially self-defeating; it is also a formula for greater difficulties when such conflicts and crises can, finally, no longer be ignored. In our schema, the security problem arises as communities of identity are manipulated into exclusivist opposition, with the result that political institutions and states are torn apart.

Our account does not rest on the collapse of Communism as the determining factor. While a weakened state or the collapse of a central control is a permissive condition for the emergence of ethnic identity in a form that may lead to violent conflict, it does not follow that such a process is somehow natural. Ethnicity and religion are politicized through a set of historical processes. In specific historical periods, society offers raw material for multiple *social* divisions to become issues of contention; only some of those social cleavages are translated into *political* divisions that turn violent. Thus, despite a potential for ethnic conflict in Latin America, for example, ethnicity has, for the most part, remained largely unpoliticized. Instead, social class historically has provided the main basis for political divisions there.

We argue that exclusive and oppositional identities are politically constructed during periods of upheaval by certain members of political and economic elites, who we can call "political entrepreneurs." Such political entrepreneurs practice the politics of identity rather than the politics of interest. These elites politicize ethnic and sectarian divisions in order to mobilize political support in their struggle with other elites for power and wealth.[31] If the rhetoric of mobilization that politicizes these identities is based on claims of superiority, exclusion, and intolerance, the potential for conflict emerges. When identity politics are accompanied by claims of collective exclusivity, xenophobia, and intolerance, they raise the potential for violence against individuals identified by ascriptive characteristics as part of the excluded group. By contrast, a politics of interest is quintessentially liberal, as it is based on the notion that individuals hold multiple and crosscutting identities and interests. Conflicts of interest can be negotiated, compromised, and settled peacefully. The identities fostered by political entrepreneurs, on the other hand, are nonnegotiable so long as the practices that follow produce generally positive returns to the practitioners. Thus, identity politics in its most extreme form increases the odds that political conflicts will escalate into repression and violence.[32]

This is not to suggest that the practice of identity politics will necessarily end in violence. Identity politics often develop in response to similar practices by other groups because the repression of a particular group based on ascriptive identities requires organizing politically on the basis of those identities, in an effort to secure rights in the political process. If these reactive groups are convinced that the political institutions governing them will protect those rights, violence might be avoided. But if those institutions are weak or simply nonexistent—and being a reaction, the chances are good that any such institutions have been undermined—the probability of escalation to violence is significant.

Below, we will provide in detail an explanation for the collapse of Yugoslavia into war. The reader might ask, however, why we present this account as an alternative discourse. Our referent object, or unit of analysis, is neither state nor tribe because we find neither to be a particularly useful organizing concept here. The discourses of state-centered war—and by extension, state security—leads one either to interstate or civil war, with the implications discussed earlier. The discourse of tribe-centered war simply places the referent object outside of history. Our referent object is best understood as society. In a society-centered war, a society becomes the locus of violence because the collapse or disappearance of all political institutions leaves behind only the structures of civil society, among which are family, religion, and culture. (Hence, it should come as no surprise that rape, indiscriminate murder of families, and the razing of churches and mosques are so common in these kinds of wars.) A society-centered explanation of the wars in Yugoslavia thus rests on the practice of identity politics under institutional arrangements that have both fostered those practices and, indeed, encouraged violence as a means of destroying any and all alternatives. Individuals suffer and kill each other because they are identified as part of a collective group.

Two questions follow from this explanation: why do political entrepreneurs choose to practice the politics of identity rather than the politics of interest? And under what conditions does the practice of identity politics lead to violence? What follows is an attempt to answer these questions in three parts: first, we describe those policies of the federal Yugoslav state that promoted identity politics by selectively promoting or retarding the economic development of ethnically defined republics—that is, the practice of ethnofederalism;[33] second, we examine the process by which liberalizing groups that had begun to promote civil society and interest-based politics within the federation and its republics were purged at the end of the 1970s, leaving few to resist those later intent on promoting the identity politics of national exclusiveness when Communism fell; and finally, we explore how a weakened economy and weakened set of federal institutions prevented politicians from distributing material resources in exchange for political support. In essence, because the political system left Yugoslav society with a fairly weak civil society, political and economic elites were left with few alternatives to the politics of identity as a basis for political mobilization and virtually no institutions to prevent the increasingly violence-prone politics from engendering the outbreak of war. This discussion is preliminary and illustrative. Its purpose is not to offer positive evidence for an argument that challenges the dominant ones described above. Rather, it is to present the rudiments of an alternative explanation—in this case, a society-centered institutional one—that, as we shall suggest, is potentially applicable even to the members of the European Union and the United States.

THE INSTITUTIONAL CONSTRUCTION OF IDENTITY POLITICS
IN FEDERAL YUGOSLAVIA

Throughout the socialist world, prior to the Soviet demise, communist ideology reduced the salience of ethnicity as a source of political identity, replacing it with a more cosmopolitan socialist political identity. Public debate on ethnic issues as political issues was largely forbidden. In Marxist regimes, the grievances of particular ethnic groups had to be articulated in economic and social terms, as these were the only ones viewed by the state as legitimate.[34] Indeed, the division of the Soviet Union, Czechoslovakia, and Yugoslavia into ethnic republics was an attempt to transform ethnicity into cultural-administrative identities and thereby prevent its reemergence as a dominant political force. But these structures were part of the state system, and not civil society; hence, they became the eventual objects of struggle.[35]

The Yugoslav case is fairly typical. Rather than risk the emergence of federation-wide political parties that could challenge communist rule, after World War II Marshal Tito established a decentralized Yugoslav federation of republics, each one named for the dominant ethnic group within republican borders drawn to this end. These republics were never intended to become autonomous bases of power for republican politicians; rather, they were meant to serve as pillars of support for the power and authority of the ruling party. Paradoxically, this was best accomplished by dividing potential opposition along regional and ethnic lines.[36]

This strategy was not, however, purely political; it included an economic component as well. The distribution of entitlements among the republics represented an attempt by the federal government to buy their loyalty to the Yugoslav state. Tito reasoned that ethnic tensions could be diffused if each republic were given comparable access to economic and political resources. He thus established an ambitious program that channeled resources to the republics and regions according to his judgment of their economic needs and level of development.

In order to avoid some of the resentments that emerged in the 1930s, the postwar constitution of Yugoslavia implied an unwritten agreement between Tito and Serbia, through which Serbian dominance in the state apparatus and in the political structure, so problematic in the interwar period, would be attenuated. The formula for neutralizing Serbia was Yugoslav centralism in a federal state, a heavy dependence on an ideology of "brotherhood and unity," and the solidarity of partisans from all the republics that had fought against fascism. But many Croat nationalists saw the centralized and unitary state as just another manifestation of Serb dominance.[37] And inasmuch as each republic had already attained a different level of economic development, ranging from developed to less developed, Tito's redistribution program—essentially a form of republican affirmative action—was inevitably unequal. This inequality gradually gave rise to tensions that eventually began to erode support for the federal state. These resentments, which already appeared within the Communist Party itself as early as the 1960s, were expressed in ethnic rather than republican terms, as ethnicity had been institutionalized in the constitution as the basis of political representation within the country as a whole.

Friction among the republics was intensified by a growing economic crisis. After the break with the Soviet Union in 1949, Yugoslavia had no patron to which it could turn for economic assistance or cheap resources. As the 1950s progressed, the country found itself increasingly isolated and dependent on the West for aid and investment, which it never received in quantities adequate for its needs. As a result of the oil shocks of the 1970s, Yugoslavia found itself in an ever more economically perilous position. During that decade and the 1980s, as a communist state—even one courted by the West—Yugoslavia received stern treatment at the hands of the international lending community. As the economy stagnated, the federal government was forced to give up its program for equalizing regional development and push instead for a nationwide policy of industrial development. This penalized those regions that produced raw materials and commodities and rewarded those that were the sources of industrial goods and manufactures, a process that exacerbated already existing tensions between more- and less-developed regions. Inevitably, of course, such discrimination came to favor some republics over others and, because ethnicity had been institutionalized as a form of political representation, it was a small matter to express resentments in ethnic terms.

Regional allocations of material resources were based on political criteria as well. Although much of the federal investment fund was allocated through a system of auctions, where interested enterprises competed on the basis of interest rates and repayment schedules, regional politicians jockeyed for investments to bolster their own regional power base.[38] Historical animosities formed an additional set of political criteria for regional investment. Montenegro, as a less-developed but Serb-dominated republic, received the most investment per capita, while Croatia, the second most developed republic in terms of its ability to maximize output per investment, barely received its fair share. Clearly, Croatia (as well as Kosovo) was being punished for its record in World War II; Montenegro, Slovenia, and Serbia received disproportionate shares, largely because of the clout of their political elites in the Communist Party of Yugoslavia.

Thus, in a reversal of Tito's intentions and hopes, the shrinking of the economic pie and the growing struggle over resources had the effect of reinforcing ethnic identities and enhancing the political power of regional and republican political entrepreneurs. The risks inherent in these processes were laid bare when the weakness of the central federal state was revealed: inasmuch as administrative republics defined ethnically became the new basis of state power, the patterns of unequal distribution of resources to these administrative republics ensured a struggle among ethnic groups over those resources. Moreover, economic pressures, both internal and external, dictated that efforts to defuse ethnicity would eventually fail. On the one hand, resentment was nurtured between republics; on the other hand, investment programs institutionalized inefficiency in the interest of inter-republic equity. This further reduced international competitiveness already severely hampered by the vagaries of central planning.

WEAKENING REFORMERS AND PURGING LIBERALIZERS

This course of events in effect revived the processes that had politicized ethnic identity before World War II. Throughout the first twenty years of the Communist regime, although ethnic identities were reified in the ways described above, there was little indication that a politics of exclusion and ethnic intolerance was brewing. This particularly violent form of identity politics in Yugoslavia resurfaced, however, with Tito's decision to purge reformers and liberals in both Croatia and Serbia in the early 1970s. Both liberalizers and hard-line communists were opposed to ethnic nationalist appeals for political support, but liberalizers, with their pressure to strengthen market forces, freedom of speech, a merit-based system of promotions, and the withdrawal of the party from the arts and from culture—all steps that would have helped to build up civil society—threatened the party's central political control. In an effort to put in place such arrangements, in 1965 these liberalizers pushed through a major reform program that sought to lessen central control by giving more political and economic clout to the republics.[39]

Tito's reaction was rapid and severe. In Serbia, he expelled from the party all leading reform-minded communists. With their expulsion, political repression and the party's hold on the economy increased markedly. By eliminating the opposition in this way, the party ensured that, in the case of its own demise, hard-line nationalists would be positioned to seize power, and there would be no civil society to absorb the shocks of a transition.

In Croatia, Tito had less power. The 1965 reform emboldened not only the liberalizers but also nationalist elements, whose rhetoric often contained separatist overtones. Local party leaders attempted to mobilize support for themselves by issuing increasingly vocal complaints about Croatia's disadvantaged position in an unfair federal system. They began to call for an end to economic exploitation by Belgrade, reform of the banking and the foreign currency systems, curbs on the wealth of Belgrade's export-import firms, and the redistribution of former federal assets that had been taken by Serbia after the reform.[40] Croatian nationalist movements were most vociferous in their demands for an end to this exploitation. These movements were centered around the *Hrvatska Matica*, a Croatian-Catholic traditionalist group that advocated cultural separatism. What worried Tito the most in this situation was the demand for a separate Croatian seat in the United Nations (as had been provided to Ukraine and Belorussia in 1945). Ironically, perhaps, he believed that if Croatia were to obtain a separate seat, it would ally itself with the Soviet Union against him.

Tito tried to discipline local Croatian party officials, pressing them to suppress the separatist movements. This, however, split the local party structure. Liberalizers supported more pluralism in Croatian society, but when faced with a crackdown, they allied with nationalist factions and formed a coalition against the center. The other republican leaderships realized that the Croatian leadership had lost control of the situation. Fearing the implications of this for their situations, they pressed Tito to suppress the nationalist elements in Croatia. The 1965 reform had weakened his political power base in Croatia, however, and he would have to use force to do so. The opportunity to do this did not appear until 1971, when there were major student demonstrations in Croatia. Tito called in the JNA to quell the demonstration and suppress the move toward political pluralism. With backing from the JNA, Tito purged the party in Croatia of both its nationalist and liberalizing elements, leaving conservative centralizers firmly in power. In turn, those centralizers acted quickly to suppress the nationalist movements.

For the moment, relative stability was restored, but the crisis ultimately deepened divisions between the Croatian republic and the federal government. The army officer corps became convinced that the central danger to Yugoslavia was not an external threat from the Soviets but internal "nationalism and chauvinism."[41] Meanwhile, Croatian soldiers balked at serving outside Croatia, and a de facto territorial army began to emerge there. Consequently, the JNA began to mirror the weakness of the federal government as a whole. In a more general sense, this crisis represented the most serious threat to the viability of the Yugoslav federation since 1948.

WEAKENED INSTITUTIONS AND ETHNIC IDENTITY AS A POLITICAL RESOURCE

In an attempt to defuse internal opposition, the new Yugoslav constitution of 1974 further weakened the federal state, creating yet more resentments that came to be expressed in ethnic terms. While Croatians believed that Serbia controlled the federal state, Serbian elites believed that they had been singled out for unfair treatment under the new constitution because it granted autonomy from Serbia to Kosovo and Vojvodina, while leaving the other five republics intact.[42]

The new constitution was aided and abetted in its weakening of the federal state by the economic situation. In contrast to what had been possible in earlier times, the weakened federal state could no longer distribute material resources in exchange for political support. Eventually, the global recession of the early 1980s dealt the fatal blow: external debt grew, export markets closed, and regional and republican conflicts over the distribution of economic resources further contributed to economic decline. Recall that the regionally based allocation of resources increased local power and the political strength of local political entrepreneurs at the expense of the central state. As the various regional political elites gained autonomy from the center, they began to follow self-protective import substitution policies, leading to important losses in economies of scale. Furthermore, the regional governments did not coordinate foreign exchange stockpiles. The absence of coordination led to fragmentation of economic activity and the reduction of the stock of available capital for new investment. The resulting losses of revenue to the central government helped to undermine its ability to resist further regional encroachments on its effort to coordinate economic activity.

This was not all. The divergent effects of the international market on the regional economies placed additional and competing demands on the central government. The relatively developed and more competitive republic of Slovenia wanted greater integration into the international economy, whereas the less-developed Montenegrins demanded protection from the vagaries of international market forces. Divergent demands further reduced the federal government's ability to deal effectively with pressing economic problems and issues of restructuring. As a state that was both weak and decentralized, Yugoslavia was not capable of withstanding the centripetal forces of conflict that were soon to break out, first along regional and then along ethnic lines.

Finally, what the regional governments did not drain from the central state, the international economy did; in the early eighties, Yugoslavia found itself with an incoherent and ad hoc system of state interventionist policies in the economy—mainly to meet the loudest and best organized demands of various political entrepreneurs—in a period dedicated to neoclassical economic reform. The state began to face a mounting debt obligation without any return on monies spent.[43] By 1983, devaluations of the currency and an orchestrated drop in domestic demand (12 percent in 1983 alone), both imposed by the International Monetary Fund (IMF), had resulted in a precipitous fall in growth rates for the country as a whole. Unemployment rose from 600,000 in 1982 to 912,000 in 1983, not including the 700,000 who had been forced to emigrate abroad, mostly to the European Community, to find work.

With its powers and resources drastically reduced, the federal state was seized by paralysis: centrifugal elements served to divert development funds to those regions with the most political clout while federalists looked on helplessly. As an example of this, consider the impact of the IMF stabilization program's requirement that the dinar be devalued. Bosnia was strongly opposed to devaluation because it was heavily dependent on imported intermediate goods from convertible currency areas. Because devaluations had to be approved by all republics, negotiations were time-consuming, bitter, and divisive. With the declining authority and power of the central state, the IMF had acquired strong leverage over economic policy, and, consequently, the federal government's scope for policy discretion became hostage to its critical need for IMF support in putting together the necessary financing arrangements that would allow it to maintain a relative degree of economic and political stability.

Under these conditions, what little loyalty remained to the federal state drained away. The drive toward regional fragmentation and autonomy helped to propagate the widespread belief that federal aid was being given on the basis of ethnic ties rather than rational allocation principles. Given the failure of the program for economic development of the less-developed republics, rapidly growing regional income disparities, and the impotence of the federal government, the rise of ethnonationalism was almost a foregone conclusion.[44]

Throughout most of the postwar period, the Serb-Croatian alliance had served as the backbone of the Yugoslav federation. This began to fall apart when political entrepreneurs on both sides, in an effort to mobilize popular support, began to manipulate the cultural and historical symbols and practices that distinguished Serbians from Croatians. On the one side, the (in)famous 1986 memo to the Serbian Academy of Sciences, penned by Dobrica Cosic, inflamed the Serbs; on the other side, the pronouncements of Franjo Tudjman, historian of Croatia and JNA former general, did likewise.[45] Playing these cards, Slobodan Milosevic in Serbia and Tudjman in Croatia rose to power, not on platforms that recommended a more equitable distribution of resources along regional lines or emphasized economic development of Yugoslavia as a whole, but on the basis of ethnic separatism, with each recasting history as one long struggle against an implacable enemy enshrined in the Other.

The rise of Milosevic was especially critical. After taking control of the federal government in 1987, he abandoned the traditional policies of the Communist Party, rescinded the autonomy granted to Kosovo and Vodjvodina in 1974, and stopped the process of decentralization. He revitalized the Serbian Orthodox Church, making it an instrument of revived Serbian nationalism. He argued that Montenegro was another branch of the Serbian nation and maintained a tight grip on that republic. He complained in public that Serbia had suffered under federalism, that huge transfers of industry from Serbia to Croatia and Slovenia had taken place between 1945 and 1951, and that now the injustices needed to be rectified. All of this added fuel to the fire of rising nationalism in Croatia and confirmation to Tudjman and others that the federation must be destroyed.

Consequently, in April 1990, with $4 million in financial backing from the Croatian émigré community, the ultranationalist Croatian Democratic Union (HDZ) won Croatia's first democratic elections since 1945. The victory opened the gateway for Croatia's new president, Tudjman, to establish a state identified with the Croatian nation and providing no minority rights to the 600,000-strong Serb population. For many Serbs in Croatia, the HDZ victory meant the revival of the World War II fascist Croatian state. In the aftermath of the elections, local Serb leaders in Croatia demanded communal autonomy, legitimating that demand through a referendum. Initially, this was not intended to mean that Serb-dominated territory would secede from Croatia, but it eventually developed into a demand for secession—if not by agreement, then by force. What followed is by now well known.

DISCOURSES OF WAR: WHO SECURES SOCIETY?

What was so striking about the wars in Croatia and Bosnia was not that they happened, but their ferocity and the determination of Serbs and Croats, in particular, to eliminate all vestiges of other cultures in the regions over which they gained control. Not only were the local institutions of government "purified"—an act that is not unusual during a time of war—but institutions and symbols of society were also reduced to rubble in the effort to terrorize and "cleanse." And this type of social warfare aimed to destroy not only the few elements of civil society that existed, but even the family through the systematic slaughter of husbands, wives, and children and the policy of rape and impregnation, practices mostly attributed to the Bosnian Serb militia but engaged in by others, too.[46]

The referent object of war in the former Yugoslavia thus has been not the state, not competitors for state power, not even the tribe, but society and the individuals who make it up. While the concept of societal security is not, as yet, very well developed, it has mostly been analyzed in terms of threats to identity within larger political units, such as the European Union.[47] In the case of Yugoslavia, however, the threat to security is not to be found in the dissolution of individual or collective identity in a larger whole but in the complete and total destruction of the carriers of identity, individuals, family, and civil society. Once such a policy is operationalized, moreover, there looks to be no turning back. No one imagines that Serb, Croat, and Muslim will ever live together again as they once did in places such as Sarajevo. In this light, the reluctance of outsiders to intervene in Yugoslavia becomes more understandable, even though it remains inexcusable. To acknowledge that the Hobbesian worlds of Yugoslavia, Rwanda, Somalia, and so on are not out of history but a product of late-twentieth-century civilization—to which all might be vulnerable—would be to look into the very maw of hell.

If our explanation for the war, and its security implications, is correct, what policy response flows from it? Clearly, the security concepts and explanations for the war that guided Western attempts to halt the carnage in Bosnia have been too few and too late; the time for meaningful action was five years ago when states and peaceful, if not civil, society, as such, still existed. But if the security of the social individual in the region is central to the policy response, then it is increasingly imprudent to pretend that implosions such as Yugoslavia are best left alone. The West needs to anticipate, and head off, such collapses, mindful that it is not fully immune from such possibilities. What, then, might we do? The prescriptions offered below are, for better or worse, liberal ones, not because we are convinced that they would necessarily work or that they overcome the contradictions between discourses and the resulting practices that we have discussed here. Rather, we offer them because the present structure of international politics remains organized around territorially exclusivist and nationally defined states. So long as this remains the case, multiethnic societies may fall prey to the logic of state building and ethnic cleansing. Alternatives are clearly necessary; how they will or might emerge is a topic for another paper or book.

Our prescription includes four elements. First, we need to recognize that the creation of a strong civil society and liberal democratic institutions in all states, not just multiethnic ones, is essential to social peace: strong civil societies create multiple identities and interests and promote the politics of interest over the politics of identity. Strong liberal democratic institutions protect both collective and individual rights. Intervention in an ethnically stratified country in order to restore peace will not help that place develop a viable civil society and liberal democratic institutions; rather, it is likely, as in Bosnia, to lead only to further separation. The story told here suggests that the early definition of the conflict as a social conflict—not a civil one, which supposes exclusivist opponents—combined with a continued effort to find a peaceful solution within the federal state while helping to strengthen civil institutions, could have saved lives. Therefore, it is critical that we develop early warning systems that are sensitive to such developing conditions and that can go into operation before a collapse has begun.

Second, we must also find ways to support local and community groups and organizations engaged in various kinds of welfare-providing activities in countries where ethnic stratification exists. Such support is already being provided by many international and governmental agencies, as well as nongovernmental organizations in the developed countries, in issue areas such as environment, development, health, and human rights. These programs must be made larger and more comprehensive without becoming politically intrusive or challenging. It may be that the best way of implementing such programs is through already existing networks of civil society in developed and developing countries.[48]

Third, we need to provide more economic aid to governments in postcommunist multiethnic societies. We need to help these societies develop democratic markets, and not just liberal ones. Under programs of liberalization, governments are finding it necessary to reduce or eliminate programs that, even in a minimal way, address the problem of the maldistribution of resources within societies. In ethnically divided societies, those who have held power, and who often come from a favored ethnic group, are often ahead at the beginning of the race and stay in the lead.[49] Rectifying such economic disparities is essential in order to create a sense of fairness. And this means that some degree of intervention into the allocative operation of markets is necessary. This, in turn, will also help to legitimate newly democratic governments. Such a process will work only if the industrialized states undertake a concerted effort to engage consciously in some degree of global reallocation of resources. This includes many of the usual elements—for example, opening developed-country markets to the goods of developing and post-Socialist countries—but also requires large increases in official development assistance, beyond the current level of around $50 billion a year, to cushion the effects of a transition to markets.

Finally, if Western states continue to put their own security first, as a guide to policy, they need to regard the prescriptions we offer here not as altruistic acts on their part, nor as a way of recycling money through the global economy. Rather, they should be seen as the protection costs necessary for maintaining a relatively stable global system after the Cold War. (Protection costs should not be regarded as shameful; after all, this was an integral part of containing the Soviet Union during the Cold War.) Peace might be divisible, or it might not be. We are better off not running the experiment. In the long run, the costs of keeping the collapsing parts of the world contained, or failing to convince rogue countries that there is more to be gained by cooperation than acquiring nuclear weapons, will be much, much more expensive than making investments now in helping to build democratic markets and nonexclusionist political systems.

NOTES

1. For explorations of the concept of security, see Barry Buzan, *People, States and Fear*, 2nd ed. (Boulder, Colo.: Lynne Rienner, 1991); and Ronnie D. Lipschutz, ed., *On Security* (New York: Columbia University Press, 1995).

2. The classical statement of this notion can be found in Hedley Bull, *The Anarchical Society—A Study of Order in World Politics* (New York: Columbia University Press, 1977). See also Jeremy Larkins and Rick Fawn, eds., *International Society after the Cold War* (London: Macmillan, 1995).

3. Richard Betts, "The Delusion of Impartial Intervention," *Foreign Affairs* 73:6 (November/December 1994), 20–33.

4. A number of useful books have been published about the origins and progress of the wars in Yugoslavia. Among them are Misha Glenny, *The Fall of Yugoslavia: The Third Balkan War* (London: Penguin Books, 1992); Rabia Ali and Lawrence Lifschultz, *Why Bosnia?* (Stony Creek, Conn.: Pamphleteers Press, 1993); Branka Magas, *The Destruction of Yugoslavia: Tracking the Break-up 1980–92* (New York: Verso, 1993); Alex N. Dragnich, *Serbs and Croats: The Struggle in Yugoslavia* (New York: Harcourt Brace Jovanovich, 1992).

5. Glenny, *Fall of Yugoslavia*, 37.

6. Ibid.

7. See, for example, Tony Smith, "In Defense of Intervention," *Foreign Affairs* 73:6 (November/December 1994), 34–46; and David A. Lake, "Powerful Pacifists: Democratic States and War," *American Political Science Review* 86:1 (March 1992), 24–37.

8. *Deutsche Presse Agenteur*, 13 February 1991.

9. On the use of the self-determination card in the two-plus-four talks, see Stephen F. Szabo, *The Diplomacy of German Unification* (New York: St. Martin's Press, 1992). On the effective use of this concept by the Christian Democratic Union (CDU) to win the internal political debate over German unification, see Gregg O. Kvistad, "Challenges to the Party State in Unified Germany," paper presented at the symposium on "Reconstruction and 'Wiederaufbau' in Germany and the United States in Comparative Perspective: 1865, 1945, and 1990," Krefeld, Germany, 20–23 May 1993.

10. John J. Mearsheimer and Robert A. Pape, "The Answer," *The New Republic* 14 June 1993, 22–25, 28.

11. These two reasons for agreement on the first option were given by four senior EC officials interviewed for this project, Brussels, 17–19 May 1993.

12. "Folter und Mord an Polizisten Zivilisten als lebende Schutzschilde" (Torture and murder of civilian police as living shields), FAZ, 5 August 1991, 3. Other examples include, "Bonn handelt nicht vorzeitig" (Bonn does not negotiate in advance), FAZ, 16 December 1991, 1; "Absurditaeten statt Politik" (Absurdities instead of politics), FAZ, 8 December 1991, 1.

13. Anne McElvoy, "Events Lead Genscher Astray," *Times Newspapers Limited*, 7 September 1991.

14. "EC to Recognize Breakaway Yugoslav Republics," *Facts on File—World News Digest*, 19 December 1991, 957 f1.

15. Interview with the authors, Bonn, 26 May 1993.

16. "EC to Recognize Breakaway Yugoslav Republics," *Facts on File*.

17. David Binder, "U.N. Fights Bonn's Embrace of Croatia," *New York Times*, 14 December 1991, 3.

18. Stephen Kinzer, "Germans Follow Own Line on Yugoslav Republics," *New York Times*, 8 December 1991.

19. Joel Havemann, "EC May Soon Recognize Separatist Yugoslav States," *Los Angeles Times*, 16 December 1991, A16.

20. "EC to Recognize Breakaway Yugoslav Republics," *Facts on File*.

21. Throughout 1990 and 1991, the Serbian press across the entire political spectrum issued anti-German reports, claiming, for example, that the Yugoslav army saw Germany as a potential opponent because of its support for Slovenian independence (*Deutsche Presse Agentur* [*DPA*], 4 December 1990), that Germany had twenty military advisers in Croatia and was training ten thousand foreign mercenaries to fight against Serbia (*DPA*, 11 November 1991), and that Germany had wanted to destroy Yugoslavia since 1918 (*DPA*, 18 August 1992). On 23 October 1991, the *DPA* ran a report from the Belgrade newspaper *Politika Express* that quoted Radovan Karadzic, the leader of the Serbs in Bosnia, as saying: "England and France think they can simply sacrifice Serbia in order to stop German expansionism. I remember how it was in 1939, the way Czechoslovakia was sacrificed. But German expansion wasn't stopped then, because expansionism is part of the 'Teutonic Spirit.' If the Western alliance wants to sacrifice Serbia, war will break out as a result of yet another act of German aggression."

22. Cited in Daniel Chirot, "National Liberations and Nationalist Nightmares: The Consequences of the End of Empires in the Twentieth Century," in Beverly Crawford, ed., *Markets, States and Democracy: The Political Economy of Post-Communist Transformation* (Boulder, Colo.: Westview Press, 1995), 43–71.

23. See, for example, Aleksa Djilas, *The Contested Country: Yugoslav Unity and Communist Revolution, 1919–1953* (Cambridge, Mass.: Harvard University Press, 1991); Jim Seroka and Rados Smiljkovic, *Political Organizations in Socialist Yugoslavia* (Durham, N.C.: Duke University Press, 1986), 34.

24. See Dragnich, *Serbs and Croats*, 46.

25. See Stevan K. Pawlowitch, *The Improbable Survivor: Yugoslavia and Its Problems 1918–1988* (London: C. Hurst, 1988); Alex Dragnich, *The First Yugoslavia* (Stanford, Calif.: Hoover Institution Press, 1983); Peter Jambrek, *Development and Social Change in Yugoslavia* (Lexington, Mass.: Lexington Books, 1975); Dusko Doder, "Yugoslavia: New War, Old Hatreds," *Foreign Policy* 91 (Summer 1993), 3–23.

26. Chirot, "National Liberations and Nationalist Nightmares," 9, 27.

27. See, for example, James B. Rule, "Tribalism and the State," *Dissent* (Fall 1992), 519.

28. Interview with the authors, EC Commission official, Brussels, 18 May 1993.

29. The conflict might also reflect postindustrial history, in which case it is also a threat to Europe. This notion is discussed in general terms in Timothy V. Luke, "Sovereignty, States and Security: New World Order or Neo-World Orders?", Adlai Stevenson Program on Global Security, University of California, Santa Cruz, Working Paper 95-1, June 1995.

30. This section draws heavily on Beverly Crawford and Ronnie Lipschutz, "Global Liberalization and the 'New' Ethnic Strife: More Yugoslavias on Order?", Center for German and European Studies, University of California, Berkeley, Working Paper 6.9, March 1995.

31. Political entrepreneurs resemble their economic counterparts in that they seek to maximize their individual interests and, in doing so, have an effect on aggregate interests. The political entrepreneur seeks to maximize political power rather than wealth. Like their economic counterpart, they engage in risk-taking behavior to maximize their returns. For additional comments on political entrepreneurs, see David Laitin, "Hegemony and Religious Conflict: British Imperial Control and Political Cleavages in Yorubaland," in Peter B. Evans, Dietrich Rueschemeyer, and Theda Skocpol, eds., Bringing the State Back In (Cambridge: Cambridge University Press, 1985), 285–316, 302. See also Paul R. Brass, "Ethnicity and Nationality Formation," Ethnicity 3:3 (September 1976), 225–39.

32. See, for example, Benjamin Schwarz, "The Diversity Myth: America's Leading Export," The Atlantic Monthly (May 1995), 57–67.

33. For an excellent discussion of this process in the former Soviet Union, see Philip G. Roeder, "Soviet Federalism and Ethnic Mobilization," World Politics 43:2 (January 1991), 196–232.

34. See Maria N. Todorova, "Language in the Construction of Ethnicity and Nationalism: The Bulgarian Case," Center for German and European Studies, University of California, Berkeley, Working Paper Series 5.5, March 1995.

35. This point is discussed in Georgi Derlugian, "The Tale of Two Resorts: Abkhazia and Ajaria before and since the Soviet Collapse," Center for German and European Studies, University of California, Berkeley, Working Paper 6.2, March 1995.

36. It should be noted that these feelings of Yugoslav nationalism were only shared by the central and regional party elites. The rank-and-file members of the party structure maintained their ethnic prejudices, and their support was bought by the creation of ethnic republics. The central point here is that the ethnic republics of Yugoslavia were never intended to serve as autonomous bases of power; they were meant to serve as pillars to support

the central power of the Communist Party, and they were created as a kind of payment for that rank-and-file support.

37. See Ivo Banac, "The Fearful Asymmetry of War: The Causes and Consequences of Yugoslavia's Demise," *Daedalus* (Spring 1992), 145.

38. Egon Neuberger, "The Transmission of International Disturbances to Yugoslavia," in Egon Neuberger and Laura Tyson, eds., *The Impact of International Economic Disturbances on the Soviet Union and Eastern Europe: Transmission and Responses* (New York: Pergamon Press, 1980), 212–50.

39. The deficit and pressure from the International Monetary Fund (IMF) led to the economic reform of 1965. The reform removed the central government from its role as the provider of investment funds to the republics by creating a network of republic-level banks that were authorized to take primary responsibility for investment finance. Cited in David Dyker, *Yugoslavia: Socialism, Development and Debt* (London: Routledge, 1990). This meant an important power shift from the federal to the regional level. That shift doomed the regional development policy that was supposed to cement loyalty to the federal system. And it weakened the federal government, already hamstrung by the requirement for unanimous consent and the republics' power of veto.

40. Their grievances were backed by the statistics. Despite the fact that Croatia brought in half of all foreign capital as of 1969, it was allocated only about 15 percent of the total credits. Croatia produced most in foreign currency earnings and enterprise profits and received much less through the redistribution process. Dijana Plestina, *Regional Development in Communist Yugoslavia: Success, Failure and Consequences* (Boulder, Colo.: Westview Press, 1992), 89. Furthermore, while Croatia produced 27 percent of Social Product, 30 percent of the industrial output, and 36 percent of the foreign currency earnings, Serbian banks controlled 65 percent of all bank assets in the country.

41. Robin Remington, "Political-Military Relations in Post-Tito Yugoslavia," in Pedro Ramet, ed., *Yugoslavia in the 1980s* (Boulder, Colo.: Westview Press, 1985), 56–76.

42. Under the new constitution, Kosovo and Vojvodina had their own representatives in the federal, state, and party bodies, and they voted against Serbia most of the time. The other five republics had complete sovereignty over their territories. See Aleksa Djilas, "A Profile of Slobodan Milosevic," *Foreign Affairs* 72 (Summer 1993), 82.

43. Finding itself unable to meet its debt obligations, Yugoslavia faced stiff IMF conditionality requirements. The federal government hoped for long-term and extensive debt rescheduling, but without the ability to create a coherent stabilization program, it was turned down. In 1982, Yugoslavia

was forced to accept a far more draconian policy of rescheduling. The IMF imposed a strict emergency package on the Yugoslav economy, greatly reducing the state's scope for policy discretion.

44. Laura Tyson, *The Yugoslav Economic System and Its Performance in the 1970s* (Berkeley, Calif.: Institute of International Studies, 1980).

45. This process is described in detail in Magas, *The Destruction of Yugoslavia*.

46. Jim Seaton, "Social Warfare: The Setting for Stability Operations," paper presented at the International Studies Association annual meeting, Washington, D.C., 29 March–1 April 1994.

47. See, for example, Ole Waever, "Securitization and Desecuritization," in Lipschutz, *On Security*, 46–86.

48. Indeed, such efforts appear to be under way in the contested areas of Croatia; see Dean E. Murphy, "A Sliver of Optimism in War-Weary Croatia," *San Francisco Chronicle*, 26 June 1995, A9 (*LA Times* wire service).

49. See Crawford and Lipschutz, "Globalization."

7

Reimagining Security:
The Metaphors of Proliferation

DAVID MUTIMER

For forty-five years the confrontation between the United States and the Soviet Union has defined the theory and practice of international security. We lived, it was assumed, in a bipolar world, with one pole in Washington and the other in Moscow. These poles oriented our thinking about security, not only between the superpowers or even in Europe, but in the world. Once the confrontation ended and the Cold War was declared over, the custodians of international security policy scrambled to make sense of a world that had lost its bearings. Their theoretical and practical compasses no longer gave direction.

In response to this loss, policy makers and students of international politics have been engaged in rethinking international security. Much of this rethinking has involved identifying interests—usually American interests—and arguing about how policy should be changed to meet those interests now that the Cold War has concluded. More thoughtful contributions to this debate have argued that the end of the Cold War provides the space for an international security agenda that is not dominated by the supposed interests of the United States and its allies, and that is not concerned solely with the leading states' military muscle. However, this very process of rethinking international security is also reshaping the security agenda. It is developing new terms in which security is being thought and is thereby structuring the problems to be tackled and the solutions that will be tried.

The Cold War security environment was thought of in terms of bipolarity and of Cold War. This image defined and ordered security problems—indeed, much of the new thinking in international security is a reaction against the exclusion and marginalization of other concerns by this image. In large part the tasks of definition and ordering are performed by the metaphorical content of the security images. Images comprise a series of metaphors, which shape our understanding of policy problems and thereby inform the solutions that are, and are not, attempted. In this chapter I consider one of the central images that is emerging from the rethinking of international security, the image of proliferation. I will show how this image is being constructed in the discourse and practice of (particularly Western) states. I will also examine the metaphors that are contained in the image and show how they are informing a particular, and flawed, policy response.

REIMAGINING INTERNATIONAL SECURITY

One noted and useful example of the rethinking of international security was provided by Charles Krauthammer, in the journal of record of the U.S. foreign policy elite, *Foreign Affairs,* in early 1991. He was responding directly to the collapse of the bipolar image of the Cold War: "Ever since it became clear that an exhausted Soviet Union was calling off the Cold War, the quest has been on for a new American role in the world. Roles, however, are not invented in the abstract; they are a response to a perceived world structure."[1] The structure Krauthammer perceived following bipolarity was a "unipolar moment." In addition to redefining international security in terms of unipolarity, Krauthammer also gave an early statement of the proliferation problem as it would come to be understood:

> The post-Cold War era is thus perhaps better called the era of weapons of mass destruction. The proliferation of weapons of mass destruction and their means of delivery will constitute the greatest single threat to world security for the rest of our lives. That is what makes a new international order not an imperial dream or a Wilsonian fantasy but a matter of the sheerest prudence. It is slowly dawning on the West that there is a need to establish some new regime to police these weapons and those who brandish them.[2]

Krauthammer's article appeared as a United States-led coalition was using Iraq as a test range for its assortment of weapons of all kinds of destruction. The aftermath of this war in the Gulf saw the

West pick up the pace of their realization that longer-term action was needed to address the proliferation of weapons of mass destruction. In addition, the massive conventional army that Iraq deployed (admittedly to little effect) was seen to tie conventional weapons to this new security agenda. Proliferation thus came to be seen as a wide-ranging problem, encompassing not only the spread of nuclear weapons, but of chemical and biological weapons, as well as the diffusion of conventional arms.

Not only did Krauthammer sound the warning on proliferation, but he also foresaw the elements of a response to this new threat, a response that would be developed by the West in the years following the Gulf War:

> Any solution will have to include three elements: denying, disarming, and defending. First, we will have to develop a new regime, similar to COCOM (Coordinating Committee on Export Controls) to deny yet more high technology to such states. Second, those states that acquire such weapons anyway will have to submit to strict outside control or risk being physically disarmed. A final element must be the development of antiballistic missile and air defense systems to defend against those weapons that do escape Western control or preemption.[3]

Over the next four years, Western states have paid increasing attention to the various problems of proliferation and developed response strategies that can be well characterized as "denying, disarming, and defending."

The first line of attack is a regime based on technology denial. The COCOM was formally dissolved in March 1994, and its members have now joined with most of the states of former Eastern Europe in a new export-control regime for conventional weapons and related technologies. Preliminary agreement was reached in September 1995 among twenty-eight states, and what is being called the Wassenaar Arrangement was formally created in April 1996.[4] More generally, regimes of technology denial are the foundation of the nonproliferation effort. Consider the communiqué of the North Atlantic Council, announcing an "Alliance Policy Framework on Proliferation of Weapons of Mass Destruction" (9 June 1994):

> 3. Current international efforts focus on the prevention of WMD and missile proliferation through a range of international treaties and regimes. . . .[5]

4. The aforementioned treaties are complemented on the supply side by the Nuclear Suppliers Group, the Zangger Committee, the Australia Group and the Missile Technology Control Regime. These regimes should be reinforced through the broadest possible adherence to them and enhancement of their effectiveness.[6]

The creation of the Wassenaar Arrangement means that there are in place technology-denial regimes for the three weapons of mass destruction (nuclear, chemical, and biological), missile-delivery systems, and conventional arms. With the exception of missile systems, there will also be some form of international mechanism addressing the spread of each of these technologies as well, as the United Nations has created a Register of Conventional Arms.

Technology denial is the backbone of the response to proliferation. At least in the case of Iraq, however, attempts have also been made to respond to proliferation through enforced disarmament. On 9 April 1991 the UN Security Council passed Resolution 687, which outlined the forcible disarmament of Iraq. It mandated a Special Commission (UNSCOM) that, together with the International Atomic Energy Agency (IAEA), would oversee the declaration and destruction of the Iraqi chemical, biological, and nuclear weapons holdings and production capabilities, as well as their missile technology.[7] Similarly, through May and June of 1994, North Korea was threatened with international sanction, and possible military conflict with South Korea and the United States, if it did not allow international inspection of its nuclear facilities.

The final element, particularly in the United States, of a security policy to counter proliferation has been the development of military capabilities to defend against what has come to be called the post-proliferation environment. The recent U.S. threats of violence in the case of North Korea are one example of such a military response forming part of the reaction to the problem of proliferation. A second is found in the NATO declaration from which I quoted above:

12. Recent events in Iraq and North Korea have demonstrated that WMD proliferation can occur despite international non-proliferation norms and agreements. As a defensive Alliance, NATO must therefore address the military capabilities needed to discourage WMD proliferation and use, and if necessary, to protect NATO territory, populations and forces.

13. NATO will therefore . . . seek, if necessary, to improve defense capabilities of NATO and its members to protect NATO territory, populations and forces against WMD use, based on assessments of threats (including non-State actors), Allied military doctrine and planning, and Allied military capabilities.[8]

It would seem, then, that it has dawned on the West that proliferation is a serious security problem. Indeed, in January 1992, an unprecedented summit meeting of the UN Security Council declared proliferation—in its new, comprehensive guise—a threat to international peace and security, opening the way for multilateral military action to respond to proliferation, under the terms of the United Nations' Charter:

> The members of the Council underline the need for all member states to fulfil their obligations in relation to arms control and disarmament; to prevent the proliferation in all its aspects of all weapons of mass destruction; to avoid excessive and destabilizing accumulations and transfers of arms, and to resolve peacefully in accordance with the Charter any problems concerning these matters threatening or disrupting the maintenance of regional and global stability. . . .
>   The proliferation of all weapons of mass destruction constitutes a threat to international peace and security. The members of the Council commit themselves to working to prevent the spread of technology related to the research for or production of such weapons and to take appropriate action to that end.[9]

This statement contains all of the key elements of the new image of proliferation in international security: a problem of all forms of weapons of mass destruction and of "excessive and destabilizing" accumulations of conventional arms. This image has been deepened and developed in the pronouncements and practices of (particularly Western) policy makers since the end of the Gulf War.[10] The importance of this new image is reflected in the academic literature on foreign and security problems. I conducted a review of the issues between 1985 and 1994 in five of the leading U.S. foreign policy journals, journals that reflect and inform the policy debate within the United States. This review bears out the contention advanced here that proliferation is a problem enunciated to fill the gap left by the Cold War and catalyzed by the experience in the Gulf. There were only seven articles on the problem between 1985 and the fall

of the Berlin Wall, of which five were concerned with nuclear proliferation. There were nine articles in the year between 1989 and the
Gulf War. In the three years following the end of the Gulf War, there
were fifty-six articles in these journals that were concerned with
proliferation.[11]

In addition to the new image, there is also a clear pattern to the
strategy being employed in response. It is a three-tiered strategy, an-
chored at the global level by formal multilateral nonproliferation
arrangements. At present there are four such arrangements: the Nuclear Non-Proliferation Treaty (NPT), the Chemical Weapons Convention (CWC), the Biological and Toxin Weapons Convention
(BTWC), and the UN Register of Conventional Arms. This leaves only
missile technology (of the identified concerns), without a global
arrangement but only a supplier-control regime, the Missile Technology Control Regime (MTCR).[12] The second tier of the control strategy
is a collection of supplier-control regimes. The MTCR is joined by the
Australia Group, which controls chemical and biological technology,
the Nuclear Suppliers Group (NSG) and the Zangger Committee,
which controls nuclear technology, and the Wassenaar Arrangement,
which is to control conventional and dual-use technology. Finally,
these supplier controls are implemented nationally by export-control
systems.

The international security environment is thus being reimagined.
The image that guided international security policy and scholarship
during the Cold War has given way to a new image centered on
proliferation. This image is informing both policy and academic
debate and is found reflected in the instruments and institutions of
international arms control and security, as well as in the written
record of the academy. What are the implications of this image?
How can we understand the way in which this image informs policy, reshaping instruments, institutions, and even interests? The images of security comprise a number of metaphors that shape our
thinking about problems and solutions; in the present case, the key
metaphors are "proliferation," "stability," and its related metaphor
"balance." In order to consider the role that image plays in international security, it is necessary to appreciate the way in which
metaphors constitute our understandings and thereby inform the
conception we hold of a policy problem, and the solutions we develop to address that problem.

IMAGES, METAPHORS, AND UNDERSTANDINGS

Scott Sagan has recently argued that the dominant approach to the proliferation problem within the academic community has been rooted in rational deterrence theory, based on an "assumption that states behave in a basically rational manner, pursuing their interests according to expected-utility theory."[13] There are a variety of problems with a theory based on the maximization of expected utility as a basis for a theory of political action. Sagan proposed to use organization theory as a corrective to some of these problems. This theory introduces two limitations on rational choice: "large organizations function within a severely 'bounded' form of rationality" and "have multiple conflicting goals and the process by which objectives are chosen and pursued is intensely political."[14] In other words, Sagan recognizes that the interests on the basis of which actors choose are not preconstituted as rational deterrence theory supposes. Ned Lebow and Janice Stein broaden this critique beyond the organizational:

> Neither theories of deterrence nor rational choice say anything about the all-important preferences that shape leaders' calculations. Achen and Snidal correctly observe that deterrence theory assumes exogenously given preferences and choice options. It begs the question of how preferences are formed. Empirical analyses of decision making suggest that individuals often identify their preferences and options in the course of formulating and reformulating a problem.[15]

The problem can be stated in general terms: rational choice theory assumes: (a) a set of preconstituted utilities (or interests), and (b) a preconstituted problem. Lebow and Stein, along with Sagan's organizational corrective, draw attention to the first but only hint at the second. The argument I am advancing is that the problem, interests, and possible solutions are shaped, at least in part, metaphorically. Lebow and Stein's "formulation and reformulation of a problem" involves adducing and refining an image. A problem is not presented to policy makers fully formed but is, rather, constituted by actors in their (discursive) practices. This practically constituted image of a security problem shapes the interests states have at stake in that problem, and the forms of solution that can be addressed to resolve it. Central to this function of shaping interests and responses is the metaphorical character of the image so constituted. To understand how an image shapes interest and policy it is first necessary to consider how metaphor shapes understanding.

Paul Chilton has provided a useful example of the role of metaphor in shaping understandings in international politics, particularly concerning the Cold War discourses around nuclear weapons and the relationship of the West to the Soviet Union. In doing so, he illustrates how the metaphor naturalizes a policy, and the apparent interests underlying it—in this case, the central security policy of Cold War Europe. Chilton works with the example of a fairly typical speech from the foreign secretary of the United Kingdom, John Nott. Nott used a metaphor of "a dying giant" to argue that there is a possibility of the Soviet Union's attacking Western Europe. He did so in order to defend the "peace through strength" policy of then Prime Minister Margaret Thatcher and her American mentor Ronald Reagan. As Chilton notes, "what Nott wants to do, it seems, is to assert the likelihood of Russia attacking Europe." On the basis of such an assertion, "proven" through the analogical reasoning of metaphor, the government can justify a policy of military hostility to insure against the lashing out of a dying giant.[16]

Chilton argues that policy makers address problems by means of what I have called "images"[17]—that is, the student or policy maker constructs a metaphorical image of problem, an issue, or even other actors.[18] This image relates the thing being imagined to another, in terms of which the first is understood. These images comprise metaphors, which are used to structure and support our understanding of a problem, and therefore our response to that problem. In Chilton's example, the key relationship is the support the image and its metaphors provide for preexisting policy. His political concern is with the bellicose nuclear strategy pursued by the Western Alliance, and the consequent danger of nuclear war that the governments foist on the people of Europe and North America through the metaphors supporting the image of the Soviet Union. However, the general relationships—between the image of a policy problem, the condition of the problem itself, and the policy solution to that problem—allow the ideas he develops to be given wider scope than Chilton provides. The metaphors entailed by a given image do more than simply support a policy choice; they structure the way in which the image holder can think about a problem and so shape that choice in the first place.

Chilton's use of metaphor is rooted in a prior argument, advanced by George Lakoff and Mark Johnson. By considering their arguments directly, we can see how metaphor shapes problems and solutions in international politics, as in other areas of our lives. The common understanding of metaphor is that it is a literary tool, allowing an author to provide descriptive depth and allegorical commentary by means of establishing a relationship between two separate objects or ideas. Lakoff and Johnson argue that metaphor is much more than this, that it is absolutely fundamental to the way in which people understand and live in the world around them: *"The essence of metaphor is understanding and experiencing one kind of thing in terms of another."*[19] They begin with an example of the way in which the concept of argument is understood in our society, suggesting that we understand argument in terms of warfare. To illustrate, they provide examples from our everyday language:

ARGUMENT IS WAR

>Your claims are *indefensible.*
>He *attacked every weak point* in my argument.
>His criticisms were *right on target.*
>I *demolished* his argument.
>I've never *won* an argument with him.
>You disagree? Okay, *shoot!*
>If you use that *strategy,* he'll *wipe you out.*
>He *shot down* all of my arguments.[20]

It is more, however, than simply using the language of war to talk about argument. Rather, our understanding of what argument is, and the way in which we then set about to argue, is in part—indeed in large part—structured by the military metaphor:

>It is not that arguments are a subspecies of war. Arguments and wars are different kinds of things—verbal discourse and armed conflict— and the actions performed are different kinds of actions. But ARGU-MENT is partially structured, understood, performed, and talked about in terms of WAR. The concept is metaphorically structured, the activity is metaphorically structured, and, consequently, the language is metaphorically structured.[21]

It would be surprising if we lived our lives, understood our most basic activities and practices, in terms of metaphor and then abandoned metaphoric reasoning and understanding at the level of social and political action. Indeed, if we take Lakoff and Johnson's arguments seriously, this is not possible, as they are making a case for metaphor as essential to human cognitive process. This makes impossible the rational choice claim that there are preconstituted state interests, or even the organizational claim that there are preconstituted, if competing, intraorganizational interests. Rather, the formulating and reformulating of a problem, to which Lebow and Stein refer, involves the formation of the metaphorical image of a problem, only in terms of which interests and policies can then be located.

It is worth examining in more detail how the images and the metaphors they comprise accomplish this structuring of action. The image, and the metaphors that are contained within that image, frame a problem in a particular way so as to highlight certain possibilities while precluding others. Lakoff and Johnson argue that:

> Every description will highlight, downplay, and hide—for example:
> I've invited a sexy blonde to our dinner party.
> I've invited a renowned cellist to our dinner party.
> I've invited a Marxist to our dinner party.
> I've invited a lesbian to our dinner party.
> Though the same person may fit all of these descriptions, each description highlights different aspects of the person. Describing someone who you know has all of these properties as "a sexy blonde" is to downplay the fact that she is a renowned cellist and a Marxist and to hide her lesbianism.[22]

The description, given to another guest, forms a key part of the image of his (for the sake of argument, I will assume a heterosexual male) fellow guest. Indeed, not having any other image on the basis of which to frame behavior toward this woman, he will base his actions on the image created by that description. It seems patently obvious that a man will behave differently to each of the people captured by the four descriptions. The image of the sexy blonde privileges certain behavior—behavior that will be downplayed, if not hidden outright, by the image of a lesbian. Our male guest is also likely to form very different conversational strategies to talk with a renowned cellist and with a Marxist. Similarly, the interests he will define in the relationship that evening will be somewhat different in response to an image of sexy blonde and an image of lesbian.

In a similar way, the characterization of the problem of proliferation highlights certain characteristics of the phenomenon, while downplaying and hiding others. That image contains three key metaphors: "proliferation," "stability," and "balance." As such, the image highlights the source-spread-recipient nature of the process of arms production and distribution. At the same time, it downplays the structural nature of the arms production and transfer system that bind the suppliers and recipients to each other, and it hides the fact that weapons and related technologies are procured for a variety of factors related to external military threat, internal regime support, and economic development.[23] I will address these features of the problem in more detail below. What is important at this point is to see that the image and the metaphors it entails privilege a certain set of policy responses—those that address the "spread" of technology highlighted by the image—while denying a place to others: policies, for instance, that would seek to address the problems of economic development, which may spur the creation of an arms industry.

Clearly, there is a difference between the image of an international problem, which draws in large part on the understandings of other international problems, and the root metaphors that are Lakoff and Johnson's focus. They speak of the "grounding" of our conceptual system in terms of simple elements of our everyday lives which we can experience directly without social mediation. Thus, for example, spatial metaphors of "up" and "down," "in" and "out" are based on our experiences of the world: we have an inside and an outside, we stand erect, we sleep lying down and rise when we awake.[24] Lakoff and Johnson have been criticized for a biological bias, and while they clearly want to ground metaphors in part in our unmediated physiological experience of the world, they also allow for social rather than biological grounding: "In other words, these 'natural' kinds of experience are products of human nature. Some may be universal, while others will vary from culture to culture."[25] Thus, Lakoff and Johnson provide an account of metaphor at the very basic level of comprehension but allow for much wider application in providing for cultural as well as physical experience to serve as a grounding for those metaphors.

The inclusion of social experience, however, does not take us far enough to serve my purposes in this discussion. My concern is with the images and metaphors that structure policy in the first instance. These obtain in discourses of policy makers, and of the policy community with which those in government interact.[26] Because the important discourse is that of a policy community, the relevant images can be grounded in both the metaphors of everyday experience and in other policy images that are common to the community as a whole. Moreover, the entailments of images and metaphors—the associations that allow metaphors to relate one kind of thing to another—that are drawn from everyday experience will grow to include other policy references, in addition to their everyday entailments. For example, balance is a concept with which we all live, and so the use of "balance" as a metaphor evokes certain common understandings. For those of us engaged in International Relations, however, balance also entails understandings associated with "strategic balances" and the "balance of power."

For this reason, we can talk of policy images in terms of a two-step image-creation process. The first step is the appropriation of a concept from its everyday meaning for application to policy. Hence, "proliferation" is appropriated from biology, where it refers to the outward spread of cells, or of organisms, by means of the reproduction of its parts—in particular, to the uncontrolled outward spread of cancer cells. Similarly, stability and its related concept balance are appropriated from our everyday experience to discuss the relations among states. Indeed, balance and stability can be seen ultimately to be grounded in the sort of unmediated biological experiences that interest Lakoff and Johnson. In standing erect, humans will see a great virtue in balance, providing them with stability. Instability, leading to a loss of balance, can cause injury or death. From these primary concerns, the metaphors of "stability" and "balance" have entered our common conceptual universe. Sanity is represented in terms of balance and stability ("she has a balanced mind" "he became unstable"), as is personality. From these root metaphorical understandings, the concepts of balance and stability are brought into the conceptual universe of students of International Relations to provide metaphors for relations among states. Indeed, these two are among the dominant metaphors of our discipline.

The second step of the process is the one with which I am most concerned. It is the use of these metaphors, "proliferation," "stability," and "balance," as they are embedded in the understandings of policy makers, to reimagine international security following the end of the Cold War, and the Gulf War of 1990–91. At this point, the metaphors are applied to the security problems of the Third World, not directly from their biological or experiential referents, but from their embedding in the experience of the Cold War international system, although this is not to say that the first-step entailments are not also present at the second step. The reimagination of international security, following the end of the Cold War, largely involves this second-step appropriation of metaphorical concepts. The implication of this, of course, is that the understandings of the Cold War will tend to re-create the practices of the Cold War as they are used to imagine the new security environment. We can see already the bipolar division between East and West beginning to be re-formed around North and South.

Finally, to understand my claim that the process detailed above is indeed a reimagining, consider the role of the superpowers in creating the problem now identified as proliferation. The huge regional arsenals (now called destabilizing accumulations) were in large part the creation of the two superpowers' providing arms to their friends and allies in different regional conflicts—"proxies," in the language of the Cold War. The Middle East is today the region of primary concern, and yet here the states that are the most problematic are the ones armed by the United States and the Soviet Union—Israel, Egypt, Syria, Iraq, and Iran.[27] It is only with the breakdown of this conceptual system that proliferation was broadened beyond the narrow field of nuclear weapons to encompass nuclear, chemical, and biological weapons, and their missile-delivery systems, as well as destabilizing accumulations of advanced conventional weapons.

This discussion provides a framework for the examination of the *proliferation* image. The centrality of that image to the contemporary international security agenda is indicated by President Bill Clinton's first address to the UN General Assembly in the fall of 1993: "I have made non-proliferation one of our nation's highest priorities. We intend to weave it more deeply into the fabric of all our relationships with the world's nations and institutions." The three metaphors of the proliferation image ("proliferation," "stability," and "balance") were neatly joined together in a recent article on proliferation from the U.S. Army Journal, *Parameters*: "The policy community uses the term 'proliferation' to define a wide array of activities regarding the spread of weapon technologies. Key to the definition is the notion that *proliferation destabilizes* the *balance* of power within a region."[28] I can now examine each of these metaphors to show what features they highlight, downplay, and hide in their formation of the *proliferation* image, and how they thereby both privilege and preclude certain policy solutions.

THE METAPHORS OF PROLIFERATION

The image of *proliferation* as an international security problem is based on a pair of unrelated metaphors. It develops a unique image by joining together the metaphors of "proliferation" with those of "stability" and "balance."

"Proliferation"

The "proliferation" metaphor, which is at the root of the *proliferation* image, comes to this image in the two-step process I outlined above. The original meanings of proliferation, the other in terms of which we begin to conceptualize and understand the emergence of nuclear power and nuclear weapons, is grounded in biology. The *Oxford English Dictionary* (OED) provides the following primary definitions for the three related words—proliferation, proliferate, and proliferous:

> Proliferation: the formation or development of cells by budding or division.
> Proliferate: to reproduce by proliferation; to grow by multiplication of elementary parts.
> Proliferous: producing offspring; procreative; prolific.

The origin of the term *proliferation* is in human and animal reproduction, indicated by the third OED definition producing offspring. However, in the discipline of biology, the term is now most commonly used to refer to the reproduction of cells; indeed, it is synonymous with cell division and cell growth. To a biologist, then, *proliferation* refers to the full range of organic reproduction, driven by cell proliferation, including budding yeasts and sexually reproducing humans. There is also a close connection with excessive multiplication of the elementary parts. Notice that the definitions from the OED conclude with prolific—that is, proliferation is rarely used to refer to small-scale reproduction. (Even "normal" cell reproduction in humans, from a single-cell zygote to an adult, yields on the average 10^{13} cells!) In the brief survey of the cell-proliferation literature I conducted to determine its nature, I found that the term is most often used in connection with cancer research, as cancer involves cells escaping the mechanisms that control their proliferation.

The connection between cell proliferation and cancer is both important and telling. Cell proliferation is a harmless, natural process—indeed, it is absolutely essential to life as we know it. This proliferation is managed by a series of biological control mechanisms, which serve to regulate the proliferation of cells so that they faithfully reproduce what is coded into their genetic material. Once these mechanisms fail, and the cells proliferate without control, cancers, often deadly to the organism as a whole, result. As Andrew Murray and Tim Hunt introduce the study of cell proliferation, "without knowing the checks and balances that normally ensure orderly cell division, we cannot devise effective strategies to combat the uncontrolled cell divisions of the cancers that will kill one in six of us."[29] Proliferation, in its base biological meaning, refers to an autonomous process of growth and outward spread, internally driven but externally controlled. Danger arises when the controls fail and the natural proliferation of cells produces excessive reproduction.

The first step of the adoption of *proliferation* as a metaphor for international security involved applying the term to the development of nuclear technology after the discovery of controlled fission in the United States' Manhattan Project. The United States' nuclear program represented the source cell or organism from which the technology would spread. Such spread was seen as a natural process, and so scholars confidently predicted that there would be thirty or forty nuclear powers by 1980. Such a condition was considered dangerous, and undesirable, and so attempts were made to establish external controls on the proliferation of nuclear weapons. These attempts resulted in the Non-Proliferation Treaty (NPT) of 1970, which remains the principal mechanism of proliferation control. The development of nuclear technology was thus imagined in terms of the "proliferation" metaphor. The first question to be asked is, what are the implications of this image, with its understandings of autonomy, spread, and external control, for the policy response to the development of nuclear technology? There are two crucial entailments of the "proliferation" metaphor as applied to nuclear weapons.

The first entailment is the image of a spread outward from a point or source. Cell division begins with a single or source cell and spreads outward from there—in the case of a cancer, both to produce a single tumor and to create a number of separate tumors throughout the host body. Similarly, the problem of proliferation is one of a source or sources proliferating, that is, reproducing itself by supplying the necessary technology to a new site of technological application. This image highlights the transmission process from source to recipient. Hence, the dominant response to nuclear proliferation has been the creation of supplier groups—the Zangger Committee and the Nuclear Suppliers Group (NSG)—which seek to control the spread of nuclear technology. Recall NATO's "Alliance Policy Framework":

> 3. Current international efforts focus on the prevention of WMD and missile proliferation through a range of international treaties and regimes. . . .
> 4. The aforementioned treaties are complemented on the supply side by the Nuclear Suppliers Group, the Zangger Committee, the Australia Group and the Missile Technology Control Regime. . . .[30]

In other words, they attempt to provide "the checks and balances that normally ensure orderly" transfer and prevent the spread of nuclear technology resulting in the "cancer" of weapons proliferation. The image is repeated even in the more extreme proposals for policy. For example, former Canadian Prime Minister Pierre Trudeau proposed a scheme to the United Nations Special Session on Disarmament for preventing the spread of weapons. This scheme included two measures currently under consideration at the Conference on Disarmament: a Comprehensive Test Ban Treaty and a Cutoff of Fissile Material Production. Trudeau's plan was known as the "suffocation proposal"—firmly in keeping with the biological referent of proliferation. To stop, rather than control, reproduction by organisms, you need to suffocate the progenitors.

The second entailment of the "proliferation" metaphor for the problem of nuclear weapons spread is an extreme technological bias. Biological proliferation is an internally driven phenomenon, and so the metaphor of "proliferation" applied to the development of nuclear technology highlights the autonomous spread of that technology, and its problematic weapons variant. As Frank Barnaby writes in a recent work, "a country with a nuclear power programme will inevitably acquire the technical knowledge and expertise, and will accumulate the fissile material, necessary to produce nuclear weapons."[31] In fact, the text from which this is drawn presents an interesting example of the autonomy of the "proliferation" metaphor. The book is titled *How Nuclear Weapons Spread: Nuclear-Weapon Proliferation in the 1990s*. Notice that the weapons themselves spread; they are not spread by an external agent of some form—say, a human being or political institution. Under most circumstances, such a title would be unnoticed, for as Lakoff and Johnson argue, the metaphors are so deeply engrained in our conceptual system that they are not recognized as being metaphorical.

This metaphor, by highlighting the technological and autonomous aspects of a process of spread, downplays or even hides important aspects of the relationship of nuclear weapons to international security. To begin with, the metaphor hides the fact that nuclear weapons do not spread but are spread—and, in fact, are spread largely by the Western states. Second, the image downplays, to the point of hiding, any of the political, social, economic, and structural factors that tend to drive states and other actors both to supply and to acquire nuclear weapons. Finally, the image downplays the politics of security and threat, naturalizing the security dilemma to the point that it is considered an automatic dynamic. The image of *proliferation* thus privileges a technical, apolitical policy by casting the problem as a technical, apolitical one. Consider one of the most important statements in the construction of proliferation as a policy problem, U.S. President George Bush's speech to the Air Force Academy on 29 May 1991:

> Nowhere are the dangers of weapons proliferation more urgent than in the Middle East.
>
> After consulting with governments in the region and elsewhere about how to slow and then reverse the buildup of unnecessary and destabilizing weapons, I am today proposing a Middle East arms control initiative. It features supplier guidelines on conventional arms exports; barriers to exports that contribute to weapons of mass destruction; a freeze now, and later a ban on surface-to-surface missiles in the region; and a ban on production of nuclear weapons material.[32]

The focus of this initiative is entirely technological: controls on the movement of technology outward from their sources, and restrictions on that technology's usages in the region.

Such a technologically focused policy is almost doomed to fail, however, for it downplays and hides the very concerns that motivate the agents of the process. Iraq was driven to acquire nuclear weapons, even in the face of NPT commitments, and so employed technology that is considered so outdated that it is no longer tightly controlled. This simply does not fit with the NPT-NSG-Zangger Committee approach. In addition, in order to gain the necessary material, the Iraqis needed access to external technology. Such technology was acquired by human agents acting for the Iraqi state and was acquired from other agents, who had their own motivational interests to provide the necessary technology. The technology does not spread through some autonomous process akin to that causing a zygote to become a person, but, rather, it is spread, and so the agents involved are able to sidestep the technologically focused control efforts.

The second step of this process, reimagining international security in terms of proliferation following the end of the Cold War, adopts the policy entailments along with the underlying biological imagery. By using the "proliferation" metaphor now to address biological and chemical weapons, missile technology, and even conventional weapons, the international community is replicating the problematic policy solutions that highlight technology and hide politics and agency. Thus, the NPT and its supplier groups are joined by the Chemical Weapons Convention and the Australia Group, a supplier group that also oversees export controls on both chemical and biological weapons technology. Missile technology is controlled by the Missile Technology Control Regime. Even conventional arms, the ones we might expect to be most closely related to understandings of politics, are conceived in terms of "excessive and destabilizing accumulations." Once more, it is the weapons themselves, rather than the political agents acquiring and using them, that are the lexical focus of discussions of conventional arms. What is ignored by this policy approach is any suggestion that there are political interests or motivations at work, which may cause human institutions to act in ways that promote insecurity (which, in other words, destabilize). A good part of the reason for this lack of understanding is that the image of the problem is one that downplays, and even hides, the involvement of the politics of human agency in both the acts of supply and acquisition.

"Stability" and "Balance"

The two related terms *stability* and *balance* are so firmly seated in the language of international relations that their metaphorical nature is seldom remembered. Thus, the use of the two in imagining the new international security agenda around *proliferation* tends to draw more explicitly on the entailments that have been generated by that disciplinary use. It is, nevertheless, still useful to remember the first step of the two-step process of metaphor creation—the understanding of international politics in terms of our common experiences of balance and stability.

While the metaphor of "proliferation" is grounded in processes that are most basic to human life, the metaphors of "stability" and "balance" are probably more firmly rooted in most people's common experiences. Both terms are used widely in the metaphors of our everyday lives, and wherever they occur, value is placed on maintaining stability and balance. Thus, we speak of people being "well balanced" or of having "stable personalities." Teams are most successful if they have a "balanced" attack, and people look for "stable" employment and to "balance" their bank accounts. Given the positive connotations of stability and balance, it should not be surprising that their use as metaphors of international politics connotes a normative commitment to the creation and maintenance of stable and balanced orders.

The balance of power is generally used to refer to the system of interstate relations created in Europe following the defeat of Napoleon.[33] The mechanism of power balancing—stabilizing relations among states by maintaining power equivalences—was progressively naturalized by theorists of International Relations. Hedley Bull argues that both an objective and subjective balance are necessary for a balance of power to operate. Nevertheless, he clearly places primacy on the objective conditions of the balance: "But if the subjective element of belief in it is necessary for the existence of a balance of power, it is not sufficient. . . . A balance of power that rests not on the actual will and capacity of one state to withstand the assaults of another, but merely on bluff and appearances, is likely to be fragile and impermanent."[34] This naturalization of the balance of power reached its zenith with Kenneth Waltz's *Theory of International Politics:*

The theory, then, is built up from the assumed motivations of states and the actions that correspond to them. It describes the constraints that arise from the system that those actions produce, and it indicates the expected outcome: namely, the formation of balances of power. Balance-of-power theory is microtheory precisely in the economist's sense. The system, like a market in economics, is made by the actions and interactions of its units, and the theory is based on assumptions about their behavior.[35]

Thus, the balance of power is not only a desired outcome; in keeping with the normative commitment of people to balance and stability, power balancing is the natural outcome of the behavior of states. There is thus strong incentive to maintain balances and to avoid anything that could destabilize them. Throughout the Cold War, the military relationship between the superpowers in particular was therefore examined in minute detail to avoid "instabilities"—either "arms race instabilities" or "crisis instabilities."

The first-step adoption of the metaphors of "stability" and "balance" to think about International Relations produced the imagination of the Cold War in terms of a balance of power and of the need to maintain that balance by avoiding instabilities. The second-step use of these metaphors has involved their adoption from the Cold War security image to apply to the new image of *proliferation*. A key element of this image is a definition of the problem posed by proliferation in terms of its effects on the stability of (regional) balances of power. This understanding is reflected in most statements on the problems of proliferation. Consider, for example, the statement of the permanent five members of the Security Council, meeting in 1991 to "review issues related to conventional arms transfers and to the non-proliferation of weapons of mass destruction":

> [They] noted with concern the dangers associated with the excessive buildup of military capabilities, and confirmed they could not transfer conventional weapons in circumstances which would undermine stability. They also noted the threats to peace and stability posed by the proliferation of nuclear weapons, chemical and biological weapons, and missiles, and undertook to seek effective measures of non-proliferation and arms control in a fair, reasonable, comprehensive and balanced manner on a global as well as a regional basis.[36]

This second step, drawing the metaphors of "stability" and "balance" into our understanding of *proliferation,* involves a number of entailments, derived both from the metaphors' initial grounding and from the specific meanings of the Cold War. The first entailment of these metaphors is that they highlight dyadic relationships. Our common experience with balancing is that of two masses offsetting one another, rendered visually by the classic scale or balance. Two masses—or in the case of International Relations, two states—offset each other in a stable fashion. The introduction of a third mass greatly complicates the problem of balancing.[37] Indeed, Waltz has raised the dyadic balance to the status of law, arguing that the ideal— that is, the most stable—balance is that between two roughly equivalent states: "International politics is necessarily a small-number system. The advantages of having a few more great powers is at best slight. We have found instead that the advantages of subtracting a few and arriving at two are decisive."[38]

During the Cold War, the dyadic understandings of "balance" were reasonably appropriate to the superpower confrontation, as there were two roughly equivalent superpowers anchoring two roughly equivalent alliances. Even then, however, the image downplayed and hid those outside the central balance, rendering non-European states or regions either as invisible or as mere appendages to the superpower confrontation. To imagine third parties as autonomous would have been to introduce problematic third- and higher-order masses into the metaphorical balance. The regional security systems, however, that are today of greatest *proliferation* concern to those (mainly in the North and West) who use the image simply do not resolve themselves into dyads. They are neither dominated by the confrontation of two overpowering opponents, nor do they divide into two allied groupings. Nevertheless, the metaphor of "balance" leads to the characterization of these regions in dyadic terms.

In the Middle East, for example, the relationships among the various states are complex, and yet even accounting for these varied relations misses the sub- and transnational dimensions of the politics of Middle Eastern security. For instance, the place of the Kurds in Iraq, and their relations to the Kurds in both Iran and Turkey, is an important element of the security relationship in the eastern Middle East, and was centrally involved in both Gulf Wars of the past fifteen years.[39] Similarly, the Israeli relationship with the Palestinians involves complex relations among Palestinians living in Israel, Jews living in Palestine, Palestinians in neighboring countries, and those countries' states. Despite this complexity, the power of the dyadic entailment shapes discussions of the region. The most prevalent dyadic construction, of course, is that which characterizes the region's complexities as the Arab-Israeli conflict. Yet the two most recent wars in the region involved an Arab state's army fighting one of another Muslim (although not Arab) state, and a broad coalition destroying an Arab state—a coalition that included both Arab states and, to all intents and purposes, Israel.

The same problems arise in other regions of concern. South Asia is, at its most simple, an intricate dance among India, Pakistan, and the People's Republic of China—a construction which ignores the Kashmiris, Tamils, and Sri Lankans. Despite the centrality of the triad of powers, there is a strong tendency to speak of the region in terms of the dyadic Indo-Pakistani relationship. Indeed, this tendency can be seen in part to have resulted in the growth of India's arsenal:

> The Indian military buildup may also be explained by the various decision-makers' political image of the state in international society. One of the problems with Indian leaders and policy-makers since the death of Prime Minister Jawaharal Nehru in 1964, is the feeling that India does not get enough respect, especially compared to China, with which it sees itself as essentially equal in size, population and economic development. Instead, India is constantly equated with Pakistan, a nation at one time one-fifth its size in population and capabilities, and only one-eighth its size since the creation of Bangladesh in December 1971.[40]

Similarly, in the North Pacific, while the relationship between North and South Korea is of central importance, the security dynamic cannot be understood outside the context of the relations among these two states and China, Japan, and the United States, at the very least. These five do not break into two neat groupings, and yet the dyadic North-against-South representation of the problem is common.

A second important entailment of the "stability" and "balance" metaphors is that they highlight numerical capabilities, while downplaying qualitative capabilities, and hiding other aspects of security—even aspects of the military other than equipment. This entailment is rooted both in the experiential basis of the metaphors and in their use during the Cold War. Balance is by and large a quantitative, not qualitative characteristic—on a scale, a kilo of feathers will balance a kilo of lead. In particular, the accounting of numbers of various kinds (although notably money), involves the metaphor of "balance." Thus it should not be surprising that the application of the balance metaphor to the relationships of arms leads to a focus on numerical capabilities. The experience of superpower arms negotiation was in large measure guided by attempts to achieve "essential equivalences"—in the number of launchers, the number of warheads, the throw weight of missiles, or the number of tanks.

What gets downplayed by the numerical entailment of these metaphors is the variation in capability among different weapons and weapon systems. This can be seen in the present proliferation-control systems. The Missile Technology Control Regime identifies technologies of concern by range and payload, entirely ignoring the reliability of the weapons, and even their accuracy (which can generally be well measured)—in other words, ignoring most of what determines whether a weapon will be delivered on target by a given missile. Similarly, the UN Register of Conventional Arms records weapons in seven categories, so that, for example, all tanks are counted together. Thus, in the first reporting cycle, the United Kingdom included several pieces of obsolete equipment that were transferred for display in museums. The comments that explain to the register's users that these entries are museum pieces were purely voluntary. For example, Britain reported two exports of tanks. Six tanks were sent to Switzerland and were marked "obsolete equipment for museums," while twenty-five were reported sent to Nigeria. Nothing more than the fact that twenty-five tanks were sent was reported by Britain, and so the character of these weapons is still formally opaque.[41]

While it is unfortunate that the numerical entailment of the "balance" metaphor downplays the quality of arms, it is much more problematic that it hides entirely aspects of the security problem other than arms—whether military doctrine and policy, or the more general politics of security.[42] Indeed, the entailments of "stability" and "balance" in this context tend to reinforce the autonomous, technological character of the problem that is entailed by the "proliferation" metaphor. Technology "spreads" through some natural process. We can count the occurrence of this spread so that we know where the technology is accumulating. We may even be able to control this autonomous process. However, it is these accumulations, if we do not prevent them, that can then upset balances; in the words of UN General Assembly Resolution 46/36L, which created the arms register, "excessive and destabilizing arms build-ups pose a threat to national, regional and international security."

There is a third, and rather ironic, entailment to the "stability" and "balance" metaphors—they can lead to the promotion of the spread of nuclear weapons to a greater number of states. The logic of the balance between the superpowers, it has been argued, is that mutually assured destruction with nuclear weapons introduces a caution conducive to stability. If the metaphors of the Cold War are adopted to imagine the new international security environment, there seems to be little way to escape the conclusions of this argument—that nuclear weapons can be stabilizers. Indeed, it has led John Mearsheimer to argue:

> If complete Soviet withdrawal from Eastern Europe proves unavoidable, the West faces the question of how to maintain peace in a multipolar Europe. Three policy prescriptions are in order.
>
> First, *the United States should encourage the limited and carefully managed proliferation of nuclear weapons in Europe.* The best hope for avoiding war in post-Cold War Europe is nuclear deterrence; hence some nuclear proliferation is necessary to compensate for the withdrawal of the Soviet and American nuclear arsenals from Central Europe.[43]

Mearsheimer suggests providing nuclear arms to Germany as part of the "managed proliferation" of nuclear weapons in Europe. On this and other points Mearsheimer's argument has been widely, and justifiably, attacked. But what is interesting about it is the way in which it makes the entailments of the "stability" and "balance" metaphors so clear. What is important is to assure that the numbers of weapons are distributed so that the balance among them is stable—regardless of who holds the weapons. The problems of history and politics that would be raised by German nuclear weapons are blithely ignored because the metaphors informing Mearsheimer's conceptualization hide them entirely. Most of us are sufficiently sensitive to these problems so that Mearsheimer's argument is jarringly uncomfortable. The problem persists in all uses of the *proliferation* image, and yet it is only when the problems are as dramatic as in this case that the implications of the image are widely rejected.

In the title of his article "Back to the Future: Instability in Europe after the Cold War," Mearsheimer also indicates the final entailment of the "stability" and "balance" metaphors—they are inherently conservative. It is not an accident that it was a conservative alliance facing a revolutionary challenge that formulated the practice we now call the balance of power. Nor is it an accident that the changes in Eastern Europe, while welcomed in the West on democratic grounds, were feared for their capability to introduce instability.[44] When a balance is stable, an asymmetrical alteration to either side introduces instability. Thus, once a stable balance is achieved, the metaphor highlights the importance of the maintenance of the status quo.

The conservative bias of the metaphors is problematic, even when considered solely in terms of arms control. The goal of policy makers seems clearly to be the reduction of weapons and their related technologies—at least in the arsenals of others! The image, however, that is informing the policy response to the problem provides no support for reduction once a stable balance is achieved. There can be no guarantee that any reduction in arsenals, even a symmetrical reduction, would produce a similarly stable balance at the lower levels of arms. Indeed, building on the received wisdom of the Cold War, there might even be a case to be made for high levels of arms, as a balance at high levels is more resistant to small changes—that is, it is more stable.

There is, of course, a more politically problematic result of the conservative entailment of "stability" and "balance." The emphasis on stability hides the struggles of the oppressed and the security concerns of any other than the regime controlling the state. Change introduces the possibility of upsetting a balance, and as stability is so highly valued, change of any kind is to be opposed. It is for this reason that we should not be surprised that the balance of power was devised by the defenders of the monarchical order in the face of the Napoleonic challenge. The conservative nature of the stress on stability can be seen in the reaction of the West in general, and the United States in particular, to the changes in Eastern Europe. As both the Soviet Union and the Yugoslavian federations fell apart, the U.S.

position was to fight to maintain the status quo, in the interests of stability.[45]

This conclusion, that security in the present international system is politically conservative, is not a new one. Indeed, the essays in this volume are, in many ways, predicated on the recognition of the problems posed by the narrow and conservative nature of international security as it is commonly understood. What I have hoped to show is that this bias is an entailment of the metaphorical images we use to construct the problems in the first place. As such, it serves to naturalize a particular set of relations of power and interest, privileging those who are able to set the metaphorical agenda, and render invisible the political basis of their claims.

THE ASSEMBLED IMAGE

The image of *proliferation* knits together the metaphors of "proliferation," "stability," and "balance" to shape the policy responses of the international community. The metaphors have certain entailments that serve to highlight, downplay, and hide aspects of the security environment. Thus, the policy responses that are being developed address primarily those aspects highlighted, while ignoring those downplayed and hidden. The image is of an autonomously driven process of spread, outward from a particular source or sources. It is an apolitical image that strongly highlights technology, capability, and gross accounts of number. As such, it is an image that masks the political interests of those supporting the present structure of proliferation control—a structure that strongly reflects this image and its entailments.

To begin with, the control efforts are classified by the technology of concern. Thus, there are global instruments for controlling the spread of nuclear, chemical, and biological weapons, and for registering transfers of conventional arms. There is no global instrument for the control of the spread of missile technology, but the Missile Technology Control Regime addresses this technology as a discrete problem and is considering the formation of a global regime. There is thus little or no recognition in the practical response to proliferation that the spread of these technologies might all be part of a common security problem. The security concerns that might drive states to acquire one or more of these technologies are hidden by the *proliferation* image. This division of the problem into discrete technologies persists, despite the fact that the connection among the various technologies of concern manifests itself in a number of ways. I will mention only two by way of illustration. The first is the common reference to biological or chemical weapons as "the poor man's atomic bomb." The implication of this phrase is that a state prevented from acquiring nuclear weapons—in this case for reasons of cost—could turn to biological or chemical weapons to serve the same purposes. The second example concerns the links being drawn in the Middle East between Arab states' potential chemical arms and Israel's nuclear arsenal. The Arab states are balking at ratifying the Chemical Weapons Convention until the Israeli nuclear arms are at least placed on the negotiating table. Conversely, supporters of the Israeli position cite the Arab states' overwhelming conventional superiority as a justification for Israel's nuclear arms.

The common approach to controlling proliferation across the technologies of concern is the limitation and even denial of the supply of technology. Each of the technologies of concern is addressed by at least one supplier group, and the major Western suppliers maintain export controls to implement the groups' lists. Such an approach is clearly informed by the entailments of the *proliferation* image. Supplier controls respond to the "spread outward from a source" entailment of proliferation. They also reflect the ways in which both the metaphors of "proliferation" and "stability" highlight technology by focusing solely on its nature and movement. In addition, these groups reflect the various entailments of stability and balance outlined above. They seek to prevent excessive and destabilizing accumulations of technologies through the application of their controls. Lost entirely in these practices are considerations of the political and economic underpinnings of security. These aspects are hidden by the image and so are not addressed by the policy responses.

The relationship among these political interests, the policy responses, and the metaphors of the *proliferation* image would form the subject of another chapter, at the very least. It is not responsible to ignore this relationship entirely, however, and so I will provide an illustration. India stands as a leading opponent of the present approach to proliferation control, with its roots in technological denial. India represents a different set of interests from those of the Northern states most concerned with proliferation as presently understood and practiced. For India, access to technology is vital, and the principle of discrimination between the have and have-not states—enshrined most notably in the NPT, but seen throughout the nonproliferation measures for denying technologies' spread—is absolutely unacceptable. As such, the Indians reject the image of *proliferation* and call, rather, for one of *disarmament*. This view is reflected in the following passage, quoted from a paper by the Indian ambassador to Japan, who was previously the Indian representative to the Conference on Disarmament:

> It would be futile to pretend that 1995 is 1970, that nothing has changed and nothing requires to be changed in the 1995 NPT. It would be a cruel joke on the coming generation to say that they will be safer with an indefinite extension of the 1970 NPT. 1995 presents an opportunity; there is great scope for non-governmental agencies, intellectuals and academics, who believe in nuclear disarmament to work towards changing this mindset and spur governments in nuclear weapon countries to look at reality, to accept that there are shortcomings in the NPT and that nations, both within and outside the NPT have genuine concerns which need to be addressed in order to make the NPT universal, non discriminatory and *a true instrument for nuclear disarmament*.[46]

What is noteworthy about this plea for change is that Ambassador Prakash Shah calls for the new NPT to be an instrument of nuclear disarmament, not of nonproliferation. In other words, he recognizes that there is a policy problem to be addressed, but it is not a proliferation problem—that is, a spread of weapons technology from those who have to those who do not presently have. Rather, the problem needs to be imagined as a disarmament problem—the possession of nuclear and other arms, regardless of who has them.

For the countries of the North, the indefinite extension of an unamended NPT was considered essential. The NPT was seen as the linchpin of the proliferation-control effort, without which the entire edifice might fall. What Ambassador Shah's comments demonstrate, reflecting the position taken in India, is the way in which that effort, tied so closely to the entailments of the *proliferation* image, serves only a particular set of interests by highlighting only specific features of reality. From where he sits, reality provides Ambassador Shah with a different approach to the problem of nuclear (and other mass destruction) weapons, an approach better captured through an image of *disarmament* than one of *proliferation*.

CONCLUSION

It is tempting to conclude this discussion by counseling the evils of metaphor for security. It is also, however, entirely impossible. We think, speak, and act in metaphors, and so proposing to eliminate them from the practice of security study and policy verges on the incoherent. What conclusion can we draw, then, as we attempt to build a critical security study?

First, we must recognize that the metaphors with which a security problem is understood will shape the nature of the problem and its solutions, focusing on the aspects that are highlighted and marginalizing or ignoring those that are downplayed or hidden in the metaphors' entailments. In a critical security *study*, our task is to reveal those metaphors and to detail their entailments. In particular, we must draw out those aspects of security problems that are downplayed or hidden by the metaphors. In doing so, we can reconnect security and security policy—so often considered as distinct and isolated realms—to the rest of the fabric of international politics and global society. The image of *proliferation* hides both the economic interests driving arms export and the location of arms production in the industrialization of the Third World. What is hidden or downplayed by the other metaphors in which we think and speak security? Indeed, what are the entailments of the metaphor of "security" itself?

The highlighting and hiding of aspects of complex security problems by the metaphors in which they are thought and acted are not innocent. Thus, for a *critical* security study, the examination of metaphors provides the basis for political involvement. Such an examination can form the basis of an immanent critique. Efforts at proliferation control are liable to fall short of expectations because the aspects of the problem hidden by the *proliferation* image will undermine supply-side controls. There is, however, also the basis for a more profound, transformatory critique. The image of *proliferation*, constructing a problem of technological movement outward from a source that is to be addressed by restricting that technology to the source, clearly masks the interests of the advanced industrial states. These states have the technologies of concern, providing them with economic and military advantages, and these states will continue to enjoy these advantages under a policy of supplier control.

Analysis of the metaphorical basis of security policy can thus serve to reveal the constructed nature of international security. It is a construction of the imagination, but of the political imagination. It therefore matters a great deal who is doing the imagining, and what the implications are of the resultant image. We cannot eliminate metaphor from the practice of security. However, by including its analysis within the critical study of security, we can reveal these foundational imaginings and normative commitments of those choosing particular metaphors. Ultimately, the analysis of metaphor is a route to the opening of alternatives in international security, alternatives that are rooted in the commitments of those making the choice of metaphors. The focus on metaphor, then, begins to address at least two of the concerns of a critical security study: it provides a methodological tool for understanding security as a historically specific construction, and it serves to return politics to a study depoliticized by the epistemological assumptions of the traditional approaches.

NOTES

1. Charles Krauthammer, "The Unipolar Moment," *Foreign Affairs* 70:1 (1991), 32–33.

2. Ibid.

3. Ibid., 33.

4. For the text of the agreement, see "New Multilateral Export Control Arrangement," press statement issued after the High Level Meeting of 28 States, Wassenaar, 11–12 September 1995. Russia was one of the twenty-eight, along with the Czech Republic, Hungary, Poland, and the Slovak Republic, as well as the former members of COCOM.

5. The communiqué cites the regimes as the NPT, the CWC, and the BTWC. The NPT is the Nuclear Non-Proliferation Treaty. It entered into force in 1970 and recognizes five nuclear weapons states, forbidding all other states to acquire nuclear weapons or to help others in their acquisition. The CWC is the Chemical Weapons Convention. It was signed in January 1993 and is expected to enter into force by 1997. It bans chemical weapons and their production and, unlike the NPT, is universal and nondiscriminatory. There are no "chemical weapons states." The BTWC is the Biological and

Toxin Weapons Convention. It entered into force in 1975 and bans the production and holding of biological weapons of all kinds. Unlike the other two, there are no verification measures associated with the convention, although the States Party are considering adding a verification protocol.

The regimes to which the North Atlantic Council refers in section 4 of the communiqué are each limited-membership supplier regimes. They jointly agree to lists of technologies on which export controls are to be maintained, although the controls themselves are applied nationally by the members. The Nuclear Suppliers Group (NSG) and the Zangger Committee both control nuclear technology and material. The Australia Group applies controls to technologies related to chemical and biological weapons. The Missile Technology Control Regime (MTCR) applies controls to ballistic and cruise missile technology, with a range greater than 300 km and a payload greater than 500 kg.

6. "Alliance Policy Framework on Proliferation of Weapons of Mass Destruction," issued at the ministerial meeting of the North Atlantic Council held in Istanbul, Turkey, 9 June 1994, M–NAC–1(94)45, 2.

7. United Nations Security Council Resolution 687 (3 April 1991), section C, paragraphs 7–14.

8. "Alliance Policy Framework," 4–5.

9. "Summit at the UN: Security Council Summit Declaration—'New Risks for Stability and Security,'" *New York Times*, 1 February 1992, 1, 4.

10. The limitations of space prevent me from detailing the development of this image in and through those pronouncements and practices. A more complete discussion can be found in David Mutimer, "Reimagining Security: The Metaphors of Proliferation," YCISS Occasional Paper Number 25, (Toronto: York Centre for International and Strategic Studies, August 1994), 5–14.

11. The journals surveyed were *International Security, Foreign Affairs, Foreign Policy, Orbis*, and the *Washington Quarterly*. The issues included those published from 1985 to June 1994.

12. In 1993, the MTCR members began considering the way in which the group could be developed into a global convention governing the nonproliferation of missile technology, in order to complete the technological coverage of these global regimes. See "Missile Technology: Looking Beyond Supply-Side Control," *The Disarmament Bulletin* 21 (1993), 5.

13. Scott Sagan, "The Perils of Proliferation: Organization Theory, Deterrence Theory, and the Spread of Nuclear Weapons," *International Security* 18:4 (1994), 71.

14. Ibid., 71–72.

15. Richard Ned Lebow and Janice Gross Stein, "Rational Deterrence Theory: I Think, Therefore I Deter," *World Politics* 41:2 (1989), 214.

16. Paul Chilton, "Revealing Metaphors," in Paul Chilton, *Orwellian Language and the Media* (London: Pluto, 1988), 58.

17. Throughout the remainder of this discussion it will be necessary to indicate words that denote images and those that denote metaphors, and so I will place the name of images in italics, while enclosing metaphors in quotation marks. The image with which I am concerned, then, is that of *proliferation*, which comprises three key metaphors: "proliferation," "stability," and "balance."

18. Chilton uses two terms, *scripts* and *frames* to refer to the concept I have developed as image. For consistency, throughout this chapter I use the single term *image*.

19. George Lakoff and Mark Johnson, *Metaphors We Live By* (Chicago: University of Chicago Press, 1980), 5. Emphasis in original.

20. Lakoff and Johnson, *Metaphors We Live By*, 4. To illustrate that this image is not simply a linguistic convenience, they suggest imaging a culture in which argument is considered in the terms of dance rather than war: "We would probably not view them as arguing at all: they would simply be doing something different" (5).

21. Lakoff and Johnson, *Metaphors We Live By*, 5.

22. Ibid, 163.

23. The structure of the arms transfer and production system is analyzed by Keith Krause in *Arms and the State: Patterns of Military Production and Trade* (Cambridge: Cambridge University Press, 1992). The term *arms transfer and production system* is also Krause's. I have elsewhere considered the variety of political and economic motivations driving states both to supply and demand weapons and their related technologies. Mutimer, "Understanding the Process of Proliferation: The Way Forward for Control and Verification," research report submitted to the Verification Research Unit, Department of Foreign Affairs, May 1994.

24. Lakoff and Johnson, *Metaphors We Live By*, 56–60.

25. Ibid., 118. Deborah Cameron accuses Lakoff and Johnson of biologism in her "Naming of Parts: Gender, Culture, and Terms for the Penis among American College Students," *American Speech* 67:4 (1992), 377–78. Cameron does recognize, however, that Lakoff becomes more sensitive to this concern in his later work on the subject, George Lakoff, *Women, Fire and Dangerous Things: What Categories Reveal about the Mind* (Chicago: University of Chicago, 1987).

26. A noted recent attempt to examine the impact of policy communities outside government on the policy process addresses the question in terms of "epistemic communities." See Peter Haas, "Introduction: Epistemic Communities and International Policy Coordination," in Peter Haas, ed., "Power, Knowledge and International Policy Coordination," a special issue

of *International Organizations* 46:1 (1992), 1–35. The concept is further elaborated by the other contributions to that volume.

27. The United States Office of Technology Assessment produced three lists of countries "trying to acquire nuclear weapons," "having undeclared chemical warfare capabilities," and "having undeclared biological warfare capabilities." The countries I named appear on at least one of the lists, and three—Israel, Iraq, and Iran—appear on all three. See U.S. Congress, Office of Technology Assessment, *Proliferation of Weapons of Mass Destruction: Assessing the Risks*, OTA-ISC-559 (Washington, D.C.: U.S. Government Printing Office, 1993), 64–65.

28. Frederick R. Strain, "Nuclear Proliferation and Deterrence: A Policy Conundrum," *Parameters* 23:3 (1993), 86. Emphasis added.

29. The sentence concludes the authors' introductory paragraph to an overview of the contemporary study of cell proliferation: "This book is about the cell cycle, the ordered set of processes by which one cell grows and divides into two daughter cells. Cell growth and division is a cornerstone of biology. Without understanding how the cell cycle works, we cannot understand how the fusion of two cells, an egg and a sperm, and the subsequent divisions of the fertilized egg produce an adult human composed of about 10^{13} cells. Without knowing the checks and balances that normally ensure orderly cell division, we cannot devise effective strategies to combat the uncontrolled cell divisions of the cancers that will kill one in six of us." Andrew Murray and Tim Hunt, *The Cell Cycle: An Introduction* (New York: Freeman, 1993), 1.

In case it seems that they are not discussing cell proliferation, consider the following: "Although we know much about some of the steps involved in the regulation of proliferation, our ignorance about others keeps us from fitting the steps together into a coherent picture of how cell multiplication is regulated in tissue culture, let alone in intact organisms" (106). Furthermore, in conversation with the author, a molecular biologist at the University of Guelph confirmed that *proliferation* is used as a general term to refer to the growth of cells by division.

30. "Alliance Policy Framework," 2.

31. Frank Barnaby, *How Nuclear Weapons Spread: Nuclear-Weapon Proliferation in the 1990s* (London: Routledge, 1993), 2.

32. "Bush Proposes Arms Control Initiative for Middle East," text of a speech by President George Bush to the Air Force Academy, 29 May 1991.

33. This is not to say that there have not been other instances of power balancing in international politics. David Hume argued that the balance of power was a feature of the classical world. Herbert Butterfield opposed this view, suggesting that "the idea of the balance of power is associated with the modern history of our part of the world, and envisages the political units of

the Continent as forming what used to be called 'the European states-system.'" Herbert Butterfield, "The Balance of Power," in Herbert Butterfield and Martin Wight, eds., *Diplomatic Investigations* (London: Allen and Unwin, 1967), 133. Similarly, Hedley Bull provides examples from six-teenth-, seventeenth-, and eighteenth-century Europe of the balance-of-power mechanism. Hedley Bull, *The Anarchical Society: A Study of Order in World Politics* (London: Macmillan, 1977), 101–2.

34. Bull, *The Anarchical Society*, 104.

35. Kenneth Waltz, *Theory of International Politics* (Reading, Mass.: Addison-Wesley, 1979), 118.

36. "Statement of the Five Countries," Paris, 9 July 1991, reprinted in Richard Dean Burns, ed., *Encyclopedia of Arms Control and Disarmament*, vol. 3 (New York: Scribner's, 1993), 1481–83.

37. The relationship among three bodies under the influence of gravity—the famed three-body problem—is one of the most difficult in the history of Newtonian physics. While two bodies will settle into a stable orbit, the addi-tion of a third body introduces complex and possibly chaotic interactions among the three. Waltz uses the three-body problem to bolster his claim that a two-power system is the most stable: "The three-body problem has yet to be solved by physicists. Can political scientists or policy-makers hope to do better in charting the courses of three or more interacting states?" Waltz, *Theory of International Politics*, 192.

38. Waltz, *Theory of International Politics*, 192. In addition, see chap. 8 (161–93), to which this sentence forms a synopsis: "Chapter 8 will show why two is the best of small numbers. . . . Problems of national security in multi- and bipolar worlds do clearly show the advantages of having two great powers, and only two, in the system" (161). On the essentially dyadic nature of the balance of power, see also Bull, *The Anarchical Society*, 102, and Martin Wight, "The Balance of Power," in Butterfield and Wight, eds., *Diplomatic Investigations*, 152.

39. For a discussion of the relation of the Kurds and other sub- and transnational social groups in the Iran-Iraq war, see W. Thom Workman, *The Social Origins of the Iran-Iraq War* (Boulder, Colo.: Lynne Rienner, 1994).

40. Raju Thomas, "The Growth of India's Military Power: From Suffi-ciency to Nuclear Deterrence," in Ross Babbage and Sandy Gordon, eds., *India's Strategic Future* (New York: St. Martin's, 1992), 38.

41. *United Nations Register of Conventional Arms: Report of the Secre-tary General*, General Assembly, A/48/344 (11 October 1993), 105. This is not to say that there are not alternate sources of information. Before the reg-ister was formed, both the Stockholm International Peace Research Institute and the International Institute of Strategic Studies tracked arms transfers

and remain able to provide information that is not included in the official data of the register.

42. A similar conclusion, although from very different assumptions, is reached by Colin Gray in his recent article, "Arms Control Does Not Control Arms," *Orbis* 37:3 (1993), particularly 341–42.

43. John Mearsheimer, "Back to the Future: Instability in Europe after the Cold War," *International Security* 15:1 (1990), 54. Emphasis added.

44. By instability, Western policy makers probably meant political and strategic instability, not the psychological instability of Vladimir Zhirinovsky.

45. Consider, for example, President Bush's "Chicken Kiev" speech in December 1991, in which he spoke out against Ukrainian independence to the Ukrainian Parliament. Reported by John Thor-Dahlburg, "Bush's Chicken Kiev Talk—An Ill-fated U.S. Policy," *Los Angeles Times*, 19 December 1991, A17. On the conservative bias in the policy to Yugoslavia, see Ralph Johnson, Principal Deputy Assistant Secretary for European and Canadian Affairs, "U.S. Efforts To Promote a Peaceful Settlement in Yugoslavia," *Department of State Dispatch*, 21 October 1991, in which he defends characterizing American goals in terms of the continued "unity" of Yugoslavia.

46. Prakash Shah, "Nuclear Non-Proliferation Implications and the NPT Review: An Indian Perspective," paper presented to the international workshop, "Nuclear Disarmament and Non-Proliferation: Issues for International Action," Tokyo, 15–16 March 1993, 3. Emphasis added.

8

Changing Worlds of Security

KARIN M. FIERKE

In recent years scholars of International Relations have been pre-occupied with redefining security, which implies that the meaning of this concept as used in the Cold War context has changed.[1] The pur-pose of this article is to return to the rough ground of the everyday language of the Cold War and its aftermath to trace the changes that gave rise to these definitional questions on the part of scholars. The task is not to ask how we should redefine security but, rather, what the meaning of security for actors was within this context and how this world was transformed, given the regularities and constraints assumed by the logic of security dilemmas.

Arguments that the West won the Cold War have become a stan-dard feature of public and academic discourse. In a recent article, Charles Kegley raised questions about this or other overly hasty and single-cause explanations for the transformation of the East-West re-lationship.[2] He calls for a more thorough investigation, an openness to multiple causal relationships, and presents a metaphor of autopsy to lend coherence to a set of procedures for future coroners to fol-low. While sympathetic to Kegley's critique, and the need to look more broadly at this context, I argue that the autopsy metaphor, in-sofar as it relies on procedures adopted from the natural sciences, will not solve the problem he identifies because, based on these pro-cedures, the scientist brings a set of meanings to the world he or she analyzes. The task in this case is to trace a change in the meanings political actors attached to practices of security.

The scientist, like Kegley's coroner, begins by positing the object of explanation (identifying the body), fixing the meaning of terms, and establishing relationships, after which he looks at the world. To fix is to hold the meaning of words in place on the basis of the scientist's definitions. Another way of proceeding, more appropriate to the analysis of change, is to approach the context, that is, the social relationships in which meanings are embedded, directly. This involves examining the positioning of subjects or objects in relation to others, their meaning within a whole: how the actors themselves establish boundaries and act within a particular time and place, what kinds of distinctions are made, what kinds of relationships are contrasted, what types of language games are played, what actors in different positions do, and the meaning of these acts within a context. In undertaking this analysis, I draw on several themes from the work of Ludwig Wittgenstein, particularly his *Philosophical Investigations*.[3]

RULES AND LANGUAGE GAMES

A central point of the hermeneutic critique of positivism was that social activity could not be simply observed without taking into account the meanings that social actors attach to their actions. Rules are a part of social life, as well as meaningful speech and other forms of action, and we cannot begin to have knowledge of a context in the absence of knowledge of the conventions by which practice is constituted. Rules often makes us think of games. Because game metaphors have been so important in the field of International Relations, this may be a useful place to explore briefly a contrast between the assumptions of procedures drawing on a natural science model as opposed to a more explicitly social alternative.

Kenneth Waltz's neorealism has often been conceptualized in terms of a billiard game. The metaphor tells us something about the assumptions of this model of interstate relations. The billiard ball has a hard crust. We cannot see inside it. The insides of each ball are identical, as far as the observer can see. Any movement of a ball on the table arises not from the ball itself; it is, rather, propelled across the surface on impact from another ball or changes course as it collides with the rim of the table. The cause of action is outside and independent of any one billiard ball.

A different game illustrates the underlying assumptions of an approach that begins with a notion of social rules. In a game of chess individual players have to think strategically in making moves. Notice already that the focus is on the players, not on the objects, as in the billiards metaphor. When applied to International Relations, no mention is ever made of those who initiate the movement of the billiard balls. In a game of chess, movement of the pieces is not determined, as in the example above; rather, in making any move from a particular place on the board or with a particular piece, for instance, a knight or bishop, the player employs the rules of the game. This is not to suggest that she cannot cheat or break a rule—this is given by its existence—instead, as long as two players are playing chess, any meaningful or strategic move will depend on the rules by which the game is constituted, which may be either followed or broken. If one player does not know the rules and says he wants to learn them, but the other says, "Sorry, they are a secret," it is not possible to proceed with the game. If one player starts playing according to the rules of Monopoly, we cannot say that this is a game of chess. The point is that the rules are public in nature, shared by both players. In playing, action is not determined by the rules, but players follow rules in acting.

One question one might ask is why a particular move rather than another was made, that is, what were the intentions of the player. This has been the focus of many hermeneutic approaches. My focus, however, is the public nature of the rules themselves and how these rules provide a tool for mapping moves in a changing game in order to gain knowledge of the nature of the game and its transformation over time.

The public nature of these rules points to the centrality of language in either learning or knowing how to proceed with a particular kind of game. *Public*, in this case, refers to the social nature of meaning and language, in contrast to arguments that both originate with mental processes. Wittgenstein argued against the idea of "private language."[4] While experience may be individual, it can only be meaningfully understood or communicated to others on the basis of a language whose rules are shared. These rules must continuously be projected into new contexts in which their meaning may change. It is not possible to simply observe behavior, to understand its meaning, without analyzing the language games by which action is structured, any more than we know or can learn the meaning of various pieces of chess or the rules by which they are used in the absence of language. Language is woven into the range of acts constituting a game, and language is the vehicle by which we are socialized into or learn the rules of how to proceed in any context. Analysis of this kind, of changing language games, makes it possible to identify a degree of coherence, at least in the contexts analyzed here, that is often presumed to be missing at the international level. This coherence cannot simply be observed in nature; it has to be recovered from a context, by returning to the rough ground to see what actors are doing, what rules they follow, and how they make different kinds of moves from any one position in social space.

LANGUAGE GAMES AND FORMS OF LIFE

The language games of a specific culture, the fact that they are shared games, rich with meaning, tell us something about the contours of a world. Within the culture of the Cold War, security is the glue by which multiple language games are bound. The English term *domestic* derives from the Latin *domus,* meaning home or house. Similarly, the Russian word for house is *dom.*[5] The use of the word *domestic* to describe the internal sphere of the state is rooted in the grammar of a particular kind of space, a home, which is occupied by particular kinds of human beings, that is, families. Security within this world belongs to the same grammar. The use of the word *social* with security emerges along with the increased role of the state in providing certain types of services or care traditionally left to the family, and in the post-World War II world, it was followed by the language of national security, defining an explicitly protective relationship between a state and its citizens. The elevation of security to the state level involved conceptualizing states in terms of families, homes, and the protection and security they are presumed to provide.

Metaphors of homes providing security to a family are not specific to the Cold War but relate to a longer tradition of conceptualizing security in terms of particular kinds of structures whose boundaries distinguish the intimate relations inside from those who threaten from outside. What now finds expression in metaphor can be traced back to historical forms of life that continue to be meaningful in conceptualizing relationships between more abstract entities such as states. The medieval fortress was composed of impenetrable walls intended to keep out enemies. The impenetrable walls of the fortress or castle existed to protect the more intimate relations inside from those outside who potentially threatened to penetrate those barriers. When deterrence, during the Cold War, was referred to as a foundation of Western security, the structural metaphor conveyed a similar meaning that the nuclear threat worked to keep the Eastern enemy out of the nuclear fortress occupied by the transatlantic alliance. When General-Secretary Mikhail Gorbachev conceptualized changing security relations in terms of a common house, or when NATO proposed a new architecture, the structural metaphor spatialized the security relationship, insofar as structures construct walls distinguishing those inside from those outside. The insides and outsides of Gorbachev's "common house" were quite different from those of the architecture, and it was precisely the boundaries and definition of Europe, as well as who was inside and who out, that were at stake.

Marriage and courtship are also forms of human life that in an earlier period were practices constituting diplomacy. Conceptualizations of the classical European balance of power rely on related language games. Take, for instance, the following discussion of the working of that system:

> With more than two states, the politics of power turn on the diplomacy by which alliances are made, maintained, and disrupted. Flexibility of alignment means that the country one is *wooing* may *prefer another suitor* and that one's present alliance partner may defect. A state's strategy *must please a potential or satisfy a present partner....* Similarly, with a number of approximately equal states, strategy is at least partly made for the sake of *attracting and holding partners. Suitors alter their appearance* and adapt their behavior *to increase their eligibility....* Ever since the Napoleonic wars many had believed that the "Republic" and the "Cossack" could never *become engaged*, let alone *contract a marriage.* The *wooing* of France and Russia, with each adapting somewhat to the other, was nevertheless *consummated* in the alliance of 1894 and duly *produced* the Triple Entente as *its progeny.*[6]

While the language of courtship structures our understanding of the classical European balance of power, language games relating to intimacy also constituted alliance relations during the Cold War, and by comparing the two, both the common origin and the distinction in the rules structuring the two eras become evident. Within the context of the Cold War both NATO and Warsaw Pact refer to each other as neighboring "families." The NATO discourse is filled with language games relating to the commitment between two partners, the United States and Western Europe, which is directly related to the central speech act by which they are united, the promise of the nuclear guarantee. The following is one of the more blatant examples of this language game:

> The United States and Europe are an *old couple*. Almost *forty years of marriage* is a long time at the end of the twentieth century. The *knot was tied* at the end of the 1940s *in a storm of passion*. . . . The U.S.-European relationship has never really fully developed; it has never acquired the calm resignation of those couples who understand that, while their love is imperfect, wisdom and happiness in some ways involve a readiness to live with the faults and shortcomings of the other party. . . . The U.S.-European *couple cannot be divorced*. For the United States, such a divorce would mean surrendering the role of superpower; for Europe, it would mean re-examination of everything which it has been since 1945. But can this *couple devise a relationship which, while no longer exclusive*, would remain privileged?[7]

While security during the Cold War is heir to an earlier culture of international relations, it shares only a family resemblance, as they are structured by two different sets of rules that are quite opposite. The classical European balance of power worked largely to prevent a major power from securing the space of a smaller state in anything more than a temporary sense. The language of the classical balance of power was one of courtship and wooing, not permanent alliance. It is only with the Cold War that this game of courtship is replaced by one of commitment and marriage and with it the securing of spaces larger than particular states on what seemed to be a permanent basis. Most noteworthy about the map of Europe during the forty or so years of the Cold War was that it was frozen or secured in place. There was no movement from one alliance to another; to have done so would have been to risk nuclear war.

Both the difference and the commonality of the two eras are expressed in a grammar of intimate relations. Here I use *grammar* to refer to a particular region of language involving clusters of related concepts, including adjectives, nouns, and verbs that we recognize as related on the basis of a particular language, in this case English, and that contain the range of possible moves from any one position. The notion that a grammar structures knowledge of alliance formation in different historical contexts is significant on two levels. First, the distinctions illustrate the relationship between contextual games and particular cultural forms. As will be explored below, NATO's nuclear family is structurally similar to cultural representations of the nuclear family in the West in the post-World War II context. Knowledge of actors and action at the international level relies on cultural forms; language games from one level of human experience are projected metaphorically to the realm of interstate relations.[8] Second, these language games construct particular spatial distinctions that emphasize certain aspects of identity while obscuring others. The heterogeneous national landscape of Europe, or its numerous divisions into separate states, fades against the background of a spatial division between two blocs, East and West. Western and Eastern Europe are homogenized, constructed as members of a single family, sharing a single set of values, contrasted with those of the "other" family. This particular distinction between families relies on a much different division of space than the courtship games of an earlier period, within which separate European states wooed or attempted to remain attractive in a context of ever-changing affairs. The point is that language games construct a field of action that is defined by specific possibilities.

The remainder of this essay is based on an analysis of changing grammars related to language games of structure and intimate relations spanning a period from the mid-1970s to the first half of 1994. The analysis is drawn from a large number of texts from several actors, both state and nonstate, in the East and West. The analysis is presented in a narrative form in which I attempt to demonstrate the forms of action characteristic of each player at particular points in time and how the games begin to change as actors make different moves, drawing on the possibilities belonging to one grammar or the other. Only direct quotations have been documented, but all references to attributes or actions belonging to one grammar or the other are based on their recurrence in text after text by different authors at particular points in time. It is not possible for purposes of publication to include either the detailed references or the complete bibliography. Readers interested in this information are encouraged to consult the larger study.[9] The exercise is primarily descriptive in nature, attempting to trace changes in language games related to security and thereby to say something about the context from which current questions about redefining security have emerged.

FAMILY AFFAIRS

Language games of family structure the public texts of both alliances during the Cold War in slightly different ways. Both rely on a grammar of security, but the structuring rules of each family are different. This does not mean that any one writer is forced to use exactly the same words, but that they draw on a shared language comprising clusters of concepts belonging to a grammar of families and security. The following story illustrates the structure of relationships underlying this versatile grammar at the beginning of the 1980s. A main point is that these do not represent the interpretations of individuals but, rather, a public language that reappears again and again and, subsequently, constitutes the identities of NATO and the Warsaw Pact as well as knowledge of what they do.

The relationship between the NATO discourse of security and the construction of NATO as a family is evident from the texts of this organization in the early 1980s. The nuclear family of the West is built on a commitment between a stronger partner and a weaker one. The title of one article in the NATO *Review*, "The Atlantic Family—Managing Its Problems," names the metaphor directly.[10] This family includes partners whose stable relationship is characterized by commitment, faithfulness, duties, responsibilities, common burdens, and obligations. The stronger partner has gotten into the habit of making most of the decisions, however, partly because of his more global responsibilities, in contrast to the primarily domestic responsibilities of the other. This relationship, which "is now an old one,"[11] has become no less intense over the years. The partners are bound by what bound them forty years ago, and they would not feel safe if they could not rely on each other. As one partner described it, "their safety and ours are one."[12]; "we were with you and are with you now, our hopes are your hopes, your destiny is our destiny."[13]

The stable and secure relationship of NATO's nuclear family is based on a foundation of values and friendship, as well as inequality, given that the two differ in capabilities. The stronger one offers protection and ensures the security of the weaker, who cannot feel secure on her own, in the face of the Soviet Union, who wants to isolate the two, making the feminine partner docile, productive, and supportive. The main objective of the Soviet Union is to split or decouple the partners.

The neighboring enemy to the East also refers to its unit as a family, although based on different values. They occupy a home, but it seems to be a very masculine family, fraternal and attached to a fatherland, where everyone is said to be equal. It is a particular kind of individual that is protected by the fraternal family, the laborer, and the socialist system in which he labors. Like NATO, the Soviet Union is concerned with preventing a shattering of the unity of this family by an interference in its domestic space. Poland, in the early 1980s, is a key concern precisely because it is the place where this interference is said to be most evident, and a space most vital to the maintenance of international security. Actors in both households are concerned that their unity is being shattered; both are protecting a set of values. This difference in values is said to be the cause of conflict between them.

In the West, security was inseparable from the need to secure the space of Western Europe, the securing of a feminine object by a masculine subject, the United States. The relationship was consensual, based on a shared history and culture, and less imposed by the Americans than desired by the Europeans—although the balance between these two was precarious—but the relationship, nonetheless, involved the securing of a larger continental space by an external power. While the Warsaw Pact also presents itself as a family, the Soviet Union actually focuses its gaze, like the United States, on Western Europe and its relationship with the United States. The Soviet Union transforms the hierarchical commitment and need expressed by NATO into the imposed obedience of Western Europe to the diktat of the United States. For the Soviet Union, the Western alliance is a form of imprisonment, done by people overseas, not present, not part of the European continent. While Western Europe was the feminine object that held each superpower's attention, Eastern Europe lacked any identity whatsoever, largely invisible, nondescript, historically abandoned, visible only as a domestic space in which the West should not interfere. The two family spheres in East and West, as well as the security dilemma constituted between them, were mutually reinforcing, a family feud in which the Other was not to be trusted because of the lack of correspondence between words and deeds.

In the early 1980s, both East and West are consumed by the need to keep their families together, in light of a renewed threat from the Other and the activities of a "younger generation," which begins to question the fundamental values on which each family is based. The naming of oppositional movements as a younger generation is particularly evident in NATO documents, in which the Western peace movement is characterized, among other things, as "immature, naive, and irresponsible."[14] The connotation of this particular label is that these movements are made up of rebellious kids reminiscent of the 1960s.[15] Participants in the peace movements have not been necessarily young, however, as various opinion polls have demonstrated.[16] This labeling effort on the part of NATO communicates a particular image of these movements and what they are about, that is, overturning a set of values by which peace has been maintained in Europe since World War II. While Eastern European dissidents are cast in less familial terms by state officials, the conflict has been discussed by many as the difference between the World War II generation and those who grew up in the relative wealth and security of the postwar period.[17]

While the two families are concerned with providing security for their domestic spaces, the younger generation in each house is attempting to emancipate itself from the destructive practices of its respective family. In this sense the critical movements take these language games of security very seriously: while the families claim to provide security, the oppositional movements expose or rename this security as a source of insecurity. Their actions relate to this same grammar of families or intimate relationships, but they make a different move in the game, based on a renaming of the relationship. Emancipation, and the cluster of concepts belonging to it, is a game that can belong to a grammar of families,[18] but it is not within the realm of possibility in alliance games based on the permanence of a particular family structure. The structuring role of these concepts is evident in the texts of Solidarity and the Western European peace movement.

The central value of the Eastern house is protecting workers in the process of building socialism. Yet as the protector becomes a source of threat to workers, KOR (Worker's Defence Committee), and later Solidarity in Poland, attempt to expose abuse by the party and state of those rights that the latter has promised to protect, both in its own constitution and in signing the international Helsinki accords. The younger generation is revolting against the oppressive control of the family over all spheres of life and wants to open up a dialogue with the government so that society can take its fate into its own hands, speak with its own voice, and develop its own self-governing and independent institutions.

In the West, while the alliance partners claim to be protecting the Western family, the acquisition of more and more sophisticated weapons as well as heightened tensions between the two families are making many feel insecure. While the family names the neighbor as the source of threat, the peace movement names the deployment of a new generation of weapons, as well as nuclear weapons and deterrence in general, as the primary threat. Like Solidarity, the Western peace movement is busy exposing a distinction between the words and the deeds of the older generation.

Social movements in both houses are calling for emancipation from a particular form of politics, a politics that has become a source of insecurity. At the international level, talk between the two households, in its present form, serves only to fix the antagonistic relationship between them. The main function of this antagonism, and the negotiations by which it is preserved, is in their view to discipline the younger generation and the alliance partners. That which the alliance names a relationship of security and protection, the Western European peace movement renames a relationship of dependence and submission. They call on Europeans within each alliance to reclaim responsibility for their own lives by taking a more independent role, disengaging from the military side of the relationship, and liberating themselves from the ideology of the Cold War. Common security between East and West requires loosening the hold of the two families and opening up spaces for more voices to speak.

The foundations of each bloc enclose two different kinds of families—neighbors who cannot get along because of a difference in values. In both houses the younger generation is making different moves within these family games, pointing out the distinction between the claim to provide security and protection and what is in fact being done. The analysis can be broadened by looking at the relationship between these family games and a structural change over a longer period of time. The structural grammar was recovered from a larger range of documents, involving the same actors, covering the period from 1975 to 1991, when the Soviet Union collapsed. This involved pulling out predicates related to a range of attributes, from ceilings to walls to foundations, as well as a range of possible moves, both active and passive (for instance, maintaining, building, eroding, undermining, restoring, and so on), and attempting to delineate patterns of action attached to specific actors. What follows is a rough sketch of moves in language games by which the structures of the Cold War were dismantled. Following this I will return to the further transformation of both security grammars in the post-Cold War world.

DISMANTLING THE COLD WAR STRUCTURES

In the mid-1970s, at the height of detente, following the signing of the Helsinki Final Act by the states participating in the Conference on Security and Cooperation in Europe (CSCE), both superpowers engage in acts of structural maintenance. The North Atlantic Treaty Organization provides a framework that rests on the foundations of deterrence capability and transatlantic ties; NATO is a political structure furnished with military means, a structure whose central task is one of maintaining deterrence, defense capabilities, and the political cohesion that provides the cement of the foundation. Likewise, the socialist family of the Eastern bloc also provides a framework that rests on the foundations of socialist production, Marxism-Leninism, and the unity of the socialist countries. The socialist alliance is the cornerstone of relations between the Soviet Union and Eastern Europe. As in NATO, maintenance is a central task of the Warsaw Pact, in this case the object of which is socialism, peace, and equilibrium. Detente also provides a framework that needs to be maintained.

Within the detente framework the West is facing several problems maintaining its own security structure; it is proving difficult in the context of a deteriorating economy to convince Western publics to pay for defense, against the background of relaxed superpower relations. Despite these economic problems, no one at this point believes the welfare state, which is seen as a barrier to Soviet political intentions in Western Europe, can be dismantled. The North Atlantic Treaty Organization is concerned that the Soviet Union, in the meantime, is building up its military potential and attempting to undermine the internal politics of the West. It is believed that this combination of factors may make it possible for the Soviet Union to fulfill its ultimate objective of dismantling the NATO alliance and separating Europe from America.

The Soviet Union expresses confidence at this point that socialism is being built in Eastern Europe and maintains a consistent policy that the military organizations of the two blocs should be dismantled. By 1977, however, the Soviet Union becomes increasingly concerned that the Eastern foundations, as well as the framework of detente, are being undermined by the West. One source of concern is the development of momentum in the United States to restore the deteriorating foundations of deterrence. In conjunction with this, the SALT II Treaty is being undermined, as are the social and political systems in the East, as evidenced by Charter 77 and other human rights groups, whose activities are said to be orchestrated by the United States.

At about the same time, KOR forms in Poland, followed a few years later by Solidarity, and with it a conflict between workers attempting to dismantle totalitarianism and the party attempting to restore order. Notice the relationship between dismantling and restoring. There is an oppositional relationship between the two forms of action, accompanied by a different naming of the object of action, which for Solidarity is totalitarianism and for the government, socialism. According to the government, the foundations of socialism are eroding as a result of this conflict. The government argues that the West is attempting to undermine socialism and that the leaderships of KOR and Solidarity, as distinguished from the mass of workers, are its puppets. As it is forced underground with the implementation of martial law, Solidarity continues with its efforts to construct independent Polish institutions.

In the West in 1979, NATO begins the restoration effort with the decision to deploy cruise and Pershing II missiles in five European countries. Ronald Reagan is elected to office in the United States on a platform to restore both the American defense posture and the economy. The restoration effort involves movement toward a countervailing strategy, based on arguments that a MAD (mutually assured destruction) posture is an inadequate basis for the American strategic commitment to Europe. In response, a mass peace movement emerges in Europe, particularly in the five NATO countries slated for deployment. At the basis of many of these movements is a rejection of deterrence and of arguments that peace can only be built on trust. In contrast to NATO claims that nuclear deterrence preserves peace, the peace movements question whether the arms race contributes to security or undermines it, given the movement toward a first-strike strategy and the increasing destructive power of nuclear weapons. The peace movement is attempting to build a new power base within Western European societies, and similar to Charter 77 and Solidarity, it argues that this base has to be built outside established political institutions.

President Reagan and NATO, following on the coattails of the Committee on the Present Danger, undertake efforts to restore the nuclear deterrent. Related to this, Reagan sets out to restore the American economy by cutting back on government bureaucracy. In order to restore America's position in the world, it is necessary to increase spending for defense in order to rebuild systems that have become antiquated through years of neglect. This can only be done by restoring the economy, which is held back by bureaucratic stagnation.

While the initial concerns stimulating this restoration effort were a Soviet buildup and erosion of the nuclear deterrent, by 1982 and 1983 it is the "unilateralist" peace movement that is undermining and eroding the Western foundation, and the Soviet Union, it is claimed, will use this to its advantage. NATO is increasingly pulled apart by the conflicting demands of public opinion and the rhetoric and policies of President Reagan. The source of the renewed fear of nuclear war is, however, attributed to a change of consciousness, which is part of a psychological war waged by the Soviet Union against the West, aimed at undermining its will to preserve its way of life.

As the deployments in Europe begin in 1983, Reagan is confronted with his own domestic battles over the Nuclear Freeze proposal that has been introduced into Congress. In April he announces the Strategic Defense Initiative (SDI) as an alternative to nuclear deterrence, stating, "What if free people could live secure in the knowledge that their security did not rest upon a threat of instant retaliation."[19] He presents a future when security would not rest on the foundation of deterrence but argues instead that it is necessary in the meantime for the United States to remain constant in preserving and maintaining deterrence. The deployments proceed and Reagan is reelected by a landslide, but the alliance continues to be threatened with the erosion of its foundations. The concern of 1980 and 1981 about erosion of the deterrent resulting from Soviet actions is replaced by concern about the erosion of public support on which that deterrent is based. The conflict is qualitatively different from past conflicts within the alliance; it is not just a routine conflict between states within NATO but points to the crumbling framework within which defense debates have been conducted throughout the postwar years. The deployments have gone ahead, but the consensus on which alliance policy is based has all but collapsed.

Part of the Western European peace movement has a two-pronged strategy, and as deployments begin they shift attention to the other part of this strategy. The focus prior to 1983 was attempting to persuade national governments to refuse deployments. The second objective, articulated in the END (European Nuclear Disarmament) appeal of 1980, begins with a renaming of the two mutually sustaining structures of the Cold War. It is not one side or the other that is maintained by the practices of the superpowers, but the Cold War itself. The objective is to dismantle this structure and break down the barriers separating East and West. While the central actions of the two superpowers—restoring, maintaining, undermining—are acts undertaken with military tools, the dismantling actions of independent movements are directed more at the ideological structures in which the military actions of the arms race are embedded. Dismantling takes the form of beginning a dialogue with independent counterparts in Eastern Europe.

Within the context of the Cold War, movements on the two sides are by definition at cross-purposes with each other. Western authorities see the population as prey to a psychological war, on the part of the Soviets, relating to issues of peace; Charter 77 and Solidarity, according to the Soviet Union, are stimulated by a psychological war on the part of the West. The United States cheers on the latter; the Soviet Union the former. There is a direct relationship between the maintaining and the undermining efforts of each bloc—these are the rules structuring the interbloc relationship. The dismantling effect of this dialogue can be understood within the framework of Václav Havel's argument that the dissident's act of breaking the rules disrupts the game itself and exposes it as a game, as convention, rather than permanent necessity.[20] From the perspective of the Soviet Union this dialogue effort by END is aimed at undermining the antiwar movement and the socialist system. The attempt to de-

velop a dialogue between Western peace movements, whose disarmament demands have been cheered on by the Soviet Union, and
independent initiatives in the Eastern bloc creates a blurring of the
distinction between friend and enemy.

Part of the dialogue effort is to restore the Helsinki Final Act to
its original meaning. Although Helsinki has been interpreted as ce-
menting the status quo and the Cold War division, it contains possibilities for breaking up the bipolar structures. Helsinki does not cement the division of Europe but opens the door for change toward a
pluralistic Europe. This involves building a civil society that tran-
scends national frontiers while dismantling the Cold War.

As this restoration effort is under way, NATO is increasingly divided in 1985 and 1986 by concerns that SDI is undermining arms
control, while the Soviet Union is concerned that it will destroy
the foundations for a normal relationship between the two sides. In
response, the Soviet Union begins to talk of restoring the balance
through reciprocal actions. Reagan, on the other hand, is increasingly concerned that his plans are being undermined by domestic
critics and particularly those who hold the purse strings in Congress.

Reagan's SDI creates new divisions in the alliance at a time when
it has not yet recovered from the domestic battles over the cruise and
Pershing II missiles. The NATO house is still suffering from erosion,
and this erosion and the deep cracks in the structure are recognized
by the Soviet Union. By 1986 the bipartisan support on which the
foreign policy consensus in Europe rested has collapsed, there is an
increasing distance between the United States and Europe (in part
because of SDI), and the Soviet Union is aware of this erosion. In
addition, the image of the Soviet Union as a threat has begun to disappear, which is a further blow to NATO cohesion: "Without a common perception every NATO activity is undermined."[21] The common
perception of a Soviet threat is fading among the Western public—
a trend that Mikhail Gorbachev encourages—and for many, the
United States poses an equal threat. On the one hand, Gorbachev is
undermining enemy images by taking unilateral steps, such as the
eighteen-month moratorium on nuclear weapons tests, and shattering old views about nuclear deterrence and balance-of-power politics. In addition to the double burden of maintaining a deterrent and
public consensus, NATO also has to concentrate on maintaining its
image. Further confusion emerges within the alliance as a result of

the unexpected outcome of the Reykjavík summit between the super-powers, which is depicted alternatively as an assault on the foundation of postwar strategy of both pacts or as a potentially disastrous blow to Western security.

As the Western security consensus crumbles, Gorbachev makes a move to rename the future contours of the European security structure by proposing to construct a European house, including both East and West, which is closely related to the restructuring of the domestic and foreign policies of the Soviet Union. Since 1983, NATO has begun to emphasize a more European, as opposed to Atlantic, identity. In 1984 attempts are made to breathe new life into the dormant West European Union, and in 1985 Jacques Delors, chair of the European Commission, launches a campaign for a new Europe free of borders. Two models of Europe are being discussed at this time: one building on Western institutions and the other, Gorbachev's house, emphasizing a historical European culture transcending the East-West divide.

The SDI plan is undermining arms control; the popular consensus that had underpinned NATO's deterrent in the post-World War II era is eroding; Reagan is concerned that Congress is undermining SDI; there exist blueprints for two different European structures. It is against this background that the peace offensive between the two superpowers must be understood. At earlier stages, the superpowers were doing the same things: maintaining and undermining. Now they both are making moves in a different game belonging to the same grammar. Gorbachev is restructuring, an action that shares a family resemblance with restoring, but the building blocs are political rather than military. His peace offensive is launched against balance-of-power and deterrence thinking as a foundation of international relations. Reagan focuses his offensive on breaking down the division of Europe, but the condition for his change of course is the technological and military solution of SDI. Both superpowers are now negating the foundations of traditional deterrence, focusing on the insecurity and fear on which it is based. Two different kinds of solutions are offered: the technological solution of SDI and the political solution of Gorbachev. Neither position is inconsistent with past positions of their respective bloc: Reagan, emphasizing human rights, wants to tear down the Berlin Wall, and Gorbachev, focusing on disarmament, wants to dissolve the two alliances. What has changed is the context in which the game is being played. The crossbeams that kept the two separate parts of the Cold War structure standing side by side are shifting: Eastern advocates of human rights and Western advocates of peace—representing movements that challenged the foundations of their respective blocs—are talking to each other and are doing so on the basis of principles agreed to by states within the framework of Helsinki. That which was viewed as merely a principle in 1975, given concerns about the possibilities for implementation, has become the backdrop for action, in which human rights and security, as well as a notion of detente characterized by cross-bloc citizen contacts, are not weapons in the superpower conflict but become a common frame of reference for actions aimed at dismantling the Cold War and building a democratic and peaceful Europe.

By the beginning of 1989 change is in the air but an end to the division of Europe is not yet in sight, although there are hopes on both sides for a gradual effort to overcome the bloc division. An infrastructure of cooperation is being constructed between East and West, in the form of treaties and accords both between the superpowers and within the Helsinki process, but with the exception of Poland, where roundtable negotiations between Solidarity and the Communist Party begin, and Hungary, the Eastern European Communist Parties, against the urgings of Gorbachev, are resisting change. As the iron curtain between Hungary and Austria is dismantled in September 1989, thousands of East Germans make their way to the Federal Republic of Germany via Austria. Throughout the autumn the flow of East Germans to the West continues, as massive demonstrations calling for the dismantlement of the various East European Communist regimes develop.

As the Berlin Wall collapses and remnants of the iron curtain are dismantled in November 1989, followed by the dismantling of the Warsaw Pact a little more than a year later, NATO is faced with the task of defining a new identity. The collapse of the Eastern bloc also means the breakdown of the Cold War structure, within which NATO's raison d'etre had been defined. In this sense, NATO has come full circle from the beginning point of this analysis in the mid-1970s, when many were questioning the future need for the alliance in a context of relaxed tensions between East and West. NATO is wondering whether it will survive in the absence of an enemy but is quite clear that it should not be dismantled. Despite Soviet claims that both alliances should be dissolved, NATO argues that the Soviet Union remains a military power and therefore that NATO has to remain intact.

As in 1975, there is agreement about the need to build a European security structure, but the foundations of this framework remain unclear. There is a consensus that the structure should be based on the rule of law and human rights. Nonetheless, the ground on which the building should be constructed has not yet been established. While Gorbachev continues building support for a common European house, NATO has brought out its tools to contribute to the construction of a new European architecture. Although there is no agreement about the blueprints for the European structure in either bloc, the two general themes are distinguished by the emphasis on the construction of a new structure encompassing all of Europe, as opposed to eventually constructing additions onto the Western framework. Both the common house and the architecture are meant to be multidimensional structures containing several different sections. Besides the greater connotation of intimacy suggested by the metaphor of a house, the difference may be that all the rooms in Gorbachev's house would be equal, although based on different societal models of which socialism would be one, while the proposed architecture is designed on the basis of a Western model, with a Western European pillar standing at the center that interlocks with a variety of different institutions drawing the former Eastern European satellites into dialogue and potential future membership. The role of the Soviet Union in the architecture is ambiguous.

The CSCE would provide the infrastructure of the common European home, while it would be a central but not the defining feature of the new architecture, within which it would complement NATO. In 1990, the independent citizens' initiatives in both blocs institutionalize the detente-from-below process, by creating a parallel citizens' parliament of the official CSCE process, as a basis for developing a pan-European civil society. The blueprint for this parallel institution was drawn in 1988 at a seminar in Prague, which would be the eventual setting of the new institution. Jiri Dienstbier, one of the founders of this nongovernmental institution who after the Velvet Revolution became Czech foreign minister, described this Helsinki Citizen's Assembly as "typical of the dramatic pressure which has arisen due to the penetration of awakening freedom and responsibility into the ossified structures of the Cold War."[22] While the hope of the former Eastern European dissidents, many of whom have now become members of government, had been for the transformation of NATO as it merged into an all-European security structure covering the whole of Europe as well as North America and the Soviet Union, they now approach NATO for the necessary support for the fragile democracies of Eastern Europe, whose economies are threatened in the aftermath of the collapse of the COMECON (Council for Mutual Economic Assistance).

Both NATO and the former Eastern European satellites are aware of the possibility that forces in the Soviet Union may attempt to restore an authoritarian system, a possibility exemplified by the failed coup against Gorbachev. Gorbachev, attempting to preserve the foundations of socialism while restructuring the framework, is pulled in two opposing directions by, on the one hand, the conservative forces of the old Communist guard and, on the other, by demands for more dramatic market reforms. In light of the further disintegration of the Soviet economy and predictions of its breakdown, his policies, both internal and external, are increasingly viewed as a source of the Soviet Union's economic problems. In 1991, as the economy and the Soviet state further crumble, and the Soviet Republics begin to dismantle the Union, the collapse of the Soviet Union becomes inevitable.

REBUILDING THE STRUCTURE

Foundational metaphors played an important role in the naming and construction of the Cold War. The stable foundations of deterrence were responsible for preserving the security of the transatlantic family for four decades. As the boundaries distinguishing East and West begin to fade, a new competition emerges between two different European spaces, each of which is bound in different ways. In response to Gorbachev's common house, including all the CSCE countries, and a variety of rooms based on different models, NATO proposes its European architecture within which it would provide the central pillar of stability in a network of interlocking institutions.

Another structural metaphor emerges about the same time that serves to recast the shape of the architecture. The structures of the Cold War in both East and West contained families who provided security, two families whose acts of mutual maintenance held the

Cold War relationship in place. The form of life attached to the architecture is quite different. The architecture has an anchor, a solid core, and a center from which bridges emanate in several directions, connecting the core Europe to its previous-protector-become-equal-partner (the United States), as well as the new neighbors in Eastern Europe who want to rejoin Europe.

The relationships connected by these bridges are somewhat less intimate than the transatlantic family; in place of the security and protection provided by the American nuclear guarantee, the field shifts to one defined by membership in a Western club, which is an investment providing security benefits. In order to join NATO, potential members must demonstrate that they possess assets. Membership in the Western club is attached to conditions. Potential members, to become "normal," must demonstrate that they hold and act on a set of values growing out of a common cultural heritage and attached to the Judeo-Christian and Enlightenment tradition, which is said to be the opposite of nationalism.

It should be noted that there is an intermediary step in the transition from a security relationship structured by protector and protected to one of club membership, based on assets and investments. In 1989 to 1990, as the Eastern bloc was transformed and as Gorbachev won the trust of the West, NATO's security becomes an insurance policy. The logic of insurance demonstrates its role in this context as part of an effort to convince public opinion of the need to continue to pay for defenses at a time when the threat from the East seems to have dissolved. One purchases insurance while healthy as a way of being prepared for future sickness.

With the dissolution of the Soviet Union, the threat is no longer another family, as in the Cold War, but the dangerous swirling waters surrounding the bridge that threaten to engulf the West if not for the NATO anchor. The dangers are now more likely to come from out of the area, lacking any specific identity, or from nationalist conflicts, especially in the former Yugoslavia, and the threat of renationalization, which, it is feared, will spread to Western Europe. The main concern is survival in these troubled waters, given the diffuseness of the threat, its unpredictability, and the difficulty of making populations understand the necessity of maintaining an active defense policy given the disappearance of the Soviet threat.

The anchor, the bridge, the architecture, and the pillar are fixed structures in dangerous seas, yet in 1993 these stable bounded images begin to fade until they largely disappear (for the time being) in 1994. There is too much tension between the erecting of structures and the language games being played in the new Russia. Lurking in the background of NATO texts are alternative images of webs, fabrics, networks. The webs or networks lack any clear boundaries distinguishing outside and inside. Yet they are not without structure or form. They are characterized by different, more intricate and complex forms, with many beginnings and endings, many interconnections. Structure is an objective, a rule from the past framing knowledge of what makes for security, a rule projected into a future where it is not working, where there is tension between these language games and others within the world order.

STRUCTURES AND PARTNERS

Action, and particularly military action, requires a unitary identity that is capable of projecting power outward. The United States and the Soviet Union were such identities in the Cold War, but Europe, after the collapse of this relationship, is having problems constructing itself as a similar kind of unitary actor. Europe, as an identity, overlaps with too many other identities that hold a tension between them, more like the fabric whose boundaries are interwoven. This problem of overlapping identities is a central tension in post-Cold War Europe, a tension most evident in the relationship to the Soviet Union. The architecture of NATO first arose as an idea in competition with Gorbachev's common house. The common house, which would have enclosed the Soviet Union within Europe, was viewed by the West as an extension of the traditional Soviet objective of decoupling Europe from the United States, leaving it alone on the European continent with the dominant military presence of the Soviet Union, even though Gorbachev's house, based as it was on the CSCE model, would have included the United States and Canada. The architecture shifts the center of gravity toward Western Europe. After the collapse of the Soviet Union, questions arise about the appropriateness of Russian membership in the European club. On the one hand, it is argued that the Russian presence would overwhelm and dominate the smaller countries of Eastern and Western Europe. On the other, there are concerns about the consequences of isolating this large historic power. Whether Russia should be inside or outside the architecture is central in this division. The question itself is inseparable from the foundational metaphor, insofar as structures constitute strict boundaries distinguishing an inside and an outside in a way that webs or networks do not. Concerns about isolation in the post-Cold War world, however, relate not only to Russia. The Europeans are concerned that the Americans will return to isolationism now that the Cold War is over; the Eastern Europeans fear that the West Europeans will isolate themselves behind a new cordon sanitaire, leaving them once again forgotten and alone.

The language games of the post-Cold War period, like those of the Cold War, construct insides and outsides. One is either inside or outside a structure, although in this case several are standing at the doorway waiting to get in. While one can, with some difficulty, join a family, joining or bringing in new members is a regular practice of clubs. One can move from the outside to the inside of a club, and this issue of who belongs and where precisely the boundaries of Europe will be drawn is the source of tension.

The possible placement of Russia outside Europe, and the emphasis on the West winning the Cold War, provides fuel to nationalists and former communists in Russia who play on themes of reviving Russia's lost empire and place in the world. On the one hand, these actors reinforce Russia's isolation. On the other, there are clear signs that a decision to move the boundaries of Europe eastward to include former Soviet satellites would harden anti-Western feelings among the Russian public and increase support for nationalists such as Vladimir Zhirinovsky.

The responses of the former Eastern bloc countries, recently having escaped the yoke of Soviet power, are anxiety and increased urgency in their need to get inside the Western club. It is at this point that the attempt to construct a European structure with clear insides and outsides becomes problematic. To accept the Eastern Europeans into NATO would only contribute to the construction of a new security dilemma with the former superpower. It risks making Europe, and the space occupied by former Eastern Europe, a place from which new divisions and conflicts, potentially more dangerous than those of the Cold War, may arise. Drawing lines in this context would contribute not to the preservation of peace, as in the Cold War, but the exacerbation of conflict at the heart of Europe.

In the first half of 1994, as this tension increases, the structural metaphors fade into the background of NATO's conceptualization of European security and are replaced by the Partnership for Peace, in which the boundaries of Europe are more flexible, and the drawing of lines distinguishing identities less important than the opening of communication, dialogue, and the development of cooperation. The purpose of the partnership, like the North Atlantic Cooperation Council (NACC), is to draw Russia, as well as Eastern Europe, closer to NATO.

Two different language games are being played by NATO, and there is a tension between them. On the one hand, NATO projects a rule from the past into this new context, that is, the rule that security is equal to the construction of unitary identity surrounded by hard boundaries, as reflected in the structural metaphors—an identity capable of projecting power outward to stabilize and bring areas of conflict under control. In 1994, for the first time in its history, NATO uses its military power, in the context of the Bosnian conflict.

On the other hand, NATO makes a decision for the time being to avoid drawing new lines around Europe. Instead of fixed spaces connected by bridges, relationships are conceived, among others, in terms of overlapping rings of love.[23] The rings of love denote a form quite different from that of either the courtship games of the classical European balance of power or the Cold War families. The former involved courtship and wooing, remaining attractive in order to be able to change partners. In contrast, the Cold War was a permanent commitment to one of two families representing quite different values and gender relationships. With the rings of love, Europe (or at least several countries of Europe) remains at the center but is woven in a range of different partnerships that overlap, making it difficult to distinguish its boundaries. The relationship between the intersection of the rings in Europe to the United States, now in the periphery, is quite different from the relationship to either Russia or the Eastern European or European Economic Area countries. Europe is constructed at the intersection of countries in the Western European Union, NATO, the European Union, and the CSCE, and it is also embedded in the UN. There are many overlapping identities and relationships that limit freedom of movement but do not fix a space. While military projection remains a possibility and is in fact being undertaken for the first time, it is not the most evident choice in the conflicts confronting NATO. Where it seems necessary, as in Bosnia, it is difficult to construct sufficient unity to make military action possible. The political side of identity and the necessity of dialogue are emphasized, given that the redrawing of lines would only create the conditions for a new security dilemma, a realignment of identity, and perhaps the renationalization of Europe. There is a tension between the need to respond to the humanitarian disaster in Bosnia and the desire to avoid hardening the lines between the West and Russia or within the Alliance, given the range of different interests and concerns that intersect in this conflict.

In the immediate aftermath of the Cold War, European state leaders engage in a process of reconceptualizing Europe, a renaming that they recognize is essential for defining their own possibilities for action in the world, for knowing how to proceed.[24] This reconceptualization, while different from that of the Cold War, draws on familiar conceptualizations of security in terms of some form of structure. On the one hand, the possibility of a more equal marriage between the transatlantic partners, as well as the possibility of divorce, is entertained. On the other, the transatlantic partnership fades in significance against the background of an expanding club and overlapping rings of love. The new structure becomes increasingly shaky as NATO is pulled between conflicting objectives or interests. The problem is that this attempt to reconstitute a structure is in conflict with other processes and potentialities in the "new world order" that require a different kind of response, a different form of relationship from the military relationships of the past.

CONCLUSION

Cold War language games of security are paradoxical. While the American promise to use nuclear weapons in defense of Europe is an expression of potential violence and destruction, it is framed in a context of stable foundations enclosing families bound by commitment. In this semantic disarrangement, properties conventionally ascribed to one form of life, a family, are unconventionally ascribed to another, a military alliance. In this act an otherwise abstract experience of a promise binding populations on two distant continents is described in the more understandable everyday language of the protection provided by families. The act is not simply one of description, however; it also replaces the destructive, fearful emotions associated with nuclear war with positive emotions of safety and belonging.

Traditional game theory has been criticized for trivializing life-and-death experiences at the international level by drawing on game metaphors. By contrast, the language games explored here are not mere games but, rather, acts by which we are connected and reconnected to a particular kind of experience.[25] Alliance games connect us to an everyday cultural experience of home. At the same time, these language games organize and construct the identity of NATO or the Warsaw Pact, creating and maintaining the sensibility on which these "imagined communities" depend.[26] The emancipatory acts of social movements reverse the paradox, exposing the violence and dependency underlying this external image of commitment and protection.

Alliance identities within the Cold War were constructed as given, that is, as belonging to a relational field defined by the permanence of committed families occupying stable structures. It is the necessity of these hierarchies that is called into question by emancipatory movements. The cohesion of each alliance relationship depends on acts that name the family as a source of security. In the early eighties, each family is engaged in actions—movement toward a first-strike strategy in the West and human rights abuses in the East—that the movements rename as a source of insecurity. These acts of renaming introduce a conflict over the interpretation of the meaning of acts by each family. Once the necessity of a particular spatial field begins to dissolve, new acts of naming recast the boundaries of possibility and action in multiple ways.

This analysis has demonstrated an underlying continuity to changes in the meaning of security. The central role historically of grammars of structure and intimate relations, as well as the various forms in which they have been expressed in different historical eras, is the basis for distinguishing that which has changed. In contrast to the deterministic notion of games or structure employed in theories of International Relations—which not incidently emerged in the context of the Cold War—the more fluid notion of language games makes it possible to recognize that the current need to redefine security is inseparable from practices in the real world by which the structures and relationships of the Cold War were called into question.

In the process of challenging assumptions that the walls or intimate relations provided security, social movements begin making different moves—the maintenance activities of states are countered by the dismantling acts of movements, accompanied by a renaming of the relationships as sources of dependence, hierarchy, and danger. These challenges from outside recast the terms of the game. Both superpowers begin to negate the foundations of deterrence, and Gorbachev proposes a security structure based on a renaming of the outsides and insides of Europe, which, like the social movement efforts to restore the meaning of Helsinki, is based on the CSCE model. The North Atlantic Treaty Organization also engages in an act of renaming the boundaries that results in a new competition between two different structures. With each move, as the game is politicized or the space renamed, the relationships within or outside spaces are also recast. As competition over the naming of the European space emerges, the relationships become less intimate—clubs rather than families—accompanied by the emergence of different degrees of intimacy, as characterized by the rings of love and the absence of clear boundaries between intimates and others. It is difficult in the post-Cold War context to redefine the meaning of security precisely because this concept has traditionally required the drawing of lines and the building of walls to distinguish the space occupied by intimates and others outside. We are faced with a choice between security in this form as traditionally defined, a choice that has become increasingly dangerous, or finding new forms of security more fitting to a world of overlapping identities.

NOTES

1. I would like to thank the Amsterdam School for Social Science Research (University of Amsterdam) for their generous support of this project. This article is based on a much larger study, "Excavating the Ruins of the Cold War: Recovering the Contours of a Changing Security Culture" (Ph.D. diss.: University of Minnesota, 1995).

2. Charles W. Kegley, "How Did the Cold War Die? Principles for an Autopsy," *Mershon International Studies Review*, supplement to the *International Studies Quarterly* 38 (April 1994), 11–41.

3. Ludwig Wittgenstein, *Philosophical Investigations* (Oxford: Basil Blackwell, 1958).

4. For an in-depth analysis of Wittgenstein's private-language argument, see Saul A. Kripke, *Wittgenstein on Rules and Private Language* (Oxford: Basil Blackwell, 1982).

5. Paul Chilton and Mikhail Llyin have written a fascinating analysis of

the difference in meaning between these two concepts in East and West as they related to interpretations of Gorbachev's common-house proposal. Paul Chilton and Mikhail Llyin, "Metaphor in Political Discourse: The Case of the 'Common European House,'" *Discourse and Society* 4:1 (1993).

6. Kenneth N. Waltz, *Theory of International Politics* (Reading, Mass.: Addison-Wesley, 1979), 165–66. Emphasis added.

7. Philippe Moreau-Defarges, "Anti-American Feeling in Europe: Between Fear of War and Obsession with Abandonment," NATO *Review* 35:2 (April 1987). Emphasis added.

8. Martin Hollis and Steve Smith have also made a connection between the dominance of chicken as a cultural game in 1950s America and the emergence of chicken as a model for conceptualizing the nuclear relationship between the superpowers at about the same time. Martin Hollis and Steve Smith, *Explaining and Understanding International Relations* (Oxford: Clarendon Press, 1991), 127.

9. See Karin Fierke, "Excavating the Ruins of the Cold War." The analysis draws on the following sources: NATO *Review; Current Digest of the Soviet Press;* speeches of President Ronald Reagan; documents of the Western European peace movement taken primarily from END *Journal* and the archives of the International Peace Coordination and Cooperation Centre; documents of Solidarity, published primarily in the *Labor Review on Eastern Europe;* documents of Charter 77, published primarily in the *Bulletin* of Palach Press; and documents of the Committee on the Present Danger, published in *Alerting America: The Papers of the Committee on the Present Danger* (Washington, D.C.: Pergamon-Brassey's, 1984).

10. Ernst Hans van der Beugel, "The Atlantic Family—Managing Its Problems," NATO *Review* 34:1 (February 1986).

11. "The American relationship with Europe is now an old one. . . . The US has been fully joined with Western Europe in the security process." W. Tapley Bennett Jr., "The US and the Atlantic Community," NATO *Review* 31:2 (July 1983).

12. "Peace and National Security: A New Defense," speech by Ronald Reagan, delivered at the White House, Washington, D.C., 23 March 1983, printed in *Vital Speeches of the Day* 49:13 (15 April 1983).

13. Speech by Ronald Reagan, delivered at the U.S. Ranger Monument in Pointe du Hoc, France, 6 June 1984, published in his *Speaking My Mind* (New York: Simon and Schuster, 1989).

14. "It is our task to explain to the new generation what we consider as self-evident truths, as basic values in our lives, and which they may disregard out of ignorance or neglect, as if it were sufficient to want something and shout for it in a street demonstration in order to get it." Arrigo Levi, "NATO, Key to Peace and Security," NATO *Review* 31:6 (January 1984).

15. Interestingly enough, if one looks back at NATO documents from this earlier period, the younger generation is handled in a much different way. Within the European context, the student movements of the 1960s were more focused on transforming the universities. Vietnam, while an issue, has a much different tenor in this context from that within the United States; in any case, it is not a NATO issue. Texts at the time focus on grooming future leaders who are afforded space to speak within the magazine. They are praised for making certain kinds of distinctions between East and West against the background of the Soviet invasion of Czechoslovakia. See, for instance, Edmund Nessler, "Explanatory Memorandum" (extracts), and Oscar de Wandel, "NATO's New Frontier: A Student's View of NATO," NATO Review 17:2 (1969); Kaare Sandegren, "The New Generation and NATO," NATO Review 17:9 (1969).

16. Opponents of the cruise and Pershing II deployments were in fact distributed across the age spectrum. A poll in February 1983 in the Federal Republic of Germany (FRG) showed 57 percent of age groups from twenty-five to thirty-nine and sixty and older agreeing with the demand not to deploy any new missiles in the FRG. The other age groups differed only by a few percentage points, including 59 percent of the eighteen to twenty-four year olds, 51 percent of those forty to forty-nine and 53 percent of those between fifty and fifty-nine. Hans Rattinger, "The Federal Republic of Germany: Much Ado about (Almost) Nothing," in Gregory Flynn and Hans Rattinger, eds., The Public and Atlantic Defense (London: Croom Helm, 1985). In Italy the differences were more noticeable. Among educated Italians, 71 percent of university students opposed the INF (Intermediate-Range Nuclear Forces) deployments, followed by 69 percent in those up to age thirty-four; 58 percent of those from thirty-five to forty-four; 48 percent of those forty-five to fifty-four, and 34 percent of those above fifty-five. Sergio A. Rossi, "Public Opinion and Atlantic Defense in Italy," in Flynn and Rattinger. In Britain, a poll from January 1983 showed the following percentages of those disapproving of the government decision to deploy American cruise missiles on British soil: ages fifteen to twenty-four, 64 percent; ages twenty-five to forty-four, 66 percent; ages forty-five to sixty-four, 57 percent; ages sixty-five and older, 58 percent. Ivor Crewe, "Britain: Two and a Half Cheers for the Atlantic Alliance," in Flynn and Rattinger.

17. "The direction the ideological thinking of the young generation will take—as well as the drift of political change in Poland and in other countries of Eastern Europe—will depend on the convergence of these groups with the activities of the working class." Adam Michnik, "A New Evolutionism," (1976) in his Letters from Prison and Other Essays (Berkeley and Los Angeles: University of California Press, 1985). Michael Waller discusses the emergence of a generational cleavage in Eastern Europe that favored develop-

ment of "anti-politics." Michael Waller, *The End of the Communist Power Monopoly* (Manchester: Manchester University Press, 1993).

18. One need only think back to the type of language games on which the women's movement relied. Emancipation is, of course, not exclusive to this type of context. Emancipation games are also played by other types of resistance movements.

19. "Peace and National Security: A New Defense," speech by Ronald Reagan.

20. See Václav Havel, "The Power of the Powerless," in Václav Havel et al., *The Power of the Powerless,* John Keane, ed. (London: Palach Press, 1985).

21. Van der Beugel, "The Atlantic Family."

22. Jiri Dienstbier, "The Helsinki Citizen's Assembly," in Mary Kaldor, ed., *Europe from Below: An East-West Dialogue* (New York: Verso, 1991).

23. This metaphor appeared, along with a nice diagram, in "Europe: Partners for What?", in *The Economist,* 24 September 1994, 29–30.

24. "The alliance has made impressive progress, at least at the level of conceptual clarification. Understanding must precede action. However, understanding does not take us very far unless it is followed by action. Conceptual agreement must lead to concerted implementation, to a commitment to resources and forces." Johan Jorgen Holst, "Pursuing a Durable Peace in the Aftermath of the Cold War," NATO *Review* 40:4 (1992), 10.

25. Clifford Geertz articulates this notion best in his analysis of the Balinese cockfight: "It is this kind of bringing of assorted experiences of everyday life to focus that the cockfight, set aside from that life as 'only a game' and reconnected to it as 'more than a game' accomplishes, and so creates what, better than typical or universal, could be called a paradigmatic human event. . . . Enacted and re-enacted, so far without end, the cockfight enables the Balinese, as read and reread, Macbeth enables us, to see a dimension of his own subjectivity. . . . Yet, because—in another of those paradoxes . . .— that subjectivity does not properly exist until it is thus organized, art forms generate and regenerate the very subjectivity they pretend only to display. Quartets, still lifes, and cockfights are not merely reflections of a pre-existing sensibility analogically represented; they are positive agents in the creation and maintenance of such a sensibility." Clifford Geertz, "Deep Play: Notes on the Balinese Cockfight," in his *The Interpretation of Cultures: Selected Essays* (New York: Basic Books, 1973), 450–51.

26. Benedict Anderson, *Imagined Communities: Reflections on the Origin and Spread of Nationalism* (New York: Verso, 1991).

III

*World Order
and Regional Imperatives*

9

Between a New World Order and None: Explaining the Reemergence of the United Nations in World Politics

THOMAS RISSE-KAPPEN

INTRODUCTION

This chapter has two purposes, one theoretical, the other empirical.[1] First, I try to show that the divide between mainstream International Relations theory and so-called critical approaches is not as deep as many authors, including some in this book, assume. In particular, I argue that competing hypotheses can be derived from sophisticated rationalist approaches to world politics as well as from social constructivist assumptions and that these propositions can well be evaluated empirically. It follows that I disagree with the commonly held argument that the rationalist-constructivist divide pertains to both ontological (that is, substantive) and epistemological assumptions, as earlier work in the field claimed.[2] Rationalists and social constructivists can well agree with the logic of the "double hermeneutics" (Hans-Georg Gadamer; Anthony Giddens) and maintain that rigorous testing of competing assumptions is possible and that the resulting truth claims can be decided through the intersubjective discourses of the scholarly community. To denounce the latter as positivist is to ignore at least the last twenty years of epistemological debates in social sciences. This is not to deny that there is no epistemological divide. But this divide resides inside the social constructivist camp itself between those who maintain that truth claims can be decided by intersubjective discourses and those who do not share that view (many poststructuralists).

This chapter tries to make sense of the recent emergence of the United Nations Security Council as a serious player in world politics and the difficulties it faces to enforce a "new world order." I argue that traditional power-based approaches pertaining to U.S. hegemony in the post-Cold War era or to strategic interests of the great powers cannot adequately account for the evolution of UN activities. A norm-based explanation emphasizing the gradual evolution of principles of multilateralism and humanitarian intervention captures the empirical evidence of increasing Security Council words and ambivalent deeds in terms of peacekeeping and peacemaking to some extent. A social constructivist interpretation can nevertheless account for the present confusion by pointing to inherent contradictions in the liberal internationalist worldview on which these norms of a new world order are based.

The chapter proceeds in three steps. First, I contrast two rationalist theories—U.S. hegemony and cooperation among great powers—with a social constructivist approach to multilateral cooperation. The discussion leads to three propositions to be evaluated in the empirical part of the chapter. Second, I examine the gradual evolution of Security Council resolutions pertaining to humanitarian interventions and threats to international peace and security. Third, these words are contrasted with UN deeds concerning peacekeeping in general, as well as UN involvement during the Gulf War, in Somalia, and in the former Yugoslavia.

THEORETICAL APPROACHES TO MULTILATERAL COOPERATION: RATIONALISM VERSUS SOCIAL CONSTRUCTIVISM

In this part of the chapter, I contrast two approaches to multilateral cooperation based on divergent paradigms of International Relations theory. On the one hand, rational choice models exogenize the preferences of actors and then theorize about the conditions under which cooperation among self-interested and egoistic actors is possible. On the other hand, social constructivist approaches argue that the preferences of actors need to become part of the explanation if we want to understand the emergence and the failure of international cooperation. The two paradigms lead to diverging assumptions about the prospects of multilateralism that can be evaluated empirically.

Following John G. Ruggie, I define *multilateralism* as a specific form of international cooperation based on the principles of "indivisibility" (of the goods and values to be achieved, such as peace and security), "nondiscrimination" (all parties to an agreement to be treated equally), and "diffuse reciprocity" (parties do not rely on specific balanced exchanges, but on the long-term expectation of equivalent gains).[3]

Rationalism: U.S. Hegemony or Minilateralism?

From a rational choice perspective, implementing the collective security measures of the UN Charter poses a collective action problem that can be represented as an n-person "prisoners' dilemma."[4] Assuming that states calculate their own and the other players' interests in rational cost-benefit terms (strategic rationality), collaboration to provide the public good of international peace and security should be unlikely in a multilateral environment. First, the large number of players increases incentives for free riding. Second, enforcing the cooperation necessary to produce the public good in a multilateral setting requires excessive monitoring and compliance capabilities. Third, the above-stated principles of multilateralism on which the UN relies are unlikely to ensure enduring cooperation. Studies of prisoners' dilemma situations have shown, for example, that strategies of *specific reciprocity* such as tit-for-tat combining of incentives to cooperate with retaliation in case of defection are more conducive to collaboration than reliance on some generalized obligations. The norm of indivisibility also increases the incentive to free ride, as members of the organization cannot be excluded from the benefits provided by the institution.

In sum, an increasing role of the UN in maintaining international peace and security is counterintuitive from a rational collective action perspective, while lack of action (the former Yugoslavia) or retreat in the face of difficulties (Somalia) could be easily explained. But rationalist cooperation theory offers two perspectives on the conditions under which such collective action problems could be solved—hegemonic stability and convergence of interests among key actors.

American Hegemony in a Unipolar World?

Can the revival of the UN be explained as a function of reasserted American hegemony in a unipolar post-Cold War world?[5] And if so, why would the American hegemon need multilateral institutions to legitimize its foreign policy, thereby risking constraints on its own freedom of action through entanglement in the UN?

Hegemonic stability theory argues that international order can be maintained if there is a hegemonic leader with such overwhelming power capabilities that she can impose cooperation among the lesser states.[6] The hegemon can do so either through coercion or persuasion. In the latter case, "benign hegemons" provide the public good in question—for example, supplying the troops to drive Saddam Hussein out of Kuwait or creating stability in Somalia. Her overwhelming power also enables her to use side payments, issue linkage, and bribery to induce the lesser states to acquiescence. Benign hegemony works because (1) maintaining the international order is in the hegemon's interest because it confirms its power status; and (2) the hegemon provides the public good—international stability—for the lesser powers so that the latter can free ride on the former and have incentives to acquiesce in the hegemonic power position.

This argument leads to the following proposition:

> *The more the U.S. considers its national interests at stake, the more the UN Security Council will be willing to declare inter- and intrastate conflicts as threats to international peace and security (Chapter VII of UN Charter) and to implement such resolutions.*

The variation in the willingness of the Security Council to enforce its resolutions would then be a function of U.S. foreign policy decisions. If we want to understand Security Council activities, we need to examine activities in Washington, not in New York.

An empirical assessment of the proposition notwithstanding, there are problems with the argument. Hegemonic powers have choices of how to deal with smaller states. They can maintain international order and stability through unilateral strategies, bilateral, or multilateral arrangements. Why then does the United States opt for multilateralism in the UN, thereby inevitably reducing its freedom of action? One could argue that empire by consent pays off in the long run, while malign hegemony relying on unilateral strategies involves continuing punishment of smaller states and the constant expenditure of resources to suppress potential rebellions.[7] Because multilateralism gives at least the appearance that smaller states are being heard, they are more likely to acquiesce to hegemonic leadership in such a setting than in an imposed regime.

But this argument only makes sense if the hegemon is willing to encounter short-term losses (in terms of reduced decision-making power) in the interest of long-term gains. In other words, benign hegemony in a multilateral setting such as the UN hinges on whether or not the hegemon has a low discount rate for the future and her preference structure is geared toward long-term considerations. At this point, rational choice considerations about hegemonic stability reach their limits. The hegemon's preference structure needs to be analyzed. As John Ruggie puts it, "to determine why *this* particular institutional agenda was pursued, it is inescapable at some point to look more closely at *this* particular hegemon."[8]

The second problem of hegemonic stability theory—either the realist or the Gramscian version—pertains to its starting assumption of a huge asymmetry between the material capabilities of the hegemon and the rest of the world. It is highly questionable that the United States currently holds such a hegemonic status. In 1987, for example, the U.S. share of the world gross national product was 25 percent, while the combined share of the other permanent members of the Security Council plus Germany and Japan was 45 percent. As to global military expenditures, the U.S. share was 30 percent as compared to 45 percent of the other six leading states.[9] With regard to nuclear weapons, Russia remains a formidable power retaining its second-strike capability. Only if the ability to project conventional military force globally were all that counted today would the United States be in a superior position compared to other states. While this latter capability provides the United States with some unique bargaining leverage as to the implementation of Security Council resolutions, it does not constitute hegemonic status in the sense of the theory.

But rational choice arguments are not finished because of the theoretical and empirical pitfalls of hegemonic stability theory.

Minilateralism: Cooperation among Core Powers

The assumption that hegemonic stability provides the only solution to collective action problems of utility-maximizing and self-interested actors has been successfully challenged by *rationalist regime analysis*. Game theory has shown theoretically that there are nonhegemonic cooperative solutions to collaboration problems of the prisoners' dilemma variety depending on the "shadow of the future," the number of players, and the strategies used.[10] Regime analysis has demonstrated that international institutions can facilitate cooperation by providing rules, norms, and procedures for negotiating agreements, by lowering the transaction costs of cooperation, and by supplying information to reduce uncertainty about motivations of actors.[11]

One could argue that UN peacekeeping operations have evolved over the years into a partial security regime with specific rules and decision-making procedures. Peacekeeping forces have been used for a variety of purposes—from monitoring armistice agreements and the provision of humanitarian assistance to the supervision of elections. The irony is that peacekeeping originated as an institutional response by the secretary-general to the Security Council's lack of ability or willingness during the Cold War to fulfil its collective security functions envisioned in the Charter.[12]

The development of a UN peacekeeping regime during the Cold War provided an institutionalized solution to the collective security problems with which the Security Council was confronted in the post-Cold War era. It was, therefore, only natural that the revival of Chapter VII measures by the Security Council used the peacekeeping instruments as its starting point and then expanded the scope and the tasks of the regime. While the existence of a regime explains the institutional pathway that the Security Council chose to become more activist in terms of Chapter VII, it does not explain the renewed activism itself.

Game theory has argued that collaboration problems involving a high number of players can be overcome, if a *k group* can be identified, a small number of key players "whose cooperation would ensure resolution of the dilemma, no matter what the others (n-k) did."[13] Such a core group for whom the benefits of cooperation outweigh the costs independently from the behavior of the others exists in many multilateral settings. Public choice theory also talks of "minimal contributing sets" as the group of actors that together may provide a public good if they cooperate. Miles Kahler has shown that many post-World War II multilateral institutions depended on such "minilateral" solutions of great power cooperation.[14]

The Security Council provides an institutionalized basis for a k-group solution to the collaboration problem involved in a large multilateral setting. First, it privileges the great powers by providing them with a permanent seat plus the right to veto. Thus, the setting ensures that the minimal contributing set in world politics is represented and cannot be overruled (except for Japan and Germany, of course). Second, the Security Council embeds the minilateral solution of great power politics into a larger multilateral framework through an elaborate scheme of representing countries from various regions of the world on a rotating basis. As a result, a representative sample of about 10 percent of the UN member states is constantly participating in Security Council decisions.[15]

The discussion then leads to a second proposition:

> The more the permanent members of the Security Council consider their national interests at stake, the more the Security Council will be willing to declare inter- and intrastate conflicts as threats to international peace and security and to implement such resolutions.

Institutionalizing a core group solution to the collective action problems of maintaining international peace and security does not ensure cooperation among the core states. The lack of agreement among the permanent members (P-5) during the Cold War rendered the Security Council virtually inoperative for decades, at least as far as its main purpose according to the UN Charter was concerned. The first attempt to overcome this problem—the 1950 Uniting for Peace resolution, transferring the authority to determine a threat to peace from the Security Council to the General Assembly—only worked as long as the Western powers could build winning coalitions in the General Assembly. The second effort—peacekeeping under the authority of the Secretary General—was more effective, but only in cases in which the P-5 did not consider an international security issue as either an interbloc or an intrabloc affair.

Rationalist regime theory and the argument about the necessity of a core group only help to challenge the point that a hegemonic power is needed to facilitate cooperation in a multilateral setting. The argument takes it for granted that the great powers in the Security Council have concluded that cooperation to maintain international peace and security is in their best interest. But where did these cooperative interests come from? Scholars using the "cooperation under anarchy" perspective agree with realist authors that national interests are ultimately defined by material power-based calculations. The disagreement between the cooperation-under-anarchy perspective and structural realism of the Waltz/Grieco variety is not about the definition of national interests, but about the conclusions concerning the prospects of international cooperation.[16]

Rationalist regime theory and the k-group solution to collective action problems in a multilateral setting then leave two possibilities. First, if state interests are treated as exogenous to the argument, we are back at square one. As in the case of hegemonic stability theory, we would need a theory of interests and preferences to explain the contrast between the Security Council's multilateral words and the variation in the degree to which the resolutions are enforced. Second, if we assume realist arguments about national preference formation, we would posit that the variation can be explained by the extent to which the P-5 considered their power-based interests at stake.

Social Constructivism: Contested Norms of Liberal Internationalism

Hegemonic stability theory and the cooperation-under-anarchy perspective agree on the core assumptions about world politics. They conceptualize international relations as an anarchic self-help system in which rational states struggle for survival and calculate their interests with regard to the power distribution in the system. The two approaches disagree with regard to the prospects of international cooperation.

Social constructivists hold different core assumptions about international relations.[17] First, they endogenize the interests and preferences of actors. These interests are not fixed by some presocial calculation of costs and benefits but emerge from processes of social interaction and communication. Domestic, international, and transnational discourses provide the framework in which actors define their preferences and build consensus-based coalitions. As a result, these discourses are causally consequential for the resulting practices and behavior. Second, structures and agency are mutually constitutive. International and domestic structures constrain and enable the practices of actors, while these practices enact and change the structures.[18] Third, material capabilities and structures are indeterminate with regard to interests or policy preferences. Ideas— worldviews, principled beliefs, and knowledge[19]—not only define the meaning of power but also affect the reasoning process by which state actors define their interests. Fourth, anarchy understood as a self-help system is not the defining feature of international relations.

World politics is heavily regulated by norms that prescribe appropriate behavior and are embedded in formal and informal institutions. These institutions form the social structure of international relations. The logic of anarchy itself is socially constructed, as presocial actors do not need to be conceptualized as potentially hostile.[20] The "democratic peace," for example, constitutes a social relationship in world politics where the logic of anarchy and of the security dilemma is virtually absent.[21]

From this perspective, international cooperation has to be analyzed in the framework of norm change and norm creation through the social and communicative practices of actors—whether states, domestic, or transnational groups. If we take the impact of norms in international relations seriously, we cannot just examine the decisions and resulting actions of state governments. Strictly speaking, norms only have independent causal effects on actors' behavior if they start believing in their validity and significance through processes of communication and persuasion. It is noteworthy in this context that the new consensus definition of international regimes emphasizes prescriptive status of normative ideas as a precondition of rule-consistent behavior.[22] *Prescriptive status* means that actors regularly refer to the respective norm to comment on their own behavior and that of others. Thus, if we want to understand the causal impact of norms, we need to concentrate on processes of persuasion and to analyze the discourses of actors. The validity claims of normative ideas are contested in communicative processes during which specific ideas win out against others and then influence the behavior of actors.

In the case of the UN Security Council, the two norms at stake are the principles of multilateralism (see above) and the obligation to intervene for humanitarian reasons in cases of gross violations of human rights.[23] The norm changes in question refer (a) to the decreasing validity of the right of individual or collective self-defense (Article 51 of the UN Charter) in favor of the collective security provisions in Chapter VII of the Charter, and (b) to an increasing collective understanding of the international community that human rights standards overrule the principle of noninterference in domestic affairs (Article 2(7) of the Charter) and, thus, a change in the traditional notion of national sovereignty.

These considerations lead to the following proposition:

The more norms of multilateralism and humanitarian intervention gain prescriptive status in the communicative practices—domestic and transnational—of the dominant members of the Security Council, the more the Security Council will be willing to declare inter- and intra-state conflicts as threats to international peace and security and to implement such resolutions.

"Dominant members" of the Security Council are, of course, the permanent five whose consent (at least implicit through abstention) is institutionally required for the UN to take action. Norms do not fall from heaven, however, but their origins are historically contingent. In the cases of multilateralism and humanitarian intervention, these norms originated from the liberal internationalist worldview that constitutes one dimension of public and elite opinion in the West.[24] Principles of multilateralism have long shaped the interactions among the members of the democratic peace (that is, the Organization for Economic Cooperation and Development world).[25] The current domestic and transnational discourses on both sides of the Atlantic concern primarily the extent to which these norms should be extended globally and govern relations among the UN members as well as the specific obligations resulting from the principles of multilateralism. As to humanitarian intervention, the idea that human rights norms supersede the principle of national sovereignty also forms part of the liberal worldview. The controversy centers around the extent to which human rights norms should govern the foreign policies of states and the degree to which they should override power-based interests traditionally defined.

From a perspective emphasizing communicative practices and norms, one does not need to assume U.S. or Western hegemony in terms of overwhelming power capabilities to presuppose Western leadership in the UN. While leadership is necessary in multilateral institutional settings to build consensus, superior power is not.[26] If there is Western leadership in the UN, it is based not so much on material capabilities, but on liberal internationalist values and norms containing consensual validity claims that can be challenged by lesser states. "Followership" would then be based on the persuasive power of the ideas promoted by the West.[27]

How do these discourses affect the Security Council decisions and the degree to which they are implemented through peacekeeping and peacemaking operations? Does the third proposition offer a better explanation of the expansion and the limits of current UN activities than the two rationalist assumptions?[28] The empirical part of this chapter starts with a discussion of the increased activities of the Security Council concerning Chapter VII resolutions and humanitarian interventions. I then move from the words to the deeds and analyze the extent to which Security Council decisions have been implemented. I focus on the cases of UN involvement in the Gulf conflict, in Somalia, and in the former Yugoslavia.

WORDS: THE POST-COLD WAR SECURITY COUNCIL AND ITS NEW CONSENSUS

The quantitative increase in Security Council (SC) activities is dramatic. From 1980–85, the SC passed 119 resolutions of which 72 were unanimous (61 percent). The percentage of consensual resolutions increased to 84 percent from 1986–90 (86 out of 103). In 1991–92 alone, the SC passed 116 resolutions, 98 of them unanimous (84 percent). With regard to the permanent members, there were 29 vetoed resolutions in 1980–85 (24 percent); the number decreased only slightly for the 1986–90 period (23, or 22 percent). No veto was cast in the Security Council in 1991–92. Most vetoes in the 1980s were cast by Western powers, particularly the United States, mainly with regard to issues pertaining to the Middle East and the Palestine question or concerning U.S. military involvements in Latin America. Only two vetoes have been cast so far in the 1990s.[29]

As to the content of these statements, an equally dramatic increase in Chapter VII resolutions can be observed. From the formation of the UN until 1989, the Security Council only passed six resolutions determining "threats to the peace, breaches of the peace, and acts of aggression." From 1990–92, thirty-three such resolutions were approved, twenty-one on the Iraq-Kuwait situation alone, eight on the former Yugoslavia, two on Somalia, and one each on the civil war in Liberia and against Libya sponsoring terrorism.

More important, the Security Council extended the definition of what constitutes "threats to peace" by explicitly including gross violations of human rights. This is not completely without precedent given the Chapter VII resolutions against Rhodesia in the 1960s and against South Africa in 1977. But these resolutions did not explicitly determine that apartheid represented a threat to international peace but focused, instead, on other actions (the unilateral declaration of independence by Rhodesia and South African military activities against frontline states). In April 1991, however, Security Council Resolution 688 set a precedent and identified the Iraqi repression of the Kurds and the Shi'ites as threats to international security and peace, legitimizing the creation of safe havens for the Kurdish population. Resolution 688, thus, not only determined that the principle of noninterference in domestic affairs (Article 2[7] of the Charter) did not apply to human rights concerns but also established that governmental "mistreatment of a minority group is a legitimate concern of the Security Council if that mistreatment raises broader international security concerns."[30] In January 1992, the summit meeting of the Security Council went even further and declared explicitly that "non-military sources of instability in the economic, social, humanitarian, and ecological fields have become threats to peace and security."[31] In August 1992, Resolution 770 authorized—under Chapter VII with its mandatory powers—states or regional agencies to take "all measures necessary" to facilitate the delivery of humanitarian aid to Bosnia-Herzegovina. The expression referred to Resolution 678, which had used similar words to authorize the use of force by the coalition forces against Iraq. In December 1992, Resolution 794 went one step further and explicitly authorized the "use [of] all necessary means" for establishing a safe environment for humanitarian relief operations in Somalia. A similar resolution legitimized the French humanitarian intervention in Rwanda at the end of June 1994. One month later and on American request, the Security Council even authorized the use of force "to facilitate the departure from Haiti of the military leadership" and to reinstate to power the ousted president Jean-Bertrand Aristide.[32] In this case, the principle of humanitarian intervention was not just confined to enable the delivery of humanitarian aid or to counter gross violations of human rights but extended to include the restoration of democracy.

In sum, the Security Council has not only dramatically increased its involvement in world affairs since the mid-1980s; it has also established two norms in the post-Cold War era since 1990:

1. Military interventions and the use of force in general are no longer considered legitimate outside explicit approval by the Security Council. This norm effectively constrains the invocation of Article

51 (right to individual or collective self-defense), thereby establishing the principles of multilateralism in the domain of international security.

2. The mandatory powers of the UN Charter's Chapter VII explicitly include the right of the international community to interfere in the domestic affairs of states in cases of humanitarian disasters, gross violations of human rights, and even the repression of democracy. This norm effectively constrains Article 2(7) of the Charter, thereby transforming traditional notions of national sovereignty.

These two principled beliefs have gained prescriptive status in the above-defined sense through a gradual process of norm creation and norm change. (Whether states behave in a rule-consistent manner is a different question and will be dealt with later in this chapter.) How can the evolution of Security Council resolutions and the voting behavior of its members be explained? Why did the non-Western SC members and the international community in general agree to essentially liberal internationalist norms?

With regard to the first rationalist proposition (U.S. hegemony), one could argue from a Gramscian perspective that reference to norms with universal validity claims (human rights, multilateralism) serves the purpose of maintaining American power in international society. The norms are consistent with a concept of benign hegemony or rule by consent that gives at least the appearance that minor states are being heard (see above). It is not at all clear from a rationalist perspective, however, that the benefits (American power status) outweigh the costs (reduced decision-making power) in this case. The norm prohibiting the use of force without UN approval should only be tolerable for the United States, for example, if it can be sure that it still commands sufficient power resources to bribe or coerce lesser states into acquiescence whenever U.S. leaders consider the use of force to pursue the American national interest. This assumption does not make sense. It is probably safe to argue that the Security Council is powerless without American cooperation (irrespective of the right to veto) in the domain of Chapter VII resolutions or humanitarian interventions. But this does not mean that the United States can dictate or even lure the other Security Council members to follow its will.[33]

Moreover, Washington's attitude toward the UN changed significantly from Ronald Reagan's to George Bush's administration and has become even more positive during Bill Clinton's term.[34] The change occurred prior to the end of the Cold War and can thus hardly be explained by a shift in the international distribution of power and a subsequent change in the U.S. national interest. Finally, we would expect from a benign hegemony perspective that the United States not only provides norms of cooperation for the international community, but also the public good of international security itself. This is not at all the case.

The second rationalist proposition assumes that the norms of multilateralism and of humanitarian intervention are consistent with the national interests of a core group of powers that then establishes its prescriptive status. One could then explain the newfound consensus among the permanent SC members with the end of the Cold War, in particular the end of the American-Soviet rivalry. The end of the East-West conflict terminated the stalemate in the Security Council that prevented it since the Korean war from dealing with interbloc or intrabloc conflicts.

But it is important to specify what we mean by the "end of the Cold War." The 1989 revolutions in Eastern Europe, the subsequent fall of the Berlin Wall, and the collapse of the Soviet Union itself in 1991 was not significant with regard to UN Security Council activities. The above-stated increase in unanimous SC resolutions occurred earlier and coincided with both the change in Soviet foreign policy under Mikhail Gorbachev and with a more favorable U.S. attitude toward the UN during the Bush administration. As to the Soviet Union, it announced in early 1986 that it would pay its peacekeeping dues and subsequently adopted a more constructive approach toward the UN. In late 1986, the British ambassador to the UN took the initiative to propose regular meetings among the P-5 to coordinate their positions before SC meetings. This led to a habit of consultation culminating in the attempt by the Security Council to end the Iran-Iraq war in 1987.[35] The P-5 consensus on SC Chapter VII Resolution 598 set a precedent that explains to a large degree the smooth operation of the Security Council in condemning the Iraqi aggression against Kuwait in 1990.

The sequence of events shows that it is not clear what was cause and what effect concerning the end of the Cold War and the new consensus among the P-5 in the Security Council. First, the evolution of a habit of consultation between the three Western permanent members and the Soviet Union was among the elements that contributed to ending the East-West rivalry. Second, the Gorbachev revolution in Soviet foreign policy that set in motion events leading to the end of the Cold War included a change in the Soviet attitude toward the UN. Third, while the emergence of cooperative and friendly relations between the former Cold War opponents was a necessary condition for the new SC consensus, it was certainly not sufficient, given that the P-5 faced choices in their foreign policies with regard to the UN. It is not clear why it was in the national interest of the five permanent members to revive the Security Council in the post-Cold War era, thereby entangling their great power interests. This particularly pertains to the norm of multilateralism that constrains the freedom of action of great powers. If rationalist considerations cannot explain the change in the American attitude in this regard, this is even more true as regards the other permanent members who command lesser power resources that might enable them to manipulate the international community.

In sum, it is hard to see how the increased activities of the Security Council and the emergence of norms of multilateralism and humanitarian intervention can be explained from a rationalist and power-based perspective exogenizing national interests and preferences. To do so would require one to demonstrate that the convergence of national interests around these norms can be accounted for solely on the basis of unilateral cost-benefit calculations by not only the great powers in the Security Council, but also the nonpermanent members. It is easier and more parsimonious to explain the same result referring to processes of communication and persuasion among the SC members. First, the norms of multilateralism and of humanitarian intervention to restore human rights originated in the West as part of the liberal internationalist worldview. The closer cooperation among the SC members (which the British ambassador initiated in 1986) then provided a forum where norm change through persuasion could occur.

Second, the gradual emergence of a norm of humanitarian intervention that even includes the restoration of democracy by force (as in Haiti) probably did not entail a process of conscious choice by the SC members. As the above-stated evolution of Security Council statements shows, these resolutions responded to specific situations in world politics. The wording then set a precedent for the next occasion, which also developed the norms further. Such processes are typical for international lawmaking through legal argumentation and persuasion but can hardly be captured by rational choice models based on instrumental rather than communicative rationality.[36]

Third, the Russian support for Western liberal norms in the Security Council deserves further elaboration. Moscow might have calculated that it would gain material benefits from supporting U.S. leadership in the UN, given its needs for Western assistance in its domestic economic transformation. But one would then have expected a decreasing Russian willingness to back Western proposals in the Security Council, the less forthcoming Western aid turned out to be. It is equally plausible that the Russian attitude in the UN can be explained in terms of the ongoing struggle over the country's identity in the post-Cold War world. Does Russia belong to the West, to Europe, and the democratic peace of the Organization for Economic Cooperation and Development world, or is it part of Asia? At issue is not just the degree to which liberal and cooperative internationalism should guide the foreign policy, but the core values of liberal internationalism are themselves contested. Nationalist foreign policies have been advocated by the opponents of reform and democratization all along—from Mikhail Gorbachev's to Boris Yeltsin's era. Current Russian foreign policy (including its role in the UN) might be explained to a large degree by the controversy about identity entailing both domestic and international dimensions.

I have tried to demonstrate so far that the social constructivist approach offers a better explanation for the dramatic increase and change in Security Council resolutions pertaining to Chapter VII and humanitarian intervention than rationalist accounts. However, the analysis has concentrated on words rather than deeds. Power-based approaches to world politics might even agree with the argument but maintain that the multilateral and humanitarian words represent the icing on the cake of foreign policies motivated by traditional national interests. The UN with its norms of multilateralism might serve as a legitimizing agency to avoid the onus of unilateral interventions, but the real motivation for the post-Cold War policies of the great powers could still be explained on rationalist grounds. If we want to establish the superior explanatory power of social constructivism, we need to move from words to deeds. I will do so by first taking a brief look at the evolution of UN peacekeeping operations and then discussing the cases of the Gulf War, Somalia, and the former Yugoslavia. A complex picture emerges that cannot fully be captured by any of the three propositions.

DEEDS: CONTRADICTIONS AMONG NORMS AND THE SOCIAL CONSTRUCTION OF STRATEGIC INTERESTS
The Evolution of UN Peacekeeping

The quantitative increase in UN activities pertaining to preventive diplomacy, peacemaking, peacekeeping, and peacebuilding is impressive. Between 1948 and 1978, only thirteen UN peacekeeping operations were established, five of which are still in effect. From 1988–92, fourteen new operations were started; by mid-1994, about 70,000 blue helmet troops from seventy countries, more than 2,300 military observers, and more than 1,100 police officers working for the UN were deployed worldwide—in Somalia (UNISOM II), the Western Sahara (MINURSO), Angola (UNAVEM), Iraq and Kuwait (UNIKOM), El Salvador (ONUSAL), Cambodia (UNTAC), the former Yugoslavia (UNPROFOR), and elsewhere. The UNPROFOR effort constituted the largest contingent—45,000 troops from thirty-six countries.[37]

The dramatic increase in peacekeeping activities contrasts sharply with the still pathetic organizational capacities of the UN to carry out these missions. There is a serious lack of early-warning mechanisms and of advance planning, resulting in an ad hoc administration of the various operations. So far, the Security Council has mostly failed to act on the recommendations by the secretary-general in his *An Agenda for Peace*.[38] The budget for UN peacekeeping missions in 1992–93 was just $4 billion; in other words, UN members paid about $5 on peacekeeping for each $1,000 for military expenditures. Only about three hundred officials at the UN work permanently on conflict management and peacekeeping issues. A situation room coordinating and overlooking peacekeeping was recently installed with about a hundred officers monitoring all peacekeeping missions.[39] Boutros Boutros-Ghali's proposal for a small number of special forces under UN command for peacemaking and peacekeeping purposes is far from being realized because of the lack of consensus among the P-5.[40]

Participation in or contribution to UN peacekeeping operations is inconsistent with the rationalist notion that either hegemonic power or a core group of actors provides the public good, enabling the lesser states to free ride on the institutions. Ironically enough, the two most powerful members of the Security Council—the United States and Russia—continue to free ride on UN peacekeeping. As of mid-1994, six developing countries (Pakistan, India, Jordan, Bangladesh, Malaysia, and Egypt) were among the ten nations providing the most UN peacekeepers, with permanent SC members France and Great Britain achieving a second and a fourth place, respectively. As to financing, the two great powers that are not permanent SC members—Germany and Japan—contribute comparatively far more to UN peacekeeping than the P-5 (in 1991 data, this is calculated in terms of the ratio between peacekeeping contributions and military expenditures).[41] The U.S. hegemon used to pay less than the world average for peacekeeping operations and has only recently increased its contribution.

Hegemonic stability theory assumes that hegemony is tolerable for the lesser states, insofar as the superpower provides the public good. The minilateral solution to collective action problems maintains that a core group of powers provides the public good. Neither is the case with regard to UN peacekeeping. Rather, the key group of actors in the Security Council decide on the peacekeeping missions, while the lesser states (except for France and Britain) implement these decisions. Hence, the lack of organizational capacities! From a rationalist point of view, one could argue, of course, that it is cheaper for great powers to free ride on a multilateral organization than to pay the burden themselves. Because most peacekeeping missions do not affect power-based national interests of the great powers in the Security Council, such buck passing might be convenient.

But this account leaves two questions. First, why do the great powers feel obliged to increase the number of peacekeeping operations by the UN and to engage in a rhetoric that is dangerous in the sense of being caught in the long run? Second, why do lesser states feel obliged to implement the decisions of the great powers, even though the latter contribute less than their fair share? There should be no incentive for troops from Bangladesh, one of the poorest countries in the world, to serve in Bosnia-Herzegovina, if the U.S. superpower continuously refuses to provide ground troops.

Of course, the findings with regard to UN peacekeeping in general is equally inconsistent with the third—social constructivist—proposition, according to which prescriptive status should lead to rule-consistent behavior, at least over an extended period of time. As of now, only France and Britain behave consistently with their rhetoric in the Security Council when it comes to UN peacekeeping, while the United States—the originator of the principles of multilateralism in the post-World War II era—mostly passes the buck. Washington's behavior is inconsistent with the norm of multilateralism, but the United States appears to be more forthcoming than the other permanent members with regard to enforcing the norm of humanitarian intervention. In other words, we can observe different degrees of norm compliance by the P-5 that can be explained neither on rationalist grounds nor by emphasizing processes of communication and persuasion in the Security Council. Rather, the domestic discourses have to be included in the picture, as the following cases demonstrate.

The Intervention in the 1990–91 Gulf Conflict

The 1990–91 Gulf conflict seems to confirm realist and/or rationalist cooperation theories. First, power-based national interests were at stake for the United States, France, and Great Britain. Iraq's invasion of Kuwait and the resulting threat to Saudi Arabia jeopardized the oil supply and, thus, the life line of the industrialized world. The stability of the Middle Eastern region was also at stake.

Second, the United States played the role of the hegemonic stabilizer providing the public good of collective security. George Bush drew "the line in the sand," regardless of the reluctance of his military advisers, and committed U.S. troops to the defense of Saudi Arabia.[42] He assembled an international coalition against Iraq and put U.S. forces in an offensive posture to drive Iraq out of Kuwait. The United States planned, controlled, and carried out the successful military effort of defeating Saddam Hussein's troops.

Third, the UN Security Council was only brought into the picture after American decisions had been made. The famous Resolution 678 of 29 November 1990, legitimizing the use of force against Iraq, was agreed on after the U.S. administration had committed itself to an offensive posture that left almost no alternative to military action. The Security Council had no control over the military effort by the coalition forces. Was the UN a multilateral rubber stamp for unilateral American foreign-policy decisions?

Fourth, the Soviet decision to follow the American lead can also be explained by power-based considerations. Gorbachev needed Western economic support as well as a benign foreign policy-environment to carry out his domestic reform program. The United States also used bribery by arranging a $4-billion credit from Kuwait, Saudi Arabia, and the United Arab Emirates.[43]

A closer look at the available evidence reveals a more complex picture. As to American policies, a power-based account assuming fixed interests needs to explain why the American interest apparently changed within a few days in August 1990. When Iraq started threatening Kuwait, the U.S. ambassador in Baghdad reassured the Iraqis that the conflict with Kuwait was their own business and that the United States would not get involved. The first National Security Council meeting following the invasion also ended inconclusively. It was British Prime Minister Thatcher who apparently talked Bush into taking a tough line against Saddam Hussein when she met with the president on 2 August. It should also be noted in this context that the U.S. military, the Pentagon, and the State Department did not endorse the use of force but advised caution. As one, albeit exaggerated, account has it, "this was George Bush's war."[44] If U.S. strategic interests dictated American behavior during the conflict, one would not assume that the president was the only actor in the administration to fully grasp its implications and that he himself had to be pushed by a major ally into recognizing the U.S. national interest.

A power-based explanation of the Soviet support for the American-led coalition is more questionable. Iraq was one of Moscow's traditional allies bound by treaty. The $4-billion credit by Saudi Arabia and others was more than offset by the losses from Iraqi nonpayment of a more than $5-billion debt and from trade including various oil deals as a result of the economic sanctions.[45] Under such circumstances, one would have expected the Soviet leadership to calculate carefully the costs and benefits of siding with the West before making a firm decision. Instead, Moscow condemned the Iraqi action right away, demanding the "immediate and unconditional withdrawal of Iraqi troops from Kuwaiti territory."[46] Foreign Ministers James Baker and Eduard Shevardnadze issued a joint declaration on 3 August 1990, castigating the Iraqi invasion and calling for an international cutoff of arms supplies to Iraq. This joint appeal was the beginning of close U.S.-Soviet cooperation throughout the crisis, culminating in a joint statement by Presidents Bush and Gorbachev at the Helsinki summit on 9 September that they were prepared to take "additional steps consistent with the UN Charter" if the efforts to get Iraq out of Kuwait failed.

The behavior of the Soviet leadership during the Gulf conflict was fully consistent with the principles and norms of "new thinking," emphasizing the peaceful resolution of conflicts and multilateralism and, thus, with liberal internationalist values. The Soviet course of action during the conflict can be easily explained as an outgrowth of new thinking, which then redefined Soviet strategic interests as better served by aligning with the West rather than siding with a traditional ally.[47]

Gorbachev and Shevardnadze's policies were internally contested from the beginning. The relevant departments in the Soviet Foreign Ministry as well as influential advisers to Gorbachev such as Yevgeny Primakov resisted the change in Soviet policies toward the Middle East. During the crisis, the opposition to Gorbachev's pro-Western policies in the Gulf grew stronger in conjunction with the deteriorating economic situation of the country. Gorbachev's freedom of action narrowed considerably, and he had to make concessions to the conservatives. The opposition to Gorbachev's liberal internationalism during the Gulf crisis resulted, first, in a stiffening of the Soviet position in the Security Council and, second, in various Soviet attempts to mediate between Iraq and the United States. Primakov paid various visits to Saddam Hussein, while Gorbachev met with Iraqi Foreign Minister Tariq Aziz on several occasions. If Saddam Hussein had understood the interaction between Soviet domestic and foreign policy during the conflict, he could probably have unraveled the international coalition against him quite easily, in particular the P-5 consensus in the Security Council. His failure to compromise not only strengthened Gorbachev's internal position, but also the U.S.-Soviet alliance during the crisis.

This leads to the role of the UN Security Council. Was it just the instrument of U.S. and, to a much lesser extent, Soviet policies during the crisis, or did it play an independent role? As noted above, close consultations among the P-5 had started earlier and had been initiated by the British ambassador, leading to the SC attempt to end the Iran-Iraq war in 1987. When the Gulf conflict began, a habit of consultation among the P-5 was already in place. The swift response to the Iraqi invasion resulting in an unprecedented series of resolutions has to be seen against this background.

The British not only played an important role in convincing the United States to react, but they were also crucial in getting the Security Council into the picture right away. President Bush and Prime Minister Thatcher discussed the need to assemble a broad UN coalition against Iraq during their meeting on 2 August. Bush, supported by Secretary of State Baker, overruled his National Security adviser, Brent Scowcroft, who argued that the United States would lose its freedom of action by getting too entangled in Security Council actions. Even before the president had made up his mind, the British and American ambassadors to the UN were drafting an SC resolution, which was discussed during an SC emergency meeting on 2 August. Resolution 660 strongly condemned the Iraqi invasion of Kuwait and demanded the immediate withdrawal of Saddam Hussein's forces. It was followed only four days later by Resolution 661 imposing comprehensive economic sanctions against Iraq.[48] Never before had the Security Council reacted so swiftly and decisively.

Thus, the initial involvement of the UN did not so much result from conscious decisions of the great powers, particularly the United States, but was the almost natural outflow of institutionalized contacts among the P-5. Norms of multilateralism did not have to be invented for the occasion but were already guiding the behavior of the main actors. Moreover, the habit of consultation among the Western governments, in this case the "special relationship," was extended into the Security Council, particularly the P-5.

But to what extent were the activities in the Security Council causally consequential for the behavior of the great powers during the Gulf conflict? I concentrate on the United States because it led the coalition against Iraq. While George Bush got himself entangled in SC activities without much debate (note his past experience as U.S. ambassador to the UN!), he quickly found out that he desperately needed UN approval for domestic reasons. Assembling an international coalition against Iraq was one thing; gathering a domestic winning coalition was at least equally difficult. As Bruce Russett has pointed out, the multilateral strategy chosen by the U.S. government was necessary to ensure public support for the American-led effort in the Gulf, as the U.S. public no longer backs the unilateral use of American force in the post-Cold War environment.[49] By the same token, the administration would probably not have been able to win a majority in Congress if it had not pursued its policies within a multilateral and liberal internationalist context, given the skepticism of leading Democrats such as Senator Sam Nunn (Dem., Ga.). The congressional resolution of 13 January 1991 explicitly legitimized U.S. military action "pursuant to United Nations Security Council Resolution 678" (the UN authorization of the use of force).[50] This part of the story is consistent, however, with a rationalist "two-level game" account, according to which the UN consensus is used to gather a domestic "winning coalition" for a policy motivated by national security concerns.[51] In other words, a clever U.S. president used the UN Security Council for instrumental reasons.

But various UN Security Council resolutions not only legitimized the U.S. courses of action during the Gulf conflict; they also constrained them. The first cracks in the P-5 consensus occurred, for example, when the United States and Britain wanted to impose a naval blockade against Iraq in mid-August, arguing that Resolution 661 had already authorized it. Secretary-General Javier Perez de Cuellar publicly warned that U.S. unilateral action would violate the UN Charter. Among the P-5, the Soviets and the Chinese were the most reluctant to agree to the use of force. When Iraq took action against foreigners in Baghdad and against foreign embassies in Kuwait, however, Britain and the United States succeeded in getting P-5 consensus on 25 August for Resolution 665, which legitimized "measures commensurate to the specific circumstances" to halt shipping and, thus, authorized using force for the first time during the crisis.[52]

While Resolution 665 placed no serious constraints on U.S. actions, the deal surrounding Resolution 678 did. By October, and in light of the critical debate in Congress about U.S. policy in the Gulf, the administration recognized that it needed another UN Security Council resolution authorizing the use of force to ensure sufficient domestic support. The main bargaining took place between the U.S. and the Soviet leaderships, the latter of which was acting under increasing pressures from conservatives in Moscow. The Soviets insisted on a "pause for peace" to have time for diplomatic initiatives and for the sanctions to work. As a result, a deadline was inserted in the resolution before which no force was to be used. By Soviet demand and French urging, the deadline was moved to mid-January rather than 1 January 1991, as the United States would have preferred.[53]

Resolution 678 of 29 November 1990 authorized member states

to "use all necessary means" to get Iraq out of Kuwait and, at the same time, allowed for last efforts to prevent a war. Had Saddam Hussein taken the opportunity to make concessions, the P-5 consensus in the Security Council would have unraveled, not even to mention Arab support for and participation in the U.S.-led coalition. As the U.S. Ambassador to the UN at the time, Thomas Pickering, put it:

> One of the reasons we were so successful in dealing with Iraq's aggression was the way Saddam himself handled the flow of events. In terms of Security Council cohesion, he was one of the key factors in keeping the council together and implementing its decisions.[54]

By using the UN to cobble together domestic and international winning coalitions against Iraq, the United States had entangled itself in a multilateral setting that became further apparent after the war. On 3 April 1991, the Security Council passed Resolution 687—the "mother of all resolutions"—establishing unprecedented and severe punishments for Iraq's actions and forcing it to accept intrusive inspections monitoring compliance with the disarmament provisions. Resolution 687 also involved the UN and its suborganizations in the settlement to an extraordinary degree. While the UN had no control over the military effort, it was fully in charge of implementing the SC measures after the war.[55]

The aftermath of the Gulf War also moved the Security Council authority with regard to Chapter VII toward humanitarian intervention. Saddam Hussein's repression of the uprising by the Shi'ites and the Kurds had led to an increasing refugee crisis inside Iraq. Following a French initiative and pressure from many Third World states, the Security Council adopted Resolution 688 on 5 April authorizing a humanitarian intervention to defend the Kurds and forcing Iraq to provide immediate access to humanitarian organizations. President Bush was caught in his own liberal rhetoric, as he had publicly called on the Iraqi people to overthrow Saddam Hussein. When some of them tried to do just that, the international community could not stay on the sidelines. Resolutions 687 and 688 established in essence what Paul Taylor and John Groom have called a "functional occupation of Iraq" by the UN.[56]

In sum, the initial involvement of the great powers, particularly the United States, in the Gulf conflict can largely be explained on rationalist, power-based grounds. Instrumental reasoning can also account for the U.S. decision (although not for the British advice) to refer the matter to the Security Council from the beginning. Norms of multilateralism and—later—of humanitarian intervention, however, caught up with the United States in the course of the conflict and increasingly constrained American actions. Had Saddam Hussein used the UN in a more clever way, he could probably have avoided the war and would have isolated the United States in the Security Council. Finally, Security Council involvement in the Gulf conflict established a precedent relevant for the next case, the humanitarian intervention in Somalia.

Somalia: The Pitfalls of Humanitarian Intervention

A power-based account of the U.S.-led humanitarian intervention in Somalia would probably emphasize that the lack of strategic interests explains the faint-heartedness with which this intervention was carried out in contrast to the Gulf War. The great powers led the intervention as long as they did not incur major losses of life. When the costs of the military action increased, the Clinton administration—followed by the other great powers—decided to withdraw U.S. troops from an increasingly dangerous situation.

Even a power-based explanation cannot deny that the decision to intervene in Somalia is hard to explain by strategic or geopolitical interests.[57] It was motivated on humanitarian grounds; the Security Council resolutions leading to it represented a further evolution of the pathway established during previous occasions, particularly Resolution 688. In early 1992, the Security Council passed a series of Chapter VII resolutions declaring that the Somali domestic situation constituted a threat to international peace and security. It then asked the secretary-general to increase humanitarian assistance to Somalia, as a result of which the UNISOM peacekeeping mission was established. During the summer of 1992, the situation in Somalia further deteriorated, leading to the starvation of roughly half a million Somalians.

In the meantime, an almost successful diplomatic mission by the UN special envoy Mohammed Sahnoun to secure cooperation for the humanitarian operation by the competing warlords and clans had failed because it was undercut by the secretary-general. Sahnoun resigned, and the situation quickly worsened. African states and Boutros Boutros-Ghali requested that the Security Council authorize another humanitarian intervention. Many Third World countries argued that the UN had been used during the Gulf conflict to legitimize Western strategic interests. The new assertive role of the Security Council in the post-Cold War environment would lack credibility if the interests of the South were continuously overlooked. Boutros-Ghali even risked an open confrontation with the P-5, arguing that the Western preoccupation with the former Yugoslavia—"the rich man's war"—let them overlook the civil war in Somalia.[58]

During the fall of 1992, the pressures by nongovernmental organizations on the ground, African states, and the UN secretary-general increased and, together with CNN pictures of starving Somalian children, changed the Western attitude toward humanitarian intervention. On 24 November Boutros-Ghali informed the Security Council that the situation in Somalia had dramatically deteriorated. One day later, he received a U.S. offer to lead a multinational operation that would provide a secure environment for humanitarian aid to reach the victims of the war. While the secretary-general would have preferred an operation under UN control, he and the council consented to the U.S. proposal as the second-best option. On 3 December the Security Council passed Chapter VII Resolution 794 recognizing the U.S. offer to establish a secure environment for humanitarian assistance and authorizing the secretary-general and the multinational coalition "to use all necessary means" (the formula used in Resolution 678 of the Gulf conflict) to create such an environment.[59] The United Task Force (UNITAF) under U.S. command was created to be replaced later by the peacekeeping operation, UNISOM II.

President Bush had just lost the elections and, therefore, had nothing to gain or lose domestically from his decision, even though more than 80 percent of the Americans approved it. Norms of multilateralism seem to have motivated him. He was well aware of the risks because both the U.S. military and the CIA had pointed to the political dangers of the intervention, given the lack of government in Somalia.[60] The Somalian intervention further increased the American entanglement in multilateral UN-led operations. When the United States withdrew most of its forces from Somalia in May 1993, the remaining troops were placed under the command of UNISOM II. For the first time, U.S. forces participated in a UN peacekeeping mission.

If the primary purpose of the Somalian operation was to provide a secure environment for humanitarian aid to reach the population, it succeeded. Starvation and famine were brought to an end. If the aim was to end the civil war and restore political institutions, it failed. The reason was an unresolved conflict of norms, between the principles of peacebuilding through diplomatic efforts on the one hand, and peacemaking through military enforcement on the other. Peacebuilding requires that the UN not take sides in an interstate or intrastate conflict but offer good office to achieve a negotiated agreement among the opponents. Parallel to the UNITAF operation, the U.S. special envoy Robert Oakley attempted just that by inviting the rivaling clans to several meetings, thereby continuing the previous attempts by Ambassador Sahnoun.

Ironically enough, though, when the American-led UNITAF was replaced by UNISOM II, the new UN special envoy, Admiral Jonathan T. Howe, changed policies and became partisan in the internal fights among the clans by refusing to meet General Mohamed Farah Aidid. Howe was supported by Boutros-Ghali, whose personal hatred for Aidid was well known. The change in policy backfired, and Aidid's troops killed twenty-three Pakistani peacekeepers in early June 1993, as a result of which the Security Council authorized retaliatory action. It expanded the mandate of peacekeeping missions further by going beyond authorizing the use of force in self-defense. The ill-fated hunt for General Aidid began that changed the UN role in Somalia dramatically and led to the death of seventeen American soldiers. Similarly to Reagan's decision in 1982 after the bombing of the U.S. marine barracks in Beirut, President Clinton then decided to withdraw U.S. troops from UNISOM II by the end of March 1994.[61]

This decision is certainly consistent with an account focusing on the lack of strategic interest in this case. But the process leading to it can be better interpreted by emphasizing both a conflict of norms and an increasing domestic controversy over the limits of humanitarian interventions. Ironically, it was not the U.S.-led UNITAF that screwed up UN peacekeeping by abandoning diplomacy, but the UN-led UNISOM II, at least initially. As a result, the domestic-support basis for the American involvement eroded. A humanitarian intervention to prevent mass starvation enjoyed broad support, even if it entailed the loss of troops. Getting bogged down in a civil war was quite different and invoked memories of Vietnam for the U.S. public.[62] Support for humanitarian intervention and a presumption against the use of force, however, are part of the same liberal internationalist worldview. In the case of Somalia, the two norms clashed. In the case of the former Yugoslavia, they clashed even further.

Bosnia-Herzegovina: Peacekeeping versus Peacemaking and the Social Construction of (Missing) Strategic Interests

The conditions for humanitarian intervention as established in Security Council Resolutions 688 (Iraq) and 794 (Somalia) were all present in the Bosnian case—from "ethnic cleansing" to mass rape, torture, and other severe violations of human rights and humanitarian law. The peacekeeping operation in the former Yugoslavia, UNPROFOR, became the largest mission ever. But the Security Council mostly refused to enforce its many resolutions—twenty-four in 1991–92 alone, for example[63]—except for the ultimatum to the Bosnian Serbs following the massacre in Sarajevo in February 1994. How is this apparent mismatch between words and deeds to be explained?

A power-based explanation would argue that the failure to intervene forcefully stemmed from a lack of strategic interests of any of the great powers in the region. On the contrary, geostrategic interests might have dictated a decision not to intervene—given the French and Soviet/Russian historic alliances with the Serbs and the German association with the Croats. Moreover, and unlike the Somalia case, the military in the United States and at NATO headquarters believed that a successful armed intervention would require a large number of troops. They would be exposed to guerrilla warfare in a mountainous terrain far riskier than the desert warfare in the Gulf region. In the United States, this invoked memories of the Vietnam War. Europeans directly resorted to the images of war in the Balkans experienced during World Wars I and II.

A closer look at the geopolitical situation reveals that the great-power behavior in the Security Council and in NATO was consistent with perceived lessons of history but actually contradicted their long-term strategic interests in the region. Regarding Russia, only the conservative nationalists could have been interested in maintaining the historic alliance with the Serbs. The democratic forces, however, should not have tolerated the quest for a Greater Serbia, given that it ran counter to their need of developing strong ties with Western Europe, the European Union (EU), and particularly Germany. Russian foreign policy nevertheless wavered on the issue, mainly because of domestic reasons including nationalist pressures. While Moscow coerced the Bosnian Serbs to comply with the NATO ultimatum in February 1994, it constantly opposed more forceful measures against them.[64] In sum, Russia certainly had strategic interests in the region, but the direction of these interests was a matter of domestic dispute and can, thus, not be determined on geopolitical or realist grounds.

This was not at all the case for the United States, which had nothing to win or lose strategically in the Balkans. In power-based terms, the only American interest with regard to the war was to prevent its spread in other European regions that would have jeopardized the stability of the continent. Hence, the deployment of a small contingent of U.S. "tripwire" peacekeepers in Kosovo! Other than that, the U.S. lack of strategic interests would have dictated a continuation of the Bush administration's hands-off approach to the former Yugoslavia. Instead, President Clinton initially adopted a more activist, albeit half-hearted, policy. Despite its lack of strategic interests, the United States constantly advocated a tougher policy of the Security Council against the Bosnian Serbs to be implemented by NATO as the enforcer of SC resolutions.

But the U.S. approach largely failed because of British, French, and Russian opposition in the Security Council. This belies the idea that the American hegemon somehow controls the UN and can impose its will on the international community in the post–Cold War era.[65] The Yugoslav case disconfirms the proposition of U.S. hegemony in the Security Council. For example, Clinton opposed the Vance-Owen peace plan as essentially sanctioning Serb aggression against the Bosnians. But when the European Community formally approved the plan on 1 February 1993 as the only game in town, the United States gave in. Several months later, the administration tried to gain European acceptance for a proposal to lift the UN arms embargo against the Bosnians and to conduct air strikes against Serb positions. The proposal ran into fierce opposition by Britain and France, not to mention Russia.[66] Among the Western P-5, London's objections against the use of military force were particularly significant given the British role as a power broker in the Security Council. It appears then that the UN and NATO inaction in enforcing Security Council resolutions can be largely explained as a result of British influence. Whenever the United States and its European allies clashed in New York, Russia sided with the British.

The NATO ultimatum in February 1994, the subsequent Russian involvement in Bosnia-Herzegovina, and the resulting cease-fires surrounding Sarajevo and other Bosnian towns confirm the point. The momentum resulted from a (German-inspired) change in the French position toward a tougher stance. France maintains a key position in the Security Council insofar as its policies are usually regarded as crucial by Russia, China, and the nonpermanent members. Winning the French over then goes a long way in securing a majority in the Security Council.[67] With the French changing position and seeking common ground with the United States on the Bosnian situation, the British became temporarily isolated among the Western P-5. In the aftermath of the Sarajevo massacre, the United States, France, and, to a lesser degree, Germany then quickly seized the momentum. The NATO council—supported by the UN secretary-general—issued its ultimatum. Russia's Boris Yeltsin had to maneuver between the need to appease the conservative nationalists at home and to maintain the alliance with the West. He launched a diplomatic initiative and successfully delivered Serb compliance with the NATO ultimatum, while, at the same time, saving the West from having to carry it out.[68]

The momentum only lasted for some months. When the Bosnian government launched its military offensive in the fall of 1994 and the Bosnian Serbs responded with a counteroffensive threatening the UN-declared "safe area" of Bihac, the disagreements among the P-5 again blocked both the Security Council and subsequently NATO. The United States then declared unilaterally that it would no longer help enforce the arms embargo against the Bosnian government and its troops. In sum and in contrast to both the Gulf conflict and the Somalia case, sharp disagreements existed among the P-5 and included the Western powers.

Can the UN response to the situation in the former Yugoslavia thus be explained by the second proposition that the P-5 lacked not only consensus because of diverging strategic interests? There were obviously sharp disagreements among the P-5 in the Security Council, but also in NATO between France and Britain, on the one hand, and the United States and Germany, on the other, creating a stalemate among the Western powers.[69]

If lack of strategic interest explains American reluctance to intervene, then the countries of the European Union (EU) should have been the most interventionist in the former Yugoslavia. Historical ties aside, the former Yugoslavia constitutes the backyard of the EU. A change in the strategic balance in the Balkans and the emergence of Greater Serbia would represent a threat not only to the stability of the EU's southern tier, but to the EU and its Maastricht project as a whole. Moreover, the possible repercussions of the war in the Balkans for future conflicts, particularly in the successor states of the Soviet Union, should have led to the conclusion that European neglect of the former Yugoslavia was disastrous for the long-term future of European security. But Britain and, to a lesser extent, France have mostly led the opposition against a more active involvement of the Security Council, NATO, and the EU.

A closer look at the strategic interests of the European powers then reveals that nonintervention might well have contradicted their long-term interests in the Balkans. At the least, one could make power-based arguments for as well as against the use of military force not only to confine the war to Bosnia—which the West achieved quite successfully—but to try ending it altogether more forcefully. Instead, the Europeans, particularly the British government, convinced themselves that almost nothing could be done about the ethnic hatred and atrocities in Bosnia, that intervention would be too costly, and that therefore no serious strategic interests were at stake. Considerations of the costs of armed intervention drove the perception of strategic interests, not the other way around. The European perception that the war in Bosnia did not threaten the continent's stability and long-term future was itself socially constructed. Many Europeans convinced themselves that events in the former Yugoslavia happened far away and that intervention was too complicated to risk the lives of one's troops. Humanitarian assistance then served to alleviate a bad conscience about the first genocide on European soil since Adolf Hitler.

The rest was buck passing between the United States and Europe. On the one hand, Britain and France took the main burden of the UNPROFOR peacekeeping operation in Bosnia, while the United States refused to participate. The two governments then argued that American calls for tougher action were hypocritical because the risks of such a move would have to be shouldered by the UN troops on the ground. Yet London and Paris never called for a substantial increase in peacekeeping and peacemaking forces, which could have served as a deterrent against retaliatory action in the case of air strikes.

But it should also be noted that the secretary-general did not request a humanitarian intervention in the Bosnian case as he did for
Somalia. The officers in charge of UNPROFOR were always reluctant
to call in the air strikes offered by NATO. The Bosnian situation cannot be construed as one in which UN officials requested a humanitarian intervention that then was denied by the P-5. Rather, from a UN
perspective, it represents another instance in which the norms of
peacemaking through diplomacy and enforcement of Security Council resolutions clashed. A negotiated solution to the conflict required
that the UN not take sides but continue to serve as an honest broker
between the opponents. Such impartiality was more and more jeopardized by the fact that enforcing the resolutions and guaranteeing
that humanitarian assistance reached the citizens of Bosnia essentially required one to take action against the Serbs.

In conclusion, none of the three propositions stated above can
fully explain the decisions of the P-5 concerning the war in the former Yugoslavia. While the U.S. demands for more forceful action
are consistent with the norms of humanitarian intervention, America did not lead the Security Council, as one would expect from a
hegemonic power, but fully complied with the principles of multilateralism. A rationalist explanation of Russian, British, and French
behavior pointing to power-based strategic interests or lack thereof
is indeterminate at best. It is more plausible that these European
powers convinced themselves that armed intervention was neither
feasible nor necessary, as long as the conflict could be confined to
the Balkans. The lack of strategic interests was itself socially constructed. Finally, the norms of peacebuilding through diplomacy
versus peacemaking through law enforcement clashed in the Bosnian case as they did in Somalia before.

CONCLUSIONS: A NEW WORLD ORDER?

The empirical findings of this chapter reveal a more complex picture
than the propositions discussed above suggest. On balance, however,
power-based explanations pertaining either to U.S. hegemony in the
post–Cold War era or to strategic interests of the great powers in the
Security Council do not appear to capture the reemergence of the UN
in world politics and the variation in the degree to which SC resolutions are enforced (see Table 1).

Table 1. Theoretical propositions and empirical findings

	U.S. Hegemony	Strategic interests of great powers	Evolution of norms
Security Council resolutions	No	No	Yes
Peacekeeping operations	No	No	Indeterminate
Gulf War	Yes	Yes	Yes
Somalia	No	No	Yes
Bosnia-Herzegovina	No	Indeterminate	No

First, except for the U.S. resolve in the Gulf War, there is not much evidence for American hegemony in the Security Council. Neither the evolution of sc resolutions with regard to norms of multilateralism and humanitarian intervention nor the peacekeeping missions in general (and the Somalian or Bosnian cases in particular) reveal U.S. primacy based on power-based American interests. While Washington's leadership was crucial in the Somalian case, the decision to intervene cannot be accounted for by strategic interests. It is certainly true that a un-sponsored major humanitarian intervention necessitates U.S. participation because of its capabilities for conventional power projection. But this does not result in American preponderance in the Security Council.

Second, it is equally difficult to understand the evolution of un peacekeeping and peacemaking in various parts of the world by referring to the strategic interests of the P-5 alone. Why should they establish norms of humanitarian intervention and multilateralism that constrain their freedom of action in the post-Cold War era? As the Bosnian case shows, so-called strategic interests are rarely fixed, but malleable through processes of social communication. Europeans convinced themselves that their national interests were not affected by the genocide in the former Yugoslavia and that a change in the balance of power in the Balkans would not destabilize Central and Eastern Europe.

Third, the proposition concerning the evolution of norms pertaining to multilateralism and humanitarian intervention also does not fully capture the variation in the empirical findings. While these norms have gained prescriptive status through a steadily increasing body of Security Council resolutions, we are far away from rule-consistent behavior in terms of implementing and enforcing these proclamations. The great powers in the Security Council continue to contribute less than their fair share to peacekeeping missions, particularly with regard to personnel. In the Somalian case, the United States and its allies quickly ran away from their responsibilities when the internal situation deteriorated, leaving UNISOM II as a half-accomplished mission. In the case of the former Yugoslavia, severe disagreements among the P-5 together with buck passing led to a situation in which even providing minimum humanitarian assistance—let alone peacekeeping—became increasingly difficult to accomplish.

The lack of rule-consistent behavior is less true for the principles of multilateralism, however, than for the norms of humanitarian intervention. As to the former, it is more and more inconceivable that any of the Western great powers will intervene militarily to pursue unilaterally defined strategic interests in any part of the world (for example, Security Council approval for the French action in Rwanda and the U.S. involvement in Haiti). Unilateral military interventions for whatever purpose appear to belong increasingly to the past.

With regard to humanitarian interventions, however, the cases of Somalia and Bosnia reveal severe contradictions among the underlying collective understandings. It is one thing to establish a norm that gross violations of human rights constitute threats to international peace and security thus legitimizing the use of force by the international community. It is quite different to specify the conditions under which the UN or coalitions acting on behalf of the Security Council should enforce the norm. First, one cannot possibly demand armed intervention by the international community whenever human rights are disregarded in any part of the world. To that extent, double standards are inevitable and do not constitute violations of the norm, unless there are systematic biases in the variation of rule enforcement with regard to regions of the world or types of political regimes.

It follows, however, that norms of humanitarian interventions cannot explain the variation in behavior among the P-5—compare the intervention in Somalia with the noninterventions in Sudan and Liberia despite similar gross violations of human rights. Human rights violations as such do not trigger a powerful response by the international community. As a comparison between the Somalian and Sudanese cases shows, nongovernmental organization pressures in conjunction with international media attention—the "CNN factor"—appear to explain the variation in behavior.[70]

Second, UN or UN-legitimized interventions in civil wars such as in Somalia or Bosnia point to inconsistencies in the liberal internationalist worldview forming the very basis of humanitarian interventions. Traditional peacekeeping was based on the principle that the UN should remain neutral in international disputes and offer its good offices to mediate in such conflicts and to keep the peace. This principle made sense as long as mainly interstate disputes were concerned or both opponents in an intrastate conflict demanded UN involvement. If the international community decides to enforce humanitarian and human rights standards, it can no longer be neutral with regard to the violators of such standards. Conflict resolution through mediation amounts to appeasement against the victims of aggression and oppression, as the Bosnian case makes abundantly clear.[71]

Third, humanitarian principles cannot and should not be enforced at all cost. It is a legitimate concern that multilateral interventions in civil war situations might lead to high numbers of casualties among the intervening troops without accomplishing the goal of stabilizing the situation. In this case, the liberal internationalist principle supporting humanitarian interventions clashes with the presumption against the use of force in the same worldview.

These conflicts among liberal internationalist norms explain to a large extent the contrast between the communicative practices in the Security Council emphasizing multilateralism and legitimizing humanitarian interventions, on the one hand, and the variation in the degree of rule-consistent behavior by the international community, on the other. Reference to strategic interests or lack thereof does not capture the variation.

Practices, however, enact norms and institutionalize them. Disregarding norms through behavior tends to undermine them in the long run, as rule-violating behavior erodes the prescriptive status of the norm. In the case of multilateralism and humanitarian intervention, the Security Council can no longer afford to pass Chapter VII resolutions without providing the UN with the means to enforce them. A serious evaluation of recent UN action is required in order to sort out the inherent contradictions in the multilateral and humanitarian principles. Policymakers, particularly in the West, need to understand that free riding on the UN and buck passing will erode the domestic and transnational support basis for liberal internationalist policies.

The result will not be that they regain their freedom of action and are free to pursue foreign policies based on materially defined interests. Traditional unilateral policies are only backed by minorities in the Western publics, and they will almost certainly lead to balancing behavior by the lesser powers. Thus, the alternative is not between a new world order and old-fashioned great power politics. The alternative is between a new world order and none.

NOTES

1. Earlier versions of this chapter were presented at the workshop "The United Nations: Towards the Half Century," European Consortium for Political Research (ECPR), Joint Sessions, University of Leiden, 2–7 April 1993, at the annual convention of the International Studies Association, Washington, D.C., 28 March–1 April 1994, and at a conference on "Strategies in Conflict: Critical Approaches to Security Studies," York University, 12–14 May 1994. I thank the participants in these meetings for their comments. I also profited from discussions at the University of British Columbia, Harvard University, Stanford University, Yale University, and the University of Washington. In particular, I thank Michael Barnett, Paul Diehl, Keith Krause, Bruce Russett, Nina Tannenwald, Michael Williams, Jennifer Milliken, and two anonymous reviewers for helpful suggestions. For research assistance on this chapter, I am very grateful to Michelle Bellini, Susanne Kupfer, Birgit Locher, Heike Scherff, Claudia Schmedt, and Richard Tanksley.

2. See, for example, Friedrich Kratochwil and John G. Ruggie, "International Organization: A State of the Art on an Art of the State," *International Organization* 40:4 (Autumn 1986), 753–75. My own thinking on these issues has been heavily influenced by a Social Science Research Council project on "Norms and International Security," directed by Peter Katzenstein. See Katzenstein, ed., *The Culture of National Security: Norms and Identity in World Politics* (New York: Columbia University Press, 1996).

3. For this conceptualization, see John G. Ruggie, "Multilateralism: The Anatomy of an Institution," *International Organization* 46:3 (Summer 1992), 561–98.

4. See Kenneth Oye, "Explaining Cooperation under Anarchy," in Kenneth Oye, ed., *Cooperation under Anarchy* (Princeton, N.J.: Princeton University Press, 1986), 7–8, 19–20; Miles Kahler, "Multilateralism with Small and Large Numbers," *International Organization* 46:3 (Summer 1992), 681–708; Lisa Martin, "Interests, Power, and Multilateralism,"

International Organization 46:4 (Autumn 1992), 765–92; Michael Zürn, *Interessen und Institutionen in der internationalen Politik* (Opladen: Leske and Budrich, 1992), 198–209.

5. See Charles Krauthammer, "The Unipolar Moment," in Graham Allison and Gregory Treverton, eds., *Rethinking America's Security* (New York: W. W. Norton, 1992), 295–306. See also Samuel Huntington, "Why International Primacy Matters," *International Security* 17:1 (Spring 1993), 68–83. For a critique of this argument, see Ernst-Otto Czempiel, *Weltpolitik im Umbruch* (Munich: Beck, 1991), 72–78.

6. For the realist version of hegemonic stability theory, see Robert Gilpin, *War and Change in World Politics* (Cambridge: Cambridge University Press, 1981). For the public choice version, see Charles Kindleberger, *The World in Depression* (Berkeley and Los Angeles: University of California Press, 1983). For critiques, see Bruce Russett, "The Mysterious Case of Vanishing Hegemony: Or, Is Mark Twain Really Dead?", *International Organization* 39 (1985), 207–31; Duncan Snidal, "The Limits of Hegemonic Stability Theory," *International Organization* 39:4 (Autumn 1985), 579–614; Isabelle Grunberg, "Exploring the 'Myth' of Hegemonic Stability," *International Organization* 44:4 (Autumn 1990), 431–77.

7. Martin, "Interests, Power, and Multilateralism," 785. The German scholar Heinrich Triepel actually made the same point in the 1930s, that is, long before public-choice and hegemonic-stability theories had been invented. See his *Die Hegemonie: Ein Buch von fuehrenden Staaten* (Stuttgart: Kohlhammer, 1938). A similar argument is made by critical theorists using Gramscian arguments claiming that modern hegemony is based on both material capabilities and the power of consensual ideas. See, for example, Robert Cox, *Production, Power, and World Order* (New York: Columbia University Press, 1987); Stephen Gill, ed., *Gramsci, Historical Materialism, and International Relations* (Cambridge: Cambridge University Press, 1993).

8. Ruggie, "Multilateralism," 592.

9. These data are according to Andrew Bennett and Joseph Lepgold, "Reinventing Collective Security after the Cold War and Gulf Conflict," *Political Science Quarterly* 108:2 (1993), 222–23.

10. See Oye, *Cooperation under Anarchy;* Arthur Stein, *Why Nations Cooperate* (Ithaca, N.Y.: Cornell University Press, 1990); Zürn, *Interessen und Institutionen.*

11. See Stephen Krasner, ed., *International Regimes* (Ithaca, N.Y.: Cornell University Press, 1983); Robert Keohane, *After Hegemony* (Princeton, N.J.: Princeton University Press, 1984); Robert Keohane, *International Institutions and State Power* (Boulder, Colo.: Westview, 1989); Oran Young, *International Cooperation* (Ithaca, N.Y.: Cornell University Press, 1989). On the state of the art, see Harald Müller, *Die Chance der Kooperation*

(Darmstadt: Wissenschaftliche Buchgesellschaft, 1993); Volker Rittberger, ed., *Regime Theory and International Relations* (Oxford: Clarendon Press, 1993).

12. See William Durch, "Introduction," in Durch, ed., *The Evolution of UN Peacekeeping* (New York: St. Martin's Press, 1993), 1–2. On the evolution of UN peacekeeping, see Marrack Goulding, "The Evolution of United Nations Peacekeeping," *International Affairs* 69:3 (1993), 451–64; Alan James, *Peacekeeping in International Politics* (New York: St. Martin's Press, 1990); Indar Jit Rikhye and Kjell Skelsbaek, eds., *The United Nations and Peacekeeping* (New York: St. Martin's Press, 1990).

13. James A. Caporaso, "International Relations Theory and Multilateralism: The Search for Foundations," *International Organization* 46:3 (Summer 1992), 607. See also Russell Hardin, *Collective Action* (Baltimore: Johns Hopkins University Press, 1982).

14. Kahler, "Multilateralism with Small and Large Numbers." See also Caporaso, "International Relations Theory and Multilateralism," 616–17.

15. For a discussion see, for example, Peter Wallensteen, "Representing the World: A Security Council for the 21st Century," *Security Dialogue* 25:1 (1994), 63–75.

16. Compare Keohane, *After Hegemony*, with Joseph Grieco, "Anarchy and the Limits of Cooperation: A Realist Critique of the Newest Liberal Institutionalism," *International Organization* 42:3 (Summer 1988), 485–507. On the debate between the two rationalist approaches, see David Baldwin, ed., *Neorealism and Neoliberalism* (New York: Columbia University Press, 1993).

17. Social constructivist approaches are often referred to as "reflectivism" or "interpretivism." For overviews, see Caporaso, "International Relations Theory and Multilateralism," 620–30; Friedrich Kratochwil, *Rules, Norms, and Decisions* (Cambridge: Cambridge University Press, 1989); Harald Müller, "Internationale Beziehungen als kommunikatives Handeln: Zur Kritik der utilitaristischen Handlungstheorie," *Zeitschrift für Internationale Beziehungen* 1:1 (1994), 15–44; Thomas Schaber and Cornelia Ulbert, "Reflexivität in den internationalen Beziehungen," *Zeitschrift für Internationale Beziehungen* 1:1 (1994), 139–69; Alexander Wendt, "Anarchy Is What States Make of It," *International Organization* 46:2 (Spring 1992), 391–425.

18. On the agent-structure debate, see Alexander Wendt, "The Agent-Structure Problem in International Relations Theory," *International Organization* 41:3 (1987), 335–70; David Dessler, "What's at Stake in the Agent-Structure Debate," *International Organization* 43:3 (1989), 441–72.

19. On these distinctions, see Judith Goldstein and Robert Keohane, eds., *Ideas and Foreign Policy* (Ithaca, N.Y.: Cornell University Press, 1993).

20. On this point, see Wendt, "Anarchy Is What States Make of It."

21. On the "democratic peace," see Bruce Russett, *Grasping the Democratic Peace* (Princeton, N.J.: Princeton University Press, 1993); Thomas Risse-Kappen, *Cooperation among Democracies: The European Influence on U.S. Foreign Policy* (Princeton, N.J.: Princeton University Press, 1995).

22. See Volker Rittberger, "Research on International Regimes in Germany," in Rittberger, *Regime Theory and International Relations*, 10–11. For the following, see Müller, "Internationale Beziehungen als kommunikatives Handeln"; Jürgen Habermas, *Theorie des kommunikativen Handelns*, 2 vols. (Frankfurt/M.: Suhrkamp, 1981).

23. On the latter norm, see Martha Finnemore, "Constructing Norms of Humanitarian Intervention," in Katzenstein, ed. *The Culture of National Security*.

24. Eugene Wittkopf calls it "cooperative internationalism." See his *Faces of Internationalism: Public Opinion and American Foreign Policy* (Durham, N.C.: Duke University Press, 1990).

25. For evidence, see Kahler, "Multilateralism with Small and Large Numbers"; Risse-Kappen, *Cooperation among Democracies*.

26. On this point, see Oran Young, "Political Leadership and Regime Formation: On the Development of Institutions in International Society," *International Organization* 45:3 (Summer 1991), 281–308. See also G. John Ikenberry and Charles Kupchan, "Socialization and Hegemonic Power," *International Organization* 42:2 (Summer 1990), 283–315; Joseph Nye, *Bound to Lead: The Changing Nature of American Power* (New York: Basic Books, 1990).

27. On this point, see Andrew Fenton Cooper et al., "Bound to Follow? Leadership and Followership in the Gulf Conflict," *Political Science Quarterly* 106:3 (1991), 391–410.

28. I deliberately ignore China in the following, mainly because the database to evaluate its policies is rather limited.

29. For these and the following data, see Foreign and Commonwealth Office, Research and Analysis Department Memorandum, *Table of Vetoed Draft Resolutions in the United Nations Security Council, 1946–1991* (London: January 1992); Sally Morphet, "Resolutions and Vetoes in the UN Security Council: Their Relevance and Significance," *Review of International Studies* 16 (1990), 341–51; Morphet, "The Security Council and the General Assembly: Their Inter-Relationship 1980–1992," draft paper for the ECPR Joint Sessions, University of Leiden, 2–7 April 1993.

30. Peter J. Frohmuth, "The Making of a Security Community: The United Nations after the Cold War," *Journal of International Affairs* 46:2 (Winter 1993), 341–66. See also Peter R. Baehr, "The Security Council and Human Rights," prepared for presentation to the ECPR Joint Sessions of

Workshops, University of Leiden, 2–7 April 1993; Lothar Brock and Tillmann Elliesen, "Zivilisierung und Gewalt: Zur Problematik militaerischer Eingriffe in innerstaatliche Konflikte," HSFK Report 9 (Frankfurt/M.: Hessische Stiftung Friedens- und Konfliktforschung, 1993); Finnemore, "Constructing Norms of Humanitarian Intervention."

31. Quoted in Baehr, "The Security Council and Human Rights," 5.

32. See "Tightening the Stranglehold," *The Economist*, 6 August 1994, 39–40.

33. I owe this point to Paul Diehl.

34. For details, see Volker Rittberger et al., "Langsame Wiederannäherung: Das Verhältnis zwischen US and UN unter den Präsidenten Reagan, Bush und Clinton," *Vereinte Nationen* 42:2 (April 1994), 45–52.

35. For details, see Morphet, "The Security Council and the General Assembly," 4; Paul Taylor and A. J. R. Groom, "The United Nations and the Gulf War, 1990–91: Back to the Future?", Discussion Papers no. 38 (London: Royal Institute of International Affairs, 1992), 3–4, 9.

36. For an analysis, see Kratochwil, *Rules, Norms, and Decisions*.

37. Data from Boutros Boutros-Ghali, "Empowering the United Nations," *Foreign Affairs* 72:5 (Winter 1992/93), 89–90; Christoph Bertram, "Hoher Anspruch, graue Wirklichkeit," *Die Zeit*, 25 February 1994, 3; "United Nations Peacekeeping," *The Economist*, 25 June 1994, 19–21; "45000 Blauhelme im ehemaligen Jugoslawien," *Süddeutsche Zeitung*, 10/11 December 1994, 7.

38. See Boutros Boutros-Ghali, *An Agenda for Peace* (New York: United Nations, July 1992). See also the recommendations in *The United Nations in Its Second Half-Century: Report by the Independent Working Group on the Future of the United Nations* (New York: Ford Foundation, 1995).

39. For these data, see Bertram, "Hoher Anspruch, graue Wirklichkeit." See also "U.N. Is Developing Control Center to Coordinate Growing Peacekeeping Role," *New York Times*, 28 March 1993; "U.N. Is in Arrears on Peace Efforts," *New York Times*, 16 May 1993.

40. See Boutros-Ghali, *Agenda for Peace*.

41. See data in Wallersteen, "Representing the World"; "United Nations Peacekeeping," *The Economist*, 25 June 1994, 21.

42. For the following, see Bob Woodward, *The Commanders* (New York: Simon and Schuster, 1991); Lawrence Freedman and Efraim Karsh, *The Gulf Conflict 1990–1991* (Princeton, N.J.: Princeton University Press, 1993); Isabelle Grunberg, "Hegemony, Self-Interest, and Collective Security: A Postscript for the Gulf War," paper presented to the Conference on Security, Development, and the Environment, Malta, 3–7 August 1993.

43. See Galia Golan, "Gorbachev's Difficult Time in the Gulf," *Political Science Quarterly* 107:2 (1992), 219–20.

44. Jean Edward Smith, *George Bush's War* (New York: Henry Holt, 1992), 1. For more balanced accounts, see Freedman and Karsh, *Gulf Conflict*, 74–76; Pierre Salinger and Eric Laurent, *La Guerre du Golfe: Le Dossier Secret* (Paris: Orban, 1991); Woodward, *The Commanders*.

45. See Golan, "Gorbachev's Difficult Time in the Gulf," 214.

46. Quoted from Freedman and Karsh, *Gulf Conflict*, 78. For the following, see ibid., 78–80; Golan, "Gorbachev's Difficult Time in the Gulf"; Michael Beschloss and Strobe Talbott, *At the Highest Levels* (Boston: Little, Brown, 1993).

47. For a general argument on how "new thinking" led to the redefinition of the Soviet understanding of its security interests, see Robert Herman, "Soviet New Thinking: Ideas, Interests, and the Redefinition of Security," Ph.D. diss., Cornell University, 1995.

48. For details, see Freedman and Karsh, *Gulf Conflict*, 75, 80–84; Taylor and Groom, "United Nations and the Gulf War," 8–11; Beschloss and Talbott, *At the Highest Levels*, 244–67; Woodward, *The Commanders*, 218–46.

49. See Bruce Russett, "The Gulf War as Empowering the United Nations," in Edward Greenberg et al., eds., *War and Its Consequences: Lessons from the Persian Gulf Conflict* (New York: HarperCollins, 1994).

50. For the text of the Congressional resolution, see "Confrontation in the Gulf," *New York Times*, 14 January 1991, 11.

51. See Robert Putnam, "Diplomacy and Domestic Politics: The Logic of Two-Level Games," *International Organization* 42:3 (Summer 1988), 427–60.

52. Quoted from "U.N. Council Calls on Navies to Block Iraq's Trade," *New York Times*, 26 August 1990, A1. See also Taylor and Groom, "United Nations and the Gulf War," 12–15; "Security Council's Rare Unity May Be Threatened over U.S. Warships in the Gulf," *New York Times*, 11 August 1990, A7; "U.N. Chief Argues Blockade Is Hasty," *New York Times*, 17 August 1990, A12; "Envoys at U.N. Say Soviets Block Endorsement of Force against Iraq," *New York Times*, 22 August 1990, A1; "Gorbachev Warns Baghdad to Back Off or U.N. Will Act," *New York Times*, 25 August 1990, A1.

53. For details, see Freedman and Karsh, *Gulf Conflict*, 228–37; Taylor and Groom, "United Nations and the Gulf War," 16–25; "Moscow Holds Off on Backing Move for Use of Force," *New York Times*, 19 November 1990, A1; "Bush Fails to Gain Soviet Agreement on Gulf Force Use," *New York Times*, 20 November 1990, A1; "Security Council Members to Discuss the Gulf Crisis," *New York Times*, 24 November 1990, A4; "U.N. Draft Offers One 'Final' Chance for Iraqi Pullout," *New York Times*, 27 November 1990, A1.

54. Thomas R. Pickering, "The Post-Cold War Security Council: Forging an International Consensus," *Arms Control Today* (June 1992), 9.

55. For details, see Taylor and Groom, "The United Nations and the Gulf Conflict," 26–34. For the following, see ibid., 35–40; Baehr, "The Security Council and Human Rights," 6.

56. Taylor and Groom, "The United Nations and the Gulf Conflict," 36.

57. Comparing the intervention in Somalia with the nonintervention in Sudan is particularly instructive in this context. The United States had far more strategic reasons to intervene in Sudan (geostrategic location, threat of Islamic fundamentalism linking up with Iran, among others) where it did not, than in Somalia where it did. For a detailed and excellent discussion of the two cases, see Daniela Engelmann, "Humanitäre Intervention— Zivilisierung der Sicherheitspolitik oder verschleierte Interessenpolitik?", diploma thesis, Fakultät für Verwaltungswissenschaft, University of Konstanz, April 1995.

58. See, for example, "Der Pharao will nicht nur Sekretär sein," *Die Zeit*, 14 August 1992. For the history of the UN involvement in Somalia, see, for example, Baehr, "The Security Council and Human Rights," 7; Fromuth, "The Making of a Security Community," 349–50; Winrich Kühne, "Die Friedenssicherung der Vereinten Nationen in der Krise?", *Aus Politik und Zeitgeschichte*, 14 January 1994, 18–27, 21–25; Volker Matthies, "Zwischen Rettungsaktion und Entmündigung: Das Engagement der Vereinten Nationen in Somalia," *Vereinte Nationen* 41:2 (1993), 45–51; Jonathan Stevenson, "Hope Restored in Somalia?", *Foreign Policy* 91 (Summer 1993), 138–54.

59. Quoted from "Excerpts from a Resolution on Delivering Somalia Aid," *New York Times*, 4 December 1992, A14. See also "U.N.'s Chief Requests New Force to Ease the Somalis' Misery Now," *New York Times*, 1 December 1992, A1; "U.N. Council Essentially Agrees to U.S. Command in Somalia," *New York Times*, 2 December 1992, A18; "U.N. Backs a Somalia Force as Bush Vows a Swift Exit," *New York Times*, 4 December 1992, A1. See also Engelmann, "Humanitäre Intervention."

60. See "U.S. Assesses Risks of Sending Troops to Somalia," *New York Times*, 1 December 1992, A10; "Doubts at the C.I.A.," *New York Times*, 1 December 1992, A18. On opinion polls approving the intervention, see Russett, "The Gulf War as Empowering the United Nations," 7.

61. See "New Strength for U.N. Peacekeepers: U.S. Might," *New York Times*, 13 June 1993; "Hope Behind the Horror," *The Economist*, 19 June 1993, 41–42; "The Making of a Fiasco," *Newsweek*, 18 October 1993, 8–11; Kühne, "Die Friedenssicherung der Vereinten Nationen in der Krise?", 23–24.

62. Seventy percent of Americans agreed in December 1992 that making

sure that "food gets to the people" was "worth the possible loss of American lives," but 79 percent were concerned that "U.S. troops will get bogged down in Somalia's civil war." Russett, "The Gulf War as Empowering the United Nations."

63. See Karl Josef Partsch, "Belgrads leerer Stuhl im Glaspalast," *Vereinte Nationen* 40:6 (1992), 183. See also Fromuth, "The Making of a Security Community," 150–53; Nigel D. White, "U.N. Peacekeeping—Development or Destruction?", *International Relations* 12:1 (April 1994), 151–54.

64. See, for example, "A Glimmer in Bosnia," *The Economist,* 5 March 1994, 33–34.

65. One could argue from a sophisticated realist perspective, however, that the Clinton administration never held intense preferences with regard to Bosnia-Herzegovina given the lack of strategic interests. As a result, it never tried very hard to impose its will on the other members of the Security Council. Note also that the United States did not want to commit ground troops to UNPROFOR in Bosnia! The problem with this argument is that it is nonfalsifiable. It is extremely hard to infer intensity of preferences from factors other than behavior, in which case the argument becomes tautological.

66. For details, see Sidney Blumenthal, "Lonesome Hawk," *New Yorker,* 31 May 1993, 35–40; John Newhouse, "No Exit, No Entrance," *New Yorker,* 28 June 1993, 44–51.

67. On this point, see Taylor and Groom, "The United Nations and the Gulf War," 13.

68. For details, see "The West Cries Enough," *The Economist,* 12 February 1994, 25–26; "Blood Bath," *Newsweek,* 14 February 1994, 10–13; "Will We Strike Bosnia?", *Newsweek,* 21 February 1994, 8–11; "Counting Down," *Newsweek,* 28 February 1994, 6–9; "A Glimmer in Bosnia," *The Economist.*

69. For an analysis, see "The Consequences of Bosnia," *The Economist,* 3 December 1994, 31–32.

70. For details, see Engelmann, "Humanitäre Intervention."

71. The Somalian case, however, is slightly different. While the killing of the Pakistani peacekeepers could not have been tolerated by the UN, the hunt for Aidid unnecessarily prevented UNISOM II from mediating among the rivaling clans.

10

The Periphery as the Core:
The Third World and Security Studies

AMITAV ACHARYA

The primary concern of this volume is to examine how the discourses and practices of security might have changed or be changing from the dominant understanding of the concept. What constitutes this dominant understanding is perhaps easily recognized. It is a notion of security rooted firmly within the realist tradition, or what Ken Booth has termed as the "intellectual hegemony" of realism.[1] During the Cold War era, its main reference point was the concept of national security. Although marked by considerable ambiguities and fuzziness,[2] the concept of national security did provide a dominating strand of security analysis, one that tended to equate "security with the absence of a military threat or with the protection of the nation [state] from external overthrow or attack."[3]

Many recent critics of the national security paradigm have found the intellectual lens of realism too restrictive and advocated a redefinition and broadening of security studies. As a result, a debate continues over which phenomena should be included within the purview of the new security studies agenda and which should not. While the advocates of a broader notion of security call for the inclusion, among other things, of economic, ecological, demographic (refugees and illegal migration), narcotic, or gender issues,[4] others (such as Mohammed Ayoob in his contribution to this volume) warn against too much broadening, citing the danger of security becoming a catchall concept, and urging the retention of the original state-centric and war-centric focus of security studies.[5]

This chapter looks at another, less pronounced but ultimately more significant, reason why a redefinition of security is called for. The Cold War period was marked by a preoccupation of security studies scholars with issues and problems of a particular segment of the international system. As with other key concepts of International Relations, national security assumed a Eurocentric universe of nation-states and dwelled primarily on the responses of Western governments and societies, particularly the United States, to the problem of war. The issues and experiences within the other segment, collectively labeled as the Third World, were not fully incorporated into the discourse of security studies. Because the international system as a whole was seen as a "transplantation of the European territorial state," the concept of national security was taken to be a general model, "reflecting the universalization of the competitive European style of anarchic international relations."[6]

This exclusion of the Third World from the Cold War security studies agenda was evident in both policy and academic arenas.[7] Superpower diplomacy carefully distinguished the "central strategic balance" (involving superpower nuclear deterrence and their European alliances) from regional conflict and regional security (conflict and conflict-management issues arising primarily in the Third World). In the academic literature, what was considered mainstream focused on "the centrality of the East-West divide to the rest of global politics."[8] Attention to problems of regional instability in the Third World was given only to the extent that they had the potential to affect the superpower relationship. Not surprisingly, therefore, in surveying the state of the field of international security studies in 1988, Joseph Nye and Sean Lynn-Jones found that "regional security issues (apart from Western Europe) . . . received inadequate attention," a fact attributable to "ethnocentric biases" resulting from "the development of security studies in the United States more than in other countries."[9]

The tendency of security studies to focus on a particular segment of the international system to the exclusion of another is ironic given the fact that it is in the neglected arena that the vast majority of conflicts have taken place.[10] Moreover, the security predicament of the Third World states challenges several key elements of the national security paradigm, especially its state-centric and war-centric universe. The Third World's problems of insecurity and their relationship with the larger issues of international order have been quite different from what was envisaged under the dominant notion.[11]

The main argument of this chapter then is that as security studies adapts itself to post-Cold War realities, the security predicament of Third World states provides a helpful point of departure for appreciating the limitations of the dominant understanding and moving it toward a broader and more inclusive notion of security. This redefinition is crucial to understanding the problems of conflict and order in the post-Cold War period.

Against this backdrop, this chapter has two main goals. The first is to provide a broad outline of the security experience of Third World states during the Cold War period with a view to pointing out the problems of applying the dominant understanding of security in the Third World context. The second is to examine ways in which the Cold War experience will benefit our analysis of the prospects for regional conflict and international order in the post-Cold War era.

NATIONAL SECURITY, REGIONAL CONFLICTS, AND THE EMERGENCE OF THE THIRD WORLD

The emergence of the Third World challenged the dominant understanding of security in three important respects:

1. Its focus on the interstate level as the point of origin of security threats.
2. Its exclusion of nonmilitary phenomena from the security studies agenda.
3. Its belief in the global balance of power as the legitimate and effective instrument of international order.

During the Cold War, the vast majority of the world's conflicts occurred in the Third World. Most of these conflicts were intrastate in nature (antiregime insurrections, civil wars, tribal conflicts, and so on). A study by Istvan Kende estimated that of the 120 wars during the 1945–76 period, 102 were internal wars (including antiregime wars and tribal conflicts), while another study by Michael Kidron and Ronald Segal (covering the 1973–86 period) found a mix of sixty-six internal wars and thirty border wars.[12] The so-called regional conflicts in the Cold War period were thus essentially domestic in origin. Many of them were cases of aggravated tensions emerg-ing from the process of state formation and regime maintenance. The proliferation of such conflicts reflected the limited internal socio-political cohesion of the newly independent states, rather than the workings of the globally competitive relationship between the two superpowers.

The roots of Third World instability during the Cold War period were to be found in weak state structures that emerged from the process of decolonization, that is, structures that lacked a close fit between the state's territorial dimensions and its ethnic and societal composition. The concept of national security is of limited utility in this context. Udo Steinbach points out that "the concept of 'nation,' introduced by colonial powers or by small elites who saw in it the prerequisite for the fulfilment of their own political aspirations, ma-terialized in a way which went against territorial, ethnic, religious, geographical or culto-historical traditions."[13] As a result, to quote Mohammed Ayoob, most Third World states lacked a "capacity to ensure the habitual identification of their inhabitants with the post-colonial structures that have emerged within colonially-dictated boundaries."[14] The most common outcome of this was conflicts about national identity, including separatist insurgencies whose peak was recorded in the 1960s.

The relatively brief time available to Third World governments for creating viable political structures out of anticolonial struggles as well as conditions of poverty, underdevelopment, and resource scarcity limited their capacity for pursuing developmental objectives in order to ensure domestic stability. Moreover, domestic conflicts in the Third World were often responsible for a wider regional insta-bility. Revolutions, insurgencies, and ethnic separatist movements frequently spilled over across national boundaries to fuel discord with neighbors. Ethnic minorities fighting the dominant elite rarely honored state boundaries, often seeking sanctuary in neighboring states where the regime and population might be more sympathetic to their cause. Weak states were more vulnerable to foreign inter-vention, as outside powers, including the superpowers, could take advantage of their domestic strife to advance their economic and ideological interests.

These general patterns of regional instability were compounded by the particular insecurities of the ruling elite in Third World states.[15] Most Third World societies exhibited a lack of consensus on the basic rules of political accommodation, power sharing, and governance. Regime creation and regime maintenance were often a product of violent societal struggles, governed by no stable constitutional framework. The narrow base of Third World regimes and the various challenges to their survival affected the way in which national security policy was articulated and pursued. In such a milieu, the regime's instinct for self-preservation often took precedence over the security interests of the society or the nation. As Barry Buzan observes, "it is tempting to identify national security with the governmental institutions that express the state, but . . . governments and institutions have security interests of their own which are separate from those of the state, and which are often opposed to broader national interests as aligned with them."[16]

As a result, the nature of national security as an ambiguous symbol is more pronounced in Third World societies than in the industrial North. The Third World experience challenged the realist image of the state as a provider of security. R. B. J. Walker finds "the state itself, far from being the provider of security as in the conventional view, has in many ways been a primary source of insecurity . . . it is difficult to see how any useful concept of security can ignore the participation of states in 'disappearances' and abuse of human rights in so many societies."[17]

Another way in which the emergent Third World challenged the dominant understanding of security relates to the place of nonmilitary issues in the latter. As mentioned earlier, national security as articulated by Western policy makers in the immediate post–World War II period was primarily concerned with war prevention. The role of nonmilitary threats did not constitute part of the agenda of national security. To date, the dominant understanding of security resists the inclusion of nonmilitary phenomena in the security studies agenda.[18] A good example is Stephen Walt's survey of the field, which clearly rejects the inclusion of such phenomena as "pollution, disease, child abuse, or economic recessions" into security studies, because, as he puts it, this would "destroy its intellectual coherence." Walt also argues that "the fact that other hazards exist does not mean that the danger of war has been eliminated."[19] On the more specific case of ecological issues, some have argued that conflict and violence in the international system had little to do with ecological degradation.[20] This perspective "disentangles resource conflicts from those leading to war and de-links security-from-violence from security from environmental degradation."[21]

But the logic of accepting a broader notion of security becomes less contestable when one looks at the Third World experience. From the very outset, resource scarcity, overpopulation, underdevelopment, and environmental degradation were at the heart of insecurity in the Third World. These essentially nonmilitary threats were much more intimately linked to the security predicament of the Third World than that of the developed countries. Economic development and well-being were closely linked not only because "a semblance of security and stability is a prerequisite for successful economic development," but also because "it is also generally understood within the Third World that economic development can contribute to national security; an economically weak nation can be exploited or defeated more easily by foreign powers and may be exposed periodically to the violent wrath of dissatisfied citizens."[22] While problems such as lack of sufficient food, water, and housing are not part of the national security agenda of developed states, they very much hold the balance between conflict and order in the Third World. Thus, as Caroline Thomas puts it, "security in the context of the Third World does not simply refer to the military dimension, as is often assumed in the Western discussions of the concept, but to the *whole range of dimensions of a state's existence which has been taken care of in the more developed states, especially those in the West.*"[23]

The vulnerability of Third World states to resource, ecological, and other transnational threats was compounded by their lack of material, human, and institutional capacity to deal with these problems. In addition, Third World states enjoy little influence over the international context within which these problems arise. In Raimo Vayrynen's view, "because of the fragility of social systems, the marginal costs of economic vulnerability, ecological degradation and ethnic fragmentation are greater problems in developing countries than in industrialized countries (where the absolute damage may be greater, however)." Therefore, "in developing countries, the notion of national security cannot be separated from the non-military threats to security."[24]

Finally, the Third World's emergence challenged the legitimacy of the dominant instrument of the Cold War international order. The principal anchor of that order, the global superpower rivalry, was viewed with profound mistrust throughout the Third World. This is evident from the dissident role of the Third World in the system of states. Hedley Bull saw the collective aim of the Third World to lie in its desire "to destroy the old international order and establish a new one, to shake off the rules and institutions devised by the old established forces (in Sukarno's phrase) and create new rules and institutions that will express the aspirations of the new emerging forces."[25] The role of the Non-Aligned Movement (NAM) in demanding a speedy completion of the decolonization process, opposing superpower interference in the Third World, and advocating global disarmament and the strengthening of global and regional mechanisms for conflict resolution testified to the collective resistance of Third World states to the system of international order resulting from superpower rivalry.[26] While the NAM's record in realizing these objectives has attracted much criticism, it was able to provide a collective psychological framework for Third World states to strengthen their independence and to play an active role in international affairs.[27] Membership in the NAM provided many Third World states with some room to maneuver in their relationship with the superpowers and to resist pressures for alliances and alignment.[28]

The Third World's collective attitude toward superpower rivalry has important implications for realist international theory. A structural realist understanding of International Relations (as developed by Ken Waltz or John Mearsheimer) would credit the Cold War and bipolarity for ensuring a stable international order. But this perspective was misleading insofar as the Third World was concerned. The Cold War order, instead of dampening conflicts in the Third World, actually contributed to their escalation. Although rarely a direct cause of Third World conflicts, the Cold War opportunism and influence seeking of superpowers contributed significantly to the ultimate severity of many cases of incipient and latent strife in the Third World.[29] It led to the internationalization of civil wars and the internalization of superpower competition.[30] It also contributed to the prolongation of regional wars by preventing decisive results in at least some theaters, including the major regional conflicts of the 1970s and 1980s—in Central America, Angola, the Horn of Africa, Cambodia, Afghanistan, and the Iran-Iraq War.[31]

Thus, superpower rivalry, while keeping the "long peace" in Europe, served to exacerbate the problems of regional conflict and instability in the Third World. The superpowers' shared interest in avoiding direct military confrontation (with its attendant risk of mutual nuclear annihilation) might have led them to enforce a degree of restraint on the behavior of their more adventurous Third World clients and thereby avoid a dangerous escalation of certain regional conflicts (in the Middle East and East Asia).[32] But the Cold War also permitted a great deal of violence and disorder in the Third World. While nuclear deterrence prevented even the most minor form of warfare between the two power blocs in Europe, superpower interventions in regional conflicts elsewhere were "permitted" as a necessary "safety valve."[33] Some writers have argued that superpower intervention in the Third World was subject to a set of "implicit rules of the game," which contributed to order and stability in the Third World.[34] But on closer examination, it becomes apparent that a great deal of the superpowers' attempts to devise a code of conduct for Third World conflicts were ad hoc, prescriptive, and limited.[35] They left considerable room for the escalation and prolongation of local and regional wars.[36]

Similarly, the Third World security experience during the Cold War explains why mechanisms for international order that reflected (and were shaped by) superpower balancing strategies were of limited effectiveness in promoting regional security. Steven David argues that for a balance of power approach to be effective, "the determinants of alignment [must] come overwhelmingly from the structure of the international system, particularly from the actual and potential *external* threats that states face." But in the Third World, it is the "internal characteristics of states" that usually influence alignments.[37] Thus, no superpower-sponsored mechanism for international order could be effective unless it would be able to address client states' internal (including regime security) concerns. This factor explains the failure of outward-looking regional security alliances such as the South East Asia Treaty Organization (SEATO) and the Central Treaty Organization (CENTO), and the relative success of more internal-security-oriented regional security arrangements such as the Association of Southeast Asian Nations (ASEAN) and the Gulf Cooperation Council (GCC).[38] (It should be noted that while the GCC failed to deter external threats to its members, particularly the Iraqi invasion of Kuwait, it had developed more effective measures against internal unrest and Iranian-backed subversion).

SECURITY IN THE POST-COLD WAR ERA: THE RELEVANCE OF THE THIRD WORLD EXPERIENCE

The above-mentioned features of insecurity in the Third World constitute a highly relevant explanatory framework for analyzing the major sources of instability in the post-Cold War era. To begin with, they aid our understanding of the emergence and escalation of conflicts and instability in the new states of Europe and Central Asia, which now constitute some of the most serious threats to the post-Cold War international order. Even though one may debate whether these states should be formally recognized as forming part of the so-called Third World, it is quite clear that there are striking similarities between the former's security problems and those of the existing Third World category. These include fairly low levels of sociopolitical cohesion and a strong element of a state-nation dichotomy, with consequent problems of ethnic strife and regime insecurity. Ayoob notes that "in terms of their colonial background, the arbitrary construction of their boundaries by external powers, the lack of societal cohesion, their recent emergence into juridical statehood, and their stage of development, the states of the Caucasus and Central Asia as well as of the Balkans demonstrate political, economic and social characteristics that are in many ways akin to Asian, African, and Latin American states that have been traditionally considered as constituting the Third World."[39]

In a broader context, the Third World security experience suggests the need to view the majority of the post-Cold War conflicts as a product of local factors, rather than of the changing structure of the international system from bipolarity to multipolarity. Some observers have suggested that the Cold War had suppressed "many potential third-world conflicts"; its end will ensure that "other conflicts will very probably arise from decompression and from a loosening of the controls and self-controls" exercised by the superpowers.[40] But such a view obscures the unchanged role of essentially domestic and intraregional factors related to weak national integration, economic underdevelopment, and competition for political legitimacy and control in shaping Third World instability. Roberto Garcia Moritan has argued:

Many of the regional problems and/or conflicts that were essentially local expressions of the [Cold War] rivalry are now proving soluble. But there are many other conflicts rooted in other sources, among them historical, political, colonial, ethnic, religious, or socio-economic legacies, that continue to produce international tensions. Cutting across these local issues are the major disparities of wealth and opportunity that separate the industrialized nations and the developing world. These have existed for decades. The failure to deal effectively with this gap is a source of additional tension, which itself frustrates long-term efforts to provide wider prosperity. The end of the Cold War has been irrelevant for many such conflicts.[41]

The view of regional conflicts as "essentially local expressions of rivalry" also underscores the need to rethink structuralist ideas that tend to analyze regional security in terms of systemic factors. During the Cold War, the theory of "regional subsystems" contributed to a system-dominant view of regional security (because a subsystem can only be located in relation to a larger international system).[42] Buzan's concept of a "security complex" offers a more powerful and specific tool for regional security analysis by focusing on "local sets of states . . . whose major security perceptions and concerns link together sufficiently closely that their national security perceptions cannot realistically be considered apart from one another."[43] But Buzan, too, sees security complexes as localized sets of essentially anarchic relations that mirror the international system at large and whose existence is revealed and shaped largely by structural shifts. Thus, in Buzan's view, colonialism and the Cold War constituted a structural "overlay" in which regional security complexes were shaped primarily by system-wide great power interactions. This overlay had suppressed many regional conflicts, which are now set to reappear.[44] Such a structuralist bias may inhibit an appreciation of the range of social, cultural, and political forces that may be unique to different regions, and that may not be significantly affected by the end of the Cold War.

There is sufficient empirical evidence to support Fred Halliday's view that "since the causes of third world upheaval [were] to a considerable extent independent of Soviet-U.S. rivalry they will continue irrespective of relations between Washington and Moscow."[45] In Africa, which the U.S. Defense Intelligence Agency rates to be "the most unstable region in the Third World,"[46] recent outbreaks of conflict (as in Rwanda and Somalia) are rooted in old ethnic and tribal animosities.[47] In Asia, the end of the two major Cold War conflicts (Afghanistan and Cambodia) leaves a number of ethnic insurgencies and separatist movements. In South Asia, the problems of political instability and ethnic separatism continue to occupy the governments of India (Assam, Kashmir, and the Punjab), Pakistan (demands for autonomy in the Sind province), and Sri Lanka (Tamil separatism).[48] The Southeast Asian governments face similar problems, especially in Indonesia (Aceh, East Timor, Irian Jaya), Myanmar (Karen and Shan guerrillas), and the Philippines (the New People's Army). In the more economically developed parts of the Third World, the primary security concerns of the ruling regimes derive from what Shahram Chubin calls the "stresses and strains of economic development, political integration, legitimation and institutionalization."[49] A good example is the situation in the Persian Gulf, where despite the recent attention to interstate wars (for example, the Iran-Iraq War and the Iraqi invasion of Kuwait), the threat from within remains a central cause of concern about the stability and survival of the traditional monarchies. While it is tempting to explain the Iraqi invasion of Kuwait, billed to be the first Third World conflict of the post-Cold War era, as an act of opportunism in the face of declining superpower involvement in the region, the roots of this conflict can only be explained in terms of the nature and position of Saddam Hussein's regime within the Iraqi polity. The Iraqi aggression was at least partly an attempt by the regime to ensure its survival in the face of a growing economic burden imposed by the Iran-Iraq War and the consequent political challenges to its legitimacy.

There is another reason why the Third World security experience is highly relevant to post-Cold War security analysis. Conflicts in the post-Cold War era are likely to become even more regional in their origin and scope because of the changing context of great power intervention. The post-Cold War era is witnessing a greater regional differentiation in great power interests and involvement in the Third World. In a bipolar world, as Kenneth Waltz has argued, "with two powers capable of acting on a world scale, anything that happen[ed] anywhere [was] potentially of concern to both of them."[50] In a multipolar world, not all great powers would wield a similar capacity, and the only power capable of global power projection, the United States, is likely to be quite selective in choosing its areas of engagement. This will render conflict formation and management in these areas more localized, subject to regional patterns of amity and enmity and the interventionist role of regionally dominant powers. The diffusion of military power to the Third World is enabling some regional powers to exercise greater influence in shaping conflict and cooperation in their respective areas.

With the end of the Cold War, some parts of the Third World are likely to experience a shift from internal to external security concerns, while others will remain primarily concerned with internal stability. There are indications that territorial disputes could become more salient for a growing number of Third World states in Africa, Latin America (Ecuador and Peru), and Southeast Asia (especially among the ASEAN nations). The more developed states in the Third World (such as the newly industrializing countries) are reshaping their defense capabilities from counterinsurgency to conventional warfare postures. For example, the Gulf Cooperation Council members are devoting more resources to external security after the Iraqi invasion of Kuwait, while in Southeast Asia there is a distinct shift from internal security to external defense capabilities. A number of major Third World powers, such as India, Indonesia, Nigeria, and Iran, are developing extended power-projection capabilities, which is bound to alarm their neighbors into giving greater attention to external security.

In general, the end of the Cold War is not having a single or uniform effect on Third World stability. In some parts of the Third World (such as in sub-Saharan Africa), the end of the Cold War has led to greater domestic disorder, while in Southeast Asia it has led to increased domestic tranquillity and regional order (with the end of communist insurgencies and the settlement of the Cambodian conflict), and in the Middle East, to greater interstate cooperation (especially after the Israeli-Palestinian accords). In Africa, the end of the Cold War has contributed to a sharp decline in arms imports, while in East Asia, it has created fears of a vigorous arms race. The rise of domestic conflicts in Africa contrasts sharply with the settlement of its long-standing regional conflicts (especially in southern Africa). In Southeast Asia, South Asia, and the Korean Peninsula, the end of the Cold War has led to greater interstate conflict. Regional hegemonism is a marked trend in East Asia with China's emergence, but elsewhere, it is the regional powers, such as India, Vietnam, and Iraq, that have felt the squeeze by being denied privileged access to arms and aid from their superpower patrons. In view of the above, it is not helpful to interpret conflict structures in the post-Cold War period as the product of a single structural or systemic realignment; a more differentiated view of the post-Cold War disorder is required.

Finally, the Third World security experience suggests the need to focus on economic and ecological changes that are giving rise to new forms of regional conflicts. The issue of economic development remains at the heart of many of these conflicts. Although economically induced instability in the Third World has been traditionally viewed as a function of underdevelopment, such instability is becoming more associated with the strategies for, and the achievement of, developmental success. In Africa, structural adjustment and growth-oriented economic liberalization mandated by lending agencies such as the International Monetary Fund (IMF) and the World Bank have led to acute political strife and regime insecurity. On the other hand, many of the successful developing countries of East and Southeast Asia today exhibit the performance paradox. In these cases, authoritarian regimes seeking legitimacy through the performance criteria (that is, rapid economic development) are confronted with the paradoxical outcome of political instability caused by an erosion of traditional social values and/or demands for political participation by an expanded middle-class population. As a result, the security predicament of countries with considerable developmental success (such as the NICS [newly industrializing countries] and near-NICS) remains essentially Third Worldish, that is, for these states, the threat from within is arguably more severe than the threat from without. In this sense, the concept of a Third World, while losing its meaning in economic terms (given the accelerating economic differentiation within this category), remains analytically useful in security terms.

Numerous empirical studies have established that the Third World is the main arena of conflicts and instability linked to environmental degradation.[51] The view of the environment as a global commons should not obscure the fact that the scale of environmental degradation, its consequences in fostering intra- and interstate conflict, and the problems of addressing these issues within the framework of the nation-state are more acute in the Third World than in the developed states. Of the three categories of conflict identified by Thomas Homer-Dixon as being related to environmental degradation, two—

"simple scarcity conflicts" (conflict over natural resources such as rivers, water, fish, and agriculturally productive land) and "relative deprivation conflicts" (the impact of environmental degradation in limiting growth and thereby causing popular discontent and conflict)—are most acute in the Third World.[52] Moreover, environmental degradation originating in the Third World is increasingly a potential basis for conflict between the North and the South, as poorer nations demand a greater share of the world's wealth and Third World environmental refugees aggravate existing group-identity conflicts (the problems of social assimilation of the migrant population) in the host countries.

The Third World security experience is helpful not only in understanding the sources of insecurity in the post-Cold War era, but also for judging the effectiveness of global-order-maintenance mechanisms. As during the Cold War period, the management of international order today reflects the dominant role of great powers, albeit now operating in a multipolar setting. The sole remaining superpower, the United States, has taken the lead in espousing a "new world order," whose key elements include a revival of collective security and the relatively newer frameworks of humanitarian intervention and nonproliferation. But as during the Cold War period, attempts by the globally dominant actors to manage international order do not correspond with regional realities in the Third World. Moreover, these attempts have contributed to a climate of mistrust and exacerbated North-South tensions.

For example, former President George Bush's vision of a new world order promised a return to multilateralism and the revival of the UN's collective security framework. But the first major test of this new world order, the U.S.-led response to the Iraqi invasion of Kuwait, prompted widespread misgivings in the Third World. Although the UN resolutions against Iraq were supported by most Third World states, this was accompanied by considerable resentment of the U.S. domination of the UN decision-making process. The United States's military actions against Iraq were seen as having exceeded the mandate of UN resolutions, and American claims about collective security were greeted with skepticism.[53] Many in the South would perhaps agree with Zbigniew Brzezinski's remark that "once the symbolism of collective action was stripped away . . . [the war against Iraq] was largely an American decision and relied primarily on American military power."[54] The Gulf War fed apprehensions in the Third World that in the so-called unipolar moment, the United States, along with like-minded Western powers, would use the pretext of multilateralism to pursue essentially unilateral objectives in post-Cold War conflicts. Conflicts in those areas deemed to be vitally important to the Western powers will be especially susceptible to Northern unilateralism.

As with collective security, armed intervention in support of humanitarian objectives has the potential to exacerbate North-South tensions. The use of the humanitarian label in justifying intervention in failed states (as in the case of Somalia or Rwanda) or against regimes accused of gross human rights abuses has created some serious misgivings in the Third World. Many Third World regimes view this as a kind of recycled imperialism, while those taking a more tolerant view worry nonetheless about the effects of such a sovereignty-defying instrument. While these fears have not prevented the UN from undertaking humanitarian missions, those operations relying primarily on U.S. power (such as Somalia) have been particularly controversial. Moreover, the Somalia case suggests that humanitarian operations are unlikely to be effective unless they also address the underlying political sources of regional conflicts; the provision of humanitarian relief to a starving population will not by itself promote stability unless it is matched by a corresponding effort to bring about long-term political accommodation within Somalian society. The complex interplay of ethnic rivalries (weak state) and political anarchy, hallmarks of the Third World regional-conflict situations during the Cold War, continues to undermine the effectiveness of post-Cold War frameworks of international order.

A third area of North-South tension concerns the Northern approach to arms control and nonproliferation. In particular, supply-side antiproliferation measures developed by the North, such as the Nuclear Non-Proliferation Treaty (NPT) or the Missile Technology Control Regime (MTCR), which seek to restrict the availability of military or dual-use technology to Southern states, have met with Southern objections. These objections focus on the selective application and discriminatory nature of the North's antiproliferation campaign. Chubin finds that the North's antinuclear policy "frankly discriminates between friendly and unfriendly states, focusing on signatories (and potential cheats) like Iran but ignoring actual proliferators like Israel. It is perforce more intelligible in the North than in the South."[55] In a more blunt tone, the Indian scholar K. Subrahmanyam charges that "export controls divide the world into North and South, project a racist bias, and have proved to be inefficient instruments for pursuing global non-proliferation objectives."[56]

In the absence of greater understanding between the North and the South, there is a definite risk that the organizing principles of order devised and enforced by the dominant actors of the international system will have a limited impact as instruments of international order. In this context, regional security arrangements, developed by the Southern actors themselves, could theoretically provide greater opportunity and scope for regional autonomy and help the maintenance of international order.[57] During the Cold War, many Third World states accused the superpowers of ignoring, bypassing, and manipulating indigenous regional security arrangements in the Third World. Some of the most visible regional groupings, such as the ASEAN and the GCC, both reflected and contributed to Cold War divisions within Third World regions. The end of the Cold War is reinvigorating and reshaping the role of Third World regional groupings toward conflict control, peacekeeping, and preventive diplomacy functions. The role of the Contadora and Esquipulas groups in facilitating conflict resolution in Central America, the peacekeeping role of the Economic Community of West African States (ECOWAS) in the Liberian civil war, the efforts by the Association of Southeast Asian Nations as a peacemaker in the Cambodia conflict and later in sponsoring a regional forum (the ASEAN Regional Forum) to deal with the changing balance of power in the Asia-Pacific region, and efforts by the Organization of African Unity to create a new mechanism for conflict resolution and peacekeeping—all attest to a new sense of purpose and activism on the part of regional mechanisms.

But the peace and security role of regional groupings remains limited by their lack of the institutional structures required for conflict resolution or a collective military capacity needed for complex peacekeeping operations. Moreover, wide disparities of power within many existing Third World regional groupings create the risk that collective regional action will be held hostage to the narrow interests of a dominant member state. The Third World's continued adherence to the principle of noninterference undermines the prospect for effective regional action with respect to internal conflicts.[58]

In addition, regional security arrangements in areas that are deemed to engage the vital interests of the great powers have limited autonomy in managing local conflicts. In these areas, the dependence of local states on external security guarantees (hence frequent great power intervention in local conflicts) will continue to thwart prospects for regional solutions to regional problems.[59] In the Persian Gulf, for example, Kuwait's security agreements with the United States came into conflict with regional security arrangements involving the GCC after the Iraqi defeat. Similarly, most developing nations of East Asia prefer bilateral arrangements with the United States as a more realistic security option than indigenous multilateral approaches. The ECOWAS peacekeeping operation in Liberia, while ambitious and elaborate in scope, has been dogged by accusations of Nigerian domination and made only limited progress in restoring order in that country.

Nonetheless, regional approaches to peace and security face fewer systemic constraints in the post-Cold War era. They could provide a way of ensuring a greater decentralization of the global peace and security regime, which has assumed greater urgency in view of the limited resources of the UN in the face of an ever-expanding agenda of peacekeeping operations. They are also a means for achieving greater democratization of the global security regime, an important challenge in view of the Third World's resentment of the dominant role of great powers in the UN Security Council. Thus, the post-Cold War era contains an opportunity for a more meaningful division of labor between universal and regional frameworks of security in promoting conflict resolution in the Third World.

THE END OF THE THIRD WORLD?

The foregoing discussion has argued for the need for the Third World security experience as a principal reason for the broadening of the security discourse. But any such argument must face the growing criticism of the continued relevance of the term *Third World* itself. Critics of the concept have always regarded the term as being too imprecise and analytically limited. They have pointed to the physical diversity and economic differentiation within the Third World category. Moreover, despite the persistence of North-South political and economic differences, the end of the Cold War has diminished the relevance of Third World political platforms such as the Non-

Aligned Movement. Against this backdrop, can one meaningfully broaden the security discourse by generalizing from the Third World experience?

There are three principal reasons why the notion of a Third World retains analytical value. First, the existence of North-South divisions continues to be widely acknowledged among scholars and policy makers from Washington to Kuala Lumpur. It has become commonplace to find observations that the end of East-West conflict has left the North-South divide as the main challenge to collective international order. Indeed, President Suharto of Indonesia, the present chairman of the Non-Aligned Movement (NAM), has gone a step further by characterizing the continuing North-South divide as "the central unresolved issue of our times."[60]

Second, despite their diversity, the Third World countries continue to share a number of common features in the security and economic arena. These include the primacy of internal threats (as weak states) and a dependence on external security guarantees (as weak powers). Moreover, while the collective bargaining position of the Third World over international economic regimes and the redistribution of wealth might have collapsed, the economic predicament of Third World states, marked by poverty, underdevelopment, resource scarcity, and dependence, remains as a general feature of many of the states that emerged in the post-World War II period (as well as many Latin American states that had obtained independence earlier). Indeed, in many parts of the Third World, especially in Africa, these problems have become more acute. Thus, the economic success of a handful of Third World states should not be the basis for making the generalization that the Third World has somehow vanished. The diversity of the South or the disunity that has afflicted all its major platforms cannot be denied, but these features are nothing new and by themselves should not negate the Third World's claim for a collective label. Indeed, the Third World states have never pretended to be a homogeneous lot. If economic and political differentiation is accepted as the basis for rejecting the notion, then the analytical relevance of similar notions (such as the "West") should also be questioned.

Third, it should be remembered that the term *Third World* was not originally intended to denote a political bloc between the East and the West. Instead, the term was coined by French authors by analogy with the "Third Estate" of prerevolutionary France to refer to social groups other than the most privileged groups of the day, the clergy and nobility. In James Mittleman's view, the relatively inferior position of Third World states within the international system still holds true, especially as a large part of the Third World is facing greater marginalization after the Cold War. In this sense, the term Third World did and continues to refer to "the marginalized strata of the international system." Thus, "despite its pitfalls, the term *Third World* is a convenient shorthand to depict the group of countries struggling to escape from underdevelopment. As a metaphor, it describes the disadvantaged position of peoples, most of whom are of color and live in poverty in post-colonial societies, within the ambit of a rapidly changing global political economy."[61] While some sort of analytical schema providing for a more differentiated view of the Third World is called for and has indeed been attempted by some scholars, to debunk the notion in its entirety is uncalled for.

CONCLUSION

The end of the Cold War has dramatically shifted the empirical focus of security studies. Today, regional conflicts—conflicts (intra- as well as interstate) in the world's less developed areas, including the new states that emerged out of the breakup of the Soviet empire—are widely recognized as a more serious threat to international order. This contrasts sharply with the greatly enhanced stability of the central strategic relationship among the great powers (China excluded).[62] Judging from the attention given to recent conflicts in the Persian Gulf, Somalia, Bosnia, South Asia, the Korean Peninsula, and other places, regional conflicts in the world's periphery have become the core issues of concern for international security studies.

But the understanding of regional conflicts and security in the post-Cold War period also requires conceptual tools and methodology beyond what is provided by orthodox notions of security developed during the Cold War period. The primary argument of this chapter has been that the very notions of security and international order developed during the Cold War must be contested if they are to help us to understand the sources of today's regional conflicts and the prospects for their control. A notion of security rooted firmly within the realist tradition, and developed as an abstraction from the Eurocentric states system that emerged from the Peace of Westphalia, does not provide an adequate conceptual framework for understanding the security problematic of those states that entered the system at a later stage. While it is fashionable to view the contemporary international system, despite being geographically and culturally more varied, as an extension of the original Westphalian model, the experience of the latecomers constitutes a different set of realities that challenge the fundamental assumptions of realism.

During the Cold War, the exclusion of the Third World's security problems from the mainstream security studies agenda contributed to its narrow and ethnocentric conceptual framework and empirical terrain. The analysis of regional conflict in the contemporary security discourse can benefit from a framework that captures the significantly broader range of issues—involving state and nonstate actors, military and nonmilitary challenges—that lie at the heart of insecurity and disorder in the Third World. In this respect, a greater integration of Third World security issues into international security studies will facilitate the latter's attempt to move beyond its now-discredited realist orthodoxy.

The incorporation of the Third World security predicament into the security studies agenda also creates the basis for rethinking the requirements of international order. The construction of international order, including its norms, principles, and institutions, cannot solely depend on global frameworks devised by the great powers. To be effective, global norms must correspond to local and regional realities. As conflicts in the international system become more regionalized as a result of the end of the Cold War, there is a need for a more decentralized system of order maintenance. In this context, the role of regional security arrangements, including region-specific approaches to security, arms control, and disarmament, deserve greater encouragement. The containment of regional conflict requires a certain amount of deference to the principle of regional autonomy and a mutually beneficial division of labor between global and regional security arrangements. Frameworks of security and order devised by major powers usually mask the latter's narrow self-interest. In many ways, mechanisms for international order such as collective security, humanitarian intervention, and nonproliferation cannot cope with disorder if they serve to exacerbate existing North-South divisions.

For the above reasons, the end of the Cold War should serve as a catalyst for the coming of age of Third World security studies. The

true globalization of security studies should be built on a greater regionalization of our understanding of the sources of conflict and the
requirements of international order, with the Third World serving as
a central conceptual and empirical focus.

NOTES

1. Ken Booth, "Security and Emancipation," *Review of International
Studies* 17:4 (1991), 318.

2. The conceptual underdevelopment of national security and the ambiguities surrounding the concept are explored in Barry Buzan, *People, States
and Fear: An Agenda for International Security Studies in the Post-Cold
War Era* (New York: Harvester Wheatsheaf, 1991).

3. Helga Haftendorn, "The Security Puzzle: Theory-Building and Discipline-Building in International Security," *International Studies Quarterly*
35:1 (1991), 3–18.

4. See Richard Ullman, "Redefining Security," *International Security*
8:1 (1983), 129–53; Michael Renner, *National Security: The Economic and
Environmental Dimensions*, Worldwatch Paper no. 89 (Washington, D.C.:
Worldwatch Institute, 1989); Arthur H. Westing, "An Expanded Concept of
International Security," in Arthur H. Westing, ed., *Global Resources and
International Conflict* (New York: Oxford University Press, 1986), 183–200;
Jessica Tuchman Mathews, "Redefining Security," *Foreign Affairs* 68:2
(1989), 162–77; Gro Harlem Brundtland, "The Environment, Security and
Development," *SIPRI Yearbook 1993* (Oxford: Oxford University Press,
1993), 15–36; Norman Meyers, "Environmental Security," *Foreign Policy*
74 (1989), 23–41; Thomas F. Homer-Dixon, *Environmental Change and
Human Conflict*, working paper (Cambridge, Mass.: American Academy of
the Arts and Sciences, 1990); Dennis Pirages, "Environmental Security and
Social Evolution," *International Studies Notes* 16:1 (1991), 8–12; Neville
Brown, "Climate, Ecology and International Security," *Survival* 31:6 (1989),
484–99; *Environmental Security: A Report Contributing to the Concept of
Comprehensive International Security* (Oslo: International Peace Research
Institute, 1989); *Our Common Future: Report of the World Commission on
Environment and Development* (Oxford: Oxford University Press, 1987);
Hans W. Maull, "Energy and Resources: The Strategic Dimensions," *Sur-
vival* 31:6 (1989), 500–518; Edward N. Krapels, *Oil And Security: Prob-
lems and Prospects of Importing Countries*, Adelphi Paper no. 136 (London:
International Institute for Strategic Studies, 1977); F. A. M. Alting von
Geusau and J. Pelkmans, eds., *National Economic Security: Perceptions,*

Threats and Policies (Tillburg, Netherlands: John F. Kennedy Institute, 1982), 47–61; Raimo Vayrynen, "Towards a Comprehensive Definition of Security: Pitfalls and Promises," paper prepared for the annual convention of the International Studies Association, Washington, D.C., 10–14 April 1990; Klaus Knorr and Frank Trager, *Economic Issues and National Security* (Lawrence: University Press of Kansas, 1977); Stephen D. Krasner, "National Security and Economics," in B. Thomas Trout and James E. Harf, eds., *National Security Affairs* (New Brunswick, N.J.: Transaction Books, 1982), 313–28; Giacomo Luciani, "The Economic Content of Security," *Journal of Public Policy* 8:2 (1989), 151–73; Al Gedicks, "The New Resource Wars," *Raw Materials Reports* 1:2 (1982), 8–13; Joseph J. Romm, *Defining National Security: The Non-Military Aspects* (New York: Council on Foreign Relations Press, 1993), 51–80; J. Ann Tickner, "Redefining Security: A Feminist Perspective," paper presented to the annual meeting of the Northwestern Political Science and Northeast International Studies Association, November 1989; Brad Roberts, "Human Rights and International Security," *The Washington Quarterly* 13:2 (1990), 65–75.

5. For important contributions to the debate on the broadening of security, see Buzan, *People, States and Fear*; R. B. J. Walker, *The Concept of Security and International Relations Theory*, working paper no. 3, First Annual Conference on Discourse, Peace, Security and International Society, Ballyvaughn, Ireland, 9–16 August 1987; Stephen M. Walt, "The Renaissance of Security Studies," *International Studies Quarterly* 35:2 (1991), 211–39; Edward A. Kolodziej, "Renaissance in Security Studies: Caveat Lector," *International Studies Quarterly* 36:4 (1992), 421–38; Sean M. Lynn-Jones, "International Security Studies," *International Studies Notes* 16:3 (1992), 53–63; Daniel Deudney, "The Case against Linking Environmental Degradation and National Security," *Millennium* 19:3 (1990), 461–76; "Forum: 'What Is Security and Security Studies?' Revisited," special section of *Arms Control* 13:3 (1992), 463–544; Joseph S. Nye, "The Contribution of Strategic Studies: Future Challenges," in *The Changing Strategic Landscape*, part 1, Adelphi Paper no. 235 (London: International Institute for Strategic Studies, 1989), 20–34; Haftendorn, "The Security Puzzle"; Simon Dalby, "Security, Modernity and Ecology: The Dilemmas of Post-Cold War Security Discourse," *Alternatives* 17:1 (1992), 95–134.

6. The words used here are those of Barry Buzan. While Buzan himself is a strong advocate of the broadening of the focus of security studies to nonmilitary threats and to the Third World, he assumes the larger international system to be based on the universal European model. Buzan, *People, States and Fear*, 204.

7. The most important exceptions to the general neglect of Third World security issues are Mohammed Ayoob, "Security in the Third World: The

Worm about to Turn," *International Affairs* 60:1 (1984), 41–51; Mohammed Ayoob, "Regional Security and the Third World," in Mohammed Ayoob, ed., *Regional Security in the Third World* (London: Croom Helm, 1986), 3–23; Bahgat Korany, "Strategic Studies and the Third World: A Critical Appraisal," *International Social Science Journal* 38:4 (1986), 547–62; Udo Steinbach, "Sources of Third World Conflict," in *Third World Conflict and International Security*, Adelphi Paper no. 166 (London: International Institute for Strategic Studies, 1981), 21–28; Soedjatmoko, "Patterns of Armed Conflict in the Third World," *Alternatives* 10:4 (1985), 477–93; Edward Azar and Chung-in Moon, "Third World National Security: Towards a New Conceptual Framework," *International Interactions* 11:2 (1984), 103–35; Barry Buzan, "The Concept of National Security for Developing Countries with Special Reference to Southeast Asia," paper presented to the Workshop on "Leadership and Security in Southeast Asia," Institute of Southeast Asian Studies, Singapore, 10–12 December 1987; Barry Buzan, "People, States and Fear: The National Security Problem in the Third World," in Edward Azar and Chung-in Moon, eds., *National Security in the Third World* (Aldershot: Edward Elgar, 1988), 14–43; Caroline Thomas, *In Search of Security: The Third World in International Relations* (Brighton: Wheatsheaf Books, 1987); Yezid Sayigh, *Confronting the 1990s: Security in the Developing Countries*, Adelphi Paper no. 251 (London: International Institute for Strategic Studies, 1990); Mohammed Ayoob, "The Security Predicament of the Third World State," in Brian L. Job, ed., *The (In)Security Dilemma: The National Security of Third World States* (Boulder, Colo.: Lynne Rienner, 1992); Mohammed Ayoob, "The Security Problematic of the Third World," *World Politics* 43:2 (1991), 257–83; Steven R. David, "Explaining Third World Alignment," *World Politics* 43:2 (1991), 232–56. Caroline Thomas provides a succinct overview of the place of Third World issues in international security studies in her "New Directions in Thinking about Security in the Third World," in Ken Booth, ed., *New Thinking about Strategy and International Security* (London: HarperCollins, 1991), 267–89.

8. Hugh Macdonald, "Strategic Studies," *Millennium* 16:2 (1987), 333–36.

9. Joseph S. Nye and Sean M. Lynn-Jones, "International Security Studies: Report of a Conference on the State of the Field," *International Security* 12:4 (1988), 27. Major theoretical attempts to develop an understanding of Third World regional conflict and security issues in terms of their local, rather than systemic or structural, determinants during the Cold War period include Ayoob's work on regional security in the Third World and Buzan's work on "regional security complexes." Contending that "issues of regional security in the developed world are defined primarily in Cold War terms (NATO versus Warsaw Pact, etc.) and are, therefore, largely indivisible from

issues of systemic security," Ayoob convincingly demonstrated that "the salient regional security issues in the Third World have a life of their own independent of superpower rivalry." Buzan similarly urged greater attention to the "set of security dynamics at the regional level" in order to "develop the concepts and language for systematic comparative studies, still an area of conspicuous weakness in Third World studies." His notion of a "security complex," was designed to understand "how the regional level mediates the interplay between states and the international system as a whole." It should be noted, however, that while both Ayoob and Buzan called for greater attention to the regional and local sources of conflict and cooperation, Ayoob's was specifically focused on the Third World. Buzan's approach is also more structuralist, emphasizing the role of systemic determinants such as colonialism and superpower rivalry (which he called "overlays") in shaping regional security trends. This seems to undercut his earlier call for "the relative autonomy of regional security relations." See Ayoob, "Regional Security and the Third World"; Buzan, *People, States and Fear*, 186; and Buzan, "Third World Regional Security in Structural and Historical Perspective," in Job, ed., *The (In)Security Dilemma*, 167–89.

10. Evan Luard estimates that between 1945 and 1986, there were some 127 "significant wars." Out of these, only two occurred in Europe, while Latin America accounted for twenty-six; Africa, thirty-one; the Middle East, twenty-four; and Asia, forty-four. According to this estimate, the Third World was the scene of more than 98 percent of all international conflicts. Evan Luard, *War in International Society* (London: I. B. Tauris, 1986), appendix 5.

11. To say that the Third World's security predicament or experience has not been captured by realist analysis is not to say that the security behavior of Third World states has not followed the tenets of realism. On the contrary, there has been a mismatch between security analysis and security policy and praxis in the case of Third World states. Many Third World governments have pursued policies that enhance the security of the state and the regime while ignoring more unconventional sources of conflict, such as underdevelopment and ecological degradation. This state-centrism in security policy has, in turn, compounded the instability and violence in the Third World.

12. Cited in Thomas, "New Directions in Thinking about Security in the Third World," 269.

13. Udo Steinbach, "Sources of Third World Conflict," 21.

14. Ayoob, "Regional Security and the Third World," 9–10.

15. Brian L. Job, "The Insecurity Dilemma," in Job, ed., *The (In)Security Dilemma*.

16. Buzan, "The Concept of National Security for Developing Countries," 6.

17. Walker, *The Concept of Security and International Relations Theory*, 11.

18. Those who are skeptical of a broader notion of security or who caution against too much broadening include some of the leading contributors to the analysis of the Third World security predicament. Mohammed Ayoob, in his contribution to this volume, argues that "there are major intellectual and practical hazards in adopting unduly elastic definitions of security" and specifically calls for security analysts to "show greater discrimination in applying security-related vocabulary to matters pertaining to ecological or other global management issues." In his view, for the latter to be considered as security issues, "they must demonstrate the capacity immediately to affect political outcomes." I agree on the need for such caution. But even if one adopts Ayoob's criteria, there remains a wide range of nonmilitary issues that create tension and violence within and between states and destabilize state-society relations. These (such as the conflict-creating potential of underdevelopment or environmental degradation) should be considered as being legitimately within the purview of security studies.

19. Stephen M. Walt, "The Renaissance of Security Studies," 211–39.

20. Deudney, "The Case against Linking Environmental Degradation and National Security," 464–65.

21. Marc Williams, "Re-articulating the Third World Coalition: The Role of the Environmental Agenda," *Third World Quarterly* 14:1 (1993), 27.

22. H. John Rosenbaum and William G. Tyler, "South-South Relations: The Economic and Political Content of Interactions among Developing Countries," *International Organization* 29:1 (1975), 243–74.

23. Thomas, *In Search of Security*, 1. Emphasis added.

24. Vayrynen, "Towards a Comprehensive Definition of Security," 10.

25. Hedley Bull, "The Third World and International Society," in George W. Keeton and Georg Schwarzenberger, eds., *The Yearbook on International Affairs 1979* (London: Stevens and Sons, 1979), 18.

26. On the origins and role of the NAM, see Peter Lyon, *Neutralism* (Leicester: Leicester University Press, 1963); A. W. Singham and S. Hume, *Non-Alignment in the Age of Alignments* (London: Zed Books, 1986); Peter Willetts, *The Non-Aligned Movement* (London: Frances Pinter, 1978); Satish Kumar, "Non-Alignment: International Goals and National Interests," *Asian Survey* 23:4 (1983), 445–61; Fred Halliday, "The Maturing of the Non-Aligned: Perspectives from New Delhi," in *Third World Affairs* (London: Third World Foundation, 1985); Bojana Tadic, "The Movement of the Non-Aligned and Its Dilemmas Today," *Review of International Affairs* 32:756 (5 October 1981), 19–24; A. W. Singham, ed., *The Non-Aligned Movement in World Politics* (Westport, Conn.: L. Hill, 1977).

27. Pervaiz Iqbal Cheema, "NAM and Security," *Strategic Studies* (Islamabad) 14:3 (1991), 15.

28. Mohammed Ayoob, "The Third World in the System of States: Acute Schizophrenia or Growing Pains," *International Studies Quarterly* 33:1 (1989), 75.

29. Edward A. Kolodziej and Robert Harkavy, "Developing States and the International Security System," *Journal of International Affairs* 34:1 (1980), 63.

30. Shahram Chubin, "The Super-powers, Regional Conflicts and World Order," in *The Changing Strategic Landscape*, Adelphi Papers, no. 237 (London: International Institute for Strategic Studies, 1989), 78.

31. In a comprehensive survey of 107 wars in the Third World between 1945 and 1990, Guy Arnold found that "many would almost certainly have been far shorter in duration and less devastating in their effects had the big powers not intervened." See Arnold, *Wars in the Third World since 1945* (London: Cassell, 1991), xvi.

32. Mohammed Ayoob, "State Making, State Breaking and State Failure: Explaining the Roots of Third World Insecurity," paper presented at the seminar on "Conflict and Development: Causes, Effects and Remedies," The Hague, Netherlands Institute of International Relations, 22–24 March 1994, 8–9.

33. Ayoob, "Regional Security and the Third World," 14.

34. On the superpower rules of the game, see Roger E. Kanet and Edward A. Kolodziej, *The Cold War as Cooperation: Superpower Cooperation in Regional Conflict Management* (London: Macmillan, 1991); Joanne Gowa and Nils Wessell, *Ground Rules: Soviet and American Involvement in Regional Conflicts* (Philadelphia: Foreign Policy Research Institute, 1982); Neil Matheson, *The 'Rules of the Game' of the Superpower Military Intervention in the Third World* (Washington, D.C.: University Press of America, 1982); Alexander George, "Factors Influencing Security Co-operation," in Alexander George, Philip J. Farley, and Alexander Dallin, eds., *U.S.-Soviet Security Cooperation: Achievements, Failures and Lessons* (New York: Oxford University Press, 1988), 655–78; Jose T. Cintra, "Regional Conflicts: Trends in a Period of Transition," in *The Changing Strategic Landscape*, Adelphi Paper no. 237 (London: International Institute for Strategic Studies, 1989), 94–108; Stanley Hoffmann, "Watch Out for a New World Disorder," *International Herald Tribune*, 26 February 1991, 6; Robert Jervis, "The Future of World Politics: Will It Resemble the Past?", *International Security* 16:3 (1991/92).

35. See Alexander George et al., *Managing the U.S.-Soviet Rivalry: Problems of Crisis Prevention* (Boulder, Colo.: Westview Press, 1983), 367–79.

36. Amitav Acharya, *Third World Conflicts and International Order after the Cold War*, working paper no. 135 (Australian National University, Peace Research Centre, 1993).

37. David, "Explaining Third World Alignment," 233–55.

38. Amitav Acharya, "Regionalism and Regime Security in the Third World: Comparing the Origins of ASEAN and the GCC," in Job, ed., *The (In)security Dilemma.*

39. Mohammed Ayoob, "State Making, State Breaking and State Failure: Explaining the Roots of Third World Insecurity," 2–3.

40. Cintra, "Regional Conflicts: Trends in a Period of Transition," 96–97.

41. Roberto Garcia Moritan, "The Developing World and the New World Order," *The Washington Quarterly* 15:4 (1992), 151.

42. For the theory of regional subsystems, see Louis J. Cantori and Steven L. Spiegel, *The International Politics of Regions: A Comparative Approach* (Englewood Cliffs, N.J.: Prentice Hall, 1970); William R. Thompson, "The Regional Subsystem: Conceptual Explication and Propositional Inventory," *International Studies Quarterly* 17:1 (1973), 89–118.

43. Barry Buzan, "A Framework for Regional Security Analysis," in Barry Buzan and Gowher Rizvi, eds., *South Asian Insecurity and the Great Powers* (London: Croom Helm, 1986), 8; Barry Buzan, "Regional Security," *Arbejdspapirer no. 28* (Copenhagen: Centre for Peace and Conflict Research, 1989).

44. See Buzan, "Third World Security in Historical and Structural Perspective."

45. Fred Halliday, *Cold War, Third World* (London: Hutchinson Radius, 1989), 162.

46. Testimony by Lieutenant General James Clapper to the Senate Armed Services Committee, 22 January 1992, in *Regional Flashpoints Potential for Military Conflict*, (Washington, D.C.: United States Information Service, 1992), 5.

47. "Africa's Tribal Wars," *The Economist*, 13 October 1990, 50–51.

48. "Tribalism Revisited," *The Economist*, 21 December 1991 – 3 January 1992, 24.

49. Shahram Chubin, "Third World Conflicts: Trends and Prospects," *International Social Science Journal* 43:1 (1991), 159.

50. Kenneth N. Waltz, *Theory of International Politics* (Reading, Mass.: Addison-Wesley, 1979), 171.

51. For example, much of the evidence cited by Jessica Tuchman Mathews to support her arguments concerning redefining security is from the Third World. See Mathews, "Redefining Security."

52. Thomas F. Homer-Dixon, "On the Threshold: Environmental Changes as Causes of Acute Conflict," *International Security* 16:2 (1991), 76–116.

53. During the Gulf War, the U.S. pressure on the UN gave the impression that the world body was being manipulated for the narrow strategic purpose of a superpower. Although the United States sought to inject a degree of legitimacy into its actions by seeking UN endorsement, in the final analysis the United States would have pursued its strategic options irrespective of the UN mandate. Richard Falk observed that "behind this formal mandate from the United Nations [to the U.S. approach to the Gulf crisis] lie extremely serious questions about whether the UN has been true to its own Charter, and to the larger purposes of peace and justice that it was established to serve. And beyond these concerns is the disturbing impression that the United Nations has been converted into a virtual tool of U.S. foreign policy, thus compromising its future credibility, regardless of how the Gulf crisis turns out." Richard Falk, "UN being made a tool of U.S. foreign policy," *Guardian Weekly*, 27 January 1991, 12. See also "The Use and Abuse of the UN in the Gulf Crisis," *Middle East Report*, no. 169 (1991). For a more positive assessment of the UN's role, see Sir Anthony Parsons, "The United Nations after the Gulf War," *The Round Table*, no. 319 (1991), 265–74.

54. "New World Order: An Interview with Zbigniew Brzezinski," *SAIS Review* 11:2 (1991), 2.

55. Shahram Chubin, "The South and the New World Disorder," *The Washington Quarterly* 16:4 (1993), 98.

56. K. Subrahmanyam, "Export Controls and the North-South Controversy," *The Washington Quarterly* 16:2 (1993), 135.

57. Regional security organizations may perform a variety of roles and may be based on different models such as collective security systems, alliances, or common security forums. Collective security systems should not be confused with alliance-type regional security arrangements such as the Bush administration's idea of a "regional security structure" in the wake of Iraq's expulsion from Kuwait. Collective security refers to the role of a global or regional system in protecting any member state from aggression by another member state. The inward-looking security role of a collective security system is to be contrasted with the outer-directed nature of an alliance that is geared to protect its members from a common external threat. See Ernst B. Haas, *Tangle of Hopes* (Englewood Cliffs, N.J.: Prentice Hall, 1969), 94. For an appraisal of the strengths and limitations of regional security arrangements in the post-Cold War era, see S. Neil MacFarlane and Thomas G. Weiss, "Regional Organizations and Regional Security," *Security Studies* 2:1 (1992); Tom J. Farer, "The Role of Regional Collective Security Arrangements," in Thomas G. Weiss, ed., *Collective Security in a Changing World* (Boulder, Colo.: Lynne Rienner, 1993), 153–86; Amitav Acharya,

"Regional Approaches to Security in the Third World: Lessons and Prospects," in Larry A. Swatuk and Timothy M. Shaw, eds., *The South at the End of the Twentieth Century* (London: Macmillan, 1994), 79–94; Paul F. Diehl, "Institutional Alternatives to Traditional U.N. Peacekeeping: An Assessment of Regional and Multinational Options," *Armed Forces and Society* 19:2 (1993); Benjamin Rivlin, "Regional Arrangements and the UN System for Collective Security and Conflict Resolution: A New Road Ahead?" *International Relations* 11:2 (1992), 95–110.

58. MacFarlane and Weiss, "Regional Organizations and Regional Security," 31.

59. See Amitav Acharya, "Regional Military-Security Cooperation in the Third World: A Conceptual Analysis of the Relevance and Limitations of ASEAN," *Journal of Peace Research* 29:1 (1992), 7–21; Amitav Acharya, "The Gulf Cooperation Council and Security: Dilemmas of Dependence," *Middle East Strategic Studies Quarterly* 1:3 (1990), 88–136.

60. Quoted in "Goodbye Nehru, Hello Suharto," *The Economist*, 12 September 1992, 32.

61. James Mittleman, "The Third World," in *The Oxford Companion to the Politics of the World* (New York: Oxford University Press, 1994), 909.

62. In one formulation, the post-Cold War international system consists of a core sector of major powers within which interdependence and shared norms minimize the risk of armed conflict, and a periphery sector (for example, the Third World) featuring fragile regional security systems marked by a high degree of conflict and disorder. James M. Goldgeier and Michael McFaul, "Core and Periphery in the Post-Cold War Era," *International Organization* 46:2 (1992), 467–92.

11

Critical Security Studies and Regional Insecurity: The Case of Southern Africa

KEN BOOTH AND PETER VALE

If critical security studies are to flourish and lead to a revisioning of security in world politics, it is necessary that they challenge traditional security studies not only at the theoretical level—where a start has already been made—but also at the empirical level in terms of dealing with what is usually called the real world. Southern Africa is a particularly interesting case with which to test the engagement of critical security studies with practical politics, given that by many indicators it can claim to be the most distressed and insecure region in contemporary world politics.

The framework of this chapter is set by what we consider to be the main questions raised by critical security studies.[1] What are the interrelationships between theories and practices? Who controls the facts in the security debate? How do we come to and how should we understand security? What should be—as opposed to are—the referent(s) when thinking about security? What principles—as well as procedures—should security policy seek to advance? How and by whom is the threat agenda to be determined? Who should be the agents for differently conceived security practices? What institutions in particular settings will best advance regional security from a critical security studies perspective? What should the relationships be between regional and global structures and processes? What conditions can be created to deliver comprehensive regional security? Is the traditional security agenda relevant? What would a condition of

329

comprehensive regional security look like? And, finally, what is our role—as academics—in trying to advance critical against traditional security thinking?

In pursuing these questions in relation to southern Africa we hope to provide a comprehensive template for thinking about security in the region (and, implicitly, in other regions); to show how ideas about security have (and might) change; to underline the inadequacies of traditional regional security analysis; and to suggest lines of thought (principles and policies) that will promote the normative values inherent in critical security studies. For some, including several authors in this book, the meaning of this critical turn is still unsettled, and hence, the subject area of critical security studies is unsettled. The standpoint from which this chapter is written has a more focused conception of the subject area, namely, that critical security studies embrace postrealist, postpositivist approaches to security informed by an explicit commitment to emancipatory politics for a potential community of humankind. The issues raised by this conception of critical security studies can be distilled into a disarmingly simple set of questions,[2] but the answers—as the discussion of southern African situations will show—are contestable and complex.

THE PRACTICES OF THEORY

Being explicit about theory is one of the moves that separates critical approaches from traditional theory in the study of International Relations. In this chapter we want to emphasize three key functions of theory. First, theoretical inquiry will lead to searching questions about the meanings and practices of security. Second, there is a relationship in all human settings between the quality of the theory and the quality of the related practice: "There is nothing so practical as a good theory," as the old adage has it. And three, all life is lived within theories; they create the structures within which we live and they provide the facts that we take to be the real world. Apartheid was a theory, and like all humanly constituted theories, it could be changed. It was neither natural, nor inheritable, nor commonsensical, but its power was such that many people came to believe it was, and as a result it destroyed many lives. The first two functions of theory will be illustrated throughout this chapter; for the moment we will simply illustrate the last.

We talked at the beginning about engaging with the real world.

But what is it in southern Africa? To be more precise, whose real world should we discuss? Who has controlled and now controls the facts that define politics? Why have some facts been given more weight than others in discussions of regional security? Whose interests are served in bringing some facts to the surface, while suppressing others? Is there a possibility of a widely shared account of southern Africa? The problems thrown up by such questions can be easily demonstrated.

The so-called facts of history as traditionally taught throughout the schools of the region are one measure of who controlled images of the real world, and with what interest. In all southern African countries, history teaching has served a variety of social and political functions—albeit subconsciously in some cases. The stories told in school have been such as to engender patriotic sentiments and social stability. In South Africa, until recently, the teaching of history was intimately associated with the perpetuation of apartheid. In Angola and Mozambique, until independence, it glorified Portuguese colonialism. And in the region's former British colonies, all schooling was inculcated with British values and knowledge: schoolchildren knew more about the mountains and monarchs of Britain than about the geographies and histories of their own land, or those of their neighbors. After independence, the teaching of history throughout the region was skewed to advance the interests of political elites.

Theories create the real world in which people learn to act. No small part of the strategic license that enabled South Africa's minority government to destabilize the region in the 1970s and 1980s was the result of generation upon generation of South Africa's white youth learning—being taught—to look upon their neighbors as inferior and manipulated by external powers hostile to South Africa. The result was the infamous "total strategy," an attempt to mobilize the entire resources of the apartheid state to face a "total onslaught."[3] The revelations of former members of South Africa's security forces shows how all-pervasive the feelings of racial superiority were and how these—learned at school but reinforced by compulsory military service—were linked to a crude anticommunism and racism.[4] Today, the need to change this sort of indoctrination has been widely recognized. Gradually, we hope, the idea of teaching a history that stresses the importance of cooperation is coming to the fore. How the people(s) of southern Africa face up to the truth of their common history remains to be seen. The installation in South Africa itself of a Truth Commission—to look into the crimes of the country's apartheid past—as a means of helping national reconciliation will have profound effects on the region.[5] South Africa's destabilization of the region was a moment of profound destruction. Seeking the truth in South Africa, as a means of promoting healing within, will be part of creating cooperation across the whole of southern Africa because life in the region is so intertwined. President Nelson Mandela recognized this when he signed the bill that established the Truth Commission: "Our immediate neighbours . . . suffered devastation at the hands of the apartheid forces and, in these countries, many . . . died and suffered terrible losses."[6]

In any human relationship, agreeing on the shared past is a major step toward agreeing on a shared future. The contrast in the relationship between France and Germany since 1945 on the one hand, and Greece and Turkey on the other, is instructive in this regard.[7] Sharing a view of history and of the contemporary world does not guarantee security and cooperation between people(s), but it helps. In this respect, Antonio Gramsci's concept of hegemony and Robert Cox's idea of the self-interested character of knowledge are crucial for critical security studies.[8] Through these lenses critical security studies can help deliver counterhegemonic facts and other-interested knowledge on which to construct alternative images of regional security. But another lens must be fashioned, and this is a revisioned concept of security.

UNDERSTANDING SECURITY

From the critical security studies perspective, security has no objective meaning but is intersubjectively invented, an epiphenomenon of contending political philosophies. For most of the postwar years, regional security in world politics derived from a top-down, masculinized Anglo-American conception of society and politics. This conception focused on the security of states and military stability. Since the mid-1980s a growing body of opinion has favored a shift to an expanded concept of security, and this is a view we share.[9] This expanded concept can be conceived of in terms of different vertical levels (the security of individuals, relevant groups of all kinds including states, and humankind as a whole) and in terms of different horizontal dimensions (including a wider agenda of issues, such as political, economic, societal, gender, and environmental, as well as military).

The expanded concept of security is particularly pertinent to the situation in southern Africa, because top-down, statist, and militarized perspectives do not accord with either the empirical character of the region or nonstatist normative concerns. On the latter point, for example, Maxi van Aardt argues for a radically different political philosophy out of which to reformulate security in the region, namely, a "perspective of care and responsibility."[10] The normative basis of such politics can be challenged, but what few will dispute is the inappropriateness of traditional security analyses to a part of the world where the infrastructure is markedly different from Europe, the crucible of realism. The states of southern Africa, for example, do not match the textbook images of Anglo-American political science. These states have not stood as reliable watch-keepers over the security of their inhabitants.[11] In the southern African context the state is often the problem, not the solution. In southern Africa, state security has often been hostile to human security; the phrase has been a code word for the security of (usually very oppressive) political regimes and social elites.

Colonialism and apartheid are quintessential examples of this. But postcolonial African states have not been friendly to their peoples either. Nor have moves to democracy and economic reform helped much. In some African countries—Zambia is a good example—the introduction of multiparty democracy and structural adjustment policies have only managed to rearrange elites. The international economic system has not been friendly to the building of healthy societies in sub-Saharan Africa, and this has only exacerbated the despair in postcolonial Africa. The problems faced by southern Africa are legion, as will be evident from the later discussion. The region's people(s) have suffered—and continue to suffer—huge privation of rights. Particularly affected have been women and children, whose lives are ignored in traditional security studies. The Human Development Reports by the United Nations Development Programme (UNDP) attest to this and, incidentally, offer interesting and innovative approaches to understanding and trying to overcome the predicaments.[12]

The apparently simple question, "what is security?" in the context of southern Africa—as elsewhere—requires a range of decisions about broad versus narrow interpretations of the concept, political questions about the status quo and change, and the discussion of the priority of different levels (vertical) and dimensions (horizontal) of security. The ending of colonialism and now apartheid has created an opportunity for opening up this discussion and the implementation of appropriate practices, but wide acceptance of an expanded understanding of security is not guaranteed. We cannot be confident of this until we know the answer from key actors in the region to the question: whose security?

REFERENTS FOR SECURITY

Critical security studies complicate the hitherto commonsensical real world of traditional security studies by changing and often multiplying the referent object(s) in the security debate. Traditionally, states have been the primary referents because in orthodox political theory they have been seen as the guardians of their inhabitants' security from external and internal threat. But states are not the only candidates as referents. Alternatives include individual human beings, nations, ethnic and kinship groups, and the whole immanent global community of humankind. The choice being offered here is a fundamental one. Put simply, when we are talking about security in southern Africa, whose security are we addressing? Who (as well as what) is regional security all about?

These questions are important because of the terrible gap that is often present between traditional political theory and the lives of people(s) in particular settings. South Africa illustrates the problem with black-and-white clarity. During the apartheid years, security for the minority-ruled state was tied to a complex Cold War mythology that portrayed South Africa as a threatened, insecure, and embattled bastion of Western civilization. This view, in the early 1980s, drew the military to the center of the decision-making process. Meanwhile, the overwhelming majority of the country's people did not share this view of who and what threatened the state, but they were completely excluded from access to power. Nor did South Africa's neighbors see an insecure state: they saw a state that was all too strong and that, in its efforts to secure itself even further, embarked on a devastatingly offensive forward-defense strategy. The security of the apartheid regime therefore meant the insecurity of both the majority population of the South African state and the neighbors of that state. National security for South Africa meant security for the white minority, not the vast majority of citizens in the state, and it meant insecurity for South Africa's neighbors. For both the black majority and neighbors the growth of the insecurity of the South African state represented their best hope for security promised by the idea of a nonracial, freely elected government. Here, we see the peoples of southern Africa as the victims of different definitions of the primary security referent.

There is therefore a fundamental problem in the traditional realist equating of security exclusively with the security of the state, and of the associated use of the language of national security to cloak the interests of sectional groups. Critical security thinking must always as a matter of priority address the issue of the appropriate referent(s). As it happens, this issue has been under consideration in southern Africa as a result of the end of the Cold War and the transition in South Africa. Apart from a widespread recognition in South Africa of the need to give a bottom-up perspective on the question "who is security all about?", there has been a growing recognition throughout the region as a whole of the desirability of a regional dimension to the security referent. The three interstate regional groupings, particularly the Southern Africa Development Community (SADC), have been searching for ways to engage the region's people, and the promise to promote individual security has played a significant part in this appeal.[13] So far so good. But there is an obvious problem: the members of SADC are states, and as such there are limits to the extent to which they can be involved in the domestic affairs of neighboring states. Recognizing the rights of individuals is an important step forward, but willing the end does not necessarily produce the availability of the means. In this respect, as will be discussed later, the general weakness of civil society in the region is an important consideration, and a constraint on achieving the political salience of the rights of individuals.

The definition of the primary security referent(s) in southern Africa is not a value-free, objective matter of "describing the world as it is"—as it has been falsely characterized in traditional realist theory. It is, as the region's history so tragically shows, a profoundly political act. Whatever definition emerges has enormous implications for the theory and practice of regional security, and not least in terms of identifying threats.

THE THREAT AGENDA

Clearly, the more expansively we conceive of security—vertically and horizontally—the fuller the threat agenda will be. Because critical security studies favor the expansive concept, it is evident that it is a recipe for an excess of threats. This problem has to be faced squarely, and the difficulties should not in themselves be an excuse for regression into the shriveled conceptions of realism. Three points are pertinent. First, no security policy can erase the whole of life's threats. Instead, we must conceive of the search for security as a balanced attempt to try to create a less threatening structural context for life's ordinary struggles (so that people can pursue their lives in a more cooperative and less violent environment, taking on only those insecurities they choose—changing jobs, rock climbing, and so on). Second, placing threats in order of priority is a problem that has to be resolved in the political process. It cannot be settled by theoretical discussion; the latter can only clarify issues such as referents and principles. Three, the perpetuation of the traditional narrow agenda will leave security advice narrowly dominated by the traditional military and other security specialists. As was seen in the "Draft White Paper on National Defence" prepared by the (new) South African National Defence Force, these specialists would prefer to keep the security agenda limited.[14] Why? If we are serious about human rights, economic development, the lot of women, and so on—all priority security problems for somebody—then we must simply accept the problems of an expanded agenda. We must ask why some security experts might want to keep an issue such as human rights or environmental matters off the security agenda. We must ask it with more than normal curiosity if the person concerned is a supporter of the region's traditional insecurity establishments.

Most people(s) in southern Africa have lived in extreme insecurity in recent decades. Many still do, but now that the marauding apartheid state is gone it is evident that most people(s) have more to fear from dangers other than the ambitions of the armed forces of neighboring states. Typical of this is the threat represented by the linkage between water and food security in a region with a propensity for drought.[15] Until recently, such issues were not on the security agenda. The drought and near-famine of 1992 brought authorities in the region closer to understanding that without adequate planning the provision of southern Africa's basic needs is problematical. The Southern Africa Development Community was aware of the problem, but South Africa (the region's most security-conscious state at the time) was not prepared, and neither was Botswana (the region's wealthiest country), which discovered an important link between urban poverty and drought.

The threat of food scarcity is, for many, more fundamental than the threat of military violence. Achieving household food security in southern Africa has been held back; this is central for both economic development and regional security. Although the economies of the region are open, trade within the region is small. At the same time, agricultural performance has been poor in comparison with the growth of population and has had to be offset by increasing imports of cereals and the provision of food aid. When food shortages and water scarcity coincide with mass migration and the breakdown of society—remember the agony of Rwanda in 1994—the result may be cholera. This threat is more virulent because of the widespread ignorance about the development and transmission of this and other diseases. In these and other examples (drugs, violence, falling investment, and the threat to the fulfillment of peoples' expectations in South Africa) it is evident that major security threats in the region are intimately interconnected. But what ideas should guide the policies seeking to overcome the threat?

EMANCIPATION AND SECURITY

Traditional security studies have privileged power and order in security policy; inevitably, this has led to a focus on states, military power, and the preservation of the status quo. In contrast, critical studies privilege emancipation as the main value, which in turn leads to a focus on people, justice, and change.[16] The issue of emancipation is a huge and complex one, and we have no room to develop it here. In headline form, however, our view is that emancipation is synonymous with an open-ended and ethical conception of politics, the rejection of false necessities in social life, justice as fairness, empowerment and choice, mutual respect of rights, the acceptance of common humanity duties, and the promotion of world-order values such as economic justice, nonviolence, humane governance, ecological sustainability, and human rights. The way emancipation in practice might be operationalized is likely to be contested, but the critical perspective sees its achievement as synonymous with security. Emancipation has been a powerful driving force throughout the twentieth century, and there is no sign that it is waning. The most dramatic event in the history of southern Africa, the ending of apartheid, was the result of the oppressed majority in South Africa and the people of southern Africa working with the global metanarrative seeking emancipation from racism.

The processes shaping the context for emancipation take many forms and operate at a variety of levels. In southern Africa the regional level is still dominated by the relations between states. However, their character has changed radically from the apartheid era, when violent confrontation was the order of the day. More recently, we have seen nonaggression pacts and confidence-building measures. Looking beyond traditional statist approaches is only at an embryonic stage. Where groupings in the region have managed to coalesce, forms of regional solidarity have been expressed. The outstanding example is the Draft Social Charter of Fundamental Rights of Workers in southern Africa; this contains a variety of demands, including one on migrant workers.[17] Recent suggestions include the adoption of a Charter of Citizenship for southern Africa and the appointment of a respected individual from the region as a roving ambassador in the region to lower tensions and help confidence building.[18] More recently, the premier of South Africa's Mpumalanga Province has suggested the establishment of an economic bloc between his province, Swaziland, and the southern provinces of neighboring Mozambique.[19] For centuries the indigenous people of this fertile triangle of African lowveld have considered themselves united by the bonds of blood, barter, and the search for a better life; they speak a common language, the area engages in a rich exchange of goods, labor, and contraband, and as has happened so often in Africa, the border between the states was a powerful growth point. Academics have also been generating innovative ideas aimed at furthering regional security and development.[20] What all these ideas share is a recognition that the identification of common interests, the building of common identities, and the spreading of moral and political obligations are the only dependable route to long-term regional security. In short, the road to emancipation is through community.

SECURITY COMMUNITY?

Can southern Africa be considered a community in any sense, and particularly in Karl Deutsch's sense of a "security community," in which peace is predictable among a group of states?[21] Such a community grows out of the mutual compatibility of values; strong economic ties and the expectation of more multifaceted social, political, and cultural transactions; a growing number of institutionalized relationships; mutual responsiveness; and mutual predictability of behavior. The litmus test of a security community is whether or not the units target each other in a military sense.

Despite efforts to create a sense of community in southern Africa—some of which have been mentioned—the region is caught in a deep moment of insecurity. The symptoms of this are all too obvious: poverty, drugs, violence, unemployment, ethnic tensions, migration, disease, class, housing, environmental decay, human rights problems, civil war, the profusion of small arms, and limited education standards. An additional morbid symptom is the continued suspicion of South African power, and the continued ambiguity surrounding its regional policy.

By all important indicators South Africa is the strongest country in the region. One view about the country's role sees it as the regional hegemon that dominates affairs and draws the region toward economic prosperity. This posture implies, as is the case with all hegemons, the exercise of both control and interference in the affairs of the weaker countries of the region. Even a benevolent hegemon is still a hegemon. At present the direction of South Africa's regional policy is wholly uncertain. The government of national unity is buffeted by competing views. The African National Congress (ANC), for example, fashioned a policy toward the region that saw South Africa more as the helper than the locomotive of regional development. As a result, it envisaged giving far more space to the sharing of South Africa's resources with the region. A policy document states that a democratic South Africa should therefore explicitly renounce all hegemonic ambitions in the region.[22] It should resist all pressure to become the regional power at the expense of the rest of the subcontinent; instead, it should seek to become part of a movement to create a new form of economic interaction in southern Africa based on principles of mutual benefit and interdependence. The differences of opinion within South Africa about its regional policy are related in part to the lack of understanding of the extent to which its very size and potential is seen as a threat by the countries to the north. States almost always see themselves as more threatened than threatening.

It is instructive for opinion formers in today's South Africa to consider the analogy of the relationship between their own country and the former Frontline states and that of Russia and the countries of the former Warsaw Pact. Whatever the character of the governments in Moscow and Pretoria, the confidence of their neighbors in regional security requires that Russia and postapartheid South Africa—the regional states with the biggest military potential—build confidence and lessen historic fear by adopting levels of armed force and military doctrines that are seen as moving in a nonthreatening direction. The theory and practice of nonoffensive defense is helpful in this regard, and some in South Africa are mindful of its community-building potential.[23] The determination of South Africa to sell arms creates an opposite impression. This is a contentious issue. The debate around the sale of arms goes to the heart of the debate on South Africa's place in the world. Faced with poverty and hopes for reconstruction, and the need to gain foreign capital to generate economic growth, South Africa's leaders have chosen to exploit their comparative economic advantages. The years of sanctions resulted in an efficient armaments industry. Consequently, South Africa's government of national unity is propelled by the demands for reconstruction toward the economics of arms sales, now that the embargo has been lifted. Recent evidence suggests an overzealousness—to the point of criminal enrichment of individuals—on the part of those involved in the sale of South African arms: this occurred even after the installation of the government of national unity.[24]

Against the sale of arms, however, there are countervailing pressures. Those engaged in the struggle against apartheid took a series of stands on some of the central issues of our time. Among these were human rights issues and their link with the sanctity of life and what is implied by the arms trade.[25] Embedded deep within the support structures of the ANC (and the government of national unity) is strong support for the principle of disarmament. The dilemma is yet to be resolved: does South Africa export arms and use the profits to finance social programs, or does it adopt a more explicitly moral policy and perhaps not garner as much money?[26] These have been familiar predicaments in the post-Cold War world, particularly in eastern Europe. There, the dilemma was resolved in favor of economic growth. In South Africa's case, however, evidence suggests that, shorn of the subsidies it receives from the state, the defense sector contributes very little to the country's overall economic performance.[27]

The ambiguity about South Africa's regional role in the future is fed by suspicion about South Africa's regional past. Can a sense of community grow in a region in which there has been so much enmity and violence in the recent past? On first sight such situations look hopeless, but history suggests that this need not be so. The destruction of the second World War was the catalyst for the growth of the Western European community: is it equally possible that a new community can grow out of the recent history of regional destabilization in southern Africa? Whether or not it does, time is a necessary healer. Steady work needs to be done over many years to strengthen community processes and so turn the historic community of fate that has been southern Africa into a community of hope. Unprecedented opportunities now exist to develop regional consciousness. Psychological breakthroughs will be important, and political drama can play a vital part. Models exist in President Anwar Sadat's journey to Israel, Chancellor Willy Brandt's act of atonement at the Warsaw Ghetto, and the solemn Te Deum shared by Chancellor Konrad Adenauer and President Charles de Gaulle at Rheims Cathedral.[28]

In southern Africa the onus for such political breakthroughs lies with the most powerful state and the one most responsible for regional devastation: South Africa. Before apartheid ended, the white government missed an opportunity for a symbolic regional gesture. They did, of course, renounce their nuclear weapons and agree to sign the NPT, but this was aimed not so much at the region as at the international community.[29] But opportunities still exist in the region. There has been a muted debate about the possibility of South Africa paying reparations to its neighbors. The idea has been received with mixed feelings both in South Africa and the region, so the prospects for full reparations look remote. A grand gesture appears unlikely at present, but the fact that Nelson Mandela chose Mozambique for his first foreign visit after becoming president was seen as a recognition of the horror that the destabilization policies of South Africa had caused.[30] Additionally, prior to the address to South Africa's new parliament by Mozambique's president, Joachim Chissano, the parliamentary speaker apologized to Mozambique's people for the wrongdoings during the apartheid years of her countrymen.[31] The leaders of South Africa need to show further imagination about the future and a deeper appreciation about their common past. Being strong enough to face up to the troubled, controversial, and contentious history of the region will be one of the building blocks of future community building. And for some time South Africa occupies a significant moral space in world politics as a result of the transition and "Mandelamania."

During this interregnum the jury is out on the potential for the region to become a security community. One possibility in the near term is that offensive doctrines will be eschewed, and so the region could become an anomaly in Deutsch's theory. That is, as the postapartheid era deepens, southern Africa will consist of states that may not target each other but neither will they score highly in terms of economic ties, transnational links, and institution building. It is not inconceivable, however, that such a community of insecurity might evolve into a security community. Whether it does depends on the development of a common sense of purpose among the different societies across the region; as a starting point they might see themselves as common victims of structural and geographical insecurities rather than potential victims of each other. The development and spread of such a sense of common purpose requires the growth of influential community-minded agents across the region.

THE AGENTS OF SECURITY

Traditional security studies have focused almost exclusively on governments and their instruments of policy. The reification of the state found its apotheosis in Cold War strategic studies. Critical security studies cannot ignore governments, as they control important levers of power. But as the history of civil society in Eastern Europe in the 1980s shows, governments are not the only decisive agents.

Comprehensive security requires foreign policy from below, as well as at the interstate level. For this to succeed, however, will require the growth of civil society throughout the region: within individual countries it needs to deepen, but, at the same time, it needs to be transnational. There are presently attempts to strengthen civil society in the region, but several obstacles need to be overcome: the legacy of the region's colonial and apartheid past, the uneven spread of civil society through the region, the low income levels, and poor communications across the region. For the moment, much responsibility is placed on a relatively small number of individuals and small groups. But this is always the case with new ideas anywhere.

Efforts at awakening regional consciousness in southern Africa have been complicated by the experience of the immediate past.

Apartheid and colonialism made the development of transnational links difficult. The region's economic development, however, had the opposite effect: this may become a factor in the search for new contours of association in southern Africa. So mine workers from Lesotho are members of the powerful South African Mine Workers Union, and South Africa and its neighbors are dependent on the same water resources.

The region was also involved with the struggle of South Africa's majority in a multiplicity of ways, and at the same time many South African exiles made their homes in the region. These experiences may lend themselves to effective person-to-person links over the course of time. Without strong civil society across the region it is unlikely that either regional consciousness or the development of a comprehensive vision of security will grow.

What about the role of outsiders as agents of security? In Africa's past, outsiders were often the agents of insecurity. If they are to play the opposite role in the future, they must eschew imposing their own grand ideas and ambitions and instead help the region to help itself. Given the legacy of the past, there is great suspicion of outsiders, and sometimes it is thoroughly deserved. It is no better personified today than in the figure of Margaret Thatcher, who as prime minister of Great Britain opposed comprehensive sanctions and instead professed to see investment as the engine for change; in 1994, in contrast, she warned Western business against investment in South Africa.[32] In both cases profit and opposition to the interests of the majority population were the common thread. When prominent individuals behave in this way, it is not surprising that suspicion of the North is rife. But even less sympathetic outsiders than Thatcher are in a difficult position. They are damned if they try to get involved, and they are damned if they do not. But there are some things outsiders can do to help the peace process—such as financing the resettlement of demobilized soldiers or the region's mounting refugees or providing material support for lifting the land mines in Mozambique and Angola—but the key is to remember that it should be left to those in the region to identify what might be constructive external involvement.

When we consider the agents of security, whether global or regional, the potential of women should not be overlooked.[33] It is, entirely, in traditional security studies. Indeed, the theory of International Relations has ignored women while its practices have been disproportionately hostile to most women. There cannot be a radical (re)visioning of the regional security picture unless the interests of women are brought fully into the picture. This means allowing them full opportunity to acquire the economic, social, and political levers to advance their position. Education is a first and necessary step. International experience suggests that women are central to security; they are the cornerstones in the development of security policies that aim to reduce the problems that arise from overpopulation, combat the social and economic difficulties that arise from disease, and help provide the skills to assist sustainable economic progress. The plain truth is that without the emancipation of women across southern Africa there will not be regional security.

THE INSTITUTIONS OF SECURITY

Institutions give agents a context in which to learn and develop a new consciousness about security. The experience of the hitherto nationalized bureaucracies of Western Europe in the postwar years is relevant in this respect. In another respect, the European situation is very different. The second World War in a sense meant starting from scratch; the end of the apartheid era in South Africa has meant a radical change but has not created a year zero in quite the same fashion. The search for an appropriate institutional framework for new security is thereby complicated by the region's recent past.

The security of the South African state was pursued by the apartheid state at the interstate level by an offensive military strategy designed to keep the ANC as distant as possible from the country[34]—a strategy that had a devastating effect on the region—and by an attempt to underpin its position by creating a regional economic institution. The latter was the stillborn Constellation of Southern African States, which was introduced in the late 1970s. To counter this, the states of the region engaged in a process of community building that was aimed not so much at maintaining security in a military sense but at asserting their economic independence. Two separate economic groupings were formed—the Southern African Development Co-ordination Conference (SADCC) and the Preferential Trade Agreement of East and Southern Africa (PTA); the former is now known as the Southern Africa Development Community (SADC), and in 1994 it

was decided that the latter be called the Common Market for Eastern and Southern Africa (COMESA). These joined an existing economic arrangement—the Southern African Customs Union (SACU)—
that linked South Africa to its closest neighbors and dated back to
colonial times. At present, efforts are under way to develop a single
institution under which security and economic concerns, to the extent they can be separated, can be drawn together.[35] There is not
much optimism that it can work, however, as the various existing
bodies continue to clash over security policy.[36] Here, what evolved in
Europe might offer a useful model, in the sense that the delicate stability that grew in the West did so as a result of complex institutionalization as opposed to any search for a single security regime. The
Common Market, EEC, EU, NATO, WEU, CSCE, and the European
Court all played their different, and in some cases unexpected, parts.
It would be difficult to devise any single regime structure for European security to cover the range of functions served by these organizations. The same seems the case, by analogy, in southern Africa.

Paradoxically, the search for dialogue among the states of southern Africa began with the signing of the ultimately disastrous nonaggression pact between South Africa and Mozambique known as
the Nkomati Accord.[37] This event took the other governments of the
region by surprise. One outcome was the start of the regular Arusha
conferences on peace and security. The earliest gatherings were concerned with apartheid's regional aggression and its impact on the
other countries of the region. Since 1990, however, these conferences
have provided southern African scholars and policy makers with the
space to share perspectives on the region's security. Dialogue between policy makers and others—not just academics but civil society
in all its forms—is crucial if efforts to develop regional outlooks at
the interstate level in southern Africa are to avoid some of the problems in Western Europe, where the process of community building
has been hindered by the gap that has opened up between governments and their national societies. As a result an impression has developed that the EU has turned into a club for politicians and bureau-
crats and has grown distant from the sentiments of the people. This
is a warning to southern Africa that security must not only be conceived at different levels (see earlier) but must then be practiced at
different levels as well.

REGIONAL AND GLOBAL

The different levels at which security policy must be pursued include establishing a relationship between regional security structures, whether they are limited or comprehensive in scope, and extraregional (including global) bodies. While the trend toward regionalization is often seen as one of the characteristic features of contemporary world politics, so is globalization. Furthermore, the record of regional security structures has not always been impressive in dealing with regional conflicts, when one considers the European institutions and the Balkan imbroglio, the Arab League and Middle Eastern wars, the Organization of African Unity (OAU) and Somalia, and other conflicts. Extraregional assistance does not guarantee success, but it can sometimes help.

At present, the region's people seem very wary of external involvement. In principle, however, external parties can perform a variety of functions in regional conflicts. Their troops can sometimes be more acceptable as peacekeepers than intraregional forces: Angola is a good example. Their diplomats can sometimes be more acceptable as mediators. They can generate ideas (frameworks for peace) that might serve as long-term goals even if they are not presently acceptable. They can apply a variety of pressures (through diplomatic appeals to sanctions to peace enforcement). They can take action and try to isolate a conflict (by helping neighbors and drawing lines). They can try to limit the escalation of conflict by appeals and embargoes. And they can sometimes have the authority to sway local decisions one way or another in a conflict because of the calculations of the parties about the postconflict situation. Despite present wariness toward outsiders, the latter's recent record in sub-Saharan Africa is not all negative.

After newsworthy earlier failures in Angola, Somalia, and Rwanda, the UN has shown its ability to generate peaceful outcomes in both Angola and Mozambique. Internationally, credit is being given for these developments to UN mediators, but an important part of their success is their use of local models. In both countries power-sharing formulas have been adopted that follow the South African example of governments of national unity. Outsiders can only help so much. If the people on the ground do not want to live together and in cooperation, they will not, and outsiders cannot make them. The limitations were horrifically exposed in the failure of outsiders—including the temporarily deployed French forces—in the bloodletting that passed for politics in Rwanda in 1994.

Regional security, comprehensively defined, must be based on a balance of intra- and extraregional perspectives and involvement. There are no golden rules, for all situations are different, and a lesson in one place may not work elsewhere. But southern African opinion formers can learn from mistakes made elsewhere, and, at the same time, can use outsiders to help them develop their own voices and answers. This, not parochialism, is what wise leadership entails.

THE REALIST AGENDA

A comprehensive conception of security, as embraced by critical security studies, clearly has to attend to the traditional security concerns of realism. Of these, perhaps the most important in the southern African context is the security dilemma—the ostensibly irreducible mistrust that states have of each other that results in defensive preparations, uncertainties, and insecurity.[38] It is thought to be the quintessential dilemma in international politics because it results in insecurity even in situations where no state has aggressive intentions. The structure of the situation provokes fear. Are the dynamics of the security dilemma likely to flourish in postapartheid southern Africa?

Robert Jackson is one analyst who argued, before the ending of apartheid, that the security dilemma was not relevant in the sub-Saharan context.[39] In the early 1990s he argued, in contrast to the traditional (Hobbesian) European assumption that states provide security for the populations within their borders and security against external threats in a hostile world, that in sub-Saharan Africa the traditional security dilemma theory can be turned on its head. He suggests that the regimes currently in power have a high degree of external security (they are not seriously threatened from outside) and that this position is underwritten by the norms of international society, notably the idea of sovereignty and nonintervention. In addition, the level of external security is relatively high because of geographical remoteness from the center of world affairs, the indifference of outside powers, and the general powerlessness of the states of the region (assuming a reduction of the South African threat as a result of its postapartheid external policy). In international terms the regional states are relatively secure legal entities, with no significant security-dilemma pressures (a situation that has been of considerable benefit to the regimes in power). Internally, the situation has been much less satisfactory. The states of the region are not social entities in the manner of textbook states. Their sovereignty is threatened more from inside than outside (by those wanting to fragment the state), and the state does not provide security for its population (because of poverty, lack of development, drugs, high levels of local violence, and so on). In this situation internal tension and instability may be high. As a result—a point Jackson did not make but one that Barry Posen recently did—the security dilemma might be an important concept in understanding the dynamics of internal conflicts.[40]

If Jackson is correct about sub-Saharan Africa being relatively free of security-dilemma pressures (at the international level, any-way), then the implications for regional security policy are enormous. It means that priority must be given to creating stable societies rather than interstate confidence building.[41] In this region, above all, security literally begins at home.

But is Jackson entirely correct? There is no room for compla-cency. In particular, the looming power of South Africa cannot be ig-nored by the much weaker states in the region, several of whom have suffered directly from South Africa's military might in the past. Botswana's recent purchase of arms suggests that South Africa's neighbors remain nervous of its power. The earlier discussion of South Africa's role and image as regional hegemon is pertinent, as is the comparison between Eastern Europe (Moscow) and southern Africa (Pretoria). Whatever the character of the government in Preto-ria, there will be some unease among its neighbors unless clear steps are taken to transcend the pressures of the security dilemma. These must include disarmament, the shift to a structural nonaggressive de-fense policy, symbolic acts of atonement and reconciliation, and a clear commitment to partnership in regional community building as opposed to the seeking of hegemonical status.

Realist concerns must be addressed, but the record suggests that realist answers are deeply inadequate.[42] Overwhelming military power, and a willingness to use it, did not save the apartheid state. Power and order, unless informed by an inclusive notion of justice, are always against somebody and, consequently, are unlikely to offer the bases for long-lasting peace and order. Indeed, not only were the instruments of realism inadequate to save the apartheid state, but their offensive employment has created serious problems for the future prospects of postapartheid South Africa. In the social distress on which international drug dealers now feed, in the regional impoverishment that now results in massive influxes of migrants into South Africa, and in the poverty and unemployment that breeds violence, we can now see the consequences of brutal realism. The massive problems and uncertain prospects of southern Africa today are a powerful testimony to the inadequacies of traditional security theories and practices.

RAINBOW STATES

It has not been the main intention of this chapter to set out a series of prescriptions for southern Africa deriving from what we take to be the critical security perspective. General principles have emerged, implicitly and explicitly, however, as a result of what has been indicated in relation to a different concept of security, different referents of security, different agents, and so on. Ironically, the "total strategy" of apartheid South Africa was a potentially useful label, but it was the wrong approach, based on the wrong philosophy for the wrong referent, having at its core the wicked intent of preserving both a single state and white racist rule.

One of the characteristic features of traditional security theories and practices is statism, the idea that all loyalty and decision-making power should be concentrated on states. Questioning nineteenth- and twentieth-century assumptions about the moral and political authority of states is one of the major features of critical security studies. But such interrogation immediately raises a set of explosive questions in the southern African context, where issues relating to the state, identity, and territory interact in complex and contentious ways. What territorial arrangements in southern Africa will deliver (what sort of) security (for whom)?

The fear of fragmentation has shaped the politics of Africa since the end of colonialism. The favored territorial principle is therefore the status quo, and this is enshrined in the OAU. But as the events of recent years have shown, the status quo is not necessarily cost-free, satisfactory, or peaceful. Southern Africa offers a perplexing patchwork of states and identities, and the cost of getting it wrong is blood. The problems exist at all levels: can anything be unraveled without starting a process whose end point might be worse?

At the state level there have already been some debates about the region's geographic future. The independence of Namibia, for example, sparked concern over the future of the enclave of Walvis Bay, which as a result of colonial history became part of South Africa. During South Africa's occupation of Namibia, Walvis Bay was used extensively for military-strategic purposes. With Namibia's independence, and the acceptance in Pretoria that it posed no real threat to South Africa, it was accepted that the geographical anomaly could be ended, and in 1994 Walvis Bay became part of Namibia.[43] So far so good, one might think, but this experience has set a precedent, and states around South Africa have instituted a number of claims on what has been hitherto seen as South African sovereignty. Lesotho has claimed parts of the Free State and Swaziland areas of the Eastern Transvaal. Such claims have been paralleled by a debate on the future of individual countries.

This concern has particularly focused on the landlocked country of Lesotho.[44] During a state visit to Lesotho in mid-July 1995, South Africa's president suggested that discussions be opened with Lesotho on giving the tiny mountain kingdom access to the sea through South Africa.[45] Entirely surrounded by South Africa and dependent on it economically (some consider it merely a labor reserve), the prospects for its citizens looked grim even before the political crisis of early 1994. The threats to the country's independence drew the military closer to the political process, and an authoritarian civilian government was overthrown by the military. This exacerbated a series of conflicts over the distribution of resources and the lack of potential for domestic production. Lesotho's capacity to sustain its independence was further undermined when its neighbors—South Africa, Zimbabwe, and Botswana—promised to involve themselves in the settlement of its domestic disputes. Although this intervention formally restored democracy to the mountain kingdom, it ironically further whittled away its fragile hold on its own sovereignty. The initiative further weakened the state's image by devaluing the symbols of national authority. The questionably viable state of Lesotho, together with the relatively stable monarchy of Swaziland, is threatened by both the emergence and model of the new democratic South Africa.

Widespread migration in southern Africa has further undermined the viability of states and the integrity of borders. This movement creates crises in the lives of individuals and stresses in the fabric of societies. In the past South Africa's economic success rested in no small part on the migration of workers to its economic heartland. Such movement was increased in the 1980s by the wars of destabilization, especially from Mozambique. The terrible conflict in Rwanda and its knock-on effects in Zaire will continue to traumatize the public in South Africa, as some elements in the press and elsewhere drew simplistic understandings of the issues surrounding migration in the region.[46]

In the 1990s a new wave of economic migrants is occurring. In some cases they have been pushed from their own countries by devastating droughts or deepening environmental decay and are drawn to the regional magnet of South Africa. But there are also different microtrends: Angolans moving to Namibia, and Zambians moving to Zimbabwe and Botswana. In countries where unemployment is already a problem—including South Africa itself—the arrival of migrants is unwelcome and a focus of social tension. There are also ugly international dimensions, such as the mass deporting of "illegals," electric fences, and military patrols: these are not the images the postapartheid government wanted to project in the region.[47] Other problems are less immediately obvious. One such is the migration of skilled professional people from the region to South Africa, but the latter's gain represents a serious loss to countries already desperately lacking in skills.

The penetrability of borders is a necessary condition of regional community, but if other conditions are lacking it can be a factor of instability. In southern Africa, cross-border activity has developed a negative momentum, in the form of desperate and unwelcome migrants, drug smuggling, and the unimpeded spread of small arms. There is a whole new phenomenon of border economies, but not one calculated to enhance regional security.

In southern Africa, as in some other major regions in world politics, there seems to be a tension between the forces of fragmentation and integration. And when seen like this, the future seems bleak indeed. But it is not necessary to conceive of the problem in this way; indeed, to do so is to remain trapped in the old dichotomies of traditional (statist) security thinking. Why is it not possible, at the end of the twentieth century, to have both fragmentation and integration? This involves moving away from the simple patterns of statism to complex structures and processes characterized by shifting power away from the state level (upward to regional community institutions and downward to local community bodies) and moving away from nineteenth-century notions of identity toward more complex answers to the question "who am I?" Whatever the EU's current problems, the development of subsidiarity and community in Western Europe, on the ruins of centuries of nation-statism, shows what can be achieved within decades. The choice for southern Africa is stark. Should its agents of security seek to create a regional system over the next forty years of relatively homogeneous states, seeking to pursue national interests relatively autonomously? Or, alternatively, should they seek to develop a southern African community made up of nonstatist states committed to regionalism and human diversity internally and externally? From the perspective of critical security studies the former has not worked in the past and will not work in the future: the latter has not been tried and will be difficult to operationalize, but we believe that it offers the only lasting basis for security. Is it expecting too much?

The ethnic issue in southern Africa sends out conflicting signals. In South Africa it brought the process of settlement close to disaster, and it still smoulders; in Angola there is a danger of exaggerating the importance of ethnicity; in Namibia ethnicity seems to loom as a long-term source of instability despite the benign nature of the settlement; in Zimbabwe and Botswana ethnicity seems driven by socioeconomic factors; in Zaire ethnicity shows signs of fueling the trend toward devolution; and in Rwanda and Burundi ethnicity is variously seen as the spark of genocide or a contingent factor. There seems little doubt that those states and societies that can organize diversity within their own borders will be better able to adapt to the interdependent demands of world politics than those who enter the twenty-first century with the simple identity mind-sets of nineteenth-century nation-statism. This seems to be appreciated in key circles in South Africa, where Archbishop Desmond Tutu has repeatedly spoken about the miracle of "rainbow" societies and President Mandela has called for approaches that make the world safe for "diversity."[48] Despite the evident problems, when measured in historical time, rapid progress has been achieved in the region in recent years. Multiracial Zimbabwe, independent Namibia, and postapartheid South Africa all attest to the possibility of tolerance in a part of the world in which race, for centuries, was the single most determining factor in a human life— even more crucial (contra Freud) than gender. If rainbow states can develop within and across the states of southern Africa, of all places, the revisioning of security as emancipation cannot be dismissed by traditional security specialists as merely wishful thinking.

CRITICAL SECURITY STUDENTS AND REGIONAL SECURITY

It is increasingly apparent how poorly equipped traditional security studies have been in conceptualizing and handling the security situation(s) in southern Africa. If there is one matter that is uncontestable as world politics hurry through the 1990s, it is that the military factor must be considered as only one element in the mosaic of security policy. Military policy might be able to deter war, but it cannot deliver comprehensive security. But if traditional security studies are inadequate, critical security studies are only beginning. The academic infrastructure within southern Africa shows the familiar dominance of traditional approaches,[49] the limited and unbalanced distribution of academic resources, and only occasional oases of critical perspectives.

All the countries of the region have institutes that deal, in general terms, with international and regional security issues. The biggest concentration is within South Africa. There, four bodies (one business-linked, one government-linked, and two university-based) have a specialized interest in region-wide issues. Several strategic studies institutions are interested in regional security questions, mostly from the traditional perspective (one, for example, enjoyed close links with the Defense Forces of the old regime, while another is staffed by former officers of the same forces). Development issues are studied at a range of universities and institutes, far apart geographically and ideologically. Elsewhere in southern Africa there are institutions concerned with international and regional studies, although they remain invisible to northern security specialists: they exist in Botswana, Mozambique, Lesotho, Namibia, Tanzania, Zambia, and Zimbabwe. Of particular note, there is the freestanding and, in the region, uniquely sponsored (by the governments of Mozambique and Tanzania) Center for Foreign Relations (CFR). The center has organized a series of conferences under the theme "Peace and Security in Southern Africa," and it is widely agreed that these gatherings are the most important venues for the deliberations of security and development questions in the region. As yet there is no regional-level institute that deals with long-term regional questions. This gap has been identified by those seeking to foster regional integration, and the possibility has emerged of a SACD-linked Institute on Security and Development.[50]

At a time of flux it is easy for agendas to fall entirely into the hands of those with political power, and for that power to be employed only with short-term perspectives. This has happened in South Africa where the Institute for Defence Policy, a think tank dominated by former members of apartheid defense forces, has seized the policy agenda. Critical security students have an important role to play, by raising the salience of different security conceptions, referents, threats, principles, institutions, and timetables. It may not be possible to exercise any direct influence on those presently exercising power, but indirect influence and a long-term perspective can be hoped for. At the minimum, academics have some space to influence the next generation of educated people. Are they to be taught to replicate the past or are they to learn to be critical? Our answer by now should be obvious. In their research and teaching, academics can play a part in (re)forming the historical and recent facts of regional security as a necessary foundation for reforming regional security.

The first task of critical security studies is to bring about a revision of the world, and its regions, and then bring about a revision of politics. In the long run, security in the form of peace, order, and justice must come from within the people(s) of the region. At present they do not have much of a voice in their own affairs. Consequently, critical security studies must engage with practical politics in southern Africa and speak up for those without security. The latter are countless in this region at the individual level, while the voice of the region as a whole is being drowned out on the preoccupied and overloaded world stage.

NOTES

A different version of this essay originally appeared in *International Affairs* 71:2 (1995), 285–304.

1. These are identified in Ken Booth's chapter in this volume.

2. These are presented, in their briefest form, in Ken Booth, "A Security Regime in Southern Africa: Theoretical Considerations," *South African Perspectives* 30 (February 1994), 26–7.

3. This was first described in Ken Grundy, *The Rise of the Security Establishment: An Essay on the Changing Locus of State Power*, Bradlow Paper No. 1 (Braamfontein: South African Institute of International Affairs, 1983). The academic roots of this approach to South Africa's position in the world are to be found in Colin Vale and Irene van den Ende, eds., *The Loss of Innocence: International Relations Essays in Honour of Dirk Kunert* (Pretoria: HSRC Publishers, 1994).

4. See "Moment of Truth," *Time*, 31 July 1995.

5. For a discussion of the issues around this, see Alex Boraine, Janet Levy, and Ronel Scheffer, eds., *Dealing with the Past: Truth and Reconciliation in South Africa* (Cape Town: IDASA, 1994).

6. Statement by President Nelson Mandela, on the occasion of the signing of the Promotion of National Unity and Reconciliation Bill, 19 July 1995.

7. See Peter Mangold, *National Security and International Relations* (London: Routledge, 1990), 57–61, 63–65, 90.

8. See David Forgacs, ed., *A Gramsci Reader: Selected Writings, 1916–1935* (London: Lawrence & Wishart, 1988), 295, 301–11, 323–26, 422–24; Robert W. Cox, "Social Forces, States and World Orders: Beyond International Relations Theory," *Millennium* 10:2 (1981), 126–55.

9. The key work in broadening the concept of security is Barry Buzan, *People, States and Fear*, 2nd ed. (Brighton: Harvester Wheatsheaf, 1991). We share Buzan's broadened conception of the security agenda, but not the neorealist philosophy that underlies it.

10. Maxi van Aardt, "In Search of a More Adequate Concept of Security in Southern Africa," *The South African Journal of International Affairs* 1:1 (Spring 1993), 85.

11. Robert Jackson and Carl G. Rosberg, "Why Africa's Weak States Persist: The Empirical and the Juridical in Statehood," *World Politics* 35:1 (1985), 1–24.

12. See United Nations Development Programme, *Human Development Report 1994* (New York: Oxford University Press, 1994); United Nations Development Programme, *Human Development Report 1995* (New York: Oxford University Press, 1995).

13. "Workshop Resolutions," SADC Workshop on Democracy, Peace and Security, Windhoek, 11–16 July 1994, 4.

14. See "Defence in a Democracy: Draft White Paper on National Defence for the Republic of South Africa," 21 June 1995, issued by the Defence Secretary.

15. On this issue, see "Drought over Southern Africa," *The Economist*, 29 April 1995.

16. For a preliminary argument, see Ken Booth, "Security and Emancipation," *Review of International Studies* 17:3 (1991), 313–26.

17. *Perspectives on Regional Co-operation from South Africa's Mass Democratic Movement*, CSAS Backgrounder Series No. 3, compiled by Robert Davies (Bellville: Center for Southern African Studies, 1991), 7–11.

18. See *Sources of Domestic Insecurity in Southern African States: A Conference Report*, CSAS Backgrounder Series No. 12, compiled by John Bardill (Bellville: Center for Southern African Studies, 1994), 59.

19. See "Phosa to Hold Security Talks in Mozambique," *The Citizen* (Johannesburg), 10 June 1995.

20. See, for example, Renfrew Christie, *One Bill of Rights and a Single Court of Rights for All of Southern Africa*, Working Paper No. 39 (Bellville: Center for Southern African Studies, Southern African Perspectives, 1994).

21. Karl W. Deutsch et al., *Political Community and the North Atlantic Area* (Princeton, N.J.: Princeton University Press, 1957).

22. See *Foreign Policy in a New Democratic South Africa—A Discussion Document* (Johannesburg: Department of International Affairs, ANC, 1993), 10–13.

23. For a summary, see *NOD & Conversion* (Special Issue on the Global Non-offensive Defence Network), 30 (September 1994), 9–36. Also B. Moller, "The Concept of Non-Offensive Defence: Implications for Developing Countries with Specific Reference to Southern Africa," in M. Hough and A. Du Plessis, eds., *Conference Papers: The Future Application of Air Power with Specific Reference to South Africa* (Pretoria: Institute for Strategic Studies, University of Pretoria, May 1995), 48–128.

24. Report by Deidree Uren of fraud case in Pretoria Supreme Court, "AM Live," SAFM, 26 July 1995. On the wider question of arms sales, see "Dirty Secrets: South Africa's Arms Trade Legacy," *Budget Watch* (Cape Town), 26 June 1995.

25. See, for instance, "Does South Africa Need the Military?", *Weekend Argus* (Cape Town), July 22/23, 1995.

26. *The Armaments Industry Debate—A Cost-Benefit Approach: A Discussion Document*. ANC's Department of Economic Planning, 29 June 1994.

27. See "Arms Trade Costs Outweigh Gains," *Budget Watch* (Cape Town), 26 June 1995.

28. Mangold, *National Security and International Relations*, 63–64.

29. See J. W. de Villers, Andrew Jardine, and Mitchell Reiss, "Why South Africa Gave Up the Bomb," *Foreign Affairs* 72:5 (November/December 1993), 98–109.

30. See "Mandela Sees First State Visit to Mozambique as Key to Re-

gion's Stability," *SouthScan* (London), 8 July 1994, 204; "Mandela Arrives for Talks after Deal on Arms Smuggling," *SouthScan* (London), 22 July 1994, 222.

31. See "Chissano Receives Apology from SA," *Citizen* (Johannesburg), 2 March 1995.

32. "Investors Holding Back, Says Thatcher," *Business Day* (Johannesburg), 22 September 1994.

33. There is a growing list of relevant literature on this. Of particular value, see Cynthia Enloe, *Bananas, Beaches and Bases: Making Feminist Sense of International Politics* (London: Pandora, 1989); and J. Ann Tickner, *Gender in International Relations: Feminist Perspectives on Achieving Global Security* (New York: Columbia University Press, 1992).

34. See Peter Vale, "The Botha Doctrine: Pretoria's Response to the West and its Neighbours," in *South African Review Two* (Johannesburg: Ravan Press, 1984), 188–97.

35. On the competition between SADC and the PTA, see "Competition Grows between SADC and PTA as Both Take on Trade Issues," *SouthScan* (London), 17 June 1994, 183; Fernando Goncalves, "SADC and PTA/Comesa Part Ways," *Southern Africa Political and Economic Monthly* (Harare) 7:12 (September 1994), 19–21.

36. See transcript of speech delivered by H. E. President Ali Hassan Mwinyi of Tanzania to the Ministerial Committee of the Inter-State Defence and Security Committee, Arusha, Tanzania, 10 November 1994.

37. For a description of the failure of this agreement, see Joseph Hanlon, *Beggar Your Neighbours: Apartheid Power in Southern Africa* (London: James Currey, 1986).

38. See Nicholas J. Wheeler and Ken Booth, "The Security Dilemma," in John Baylis and Nicholas J. Rengger, eds., *Dilemmas of World Politics* (Oxford: Oxford University Press, 1992), 29–60.

39. Robert H. Jackson, "The Security Dilemma in Africa," in Brian L. Job, ed., *The (In)Security Dilemma: The National Security of Third World States* (Boulder, Colo.: Lynne Rienner, 1992), 81–94.

40. Barry Posen, "The Security Dilemma and Ethnic Conflict," *Survival* 35:1 (Spring 1993), 27–47.

41. See Buzan, *People, States and Fear*, on "strong states" and security.

42. See Ken Booth and Peter Vale, "Security in Southern Africa: After Apartheid, beyond Realism," *International Affairs* (London) 19 (1995), 285–304.

43. For the background to this, see Lynn Berat, *Walvis Bay: The Last Frontier* (Wynberg, Sandton: Radix, 1990). On the pressures toward the handover, see "All Parties at Talks Urge Pretoria to Yield on Status of Walvis Bay," *SouthScan* (London), 13 August 1993, 246; on the consequences of

the handover, see "Deal Secured with SA on Walvis Bay Staff," *SouthScan* (London), March 25 1994, 95.

44. On the crisis in Lesotho, see, for example, "Pressure Mounts on Mandela to Accept Security Role for SA in Region," *SouthScan* (London), 17 June 1994; and "Military and Economic Pressure from SA Forces King to Yield," in *SouthScan* (London), 16 September 1994, 270.

45. AFP *Press Clips*, 13 July 1995.

46. This issue has been reported with great hysteria in South Africa. For example, *The Argus* (Cape Town), 2 September 1994, published an article on migration from Africa under the screaming banner headline "Alien's Invasion."

47. On this issue, see "Electric Fence May Be Extended," *SouthScan* (London), 21 October 1994, 306.

48. Archbishop Desmond Tutu, *The Rainbow People of God* (London: Doubleday, 1994); Nelson Mandela, "South Africa's Future Foreign Policy," *Foreign Affairs* 72:5 (1993), 86–97.

49. See the publications of the Institute for Defence Policy and the Institute for Strategic Studies of the University of Pretoria.

50. The issue was discussed at the Eighth International Conference on Peace and Security in Eastern and Southern Africa, 22–24 August 1994. See "The Southern African Institute: A Forum for Security & Development Concerns: The Lupogo Report," *The Arusha Papers*, no. 4 (June 1995).

12

Conclusion: Every Month Is "Security Awareness Month"

BRADLEY S. KLEIN

The official magazine of the U.S. Department of State, appropriately—if unimaginatively—titled *State*, announces by way of a cover story that January 1995 is "Security Awareness Month."[1] No small pronouncement, this is, in a post-Cold War world characterized by dozens of regional conflicts, serious threats against human rights, global warming, the worldwide migration of plagues and epidemics, the instability of incipient democracies, and the spread of nuclear armaments-development programs by aggressive countries suspected of wanton irresponsibility, if not outright terrorism. But no, it turns out that this is something much less than the state's rethinking of a fundamental security agenda. Closer inspection of the cover, as well as a read of the two-page article inside, reveals this as practical advice about posts overseas that, we are warned, are increasingly subject to a variety of direct physical threats. As it turns out, rape, thefts, carjacking, murder, muggings, burglary, and purse snatching are the abiding issues of the day for U.S. personnel posted overseas. The model of security in strategic studies, seen as direct threats of force and military power, has now been reduced and concentrated into their effects on the micropolitics of modern diplomacy.

No need to trivialize this. With the collapse of the grand narrative—the Cold War—that had sustained a strategic definition of state security for some forty-five years, the field has now to get down to the nitty-gritty of its own existence under admittedly hostile global conditions.

Hardly a way to address the complexities of modern world politics—or the fact that conventional accounts of security are not up to the multiple forms assumed by global politics in the post-Cold War era. Small wonder that quarterly journals regularly subscribed to by leading decision makers inside and outside of government have been issuing expanded views of security since the walls came tumbling down across the German-German divide. Such popular voices have been echoed in the halls of power, where a spate of government officials and hopeful appointees have been variously testifying as to the enhanced construction of modern security—to the point where, on some accounts, national security information might extend to the domain of economic and industrial spying. In the highly competitive world of high-tech industry and information processing, every little byte helps, although whom it helps is not quite clear.

Not all accounts of an enhanced security agenda would appear to sanction hypermodernist surveillance and extended state power in the name of global security. There are, as it turns out, a variety of formulations available for those who would extend the current terms of strategic discourse into a dialogue about politics writ large. That, after all, is the point of the intellectual ferment within the subfields of the International Relations discipline that concern themselves with both theory and security studies. In a manner with which all of the essayists in this book are familiar, a range of disciplinary debates about the general nature of International Relations has been amplified by a stunning series of developments in recent world history to pose fundamental questions about the whole meaning and pursuit of security. Most important, these are not sectarian debates limited to a particular province of the conceptual landscape. Mainstream theorists also know that something is awry with the conventional approach and that, at the very least, it needs its own strategic defenses. Why else concern themselves, as does Stephen Walt's much-cited article "The Renaissance of Security Studies," with fortifying disciplinary boundaries against those who would expand the meaning of security beyond externally originating military threats to the state and its borders?[2]

Recognizing the limits of security studies is not just a post-Cold War phenomenon. Witness Robert McNamara's tortured attempt to explain (away) the series of shortcomings that led the United States during the Kennedy and Johnson administrations into the Vietnam War.[3] At nearly every turn of his narrative, McNamara admits that perceived weaknesses in the arguments for involvement and escalation were never seriously explored, and that the prevailing mind-set of decision makers working within the operational code of the Containment strategy allowed no room for critical inquiry. What we witness is a lack of imagination, and a resulting failure of nerve to challenge, or even explore, the most elemental components of security and its attending language of threat, perception, and response.

As a number of chapters in this volume demonstrate, however, security considerations are not objectively gleaned from a neutral road map of world politics; they are themselves socially constructed and discursively reproduced in ways that are contestable and subject to revision. David Mutimer's chapter, for instance, illustrates how various readings of the problem of arms proliferation today sustain distinct political norms about responsibility and irresponsibility in the very definition of the issue. Beverly Crawford and Ronnie Lipschutz's account of the Yugoslavia conundrum also establishes the links between interpretive norms and policies of (non)intervention. And Karin Fierke's concluding account of metaphor and cultural representation in recent European security debates shows that successive descriptions of European alliance building—in terms of courtship, family, club, house, and insurance—have all been part of the narrative politics by which security is constructed and legitimized.

Even the most dedicated realist today cannot avoid concluding that when it comes to security policy, theory makes a difference in how the world is viewed. Or, to draw out a point that animates the chapters here by Michael Williams and Keith Krause, the claims of social science objectivity and value neutrality that had long underpinned scientific approaches to realism and International Relations cannot be sustained without an appeal to the normative political commitments that made such accounts possible. Ironically, the idea of a normative commitment undercuts the self-representation of those who see themselves as pursuing security as a policy science. The claims of a science of world politics based on the primacy of a security dilemma among states in an anarchic states system emerge from tacit norms of stability, order, and the preserving of a specific moment in the evolution of hierarchy in global power. Security studies, in the guise of both realism and its neorealist variant, is the point at which a strategic discourse of organized violence becomes a hegemonic discourse of world order.[4]

The limitation of security studies is thus not simply an empirical phenomenon produced, or revealed, by the end of the Cold War and the resulting complexities of postbloc politics. Amitav Acharya argues in this book, for example, that when it comes to Third World politics, security studies has fundamentally failed to address, much less adequately explain, the overwhelming majority of wars and civil conflicts that have characterized world affairs since 1945. Security studies, after all, is not some neutral reflection of contending global forces but is itself an interpretive mode, a disposition to the world. In the parlance of recent critical scholarship, it is a constellation of discourses about world politics that has always privileged statist and military practices when confronting international developments, and it has done so in ways that rationalize the power of the dominant states while peripheralizing, or "Orientalizing," the dynamics of developing societies. If security studies managed to find for itself a safe place in liberal society as part of the policy sciences, that is because it was more sophisticated and self-conscious about its politics than was its predecessor, the more narrowly force-oriented field of classical strategic studies. The postwar shift in the United States from the War Department to the Defense Department suggests that the manipulation of force must find politically acceptable guises for itself. In a way that none of these essays quite makes clear, security studies was entirely a product of the post–World War II environment, when liberal societies undertook projects of both decolonizing and maintaining global order under Western protection and coordination. In Gramscian terms, security became a crucial element in the construction of hegemony—a hegemony that operated not simply between states but below them as a mechanism for binding the civil societies of the West and its aspiring allies. Its self-representation, in Hobbesian terms of an anarchic security dilemma, masked the deeper global politics of state building, elite recruitment, modernization, military-police training, and societal incorporation. Security, in other words, was never simply about preparing against military threats "out there." It was always intended as a way of defending common ways of life. It was an inherently cultural practice that was always about more than just the deployment of weapons systems.

Ken Booth's semiautobiographical "Security and Self: Reflections of a Fallen Realist" in this volume gives powerful voice to an element of security studies that has never received adequate attention. Security studies functioned, after all, not merely as a map of potential military threats but also as a mechanism for the construction of political community. In terms of a sociology-of-knowledge approach, for example, security studies provides an interpretive repertoire that empowers certain actors in global affairs by favoring their domain of responsibility. A crucial amplifier in this sociology of knowledge and elite recruitment was the strategic think tank and its associated community of practitioners poised at the intersection of scholarship and policy. Booth makes clear how easy it is in terms of self-confidence and ease of career advancement for the bearers of such a security outlook to replicate themselves while marginalizing dissent. Perhaps the professional rewards inherent in such a community of shared discourse explain how someone like McNamara could hold back his own discontents and continue to operate. Even when he left the United States Defense Department in early 1968, McNamara withheld from publication the scathing indictment of the community of which he was so central a figure. Of course, the mere lure of being close to power and of partaking in its benefits does not suffice to explain such prolonged self-censorship. As a reading of McNamara's book makes clear, when he finally does express his dissatisfaction thirty years after the fact, the analytical framework from which he writes affords him not the slightest glimpse of an expanded conception of security. Booth, by contrast, acknowledges—and shows through his own work—that developing a more critical perspective requires a massive reconstruction of one's disciplinary commitments.

There is a danger in any critical enterprise of its bearers announcing their particular truth as the latest and greatest newly dominant paradigm. Special issues of quarterly journals are thereby promised, and a whole cohort of scholars is thereafter anointed for a brief reign at the top of the discipline—only to be knocked off by the next coterie of theorists. Wisely, the editors of this volume have eschewed such broadsides. Their point, rather, is to stimulate contestability, interpretation, and politics instead of encasing global security within yet another lockstep perspective. Indeed, the strength of this volume is precisely its openness rather than its closure of issues that have for too long been heralded as deadly serious concerns best left to realist and neorealist students of the genre.

At the same time, the editors, perhaps in a mood of undue optimism, believe that mainstream practitioners and security insiders with a reformist (liberal) bent will take these concerns seriously. In so doing, they invoke Robert Cox's formulation of the difference between reformist and critical perspectives—a distinction adapted from Max Horkheimer's famous dichotomy between traditional and critical theory.[5] In each pairing, the former is defined as an accommodationist strategy designed to strengthen prevailing institutional arrangements. The latter attitude assigns itself the political task of a fundamental transgression and transformation—invariably in the name of some democratic and emancipatory social agent who has been excluded and/or disempowered from prevailing practices. It is one thing to denote the boundary between conventional and transformative perspectives, but quite another to have them enter into a constructive dialogue. The presumption of open interest is not always warranted, the more so in cases where those at the center of power find themselves on the defensive. As Booth's chapter here suggests, when it comes to matters of international security, there is precious little tolerance for critical space to operate. The intent of this text, after all, is to address those in positions of authority and to test the limits of established security practices in terms of political adaptability.

And yet the effort is being undertaken in large measure because responsible practitioners themselves understand the way in which the fate of the West, let alone the fate of the earth, is tied to a far wider range of issues than conventional strategic-nuclear studies have emphasized. Ecological crises, terrorist campaigns, resource shortages, economic instability, legal and illegal immigration, the drug trade, and the most elemental human rights of survival are just some of the areas ripe for monitoring, if not intervention, as states extend their strategic domain in search of practices that render their civil societies vulnerable. The appeal of such a newly expanded agenda of security is, on the surface, self-evident. Security studies in its strategic-military guise had always inflated dimensions of force, to the neglect of more quotidian dimensions that shape the tenor of public life. But as Simon Dalby's chapter here reminds us, such an expanded security agenda is not without its own risks, as the price to be paid for such post-Cold War pursuits is to sanction the state as an interventionary mechanism in vast domains of contemporary and international life. The dilemma lies not in recognizing the interconnectedness of modern industrial life, nor in acknowledging how fragile those ties are; rather, it rests in centralizing disciplinary power and in promoting state practices that are inexhaustible in their scope and ambition. Securing access to resources, or monitoring technological innovations, simply deepens interventionary practices and results in panoptic states.[6]

The problem is not simply technological. It is also inherent in the modernist legacy of the state's relation to civil society. R. B. J. Walker invokes this sensibility, even if his presentation is couched in philosophical terms rather than structural ones linking state, political economy, and what geographers call "working landscapes," both local and global.[7] Security as a set of protective practices is intimately associated with the rise of the modern state. A grand realist tradition narrowly construes this legacy in terms of a state of nature and the need for self-help in the face of anarchy. But as both critical theory and "structurationist" works have suggested, such an account presupposes precisely what needs to be explained, namely, the emergence of those states in the first place.[8]

Here, it is important to return to some classical thinkers in political theory, namely, Niccolò Machiavelli and Thomas Hobbes. Both articulate the grounds on which a state apparatus is constructed over and beyond its own civil society to preserve the possibility of certain forms of life within. Machiavelli thus becomes interesting for his defense of republican *virtù* and the need for the state to preserve and contain the nascent dynamics of urban commercial life. The difference, when measured against the reading of Machiavelli as nefarious, is that he continually warned against the expectation that either the prince or the republic would be able to secure space against the vicissitudes of time—*fortuna,* as he called it. Hobbes was more confident that time could be forestalled. He argues in the *Leviathan* that the state creates the very possibility of both commercial activity and personal identity to sustain itself over time. Realists who place Hobbes in their pantheon miss his most important point. In contrast to the version deeded to today's structural realists, Hobbes explicitly claims that international life is unlike the state of war because the condition of states is characterized not by natural equality but by artificial inequality, dominance, and empire. In other words, the analogy of international anarchy to the war of all against all in a state of nature breaks down immediately. Based on a reading of his work, the chief threat to security in international life derives less from international violence than from the loss of civic associations should the polity collapse.

This is the understanding that animates what Mohammed Ayoob calls "subaltern realism." His point is that a security studies committed to examining external contingencies upon the sovereign, territorially completed state apparatus simply glosses over the most pervasive and crippling aspects of security threats to emergent Third World states. Thus, he focuses on securing the very boundaries of the state from both external threats (regional security complexes) and internal destabilization. The process of state building is a slow, arduous, and inherently bloody undertaking, and it is disingenuous for First World representatives to overlook this in viewing Third World politics. His account of both the (political) "software" and (security) "hardware" by which regimes on the periphery of the world political economy have to sustain themselves provides a powerful complement to conventional security analysis, one colored by an appreciation for historical sociology. In Ayoob's account, such a concern for the security of subaltern states is part of a project of counter-hegemonic political resistance by which developing states hold off the more invasive aspects of a larger world system as they develop their own internal political, economic, and cultural identity.

For reasons that do not appear to derive internally from the logic of state building, however, Ayoob resists incorporating an expanded security agenda into the disciplinary matrix. Part of this has to do with preserving a certain analytical rigor—no doubt, security politics in the broader sense is a messy affair in terms of definitional boundaries. Ayoob is also worried about the divisiveness encouraged by emancipatory politics. But this is to construe emancipation only as a matter of political groups, such as ethnonational state movements, rather than in the more postmodern sense of the kind of multidimensional identity politics that informs Booth and other proponents of an expanded security agenda, and that would include issues of gender, human rights, and cultural plurality. Not surprisingly, then, one comes away from Ayoob's contribution sensing that part of his analytical concern—to constrain the constituent elements of security—is tied to hopes of not overloading the state with burdensome demands in what is admittedly a precarious stage in its unfolding. It is one thing for a critical tradition to express concern for the militarization resulting from dominant states as they extend their control of international order. It is quite another to abandon the pursuit of state security altogether, particularly when, as Ayoob notes, the resulting internal stability is a foundation for the construction of civil society in the first place.

This sets the framework in this volume for what is surely the most important conceptual debate, namely, whether the modern state—and not simply its subaltern incarnation—is at all prepared to meet the burden of securing public life. Walker thinks it is incapable, and Dalby extends the concern to warning of the dangers inherent in demanding too much of our political institutions. Meanwhile, Ayoob rules such concerns beyond the responsibility of the political sphere. Just because something is important does not mean it should become part of security. The unresolved dilemma here has to do with the tacit relationship between security and community. The realist tradition construes community as only a provisional possibility within the confines of the state—and it is something counterpoised to the lack of connectedness prevailing amidst international order. Neorealism, including much of security studies, sees limited forms of community possible only for states that constitute alliances and interdependent modes of cooperation on an issue-by-issue basis.

The task of a critical security studies would be to reformulate the foundations of security and to link it back to the forms of political community from which it has been severed by a variety of modern practices—not the least of which is militarization. Beyond basic issues of violence, both domestic and international, this new critical approach would see security as transcending the boundaries of the modern state and addressing issues of transnational vulnerability. A number of internal critics have rightly pointed to the question of political overload, asking, in effect, if in so doing, modern citizens are asking too much of their political institutions and not relying on forms of social mobilization and networking that both undergird and overlap those of the formal state. The issue is particularly appropriate insofar as, for many citizens of the Third World, the chief source of the daily insecurity they face is the state itself. But it turns out that on closer inspection, many of the same issues confronting developing societies are part of the fabric of daily life in industrial societies as well.

NOTES

1. "As Crime Mounts Overseas, State Sponsors 'Security Awareness Month,'" *State* (January 1995), 2–3.
2. Stephen M. Walt, "The Renaissance of Security Studies," *International Studies Quarterly* 35 (1991), 211–39.
3. Robert S. McNamara, *In Retrospect: The Tragedy and Lessons of Vietnam* (New York: Random House, 1995).
4. Bradley S. Klein, *Strategic Studies and World Order* (New York: Cambridge University Press, 1994).
5. Robert W. Cox, "Social Forces, States and World Order: Beyond International Relations Theory," *Millennium* 10 (1981), 126–55; Max Horkheimer, "Traditional and Critical Theory," in *Critical Theory: Selected Essays* (New York: Herder and Herder, 1972), 188–243.
6. Manuel De Landa, *War in the Age of Intelligent Machines* (New York: Zone, 1991).
7. Tony Hiss, *The Experience of Place* (New York: Vintage, 1991).
8. On "structurationist" perspectives, see Alexander Wendt, "Anarchy Is What States Make of It: The Social Construction of Power Politics," *International Organization* 46 (1992), 391–425.

Contributors

AMITAV ACHARYA is associate professor in the department of political science, York University, Toronto. His areas of interest include security in the Third World and politics and regional security of Southeast Asia. He is the author, with Larry Swatuk, of *Reordering the Periphery: An Essay on North-South Relations in the Post-Cold War Era* (London: Macmillan, forthcoming).

MOHAMMED AYOOB is professor of International Relations at James Madison College, Michigan State University. He has held faculty appointments at the Australian National University, the National University of Singapore, and Jawaharlal Nehru University (India), and visiting appointments at Columbia, Oxford, Princeton, and Brown. A specialist in conflict and security in the Third World, his articles have appeared in *World Politics, International Studies Quarterly,* and *Global Governance,* among others. His latest book is *The Third World Security Predicament: State Making, Regional Conflict, and the International System* (1995). He has also been awarded Rockefeller, SSRC-MacArthur, and Ford Foundation fellowships.

KEN BOOTH holds a personal chair in the department of international politics, University of Wales, Aberystwyth. He has been scholar-in-residence at the U.S. Naval War College, senior research fellow at the Centre for Foreign Policy Studies, Dalhousie University

(Canada), and visiting fellow and MacArthur professor at Cambridge University. His books include *Strategy and Ethnocentrism* (1979), *Law, Force and Diplomacy at Sea* (1985), and (as editor) *New Thinking about Strategy and International Security* (1991). His latest book, edited with Steve Smith, is *International Relations Theory Today* (1995). He is currently chair of the British International Studies Association.

BEVERLY CRAWFORD teaches political economy at the University of California at Berkeley and is the research director of the University of California Center for German and European Studies. She is the coprincipal investigator on the project "Redefining Global Security: Economic Liberalization, Eroding Sovereignty and Ethnic and Sectarian Conflict," funded by the Pew Charitable Trusts. Her most recent book is *Economic Vulnerability in International Relations*, published by Columbia University Press.

SIMON DALBY is associate professor at Carleton University in Ottawa, where he teaches political geography and international affairs. Author of *Creating the Second Cold War* (1990), his current research interests are in critical geopolitics and environmental security.

KARIN M. FIERKE has a Ph.D. in political science from the University of Minnesota. This article, which is drawn from her dissertation, titled "Excavating the Ruins of the Cold War: Recovering the Contours of a Changing Security Culture," was written while she was a fellow at the Amsterdam School for Social Science Research, University of Amsterdam. She is a Prize research fellow at Nuffield College, Oxford University.

BRADLEY S. KLEIN is assistant professor in the department of government and international relations, Clark University (Massachusetts), where he teaches courses in International Relations, political theory, and politics of the media. He is the author of *Strategic Studies and World Order* (1994) and is currently working on a study of architecture, political economy, and the politics of public space.

KEITH KRAUSE is professor of political science at the Graduate Institute of International Studies (Geneva) and associate professor of political science (on leave) at York University (Toronto). He has authored *Arms and the State* (1992) and coedited, with W. Andy Knight, *State, Society and the UN System* (1995). He has written numerous articles and chapters on various aspects of global arms transfers and weapons proliferation, and his current research focuses on the role of the armed forces and state formation in the Middle East.

RONNIE D. LIPSCHUTZ teaches politics at the University of California at Santa Cruz, and he is the director of the Stevenson Program on Global Security. He is the coprincipal investigator on the project "Redefining Global Security: Economic Liberalization, Eroding Sovereignty and Ethnic and Sectarian Conflict," funded by the Pew Charitable Trusts. His most recent book is *On Security* published by Columbia University Press.

DAVID MUTIMER is a lecturer in the department of International Relations, Keele University in England, where he teaches various aspects of international security. He has just spent two years as a research associate of the York Centre for International and Strategic Studies at York University in Toronto, where he conducted an ongoing research project into the control and verification of weapons proliferation. This project has produced two edited volumes, *Control But Verify: Verification in the New Nonproliferation Agenda* (1994) and *Moving Beyond Supplier Controls in a Mature Technology Environment* (1995), both published by the York Centre for International and Strategic Studies.

THOMAS RISSE-KAPPEN is professor of international politics in the department of administrative sciences, University of Konstanz, Germany, and he has also taught at Cornell, Yale, and Stanford Universities as well as at the University of Wyoming. He is the author of *Cooperation among Democracies: The European Influence on U.S. Foreign Policy* (1995) and the editor of *Bringing Transnational Relations Back In* (1995) and, with Richard N. Lebow, of *International Relations Theory and the End of the Cold War* (1995). He has also contributed articles to *World Politics, International Organization, International Security,* and others. His research interests include International Relations theory, comparative foreign policy, norms and ideas in international politics, and transnational relations.

PETER VALE is professor of Southern African studies, University of the Western Cape, and visiting professor in political science at the University of Stellenbosch. In 1996, Peter Vale was UNESCO professor of African studies at the University of Utrecht, The Netherlands. In 1994 he was visiting scholar at the Christian Michelsen Institute, Bergen, Norway. With Hans-Joachim Spanger, he has recently edited *Bridges to the Future: Prospects for Peace and Security in Southern Africa* (1995).

R. B. J. WALKER is professor of political science at the University of Victoria (British Columbia) and editor of the journal *Alternatives*. He has written widely on the limits of modern political theory, especially in relation to contemporary claims about global politics, including *One World/Many Worlds* (1988); *Inside/Outside: International Relations as Political Theory* (1993), and *International Relations/World Politics*, which is still in progress.

MICHAEL C. WILLIAMS is assistant professor of political science at the University of Southern Maine. His research interests include security studies and International Relations theory, areas in which he has published articles in *Alternatives, International Organization,* and the *Review of International Studies*. His current projects include analyses of modernist and postmodernist International Relations theory and of multilateral security institutions.

Index